MW01170151

THE ALCHEMISTS

Can courts really build democracy in a state emerging from authoritarian rule? This book presents a searching critique of the contemporary global model of democracy-building for post-authoritarian states, arguing that it places excessive reliance on courts. Since 1945, both constitutional courts and international human rights courts have been increasingly perceived as alchemists, capable of transmuting the base materials of a nascent democracy into the gold of a functioning democratic system. By charting the development of this model and critically analysing the evidence and claims for courts as democracy-builders, this book argues that the decades-long trend toward ever greater reliance on courts is based as much on faith as fact, and can often be counter-productive. Offering a sustained corrective to unrealistic perceptions of courts as democracy-builders, the book points the way toward a much needed rethinking of democracy-building models and a re-evaluation of how we employ courts in this role.

TOM GERALD DALY is a Fellow of Melbourne Law School, Associate Director of the Edinburgh Centre for Constitutional Law at Edinburgh Law School, and a consultant on public law, human rights, and democracy-building. He has previously clerked for the Chief Justice of Ireland, and has worked at the Judicial Studies Institute and Edinburgh University's Global Justice Academy. As a consultant, he has worked on Council of Europe, European Union, International IDEA (Institute for Democracy and Electoral Assistance), and Irish government projects.

CAMBRIDGE STUDIES IN CONSTITUTIONAL LAW

The aim of this series is to produce leading monographs in constitutional law. All areas of constitutional law and public law fall within the ambit of the series, including human rights and civil liberties law, administrative law, as well as constitutional theory and the history of constitutional law. A wide variety of scholarly approaches is encouraged, with the governing criterion being simply that the work is of interest to an international audience. Thus, works concerned with only one jurisdiction will be included in the series as appropriate, while, at the same time, the series will include works which are explicitly comparative or theoretical – or both. The series editor likewise welcomes proposals that work at the intersection of constitutional and international law, or that seek to bridge the gaps between civil law systems, the USA, and the common law jurisdictions of the Commonwealth.

Series Editor
David Dyzenhaus
Professor of Law and Philosophy, University of Toronto, Canada

Editorial Advisory Board
T.R.S. Allan, Cambridge, UK
Damian Chalmers, LSE, UK
Sujit Choudhry, Berkeley, USA
Monica Claes, Maastricht, Netherlands
David Cole, Georgetown, USA
K.D. Ewing, King's College London, UK
David Feldman, Cambridge, UK
Cora Hoexter, Witwatersrand, South Africa
Christoph Moellers, Humboldt, Germany
Adrienne Stone, Melbourne, Australia
Adam Tomkins, Glasgow, UK
Adrian Vermeule, Harvard, USA

Books in the Series

Australia's Constitution after Whitlam Brendan Lim

Building the Constitution: The Practice of Constitutional Interpretation in Post-Apartheid South Africa James Fowkes

Dimensions of Dignity: The Theory and Practice of Modern Constitutional Law Jacob Weinrib

Reason of State: Law, Prerogative, Empire Thomas Poole

Bills of Rights in the Common Law Robert Leckey

The Guardian of the Constitution: Hans Kelsen and Carl Schmitt on the Limits of Constitutional Law Translated by Lars Vinx, with an introduction and notes by Lars Vinx

THE ALCHEMISTS

Questioning Our Faith in Courts as Democracy-Builders

TOM GERALD DALY

University of Melbourne

CAMBRIDGE
UNIVERSITY PRESS

University Printing House, Cambridge CB2 8BS, United Kingdom

One Liberty Plaza, 20th Floor, New York, NY 10006, USA

477 Williamstown Road, Port Melbourne, VIC 3207, Australia

4843/24, 2nd Floor, Ansari Road, Daryaganj, Delhi – 110002, India

79 Anson Road, #06–04/06, Singapore 079906

Cambridge University Press is part of the University of Cambridge.

It furthers the University's mission by disseminating knowledge in the pursuit of education, learning, and research at the highest international levels of excellence.

www.cambridge.org
Information on this title: www.cambridge.org/9781108417945
DOI: 10.1017/9781108283731

First published 2017

Printed in the United Kingdom by Clays, St Ives plc

A catalogue record for this publication is available from the British Library.

Library of Congress Cataloging-in-Publication Data
Names: Daly, Tom Gerald, author.
Title: The Alchemists : Questioning Our Faith in Courts as Democracy-Builders / Tom Gerald Daly, University of Melbourne.
Description: Cambridge [UK] ; New York : Cambridge University Press, 2017. | Includes bibliographical references and index.
Identifiers: LCCN 2017018753| ISBN 9781108417945 (hardback : alk. paper) | ISBN 9781108406086 (printback : alk. paper)
Subjects: LCSH: Courts. | Constitutional courts. | International human rights courts. | Democratization. | Democracy.
Classification: LCC K2100 .D355 2017 | DDC 321.8–dc23 LC record available at https://lccn.loc.gov/2017018753

ISBN 978-1-108-41794-5 Hardback

For Grandad, Mama, Emma and Ger

CONTENTS

DETAILED TABLE OF CONTENTS

ILLUSTRATIONS

Table

Figures

Table

Figures

PREFACE

Our Court Obsession

As a young lawyer working for the Chief Justice of Ireland, I would visit his chambers almost every day – often multiple times a day. There, amidst the oak furniture, heavy curtains, and blizzard of court submissions was the unshakeable sense of judicial power; the sense of judge-made law *in utero*, to be birthed later in the more austere setting of the Supreme Court itself.

Having been the Chief Justice's chambers for almost a century, it took little imagination to picture the first Chief Justice of an independent Ireland in the 1920s, Hugh Kennedy, tackling his judicial duties under new constitutional arrangements that differed radically from the unentrenched British constitution under which all Irish lawyers had been trained. The Constitution of 1922 lay in the slipstream of more modern constitutions, with its separation of State powers, bill of rights, and, crucially, express conferral on the superior courts of the power to review ordinary law for compatibility with the Constitution. That power would be amplified under the new Constitution of 1937, adopted to sweep away most of the remaining constitutional vestiges of British rule.

It is a vanished world in which judicial power, though present, bore little relation to what we see around the globe today.[1] Despite the authority placed in their hands, continuity with the British legal tradition remained the dominant theme for two generations of Irish judges, content to play a marginal role in governance by policing the boundaries of legality in the same way as their counterparts across the Irish Sea. They did not begin to exercise their ample powers with any vigour until the 1960s, when a new approach recast the Court in a more American

---

[1] Even the US Supreme Court's use of judicial review did not become truly expansive until the post-war period. See M. Schor, 'Mapping Comparative Judicial Review' (2008) 7 *Washington University Global Studies Law Review* 257, 262.

mould, shrugging off the restraint of the British judicial style and placing the Court in a more assertive posture vis-à-vis the other branches of government.

By the time they did rouse themselves, independent Irish democracy was decades old and the judges of the Supreme Court had already started to enter a strange new world of shared constitutional supremacy with external courts. The principle in the 1937 Constitution that the Court's decisions 'shall in all cases be final and conclusive'[2] had begun to unravel in the face of the first judgment of the European Court of Human Rights in 1960, delivered over 800 miles away in Strasbourg – in an action taken against Ireland, as it happens.[3] Ireland's entry into the European Economic Community (EEC) in 1973 later required submission to the jurisdiction of the European Court of Justice. Of course, the full effects were not to be felt for some decades.

* * *

For large swathes of the world today, the notion of the highest domestic court merely policing legality at the periphery, playing a marginal role in democracy-building and, in principle, having an irrefutably final say in all constitutional matters, no longer chimes with reality.

Indeed, even before the Supreme Court of Ireland had found its voice, the European landscape after 1945 had started to undergo a profound legal and cultural transformation, with the activity of constitutional courts in Germany and Italy initiating a paradigm shift toward a central role for such courts in democratic governance. The courts of mainland Europe had more pressing reasons than the Irish superior courts for flexing their muscles. Unlike the incremental Irish steps toward full independence in a democratic (albeit thinly democratic) setting, these courts seized their task in a context of discredited parliaments and a strong hangover from the corruption of democratic processes, which had led to authoritarian rule. In a relatively short time they came to be viewed as anchors in an uncertain world, extolling the rule of law and adherence to constitutional values that voiced a stark reaction to the barbaric experiences of wartime and its immediate aftermath.

In the ensuing decades, constitutional courts and strong judicial review were established across the globe in states emerging from undemocratic

[2] Article 34.4. 6°, Constitution of Ireland 1937.
[3] *Lawless* v. *Ireland* (1979–80) 1 EHRR 1 (14 November 1960).

rule: in Southern Europe, Latin America, Asia, Central and Eastern Europe, and Africa. This has led to a tendency to conflate assertive adjudication with successful democratisation processes; reflected in the contemporary calls for a new constitutional court to aid Sri Lanka's path back to democratic rule,[4] and in Tunisia, the central position accorded to a new (though yet to be established) Constitutional Court in the democratic Constitution of 2014 adopted following the Jasmine Revolution that ousted dictatorial president Zine El Abidine Ben Ali.[5] At the international level, the intervention of regional human rights courts in young democracies has led to a multi-level judicial role in democracy-building, further enhancing the perception that courts have a central role to play in supporting and shaping democratisation processes: the elaboration of strong lines of jurisprudence by the Inter-American Court of Human Rights from the late 1980s in a regional context of democratising states; the sweeping expansion of the Strasbourg Court's territory in the 1990s to encompass Turkey and states emerging from Communist rule; and, most recently, robust decisions of the African Court on Human and Peoples' Rights since its first ruling in 2009.

* * *

How have we travelled so far from the vanished world of pre-war Ireland, and has our post-war obsession with courts as democracy-builders proven to be justified? In addressing these questions, this book seeks not only to question prevailing understandings of courts as democracy-builders, but to satisfy the author's own long-standing 'court obsession'. It is an obsession fed by six years at the Supreme Court of Ireland, three years representing that Court on the Venice Commission's Joint Council of Constitutional Justice (which has sixty member courts from Europe and worldwide), and over a decade of working with and visiting courts across the world; from Estonia to Turkey, from Brazil to Kyrgyzstan, and from Lebanon to Canada.

---

[4] See N. Jayawickrama, 'Establishing a Constitutional Court: The Impediments Ahead', CPA Working Papers on Constitutional Reform No. 13, January 2017 www.constitutional reforms.org/wp-content/uploads/2016/06/Working-Paper-13-1.pdf.

[5] N. Mekki, 'The Tunisian Constitutional Court at the Center of the Political System – and Whirlwind' *ConstitutionNet* 9 February 2016 www.constitutionnet.org/news/tunisian-constitutional-court-center-political-system-and-whirlwind?utm_source=newsletter&utm_medium=email.

As a result, this book is written – to some extent – with the sympathy of a judicial insider. The critical vein of this book should in no way be read as an unwarranted attack on the many hardworking and conscientious judges serving on constitutional courts and regional human rights courts worldwide. In particular, the term 'alchemists' in the title should not be read as 'charlatans'. Rather, it denotes the concern that courts under the existing global model of court-centric democracy-building are increasingly expected to perform an impossible feat of alchemy; to transmute the base materials of a new democracy – an incomplete political settlement, a nascent commitment to democratic rule, and imperfect constitutional and international texts – into the gold of a functioning democracy. As we will see, the decades-long trend toward ever increasing reliance on courts in democracy-building projects is based on a variety of false premises, and can at times threaten to hinder, rather than help, the achievement of a viable democratic system.

ACKNOWLEDGEMENTS

So many debts of gratitude were accrued in bringing this book to harbour that they are difficult to fully enumerate. The book started life as a doctoral thesis and I am sincerely grateful to the National University of Ireland (NUI) for awarding me a Travelling Studentship in International Law to pursue my research. Second in line are my two supervisors, Christine Bell and Stephen Tierney, for their guidance, incisive commentary, and profound expertise, and my Ph.D examiners, Denis Galligan and Neil Walker, for their close attention to the text and for a truly enjoyable experience in discussing its contents.

My colleagues at the Edinburgh Centre for Constitutional Law and staff at Edinburgh Law School also helped to shape my thinking, including Asanga Welikala, Cormac Mac Amhlaigh, Niamh Nic Suibhne, and Stephen Neff. Particular thanks go to Kenneth Campbell for his insight, camaraderie, wit, and interest in the project. Visiting speakers at the Law School's Constitutional Law Discussion Group (CLDG) also greatly enriched my thinking: Conrado Hübner Mendes and Erin Delaney merit a special mention, as well as Roberto Gargarella, Jeremy Waldron, Jim Pfander, Ted White, Alon Harel, Rivka Weill, Jeff King, Paul Blokker, Zaid Al-Ali, Catherine Dupré, Yaniv Roznai, Tamás Győrfi, and Pau Bossacoma i Busquets.

A veritable crack team provided much-needed assistance in completing the central Brazilian case-study. A most sincere vote of thanks to Conrado Hübner Mendes, who has been extremely helpful in so many ways, and to Virgílio Afonso da Silva and Marcelo Torelly for reading the final text of Chapters 5 and 6 and suggesting key revisions. A number of individuals assisted me in navigating and selecting case-law of the Supreme Court of Brazil. Oscar Vilhena Vieira at the Fundação Getulio Vargas (FGV) in São Paulo, who oriented me through the Court's phases of jurisprudence. Tiago Neiva Santos, Maria Ângela Jardim de Santa Cruz Oliveira, Luciano Felício Fuck, Vinicius Prado, and Felipe Farias at the Court, who were so generous with their time and provided training in using the Court's case-law databases. Particular thanks also to Diogo de Sousa e Alvim and Felipe Oliveira for their occasional linguistic assistance during my reading and translation of tracts of key decisions of that Court (all translations in Chapter 5 are by the author). *O meu muito obrigado a todos.*

Parts of the book were presented at a number of conferences worldwide. I am thankful to the Brazilian Society of Public Law (SBDP), conference organisers at the universities of Oxford, Cambridge, and Newcastle, the Public Law and Human Rights group at Glasgow Law School (with special thanks to Tom Raine and Marco Goldoni), and Erin Delaney and Ros Dixon, who invited me to a conference on comparative judicial review at Northwestern Law School in October 2016.

A whole host of people provided key research materials for the book, including unpublished material: Theunis Roux, Mikael Madsen, Pau Bossacoma i Busquets, Joel Colón-Ríos, Maartje de Visser, Tímea Drinóczi, Oliver Windridge, Tarik Olcay, Serkan Yolcu, Dilek Kurban, and Raul Sanchez-Urribarri. My sincere thanks also to Tom Raine, Emily Hancox, Kenneth Campbell, Martin Kelly, Jenna Sapiano, and Celia Davies, who took time to read the Ph.D text and to assist me with the *viva voce.*

Working for and with a number of organisations has fed into the book in a variety of ways, especially by connecting me with relevant developments across the globe: the Edinburgh Centre for Constitutional Law; Edinburgh University's Global Justice Academy; the Council of Europe; the Venice Commission; International IDEA; the British Academy; and the Arab Association of Constitutional Law. Working at the Supreme Court of Ireland for over six years also provided me with an invaluable 'insider' perspective on the judicial role.

The text was finalised between Copenhagen and Dublin, and on many flights to and from Turkey. Thanks to the Centre of Excellence for International Courts (iCourts) at the University of Copenhagen, where I spent six months in 2016, obtaining valuable insights from Mikkel Rask Madsen, Shai Dothan, David Thór Björgvinsson, Kerstin Carlson, Juan Mayoral, Carolina Alvarez Utoft, and Amalie Frese. Thanks also to Oran Doyle, Dean of Trinity College Dublin Law School, for arranging a Visiting Fellowship and office space on the beautiful Trinity campus in early 2017.

A particular vote of thanks goes to Cambridge University Press: to Series Editor David Dyzenhaus and Commissioning Editor Finola O'Sullivan for their enthusiastic reception of the initial manuscript; to

Editorial Assistant Rebecca J. Roberts for shepherding me through the publishing process; and to the anonymous reviewers, who provided such positive reviews and incisive feedback. Sincerest thanks also to the one and only Ognjenka Manojlovic, whose first-rate editing skills at the eleventh hour brought the text to completion on schedule, and to Stephen Daly, Edel Hughes, Helen Whately, Sean Molloy, Amalie Frese, Parisa Zanganeh, and Camila Dabrowski De Araújo Mendonça for their impressively thorough last-minute proofreading. Thanks also to Justice Susanne Baer of the Federal Constitutional Court of Germany for permission to quote from her speech to the I-CON conference in Berlin in June 2016 in the concluding thoughts.

Last, but never least, are my friends and family: Mam, Dad, Ed, Lib, Steve, Mia, Fifi, Breda, Sarah E., Ali, Helen, Sarah O'M., Stine, Stefie, James, Claire, Jane, Dellie, Sile, Noodles, Eli, Aisling, Bob and Wennie, Celia, Ben, Laura, Krittika, Louise, Michael, Grant, Chris, Eduardo, Felipe, Diogo, Ruby, Ognjenka, Eugene, Graham, Katharina, Kerstin, Barrie, Amelie, Juan, Kerstin, Pola, Salvatore, Mikkel, Jess, and many others who have provided support and lifted my spirits when needed. A special thanks to Fif, Breda, Sarah E., Sarah O., Helen, and Ali for understanding me, listening to me, and being my greatest cheerleaders, to Mam for her endless care and positivity, and to Libby and my wonderful niece Mia for telling me I'm 'too interesting to be a lawyer'. A final and particularly profound mark of appreciation goes to my twin brother Stephen: a true scholar, inspiration, and confidant, who has provided so much support, in every conceivable way, during the entire life of the project – not least in making me shake with laughter when it has been most needed. I am a very lucky man to have all of you in my life.

TABLE OF CASES

The cases listed below appear in the main text of the book. It may be noted that decisions of the Federal Supreme Court of Brazil, which are identified solely by numbers, have been assigned names to make them more recognisable, in a similar manner to the style of naming judgments of the Federal Constitutional Court of Germany. The following key relates to the Brazilian case citations:

ADI   Direct Action of Unconstitutionality
ADPF   Petition for Non-Compliance with a Fundamental Precept
MC   Provisional Measure
RE   Extraordinary Appeal

African Court on Human and Peoples' Rights

Abubakari *v.* Tanzania App. No. 007/2013 (3 June 2016)
Konaté *v.* Burkina Faso App. No. 004/2013 (5 December 2014)
Mtikila *v.* Tanzania App. 009/2011 and 011/2011 (14 June 2013)
Onyango *v.* Tanzania App. No. 006/2013 (18 March 2016)
Thomas *v.* Tanzania App. No. 005/2013 (20 November 2015)
Zongo *v.* Burkina Faso App. No. 013/2011 (28 March 2014)

Constitutional Court of South Africa

Economic Freedom Fighters *v.* Speaker of the National Assembly and Others; Democratic Alliance *v.* Speaker of the National Assembly and Others [2016] ZACC 11

Court of Appeal of Tanzania

Attorney General *v.* Reverend Christopher Mtikila, Civil Appeal No. 45 of 2009 (17 June 2010)

Court of Justice of the European Union

European Court of Human Rights

Federal Constitutional Court of Germany

Federal Supreme Court of Brazil

High Court of Tanzania

Inter-American Court of Human Rights

ABBREVIATIONS

ACHPR	African (Banjul) Charter on Human and Peoples' Rights
ACtHPR	African Court on Human and Peoples' Rights
ACHR	American Convention on Human Rights
AC	Andean Community
ADHR	American Declaration of Human Rights
ADI	Direct Action of Unconstitutionality
ADPF	Petition for Non-compliance with a Fundamental Precept
ANC	African National Congress
ASEAN	Association of Southeast Asian Nations
AU	African Union
CEE	Central and Eastern Europe
EAC	East African Community
EACJ	East African Court of Justice
EC	European Community
EDC	European Defence Community
EEC	European Economic Community
ECHR	European Convention on Human Rights
ECtHR	European Court of Human Rights
ECOWAS	Economic Community of West African States
EU	European Union
IACHR	Inter-American Commission on Human Rights
IACtHR	Inter-American Court of Human Rights
ICC	International Criminal Court
ICCPR	International Covenant on Civil and Political Rights
ICESCR	International Covenant on Economic, Social and Cultural Rights
ICJ	International Court of Justice
IDEA	International Institute for Democracy and Electoral Assistance
IMF	International Monetary Fund
MENA	Middle East and North Africa
MERCOSUR	Common Market of the South
NGO	Non-governmental organisation
OAS	Organization of American States

OAU	Organisation of African Unity
PC do B	Communist Party of Brazil
PiS	Law and Justice Party (Poland)
PT	Workers' Party (Brazil)
PV	Green Party (Brazil)
QoD	Quality of Democracy
SADC	Southern African Development Community
SADR	Sahrawi Arab Democratic Republic
STF	Federal Supreme Court of Brazil
UDHR	Universal Declaration of Human Rights
UK	United Kingdom of Great Britain and Northern Ireland
UN	United Nations
UNASUR	Union of South American States

~

Introduction

An Onerous Role for Courts as Democracy-Builders

This book seeks to question the development since 1945 of a global model of democracy-building for post-authoritarian states that places undue reliance on courts. In essence, instead of being viewed as epiphenomenal, constitutional courts and regional human rights courts[1] have come to be viewed as integral to the achievement of, or even constitutive of, a functioning democratic order. In other words, they are seen as central to successful democratisation.[2] It is an onerous role, which differs significantly from the judicial role in long-established democracies (hereinafter, 'mature democracies'). In young democracies courts are required to somehow 'judge' democratisation. They are expected to both assess what is required to support the democratisation process at any given point, especially in light of key deficiencies of the newly democratic order, and to judge when the democratisation context requires a different approach than may be appropriate in a mature democracy, such as the United States, Costa Rica, or Ireland.

The burden placed on courts tends to lead, at the extreme, to an expansion of the judicial role beyond the usual limits seen in mature democracies, and a blurring of the boundaries between judging law and judging democratic propriety. It also freights courts with weighty expectations to 'deliver' on the promises of a new democratic order, while navigating their own place in that developing order – or, in the case of regional human rights courts, inserting themselves into the democratisation process from without. However, the aim here is not merely to examine adjudication for its own sake. Rather, the effectiveness and viability of the global court-centric model for democracy-building, as it currently exists, is the overarching concern that drives this enquiry. This book, then, focuses on the evolving, interacting, and overlapping

---

[1] The terms 'constitutional court' and 'regional human rights court' are defined at the end of this Introduction.

[2] The meaning of 'democratisation' is discussed at length in Chapter 1.

roles constitutional courts and regional human rights courts play in 'building' democracy, as distinct from the governance roles such courts play in a mature democracy. By examining what we *think* courts do as democracy-builders, what they *actually* do, and what they *should* do, it is argued that the decades-long trend toward ever greater reliance on courts is based on slim evidence and that a rebalancing of democracy-building models away from excessive reliance on courts is required.

1   Origin of the Book and Key Questions

The germ of this book lay in the rather simple observation that the Supreme Court of Brazil and the Inter-American Court of Human Rights had taken divergent stances in 2010 on the validity of Brazil's Amnesty Law of 1979 – a core component of that state's transition to democratic rule in 1985. For the Supreme Court, the law was constitutional, as a valid catalyst for the democratic transition, and its amendment or repeal was a political question for the representative branches of government. By contrast, the Inter-American Court deemed the law invalid as enshrining continued impunity for serious human rights violations, contrary to the pan-regional American Convention on Human Rights (ACHR). The result on the ground was something of a fudge: the law remains on the statute books, but the state complied with a central order of the Inter-American Court; namely, establishing a Truth Commission that facilitated an official and public discussion of human rights violations under the military dictatorship of 1964–1985.

Was the Supreme Court's approach correct, by batting the decision back to the elected branches of the state? Or was the Inter-American Court's approach preferable, not only in vindicating human rights in the instant case, but also in addressing the impunity 'bottleneck' in Brazil's democratisation process left by this legislative legacy of the democratic transition – one which the state, and Brazilian society more generally, had proven unwilling or unable to address?

This discussion could all too easily become fixated solely on the question of which court should have the 'final say' regarding key societal questions, or on general concerns as to the democratic legitimacy[3] of courts of any stripe resolving questions that cut to the heart of the identity and foundations of a democratic political community. However,

---

[3] It is recognised here that 'democratic legitimacy' is a somewhat vague term. It is employed in this thesis due to its prevalence in the existing normative debate, discussed in Chapter 7.

to focus exclusively on such questions would add little to an extremely well-trodden debate concerning the rise and legitimacy of judicial governance power in democratic states since the latter half of the twentieth century, which has become a 'central obsession'[4] of constitutional scholars. In this book, a rather different set of questions raised by the Brazilian scenario is addressed. First, how have domestic constitutional courts and regional human rights courts become such central actors in post-war democratisation processes? Second, what roles do these courts actually play in democratisation processes, and how does the democratisation context shape their roles? Third, what roles should courts play to 'build' democracy in a post-authoritarian polity, as compared to a mature democracy?

A Global Resonance

Today these questions are of global resonance. In the decades since the establishment of constitutional courts in the defeated Axis powers of post-war Europe (Austria, Germany, and Italy)[5] and the inauguration of a regional Court of Human Rights for Western Europe in 1959, the court-centric legal paradigm for supporting democratisation has spread worldwide.

In the various 'waves'[6] of democratisation since 1945 a 'new constitutionalism',[7] focused on transformative constitutional texts and expansive bills of rights, saw constitutional courts and strong judicial review become 'standard equipment'[8] for states transitioning from Communist, military, and autocratic rule, across Europe, South America, Africa, and East Asia, with the perceived democratisation successes of post-war European courts exerting a strong influence.[9] Regional human rights

---

[4] E.C. Dawson, 'Adjusting the Presumption of Constitutionality Based on Margin of Statutory Passage' (2013) 16 *University of Pennsylvania Journal of Constitutional Law* 97, 100.

[5] Constitutional courts were established in Austria, Germany, and Italy in 1945, 1951, and 1956 respectively.

[6] See Chapter 1, Section 2.

[7] M. Shapiro & A. Stone, 'The New Constitutional Politics of Europe' (1994) 26 *Comparative Political Studies* 397.

[8] D. Horowitz, 'Constitutional Courts: A Primer for Decision Makers' in L. Diamond & M. Plattner (eds.), *Democracy: A Reader* (Johns Hopkins University Press, 2009) 183.

[9] Ginsburg observes: 'Germany's Constitutional Court is arguably the most influential court outside the US in terms of its institutional structure and jurisprudence.' T. Ginsburg, 'The Global Spread of Constitutional Review' in A. Caldeira, R.D. Kelemen & K.E. Whittington (eds.), *The Oxford Handbook of Law and Politics* (Oxford University Press, 2008) 85–6.

courts, in turn, have been established in two other world regions: the Americas and Africa.[10] The Inter-American Court of Human Rights is perceived as having played a key role in democratisation processes across Latin America since the late 1980s.[11] A democratisation role was conferred on the European Court of Human Rights with the enlargement of the Council of Europe in the 1990s to include Turkey and the new democracies of the post-Communist world in Central and Eastern Europe.[12] Since its first merits judgment in 2013, the African Court on Human and Peoples' Rights has taken a strident approach in cases concerning non-inclusive electoral arrangements, free speech, and fair trial (albeit not in a context of sweeping regional democratisation).[13] An Arab Court of Human Rights is reportedly close to establishment,[14] and there are growing calls for an Asian Court of Human Rights.[15]

The focus on courts as key actors in new democracies shows no sign of abating, in scholarship or practice. For instance, at a conference in 2014 on constitutional reforms in the Middle East and North Africa – bringing together judges, constitutional lawyers, and political activists from across the region, as well as international experts – discussion of legal mechanisms for enhancing rights protection and supporting nascent or potential democratisation processes in Arab states was dominated by courts.[16] Delegates debated the promise and perils of domestic courts

[10] See Chapter 3.   [11] See the quotations at the start of Chapter 3.
[12] In 1998 the Council of Europe's recently resigned Deputy Secretary General opined: 'The [Council's] new task is to play an active role in "democracy-building" in the post-communist countries'. P. Leuprecht, 'Innovations in the European System of Human Rights Protection: Is Enlargement Compatible with Reinforcement?' (1998) 8 *Transnational Law & Contemporary Problems* 313, 317.
[13] Discussed in Chapters 3 and 6.
[14] 'Plan to Establish Arab Court of Human Rights in Final Stage' *Arab News* 23 February 2016 www.arabnews.com/saudi-arabia/news/884921. Such a court had been mooted as long ago as 1986: see A.A. An-Na'im, 'Human Rights in the Arab World: A Regional Perspective' (2001) 23 *Human Rights Quarterly* 701, 714–15. See further discussion in Chapter 3.
[15] See e.g. M. de Visser, 'Cultivating Judicial Conversations on Human Rights Protection under the Auspices of a Regional Rights Regime' *The Asian Yearbook of Human Rights and Humanitarian Law* (forthcoming, 2017); S. Chiam, 'Asia's Experience in the Quest for a Regional Human Rights Mechanism' (2009) 40 *Victoria University of Wellington Law Review* 127; and the Third Congress of the World Conference on Constitutional Justice, 'Seoul Communiqué' (30 September 2014) www.venice.coe.int/wccj/seoul/WCCJ_Seoul_Communique-E.pdf. See also H.D. Phan, 'A Blueprint for a Southeast Asian Court of Human Rights' (2009) 10 *Asian-Pacific Law & Policy Journal* 384.
[16] Arab Association of Constitutional Law, Third Annual Conference, 'Enforcement Mechanisms and the Protection of Political, Economic and Social Rights', Beirut, Lebanon, 16–17 October 2014. The author attended as an invited speaker.

and the recently announced Arab Court of Human Rights as democratic or undemocratic institutions, as well as a formal Tunisian proposal to the UN General Assembly for the establishment of an International Constitutional Court, to issue decisions on mass rights violations, the holding of elections, and serious violations of international law principles related to democracy.[17] Even sessions specifically devoted to non-judicial mechanisms persistently returned to talk of judicial review, as though on a loop.

In Tunisia, the one potentially viable democracy to emerge from the Arab Spring, a new Constitutional Court endowed with an array of powers, though yet to be established, is viewed as 'the centerpiece of the Tunisian legal order.'[18] Beyond the Arab region, courts are centre stage in contemporary democracy-building processes across the globe, such as those in Nepal, Sri Lanka, Kenya, and Zimbabwe.[19] At the international level, a chorus of scholars and policy-makers supports the establishment of human rights courts in the remaining world regions (Asia and the Pacific[20]), or even a World Court of Human Rights.[21]

Thus, the promise of domestic constitutional courts and regional human rights courts as democracy-builders now forms a *fil rouge* connecting post-authoritarian states across the globe. These courts represent a central 'democratisation technology' in the minds of many scholars and in the toolkit of domestic and international constitution-makers and law-makers.

B   The Distinct Role of Courts in New Democracies

What is distinctive about the roles of these courts in new democracies, compared to their functions in mature democracies? A central claim of this book is that the democratisation context alters courts' roles, and changes our perspective on familiar questions concerning the legitimate roles courts can play in democratic governance, for five principal reasons.

---

[17] See D. Landau, 'Abusive Constitutionalism' (2013) 47 *UC Davis Law Review* 189, 257–8. See also International IDEA, 'International Constitutional Court proposed to protect democracy' 4 May 2013 www.oldsite.idea.int/wana/international-constitutional-court-proposed-to-protect-democracy.cfm.

[18] See Mekki, 'The Tunisian Constitutional Court'.

[19] For instance, Kenya's constitutional reform process, centred on the new Constitution of 2010, included the establishment of a new Supreme Court with broader jurisdiction and powers than its previous iteration. See also Jayawickrama, 'Establishing a Constitutional Court'.

[20] See the sources cited at (n 15).

[21] See e.g. M. Nowak, 'On the Creation of a World Court of Human Rights' (2012) 7 *National Taiwan University Law Review* 257.

First, in new democracies strong judicial review,[22] which accords the final say on constitutional matters to the courts, often forms a fundamental component of the political bargain underpinning the very transition to democratic rule. It is thus viewed, not as an option, but as a prerequisite for the democratic project. Second, a new democracy is paradigmatically underpinned by a new or substantially revised constitution (or a new constitutional understanding[23]) and a significant residue of authoritarian-era laws, which requires the courts to engage in wholescale constitutional construction while remaking ordinary law in the democratic image of the constitution. This differs starkly from the general constitutional 'fine-tuning' role of a court in a mature democracy. Third, submission to the jurisdiction of a regional human rights court is often viewed as a symbolic act underscoring a commitment to democratic rule, as well as a useful adjunct to support nascent domestic institutions. Fourth, the relationship between the courts at each level is itself shaped by the trajectory and vicissitudes of the democratisation process, with regional adjudication, designed as a 'back-up' system, tending to assume more prominence either through adherence by domestic courts to regional case-law, or where domestic adjudication is deemed lacking – whether due to the unwillingness or incapacity of the domestic constitutional court to engage in robust decision-making. Finally, in new democracies the capacity of other actors in the democratic order to play their part in democracy-building is limited, in a context where multiparty politics is often nascent or stifled by dominance of a single party, civil society is weak, and citizens are unschooled in democratic deliberation and the wielding of political power.

These reasons all point to some justification for strong judicial review as a necessary component of successful democracy-building, although they do not address the extent to which courts should assume central roles in democratisation processes, nor the true nature of their adjudicatory function in such processes. In the sense of 'judging' democratisation, we are faced with the crucial question of when the specific demands of supporting or navigating the democratisation process justify a court's taking a more assertive or more deferential approach than might be appropriate in the context of a mature democracy. Whether we can trust courts to carry out such a difficult task, what happens when the courts at each level disagree, and whether we can trust other state organs in new

---

[22] The term 'strong judicial review' is defined at the end of this Introduction.
[23] This is discussed in more depth in Chapter 1, Section 5.B.

democracies, or even the people, to carry more of the 'democratisation burden' apportioned to courts under the post-war model are all vital questions. This book focuses on the first two questions, but with the other questions in mind.

2 Gaps in the Literature

The key questions set out above are not systematically addressed in existing scholarship on the role of constitutional courts and regional human rights courts in democratisation processes, which is scattered across a wide array of distinct but overlapping research fields. These generally consist of a shared terrain between two key disciplines, political science and law. On even a short roll-call are legal theory, political philosophy, constitutional theory, comparative constitutional law, law and politics, judicial politics, democratisation studies, transitional justice, and international human rights law.

The core scholarship here is a small number of region-specific analyses of the roles played by constitutional courts in new democracies, including Wojciech Sadurski, Jan Zielonka, and Kim Lane Scheppele on Central and Eastern Europe; Roberto Gargarella, Siri Gloppen, Gretchen Helmke, and Irwin Stotzky on Latin America (and, to a lesser extent, Africa); Theunis Roux and Magnus Killander on Africa; and Tom Ginsburg on East Asia.[24] Others, such as Samuel Issacharoff, Andrew Harding,

---

[24] See W. Sadurski, *Rights Before Courts: A Study of Constitutional Courts in Postcommunist States of Central and Eastern Europe* (Springer, 2008); W. Sadurski (ed.), *Constitutional Justice, East and West: Democratic Legitimacy and Constitutional Courts in Post-Communist Europe in a Comparative Perspective* (Springer, 2002); J. Zielonka (ed.), *Democratic Consolidation in Eastern Europe, Vol. 1: Institutional Engineering* (Oxford University Press, 2001); K.L. Scheppele, 'Guardians of the Constitution: Constitutional Court Presidents and the Struggle for the Rule of Law in Post-Soviet Europe' (2006) 154 *University of Pennsylvania Law Review* 1757; K.L. Scheppele, 'Democracy by Judiciary (Or Why Courts Can Sometimes Be More Democratic than Parliaments)' in W. Sadurski, M. Krygier & A. Czarnota (eds.), *Rethinking the Rule of Law in Post-Communist Europe: Past Legacies, Institutional Innovations, and Constitutional Discourses* (Central European University Press, 2005); K. Lane Scheppele, 'The New Hungarian Constitutional Court' (1999) 8 *Eastern European Constitutional Review* 81; G. Helmke & J. Ríos-Figueroa (eds.), *Courts in Latin America* (Cambridge University Press, 2011); S. Gloppen, B.M. Wilson, R. Gargarella, E. Skaar & M. Kinander (eds.), *Courts and Power in Latin America and Africa* (Palgrave MacMillan, 2010); S. Gloppen, R. Gargarella & E. Skaar (eds.), *Democratization and the Judiciary: The Accountability Function of Courts in New Democracies* (Routledge, 2004); I. Stotzky (ed.), *Transition to Democracy in Latin America: The Role of the Judiciary* (Westview Press, 1993); T. Roux, *The Politics of Principle: The First South*

Peter Leyland, Daniel Bonilla Maldonado, Diana Kapiszewski, Oscar Vilhena Vieira, and Upendra Baxi provide cross-regional comparisons of constitutional courts.[25] Important scholarship using specific country case-studies (e.g. Russia, Argentina, Indonesia) has also been developed by authors including Nancy Maveety, Rebecca Bill Chavez, and Marcus Mietzner.[26]

Analysis of the specific roles played by regional human rights courts in new democracies remains rare. Europe is the principal focus, with three main works on the European Court of Human Rights: an edited collection by the transitional justice scholars Michael Hamilton and Antoine Buyse; a monograph by the transitional justice scholar James Sweeney; and a co-authored work by Christopher McCrudden and Brendan O'Leary focusing on the European Court's widely criticised judgment in *Sejdić and Finci v. Bosnia and Herzegovina*,[27] which found aspects of

---

African Constitutional Court, 1995–2005 (Cambridge University Press, 2013); T. Roux, 'The South African Constitutional Court's Democratic Rights Jurisprudence: A Response to Samuel Issacharoff' (2014) 5 *Constitutional Court Review* 33; T. Roux, 'Principle and Pragmatism on the Constitutional Court of South Africa' (2009) 7 *International Journal of Constitutional Law* 106; M. Killander (ed.), *International Law and Domestic Human Rights Litigation in Africa* (Pretoria University Law Press, 2010); T. Ginsburg, *Judicial Review in New Democracies: Constitutional Courts in Asian Cases* (Cambridge University Press, 2003); and A. Harding & P. Nicholson (eds.), *New Courts in Asia* (Routledge, 2010).

[25] See S. Issacharoff, *Fragile Democracies: Contested Power in the Era of Constitutional Courts* (Cambridge University Press, 2015); S. Issacharoff, 'Constitutional Courts and Democratic Hedging' (2011) 99 *Georgetown Law Journal* 961; S. Issacharoff, 'Constitutional Courts and Consolidated Power', (2014) NYU Public Law and Legal Theory Working Papers, Paper 459; S. Issacharoff, 'The Democratic Risk to Democratic Transitions', (2013) NYU Public Law and Legal Theory Working Papers, Paper 418; A. Harding & P. Leyland (eds.), *Constitutional Courts: A Comparative Study* (Wildy, Simmonds & Hill Publishing, 2009); D. Bonilla Maldonado (ed.), *Constitutionalism of the Global South: The Activist Tribunals of India, South Africa, and Colombia* (Cambridge University Press, 2013); O. Vilhena Vieira, F. Viljoen & U. Baxi (eds.), *Transformative Constitutionalism: Comparing the Apex Courts of Brazil, India and South Africa* (Pretoria University Law Press, 2013). See also D. Kapiszewski, G. Silverstein & R.A. Kagan (eds.), *Consequential Courts: Judicial Roles in Global Perspective* (Cambridge University Press, 2013) chs. 1–5.

[26] See N. Maveety & A. Grosskopf, '"Constrained" Constitutional Courts as Conduits for Democratic Consolidation' (2004) 38 *Law & Society Review* 463; C.J. Walker, 'Toward Democratic Consolidation: The Argentine Supreme Court, Judicial Independence, and the Rule of Law' (2006) 18 *Florida Journal of International Law* 745; R.B. Chavez, *The Rule of Law in Nascent Democracies: Judicial Politics in Argentina* (Stanford University Press, 2004); and M. Mietzner, 'Political Conflict Resolution and Democratic Consolidation in Indonesia: The Role of the Constitutional Court' (2010) 10 *Journal of East Asian Studies* 397.

[27] ECtHR, App. Nos. 27996/06 and 34836/06 (22 December 2009).

the Bosnian consociational political system to be incompatible with the European Convention on Human Rights (ECHR).[28] Literature on the Inter-American Court of Human Rights is modest,[29] but recent ground-breaking comparative work by Alexandra Huneeus has provided greater understanding of the democracy-building roles of both the European and Inter-American courts.[30] Analysis of the African Court on Human and Peoples' Rights remains scant, given that its first merits judgment was not issued until 2013.[31]

Despite providing significant insights into the roles of courts in the post-war model for judicialised democratisation, these roles as yet remain unclear and far from fully understood. The existing scholarship suffers from five central deficiencies.

First, existing scholarship does not engage sufficiently with the foundational concept of democratisation itself; in terms of what it really means, and when it starts and ends. This is essential to any discussion of how we view courts' roles in this process. Second, there is a tendency to focus on single-country case-studies, and an inordinate focus on a small number of empirical contexts (e.g. South Africa, Hungary, Colombia). Third, the literature fails to capture the very particular context of adjudication in a new democracy, and how this context shapes not only how the courts approach their adjudicative role, but also objective justifications for a role that differs from that of courts in mature democracies. Fourth, in the majority of the literature, produced largely by political scientists, and by lawyers using political science methodologies, the unique nature of courts as legal institutions is easily obscured. The

---

[28] See A. Buyse & M. Hamilton (eds.), *Transitional Jurisprudence and the ECHR: Justice, Politics and Rights* (Cambridge University Press, 2011); J.A. Sweeney, *The European Court of Human Rights in the Post-Cold War Era: Universality in Transition* (Routledge, 2013); and C. McCrudden & B. O'Leary, *Courts & Consociations: Human Rights versus Power-Sharing* (Oxford University Press, 2013).

[29] See A. Dulitzky, 'An Inter-American Constitutional Court? The Invention of the Conventionality Control by the Inter-American Court of Human Rights' (2015) 50(1) *Texas International Law Journal* 45; D. Rodríguez-Pinzón, 'The Inter-American Human Rights System and Transitional Processes' in Buyse & Hamilton (eds.), *Transitional Jurisprudence and the ECHR: Justice, Politics and Rights* (Cambridge University Press, 2011); and D García-Sayan, 'The Inter-American Court and Constitutionalism in Latin America' (2011) 89 *Texas Law Review* 1835.

[30] A. Huneeus, 'Reforming the State from Afar: Structural Reform Litigation at the Human Rights Courts' (2015) 40(1) *Yale Journal of International Law* 1.

[31] The leading work on the African regional human rights system was published before the African Court had issued its first full judgment in 2013: M. Kiwinda Mbondenyi, *International Human Rights and their Enforcement in Africa* (LawAfrica, 2011).

primary focus tends to be on judicial behaviour and strategy, using game theory, rational choice institutionalism, and other behavioural methodologies. This provides useful insights, but often fails to fully capture the nature of adjudication in a new democracy, and tends to privilege the outcome and impact of judgments over their content. We are left with an incomplete picture, which fails to appreciate the impact of doctrinal development and contestation *within* courts on the roles they assume as democracy-builders.

Fifth, and perhaps more importantly, there is a stark divide between a vast literature on domestic constitutional courts in new democracies and a much smaller literature on the impact of regional human rights courts on such states. Analysis of courts at the domestic level does not integrate the role of courts at the regional level, or *vice versa*, with the result that their interaction in the context of democratisation is never fully explored and remains underconceptualised. In addition, existing scholarship fails to capture, more generally, the multiple and overlapping systemic interaction between courts and non-judicial sites of constitutional authority across the domestic and regional levels, and how this raises a complex scenario of 'variable geometry' where assertive action at any one site has ramifications for the roles carried out by the other actors.

This glaring gap reflects the fact that the relevant literature as a whole is contained in discrete silos. There is little connection or communication between specific fields of scholarship that analyse different aspects of the roles of courts in new democracies. In particular, as we will see, normative arguments concerning the roles that courts should play in supporting democratisation processes often engage to a limited extent not only with the core debate on the judicial role in mature democracies,[32] but also, more importantly, with other normative arguments focused on the role of courts as democracy-builders. To a certain extent, this fragmentation is due to the differing preoccupations of scholars, addressing different questions to those in this book.

3   Scope of the Book

A   What the Book Aims to Achieve

Evidently, no monograph can attempt to fully address all of the deficiencies in the literature described above. This project does not aim to fully

---

[32] Discussed at the end of the Introduction.

answer all of these questions, but to ask the right questions; questions that are not addressed systematically in the existing literature.

The main aim of the book is to make a meaningful contribution to existing normative debates concerning the proper roles of courts as democracy-builders, which considers the strengths and limits of the court-centric post-war model of democratisation, integrates the role of regional courts,[33] and is more mindful of the strengths and weaknesses of adjudication at the domestic and regional levels. In order to do so, it provides a historical account of the development of the judicialised post-war model of democratisation; constructs a conceptual and analytical framework that is heuristically useful for exploring what is distinctive about the democratisation context and the role of courts in that context; and seeks to reveal the 'real world' nature of adjudication in the democratisation context at both the domestic and regional levels.

The Brazilian scenario briefly discussed at the start of this introduction remains at the heart of the book, but it is used to illuminate the post-war global model of court-centric democratisation as a whole. To do so, the book traces the origins of the post-war template for adjudication as a component of successful democratisation to the experience of post-1945 West Germany, and its global spread through the various post-war waves of democratisation across the world, which from the 1980s onwards began to include regional human rights courts as well as domestic constitutional courts. The book underscores the different roles played by the courts at each level, by conceptualising these roles in a general sense, applying this conceptual framework to examine the roles of the Brazilian Supreme Court and the Inter-American Court in Brazil's democratisation process, and placing these roles in a regional and inter-regional comparative perspective. By placing the inter-court contestation concerning Brazil's amnesty law within a much wider historical, regional, and global context, we get a sense of not only how courts in new democracies worldwide have come to be perceived as such central actors to successful democratisation processes, but also their limits in this regard and the democratic difficulties raised by their centrality.

---

[33] In this way, the book reflects calls in political science for treating the study of constitutional courts and regional human rights courts as a single field: see J.K. Staton & W.H. Moore, 'Judicial Power in Domestic and International Politics' (2011) 65 *International Organization* 553.

B Why Brazil?

As well as providing a useful example of a lack of harmony between the domestic constitutional court and the regional human rights court, Brazil has been chosen as the core case-study of the book for three additional reasons.

First, the Brazilian experience of democracy-building after the transition to democracy in 1985 has been understudied compared to states that transitioned to democracy in the post-Cold War period from 1989 onward (e.g. Hungary, South Africa), especially as regards analysis of relevant domestic and regional case-law.

Second, is the peculiar institutional form of the Supreme Federal Court: in the constitutional reform culminating in the 1988 Constitution, reformers considered – but ultimately eschewed – the creation of a 'European-style' constitutional court with exclusive powers of constitutional review. Yet, they embraced such a radical overhaul of the Court's jurisdiction, and the structure of the judiciary as a whole, that it was left looking more like a constitutional court closer to the European model than a classic American-style Supreme Court (although its work continued to be dominated by appeals). In this one court, then, we get two advantages: an institution that has faced the challenge of navigating the different roles of both types of court (which becomes clear in Chapter 5); and an excellent example of the post-war shift toward an ever greater burden on the constitutional court in a new democracy as an engine of democratisation.

Third, although many constitutional courts allow dissenting opinions, the Brazilian court's case-law is particularly revealing given that its adjudication takes place through a public *seriatim* procedure where judges provide their 'votes' in open court on the basis of a draft judgment by a rapporteur-judge, without having previously deliberated together to find common ground.[34] It therefore provides an interesting window into naked intra-Court contestation concerning democratisation and the Court's proper role as a democracy-builder.

C A Few Caveats

A number of caveats are warranted regarding the scope and orientation of this project. While the book proceeds from the premise that the roles

---

[34] See V.A. da Silva, 'Deciding without Deliberating' (2013) 11 *International Journal of Constitutional Law* 557.

of courts at both levels in democratisation processes has often been exaggerated, this is not to suggest that courts are merely epiphenomenal in democratisation processes. It is recognised that courts can play a significant role and can have a crucial impact at critical junctures in the democratisation process.

It is also recognised that to some extent the role of courts in 'building democracy' is a perennial. John Hart Ely's theory of judicial review in his seminal 1981 work *Democracy and Distrust*, for instance, argued that the US Supreme Court's core role should be to reinforce democratic governance by ensuring broad participation in electoral and decision-making processes and fair representation of all (including minorities) by those elected.[35] However, the focus here is not on courts reinforcing democratic governance in Western states that enjoyed a slow march toward democracy, such as the United States or the United Kingdom, but remains at all times on the trend since the 1970s in particular to expect courts to act as central engines of a more rapid democratisation process in the first decades of a post-authoritarian polity.

It is also acknowledged that other courts could be considered democracy-builders; for example, national courts besides constitutional courts, or international courts such as the East African Court of Justice (EACJ) or the International Criminal Court (ICC). However, this book confines its focus to constitutional courts and regional human rights courts, which have generally been presented as the central judicial democracy-builders in both scholarship and policymaking.

In addition, the book does not directly focus on the very specific case of the European Court of Justice (ECJ)'s role in enhancing the democratic credentials of the EU (e.g. by strengthening the powers of the European Parliament), on the basis that the EU and ECJ are entirely European phenomena that have not been replicated, and are unlikely to be replicated, elsewhere.[36]

Nor do I view it as a 'rights' study, in the sense that it does not analyse the role of courts exclusively through the lens of human rights; rather, it takes a structural approach that places emphasis on the need to achieve structural stability and a level of organisational functioning in a new democracy, which provides a wider analytical framework for assessing

---

[35] J. Hart Ely, *Democracy and Distrust. A Theory of Judicial Review* (Harvard University Press, 1981). See also R. Pildes, *The Law of Democracy: Legal Structure of the Political Process* (Foundation Press, 1998).

[36] This is addressed in more detail at the end of Chapter 1.

democracy-building. That said, it is fully recognised here that a core ultimate aim of successful democratisation is to improve rights protection as a whole in a society emerging from authoritarian rule, given that debasement of rights is a hallmark of such rule.

In addition, the book does not deal at any length with issues such as judicial selection and judicial independence, which are addressed in detail in other works.[37] The book also does not focus on post-conflict contexts, although much of its content may have some relevance to those contexts. While the temporal scope of the book may appear extremely long, covering some seventy years, the heart of the study concerns a time-span running from the late 1980s, when the European and Inter-American human rights courts began to operate in earnest, and the global spread of constitutional courts had started to become manifest.

Finally, it may appear odd that a book arguing against excessive focus on courts is itself centred on courts. However, there is a real need to anatomise and better understand this 'court obsession' before we can move to considering how to address and rebalance it. This book therefore dwells for the most part on the first task, only moving at the very end to considering how we might begin to approach rebalancing our current court-centric democracy-building models. Evidently, it would be impossible to do full justice to the second task in the course of one book.

D   Interlocutors

To whom is this book addressed? Despite its cross-cutting approach, perhaps the most natural home for the book is in the 'big tent' of law and politics, in the corner occupied by studies of the judicial role in democratic governance. It is therefore primarily aimed at adding to existing analyses by scholars such as Alec Stone Sweet, Samuel Issacharoff, Kim Lane Scheppele, Ariel Dulitzky, Anne-Marie Slaughter, David Landau, Rosalind Dixon, Denis Galligan, Karen Alter, Martin Shapiro, Roberto Gargarella, Alexandra Huneeus, Nico Krisch, Tom Ginsburg, Ran Hirschl, Nina Binder, James Sweeney, and Christopher McCrudden, among others.

---

[37] See e.g. A. Seibert-Fohr (ed.), *Judicial Independence in Transition* (Springer, 2012); P.H. Russell & D.M. O'Brien, *Judicial Independence in the Age of Democracy: Critical Perspectives from Around the World* (University of Virginia Press, 2001); J.C. Calleros, *The Unfinished Transition to Democracy in Latin America* (Routledge, 2009); and R.B. Chavez, 'The Rule of Law and Courts in Democratizing Regimes' in Caldeira, Kelemen & Whittington (eds.), *Law and Politics*.

There are a variety of 'entry points' to the book, whether one is interested in law and development, the interface between domestic and international law, 'judicial dialogue', post-national governance, the democratic legitimacy of strong judicial review, comparative judicial review, comparative constitutional law, or the spread of regional human rights courts. More widely, it is hoped that the study may be of use to policy-makers and organisations involved in legal reform in existing and future democratising states, as they are currently operating without any systematic account of the potential, operation, limits, and drawbacks of constitutional courts and regional human rights courts, and the inter-action between such courts. Such an account is sorely needed if they are to make recommendations that fully appreciate the complexity of these courts' relationships to both successful democratisation and good governance.

4   Structure, Arguments, and Conceptual Framework

The book contains seven substantive chapters.

Chapter 1 explores the concept of democratisation as the first step in sketching an analytical framework for examining the role of courts as democracy-builders. The chapter seeks to explain what is distinctive about democratisation, including how we define it, what temporal markers it contains, and when it might be said to end. It addresses the relationship between democratisation theory and the conceptual frame-works provided by transitional justice theory and social justice, and explains why the former framework is preferred in this book, as avoiding the terminological and conceptual confusion rife in the literature, and permitting the sequence of events typical of democratisation to be more precisely located. This allows the activity of courts to be related to, and viewed within, the overall context of democratisation. The chapter then constructs an analytical framework fundamentally based on a reading of democratisation theory (and, in particular, the sub-concept of 'democratic consolidation'), but refined through an exploration of the relation-ship between democratisation and two other key concepts: democracy and constitutionalism, at both the domestic and regional levels.

Chapters 2 and 3, which address constitutional courts and regional human rights courts respectively, narrate the development of the global model of court-centric democratisation, and the widespread perception of courts as central to democratisation processes. It is argued that the model, and the perceptions underpinning it, find their roots in a novel form of constitutional adjudication pioneered by the Federal Constitutional Court of Germany from 1951 onward, and a perception of that court as central to West Germany's successful return to full democratic governance by the 1970s. It is contended that this led not only to constitutional courts assuming prominence in constitution-making for subsequent new democracies, but also paved the way for meaningful adjudication by regional human rights courts, with the Inter-American Court of Human Rights as the quintessential 'democratisation court' at this level. Both chapters challenge the perception of the power of courts to drive democratisation as based on unsound premises, tending to elide the propitious context for democratisation in Western European states of the immediate post-war period (particularly Germany), tending to place unrealistic expectations on courts in regional contexts outside Western Europe, which have not enjoyed the same advantages, and often overstating the impact and capacities of regional human rights courts as democracy-builders.

Having challenged the often unrealistic perceptions of courts as democracy-builders in Chapters 2 and 3, Chapter 4 seeks to explore in more depth the roles that constitutional courts and regional human rights courts play in 'democratic consolidation', as defined in Chapter 1. The aim of the chapter is to conceptualise the different but intersecting roles that the domestic and regional courts play, emphasising that the significant particularities of the context of a new democracy, compared to a mature democracy, fundamentally shape the roles assumed by the courts. The chapter first conceptualises the roles of constitutional and regional human rights courts separately, asserting that the former act as primary sites of normativity embedded within a single democratisation context, whereas the latter act as secondary sites of normativity, external to any particular democratisation context, which can assume primacy where the domestic courts are perceived as failing to provide sufficient rights protection. This discussion is then refined through a fuller conceptualisation of the interaction between the courts at each level, challenging and adding nuance to the common presentation of the courts as partners in a coherent system of adjudication.

Chapters 5 and 6, which concern domestic and international adjudication respectively, apply the conceptual framework set out in Chapter 4 to a comparative analysis of the Brazilian scenario discussed at the start of this Introduction, in order to achieve a finer-grained picture of the texture and nature of 'democratisation jurisprudence' at each level based on empirical evidence. These chapters first explore the different impacts of the Supreme Court of Brazil and the Inter-American Court of Human Rights on Brazil's democratisation process and the implications of the conflictual relationship between the two courts for other actors in the democratic order. In the latter half of Chapter 6 the Brazilian context is compared to the wider regional and global contexts, through significant comparison to the African and European contexts, which shows the extent to which it exemplifies, and departs from, the post-war model of court-centric democracy-building.

Based on the empirical data and conceptual framework built up in the first six chapters, Chapter 7 explores normative debates concerning the appropriate role for courts as democracy-builders, contrasting these with the 'core' debate on the role of courts in a mature democratic order. The chapter critically reviews the existing normative stances as generally failing to integrate adjudication at the regional level, often talking past one another, and having insufficient regard for concerns regarding democratic legitimacy. The chapter then presents a normative position that departs in key ways from existing positions, particularly by integrating regional human rights courts. First, it makes an argument for how existing courts might operate more effectively separately, and as a system, to support democratisation. Second, and perhaps more importantly, it tentatively begins to explore a range of constitutional design options for the future that may improve the capacity of courts to act effectively as democracy-builders, arguing for a rebalancing of the existing democracy-building model for post-authoritarian societies away from excessive reliance on courts.

Finally, the 'concluding thoughts' at the end engage in a spot of future-gazing, asking whether the court-centric model of democratisation will persist into the future, or whether it is already ceding to a new paradigm.

5   Methodology

The methodology of the project blends elements of philosophical, doctrinal, and social analysis of courts as democracy-builders, but the fundamental purpose is to analyse the roles of these courts as social institutions,[38] and how they impact on, function in, and are affected by the particular social and political context of democratisation. If a label must be attached to the overall methodological thrust, perhaps the most

---

[38] See further, D.J. Galligan & M. Versteeg (eds.), *Social and Political Foundations of Constitutions* (Cambridge University Press, 2013).

apt is 'practical reasoning'.[39] This seeks to derive general conclusions from particular instances and to appreciate a complex reality, rather than framing a general argument and applying it to specific instances. It is not the fundamental choice of an inductive approach over a deductive approach. Rather, a reflexive relationship is maintained between both approaches. Theoretical discussion at the beginning serves to frame how we view and filter an embarrassment of empirical data on courts in new democracies. In turn, the analysis of empirical data feeds into the theoretical discussion in the final chapter. The book remains, at all times, tethered to the empirical reality.

The study is conducted through a small-n research design that combines a critical literature review with a focus on a small number of case-studies, along diachronic and synchronic axes. Necessarily, different methodological approaches predominate in each chapter: Chapters 1, 4, and 7 are conceptual and theoretical in nature; Chapters 2 and 3 are largely historical, and the central comparative case-study in Chapters 5 and 6 focuses on doctrinal analysis within the conceptual framework set out in Chapter 4.

The core case-studies, of the German Federal Constitutional Court in Chapter 2 and the comparative case-study of the Brazilian Supreme Court and Inter-American Court in Chapters 5 and 6, are used as empirical foils for discussing normative stances on the roles of such courts in Chapter 7. In particular, focusing on the Latin American context as the core case-study serves a dual purpose. First, it adds to an existing literature whose dominant focus to date has been on constitutional courts in the European context, and where only the role of the European Court of Human Rights in new democracies has been the subject of systematic study. Second, as compared to the very particular European context, the reality of regional governance in Latin America, and the institutional set-up of the Inter-American regional human rights system, is more similar to that seen in Africa. The Latin American experience therefore not only deepens our understanding of courts as democracy-builders in that region, but appears to have more resonance for the African context than the European experience, as seen in Chapter 6.[40]

---

[39] A useful summary of 'practical reasoning' is found in S. Brewer (ed.), *Evolution and Revolution in Theories of Legal Reasoning: Nineteenth Century Through the Present*, Vol. 4 (Taylor & Francis, 1998) 850ff.

[40] Indeed, the institutional ties between both systems are deepening. For instance, at its second 'Continental Judicial Dialogue' in 2015, the African Court invited judges from

The reliance on doctrinal analysis in Chapters 5 and 6 warrants some explanation, given that textual analysis of decisions appears somewhat *démodé* in research on courts, where political scientists, and their methodologies, are increasingly dominant. It is used in this book because, ultimately, it is the only way to unpack the very real contestation within courts themselves regarding the permissible limits of their role, their view of their constitutional 'mission' in the new democracy, and their perception of the democratisation context itself, as well as their systemic interaction with one another and with third party actors at the domestic level in the task of democracy-building.

In a sense, a judicial decision is the closest one can get to a 'unit' of democratisation. Each case presents a vignette, whether of political power plays, authoritarian impulses, inter-branch conflict, individual–state conflict, state–international conflict, or inter-court contestation. From the vignettes one progressively builds a collage, which – however impressionistic – illuminates the contested roles of the courts in democratisation processes, and the nature of those processes, as a whole. It is also vital to a presentation of courts that seeks to avoid representing them as monolithic entities, of one mind and voice. Such analysis is therefore 'added value' that lawyers can bring to the existing scholarship.

6   Defining Key Terms

For the purposes of clarity, it is worthwhile to define and briefly discuss key terms in the text.

A   Constitutional Courts

Typically, the term 'constitutional court' denotes a decision-making institution which is separate from the ordinary judiciary, and which has the final, and usually exclusive, say on the interpretation of the constitution, as well as the constitutional validity of laws and state action. The term 'supreme court', by contrast, denotes a judicial institution at the apex of the ordinary judiciary, which operates both as the final

the Inter-American Court to share their experiences. See O. Windridge, '2015 at the African Court on Human and Peoples' Rights – A Year in Review' *The ACtHPR Monitor* 25 January 2016 www.acthprmonitor.org/2015-at-the-african-court-on-human-and-peoples-rights-a-year-in-review.

interpreter of the constitution as well as the final court of appeal concerning various non-constitutional matters.

Although constitutional courts and supreme courts exhibit significant differences (see below), this book employs the term 'constitutional court' for both types of court, where they engage in constitutional review in the sole or final instance. This is to avoid the cumbersome reference to 'constitutional and supreme courts', or to 'apex courts', the latter term being widely used, but which, in reference to constitutional courts, is not technically correct.

For the purposes of analytical clarity, a certain ideal type has to be used. A constitutional court is defined, using Conrado Hübner Mendes' minimal formula, as 'a (i) multi-member and non-elected body that, (ii) when provoked by external actors, (iii) may challenge, on constitutional grounds, legislation enacted by a representative parliament.'[41]

Supreme Courts v. Kelsenian Courts

Notwithstanding the definition above, it is necessary to briefly observe that a number of basic typologies are employed in the literature; the most fundamental being the distinction between supreme courts in the 'American' mould (hereinafter, 'supreme courts') and 'European' constitutional courts based on the principles elaborated by the Austrian legal philosopher Hans Kelsen in the 1920s (hereinafter, 'Kelsenian courts').[42] The former have general jurisdiction while the latter specialise in constitutional adjudication. Review can be decentralised or centralised. Ordinary courts in 'American' systems are empowered to disapply laws deemed unconstitutional, while the supreme court enjoys the exclusive power to strike down laws.[43] In Kelsenian systems the constitutional court enjoys a monopoly on questions of constitutionality. In 'American' systems constitutional questions only come before the supreme court as part of a

---

[41] C. Hübner Mendes, *Constitutional Courts and Deliberative Democracy* (Oxford University Press, 2013) 11.

[42] The wide variety of systems of strong judicial review worldwide is presented by e.g. A. Mavčič, *The Constitutional Review* (2nd edn, Vandeplas Publishing, 2013); and A. Harding, P. Leyland & T. Groppi, 'Constitutional Courts: Forms, Functions and Practice in Comparative Perspective' in Harding & Leyland (eds.), *Constitutional Courts*. The diversity in Europe alone is addressed in M. de Visser, *Constitutional Review in Europe: A Comparative Analysis* (Hart, 2014).

[43] In the US system the Supreme Court technically does not 'invalidate' laws, but the effect of a finding of unconstitutionality is to bar the application of the law, leading to a very similar result.

concrete case, whereas Kelsenian courts can perform abstract review of laws as well as concrete review. Abstract review may be *a priori* (before a bill is promulgated as law) or *a posteriori* (after a bill becomes law).

Enduring and useful as this typology is, it is important to recognise that it does not capture the diversity and complexity of courts in regions such as Latin America, which defy traditional taxonomies by mixing decentralised review with centralised review, through the creation of novel constitutional review mechanisms that do not exist in other world regions, and with review powers in some states shared between supreme courts and Kelsenian courts.[44] Although often described as a hybrid of American and European models, given the venerable tradition of judicial review in the region such a characterisation can be unhelpfully reductive.

Much of the literature on strong judicial review in the new democracies that emerged after 1945 focuses on Kelsenian courts. Considered, as Sujit Choudhry notes, 'an expected component of new democracies',[45] it is true that the institution is virtually standard in Europe and is a highly popular institutional form for strong judicial review in new constitutions of the post-war era,[46] with the German, Hungarian, South African, and Colombian constitutional courts garnering the lion's share of attention in English-language scholarship. However, it is important to emphasise that outside Europe the majority of new democracies worldwide have *not* opted for this model, preferring instead to retain the existing supreme court, or to reform it by installing a new constitutional chamber, adding new powers, changing its jurisdiction, or simply purging its membership (see Table 2.1).

This is true of Latin America, Africa, and Asia, despite the misleading impression given by the fact that the majority of the most well-known courts in each region are all Kelsenian courts (those of Colombia, South Africa, and South Korea). To focus solely on Kelsenian institutions, then, would tell only part of the post-war story. Differences in institutional design are discussed at more length in Chapter 4.

---

[44] J. Frosini & L. Pegoraro, 'Constitutional Courts in Latin America: A Testing Ground for New Parameters of Classification?' in Harding & Leyland (eds.), *Constitutional Courts.*

[45] See the report by Sujit Choudhry published by International IDEA, *Constitutional Courts After the Arab Spring* (Center for Constitutional Transitions at NYU Law, International Institute for Democracy and Electoral Assistance, 2014) 16 www.idea.int/sites/default/files/publications/constitutional-courts-after-the-arab-spring.pdf.

[46] A. Stone Sweet, 'Constitutions and Judicial Power' in D. Caramani (ed.), *Comparative Politics* (3rd edn, Oxford University Press, 2014) 160.

B   Regional Human Rights Courts

The definition of constitutional courts above may also be used for regional human rights courts, with the addition of three criteria: (i) the body has been established by an international treaty; (ii) it is the final interpreter of rights enshrined in an international treaty setting out a bill of rights for a specific world region; and (iii) its competence does not go beyond rights adjudication.

This definition thus includes solely the three regional human rights courts in Europe, the Americas, and Africa,[47] and excludes other regional courts with a broader jurisdiction that includes rights adjudication, such as the apex courts of the EU or the Andean Community (AC),[48] and sub-regional entities such as the East African Court of Justice (EACJ). It also excludes global entities that cannot be considered 'regional' and whose jurisdiction goes beyond human rights matters to international criminal law, international humanitarian law, international economic law, or international law *sensu lato*.[49] For the avoidance of all doubt, the definition also excludes national human rights courts, such as the ad hoc Human Rights Courts of Indonesia.

The Three Existing Courts: Fundamental
Similarities and Differences

At present, the three existing regional human rights courts in Europe, the Americas, and Africa together have jurisdiction over ninety-six of the UN's 194 member states: the European Court of Human Rights in Strasbourg, France, conducts oversight of forty-seven states; the Inter-American Court of Human Rights in San José, Costa Rica, oversees twenty states; and twenty-nine[50] states to date have accepted

---

[47] As stated above, the Arab League has resolved to establish an Arab Court of Human Rights. In Asia, embryonic advances in the human rights architecture have been made. See D. Shelton, *The Regional Protection of Human Rights* (Oxford University Press, 2010) 1051ff. However, a push has recently been made to build a fuller regional system with a human rights court at its centre: see de Visser, 'Cultivating Judicial Conversations'.

[48] As the president of the EU's Court of Justice emphasised in 2014: 'The Court is not a human rights court: it is the Supreme Court of the Union.' S. Douglas-Scott, 'Opinion 2/13 on EU Accession to the ECHR: A Christmas Bombshell from the European Court of Justice' *UK Constitutional Law Blog* 24 December 2014 www.ukconstitutionallaw.org.

[49] The International Criminal Court (ICC), the International Court of Justice (ICJ), and the adjudicative machinery of the World Trade Organisation (WTO), for instance.

[50] In fact, thirty states are listed in the AU's statistics, but these include the Sahrawi Arab Democratic Republic (SADR) in the Western Sahara region, which is not recognised as a state at UN level.

the jurisdiction of the African Court on Human and Peoples' Rights in Arusha, Tanzania.[51]

The Inter-American and African systems owe their existence in large part to a process of legal and institutional mimesis, looking to the European experience for inspiration from the beginning. Like the European Court, each represents the apogee of an incremental process of institutional development. All three courts have contentious jurisdiction, advisory jurisdiction, the power to order relief where a rights violation is found, or even provisional measures where necessary. However, the non-European systems are far from facsimiles of the European system, having institutional machinery more similar to one another than to the European system: in particular, both continue to operate with a non-judicial commission and a judicial court. By contrast, the European system became a wholly judicial affair centred on the sole institution of the Court with adoption of Protocol 11 to the ECHR in 1998, which dissolved the European Commission on Human Rights. Differences in institutional design are discussed at more length in Chapter 4.

C Strong Judicial Review

This book is, ultimately, about the role of strong judicial review in 'building democracy' in post-authoritarian states. At the domestic level, the fundamental typology is between 'strong' judicial review, which as a matter of constitutional law accords the 'final say' on constitutional questions to the constitutional court, empowering it to invalidate legislation repugnant to the constitution, and 'weak' judicial review, under which the courts can declare laws to be inconsistent with the constitution, but where the final say on the validity of a law rests with parliament in line with the principle of parliamentary supremacy.

Worldwide, strong judicial review is by far the most common form,[52] with weak review systems primarily a phenomenon of the common law

---

[51] Obtaining reliable statistics on the African Court can be surprisingly difficult. This information was obtained directly from Oliver Windridge at the ACtHPR Monitor (www.acthprmonitor.org) on 7 June 2016, who also provided the AU's ratification table, which was up-to-date at the time of writing: www.au.int/en/sites/default/files/treaties/7778-sl-protocol_to_the_african_charter_on_human_and_peoplesrights_on_the_establishment_of_an_african_court_on_human_and_peoples_rights_17.pdf.

[52] See Chapter 2, Section 1.

world (e.g. New Zealand, United Kingdom[53]). In principle, judicial review by regional human rights courts most strongly mirrors strong judicial review at the domestic level. The respective founding treaties explicitly declare that the court's judgments are final, and enjoin states parties to comply.[54] While it remains a useful fundamental distinction for the discussion that follows, as we will see, adjudication in the real world often departs from this rather neat typology.

It is also worthwhile to briefly note at the outset that the dominant understandings of the rise of judicial power worldwide and the permissible and possible roles of constitutional courts and regional human rights courts derive from scholarship focused on courts in long-established democracies. They have thus been hammered out on the anvil of Western empirical realities, where the role of courts has either developed within an evolutionary progress toward democracy (e.g. the United Kingdom, United States, Canada), or, as in much of post-war Western Europe (e.g. Germany, Italy, Spain), has developed in a regional context aided by the post-war 'economic miracle' and the significant institutional and normative ballast of the European Community (now Union).

The core literature on the global expansion of judicial power, under the rubrics 'judicial politics'[55] and 'judicialisation of politics',[56] charts the unprecedented and increasing transfer of the power to decide on

---

[53] Although historically weak review has also been common in Latin America: see J.I. Colón-Ríos, 'A New Typology of Judicial Review of Legislation' (2014) 3 *Global Constitutionalism* 143, 145–6.

[54] See Articles 44 and 46 of the ECHR; Articles 67 and 68 of the ACHR, and Articles 28 and 30 of the Protocol to the African Charter on Human and Peoples' Rights on the Establishment of an African Court on Human and Peoples' Rights. Some view the operation of these courts as closer to 'weak' judicial review: see, e.g. A. Føllesdal, 'Much Ado about Nothing? International Judicial Review of Human Rights in Well-Functioning Democracies' in A. Føllesdal, B. Peters, J. Karlsson Schaffer & G. Ulfstein (eds.), *The Legitimacy of Regional Human Rights Regimes* (Cambridge University Press, 2013). See, further, Chapters 4 and 7.

[55] See D. Kommers, *Judicial Politics in Western Germany: A Study of the Federal Constitutional Court* (Sage Publications, 1976); M.L. Volcansek (ed.), *Judicial Politics and Policy-Making in Western Europe* (Cass, 1992); A. Stone Sweet, *The Birth of Judicial Politics in France* (Oxford University Press, 1994); H. Jacob, E. Blankenburg, H.M. Kritzer, D.M. Provine & J. Sanders, *Courts, Law and Politics in Comparative Perspective* (Yale University Press, 1996); and A. Stone Sweet, *Governing with Judges: Constitutional Politics in Europe* (Oxford University Press, 2000).

[56] See N. Tate & T. Vallinder, *The Global Expansion of Judicial Power* (New York University Press, 1995); M. Shapiro & A. Stone Sweet, *On Law, Politics and Judicialization* (Oxford University Press, 2002); and R. Hirschl, *Towards Juristocracy: The Origins and Consequences of the New Constitutionalism* (Harvard University Press, 2004). See also

fundamental political and social questions from elected representatives to courts, and is overwhelmingly the scholarly product of political scientists. It focuses on the nature of strong judicial review in Western states such as the United States, Italy, and Germany,[57] and the rise of weak review in a minority of other Western states,[58] as well as the emergence and growing power since the 1950s of judicial and quasi-judicial bodies in the international sphere. These include the Court of Justice of the European Union (EU), the adjudicative organs of the World Trade Organisation (WTO), and the European Court of Human Rights.[59]

That the birth of strong judicial review arose through the US Supreme Court's perceived arrogation of the power to invalidate unconstitutional laws[60] has cast a long intellectual shadow: scholars in this field routinely assume that courts, like other political institutions, seek to optimise and expand their power – a view often shared by scholars outside the field.[61] Indeed, examples of this expansionist tendency abound: the Irish Supreme Court's use of an 'unenumerated rights' doctrine in the 1960s to expand rights protection;[62] the European Court of Justice's unprecedented role in progressing legal integration in the European Community and 'constitutionalising' the founding treaties;[63] and the characterisation of the European Convention as a 'living instrument' by the European Court of Human Rights, which has allowed it to expand rights protection under the Convention in line with present-day under-standings.[64] In more recent years the discussion has expanded from courts' involvement in policymaking to their intervention in matters of 'pure' politics, such as Germany's relationship with the EU, the foundational definition of Israel as a 'Jewish and democratic state',[65]

G. Sturgess & P. Chubb, *Judging the World: Law and Politics in the World's Leading Courts* (Butterworth, 1988).

[57] Shapiro & Stone Sweet, *On Law, Politics and Judicialization.*

[58] Hirschl, *Towards Juristocracy.*   [59] See e.g. Sturgess & Chubb, *Judging the World.*

[60] *Marbury* v. *Madison* 5 US 137 (1803).

[61] See e.g. ch. 4 in Sturgess & Chubb, *Judging the World.*

[62] See R. Keane, 'Judges as Lawmakers: The Irish Experience' (2004) 2 *Judicial Studies Institute Journal* 1.

[63] See e.g. A. Rosas, E. Levits & Y. Bot (eds.), *The Court of Justice and the Construction of Europe: Analyses and Perspectives on Sixty Years of Case-law* (Springer, 2012).

[64] See e.g. A. Føllesdal, B. Peters & G. Ulfstein (eds.), *Constituting Europe: The European Court of Human Rights in a National, European and Global Context* (Cambridge University Press, 2013).

[65] See R. Hirschl, 'The New Constitutionalism and the Judicialization of Pure Politics Worldwide' (2006) 75 *Fordham Law Review* 721.

or the current tug-of-war between the Spanish and Catalan governments concerning Catalan independence.[66]

The dramatic post-war rise in judicial power in the domestic and international arenas has lent a particular piquancy to a long-standing debate between so-called 'political constitutionalists' and 'legal constitutionalists'. The former place their faith in the political process to protect rights and minorities, and perceive a fundamental conflict between principles of representative democracy and the enjoyment of constitutional supremacy by unelected judges. The latter support justiciable constitutional limits on governmental power and action to guard against the tyranny of the majority, viewing judicial power to invalidate unconstitutional laws as necessary to counter dangerous majoritarian impulses and to provide sufficient protection for fundamental rights. As regards state supervision by regional human rights courts, political constitutionalists perceive heightened democratic deficiencies in their operation,[67] while legal constitutionalists focus on questions of heterarchy and hierarchy, as between domestic and international courts, and the challenge of managing co-existence and co-operation in a shared transnational judicial space.[68]

As we will discover in the following chapters, the democratisation context not only fundamentally alters the roles that courts assume in democratic governance, but is also the driver of those roles, which has led to a parallel discussion of the judicial role beyond the familiar core debate about the permissible limits of judicial power in mature democracies. First, we need to explore what is meant by the foundational concept of 'democratisation', as a preliminary step toward appreciating the distinct role of courts as democracy-builders.

---

[66] See e.g. V. Ferreres Comella, 'The Spanish Constitutional Court Faces Direct Democracy' International Journal of Constitutional Law Blog 23 September 2009 www.iconnect blog.com/2009/09/the-spanish-constitutional-court-faces-direct-democracy/; and 'The Secessionist Challenge in Spain: An Independent Catalonia?' International Journal of Constitutional Law Blog 22 November 2012 www.iconnectblog.com/2012/11/the-seces sionist-challenge-in-spain-an-independent-catalonia. See also P. Bossacoma i Busquets, 'The Secession of Catalonia: Legal Strategies and Barriers' in X. Cuadras-Morató (ed.), Catalonia: A New Independent State in Europe? (Routledge, 2016).

[67] See e.g. R. Bellamy, 'The Democratic Legitimacy of Regional Human Rights Conventions: Political Constitutionalism and the Hirst case' in Føllesdal, Peters, Karlsson Schaffer & Ulfstein (eds.), Legitimacy.

[68] See e.g. N. Krisch, Beyond Constitutionalism: The Pluralist Structure of Postnational Law (Oxford University Press, 2010).

1

The Core Concept: Democratisation

What do we mean when we call courts 'democracy-builders'? Democracy-building, a term with increasing currency in international development,[1] might simply be defined as activity aimed at supporting a process of democratisation in a given state. At the centre of any discussion of democracy-building therefore lies the question of how we understand the central concept of democratisation. It is particularly central to our conceptualisation in Chapter 4 of the roles courts play in the process, and the discussion in Chapter 7 of normative stances arguing for a distinctive role for courts in new post-authoritarian democracies, as compared to their counterparts in mature democracies, due to the particular demands of the democratisation context. However, achieving clarity is no easy task.

If we generally agree that there is something distinctive about the role courts play in 'building' new democracies, when does this role begin and end? In other words, what is extraordinary about the context of a new or young democracy, how does it affect adjudication, and when does this cede to a 'normal' functioning democracy, and presumably, a more 'normal' role for courts? At present, no satisfactory theoretical account has been provided to address these questions, and contemporary thinking about courts as democracy-builders tends to be clouded by the way relevant concepts and terminology concerning democracy-building are employed.

This chapter aims to set out a workable analytical framework for exploring the roles that constitutional courts and regional human rights courts play as democracy-builders, and explains why the framework of the book is based on the concept of democratisation rather than possible alternative concepts, such as transitional justice or social justice. The chapter first examines the ways in which democratisation as a concept is used and how it relates to these other terms of art in the literature on democracy-building. The chapter then discusses the meaning of

---

[1] The term is used by a variety of organisations, including the European Union, United Nations, and International IDEA.

democratisation in democratisation theory and lays out a minimal analytical framework for discussing democratisation and the courts in the
following chapters. The framework, we will see, focuses in particular
on the concept of 'consolidation of democracy', which is refined for the
purposes of the book by exploring the relationship between democratisation, democracy, and constitutionalism, at both the domestic and
regional levels.

1   The Prevalence of 'Democratisation Talk' in Law and Policy Today

Law, policymaking, and scholarship have become increasingly suffused
with 'democratisation talk' in recent decades. Consider the following
samples:

> Democratization is a process which leads to a more open, more partici-
> patory, less authoritarian society. Democracy is a system of government
> which embodies, in a variety of institutions and mechanisms, the ideal of
> political power based on the will of the people.
>
> Boutros Boutros-Ghali, *An Agenda for Democratization*, 1996[2]

> CONSIDERING that . . . one of the purposes of the OAS is to promote
> and consolidate representative democracy, with due respect for the
> principle of nonintervention;
> . . .
> REAFFIRMING that the participatory nature of democracy in our
> countries in different aspects of public life contributes to the consolidation
> of democratic values and to freedom and solidarity in the Hemisphere;
>
> Inter-American Democratic Charter, 2001[3]

> The Council of Europe's philosophy has always been to provide a 'school
> for democracy' under which ['hybrid regimes'] would gradually deepen
> their commitment to democratic consolidation.
>
> 'Smart Power – Ways of Enhancing the Council of Europe's Impact',
> Advisory Report by the Think-Tank Task Force, 2014[4]

> [The changing role of the Inter-American Commission on Human
> Rights] reflects the part that the IACHR played in dealing with

---

[2] United Nations (New York, 1996) 1.

[3] Preamble. Adopted by the Organisation of American States (OAS) in Lima, 11 September
2001. Available at www.oas.org/charter/docs/resolution1_en_p4.htm.

[4] Strasbourg, January 2014, 20. Available at www.coe.int/t/policy-planning/think_tanks/
Smart_power_report.pdf.

authoritarian governments and during transition periods and the role it currently has with respect to the consolidation of democracy.

OAS, Tenth Anniversary of the Inter-American
Democratic Charter, 2011[5]

According to [Tom] Ginsburg quite often transition to democracy precedes the development of an independent judiciary, and courts are more likely to strengthen democratic consolidation after transition.

Anja Seibert-Fohr, 2012[6]

The purposes of ASEAN are . . .
To strengthen democracy, enhance good governance and the rule of law, and to promote and protect fundamental rights and fundamental freedoms

Charter of the Association of Southeast Asian
Nations (ASEAN), 2007[7]

13. The Assembly . . . suggests that it be ensured that lustration laws and similar administrative measures comply with the requirements of a state based on the rule of law, and focus on threats to fundamental human rights and the democratisation process.

Parliamentary Assembly of the Council of Europe,
Resolution 1096 (1996)[8]

[W]e observe judicial decisionmaking that furthers goals of democratic consolidation *by* identifying for legislators national constitutional paths along which internationally defined democratic reforms may be pursued, preserving national integrity while acknowledging international reality. This 'international reality' is the context of powerfully felt but often nationally distasteful international constraints within which democratic consolidation is taking place in post-Communist Central and Eastern Europe.

Nancy Maveety and Anke Grosskopf, 2004[9]

---

[5] 21. Available at www.oas.org/docs/publications/Tenth%20Anniversary%20of%20the%20 Inter-American%20Democratic%20Charter.pdf.

[6] Seibert-Fohr, *Judicial Independence*, 1334: citing T. Ginsburg, 'The Politics of Courts in Democratisation' in J.J. Heckman, R.L. Nelson & L. Cabatingan (eds.), *Global Perspectives on the Rule of Law* (Routledge, 2010).

[7] Article 1(4). Adopted by ASEAN on 20 November 2007. Available at www.asean.org/ archive/publications/ASEAN-Charter.pdf.

[8] Parliamentary Assembly of the Council of Europe Resolution 1096 (1996) on 'Measures to dismantle the heritage of former communist totalitarian systems'.

[9] N. Maveety & A. Grosskopf, '"Constrained" Constitutional Courts as Conduits for Democratic Consolidation' (2004) 38 *Law and Society Review* 464.

> Recognising the contributions of the African Union and Regional Economic Communities to the promotion, nurturing, strengthening and consolidation of democracy and governance;
>
> African Charter on Democracy, Elections and
> Governance, 2007[10]

> As a student who believes that I am taking a step to assist the democratisation in Turkey, I request from the Chancellor of our University that Kurdish be taught in our University, under optional courses.
>
> Excerpt from submissions of the applicants in *Irfan Temel
> and others* v. *Turkey,* 2009[11]

From this global sampling, we see that a whole language and terminology developed in the field of democratisation theory – democratisation, transition and consolidation – is widely used. Democratisation is used in the sense of moving toward participatory government, representative government, a basis for stability, peace and development, freedom and solidarity, and, in the words of the Kurdish student above, possibly as a synonym for more inclusive government. It is often linked with other concepts, such as human rights protection and governance, suggesting that they are rather natural and complementary groupings. There is a distinction made in some of the quotations between 'transition to democracy' and 'consolidation of democracy', while other documents employ different language, such as 'strengthening' democracy and 'promoting' democracy. The following sections attempt to explain the development of this democratisation terminology and chart a way through the conceptual thicket.

2   A Democratising World

Democratisation would have been a relatively unfamiliar term to the pre-war hero of our preface, Chief Justice Hugh Kennedy. Although its origins lie in the new verb *démocratiser,* coined in the heady years of post-revolutionary France, it did not come into common usage until the 1970s.[12] Certainly, its use by lawyers was rare until the 1970s, for instance, a HeinOnline search reveals only 815 publications referring to 'democratization' between 1900 and 1970, and these generally contain

---

[10] Preamble. Adopted by the African Union in Addis Ababa, Ethiopia on 30 January 2007. Available at www.ipu.org/idd-E/afr_charter.pdf.

[11] ECtHR, App. No. 36458/02 (3 March 2009) para.8.

[12] Prominent revolutionary thinkers date the verb to 1792: P.V. Vergniaud, *Oeuvres de Vergniaud* (A. Vermorel edn, A. Faure, 1867).

fleeting references to democratisation in the sense used in this book. By contrast, searching for use of the same term between 1970 and 2016 returns 16,830 publications.

The increasing prevalence of the term and our prevailing understandings of what it means were forged during the post-war period in the unprecedented moves across the world toward civilian rule through full, free, and fair elections. The conventional – albeit contested – narrative draws on Samuel Huntington's concept of 'waves of democratisation', in which multiple states took steps toward democratic rule at roughly the same time.[13] The first took place in the Western World – mainly Western European and North American states – in the nineteenth and early twentieth century (1828–1926). The second took place in the immediate post-war period as Italy, Austria, West Germany, and Japan committed to democratic rule after authoritarian periods and decolonisation took place in South Asia, Southeast Asia, and Africa. The third, most extensive, wave began in 1974 with Portugal's Carnation Revolution, followed by a return to democratic rule in Spain in 1978. It then spread to Greece, Latin America, Central and Eastern Europe (CEE), and various states in East Asia and Africa in the 1980s and 1990s, and also encompassed another round of decolonisation in the 1970s.

Each 'wave' is viewed as having been followed by a 'reverse wave': from the 1920s to the 1940s by authoritarian regimes such as the National Socialist and other fascist regimes of Europe; and in the 1960s to 1970s by the souring of democratic governance in newly independent African states and the striking emergence of military rule across Latin America.[14] Consensus is emerging that we are now witnessing a reverse wave affecting a significant number of 'third wave' democracies – Larry Diamond, for instance, uses the term 'democratic recession' to discuss democratic backsliding worldwide since 2000.[15]

---

[13] The concept of 'waves' of democratisation has been subjected to robust criticism but remains useful as a shorthand for the various global phases of democratisation: See S. Huntington, *The Third Wave: Democratization in the Late Twentieth Century* (Oxford University Press, 1991) chs. 1 and 2.

[14] Huntington, ibid. 15–17, 290ff. A key work is J. Linz & A. Stepan (eds.), *The Breakdown of Democratic Regimes* (Johns Hopkins University Press, 1978).

[15] L. Diamond, 'Facing Up to the Democratic Recession' (2015) 26(1) *Journal of Democracy* 141. Recent years have seen democratic decay in regions such as CEE, the Andean region of South America, African states such as Kenya, Nigeria, and Cameroon, and various states in Asia. See e.g. P. Blokker, *New Democracies in Crisis? A Comparative Constitutional Study of the Czech Republic, Hungary, Poland, Romania and Slovakia* (Routledge, 2013); G. Crawford & G. Lynch (eds.), *Democratization in Africa: Challenges and*

Recent convulsions in the Middle East and North Africa (MENA) – in states as diverse as Tunisia, Egypt, Bahrain, and Morocco – clearly have not resulted in a 'fourth wave' of democratisation.[16] Yet, as Cynthia Arnson and Abraham Lowenthal recently observed, due to these developments, transition from authoritarian rule is now back at the heart of international politics;[17] and, it might be added, has brought renewed relevance to scholarship and policymaking in the realm of constitutional and international law.

On the minimum criteria of free, fair, and periodic elections – i.e. *electoral democracy*, as compared to full liberal democracy – we have moved from a world where nine states in 1900 (out of fifty-five states in total; sixteen per cent) could be considered democratic, to sixty-nine states in 1989 (out of 159; forty-three per cent), to today's tally of 125 (sixty-four per cent) of the 194 states of the United Nations which today meet this requirement (see Figure 1.1).[18] However, there is an enduring tension between the minimal conception of democracy as simply allowing citizens to choose their political leaders at the ballot box, and the broader conception of that term which, as this chapter recounts, tends to include respect for fundamental rights, a commitment to democratic constitutionalism, constraints on state authority, and the dispersal of public power. There is a world of difference between, say, Norway and Nepal, or Canada and Colombia. Some states briefly achieve electoral democracy but quickly lose this status. Two electoral democracies were removed from Freedom

---

Prospects (Routledge, 2013); A.R. Brewer-Carías, *Dismantling Democracy in Venezuela: The Chávez Authoritarian Experiment* (Cambridge University Press, 2010); E.S.K. Fung & S. Drakeley (eds.), *Democracy in Eastern Asia: Issues, Problems and Challenges in a Region of Diversity* (Routledge, 2013); and A. Croissant & M. Bünte (eds.), *The Crisis of Democratic Governance in Southeast Asia* (Palgrave Macmillan, 2011).

[16] Some claim the CEE transitions to be a 'fourth wave': e.g. M. McFaul, 'The Fourth Wave of Democracy and Dictatorship: Noncooperative Transition in the Postcommunist World' (2002) 54 *World Politics* 212.

[17] C.J. Arnson & A.F. Lowenthal, 'Foreword' in G. O'Donnell, P.C. Schmitter & L. Whitehead, *Transitions from Authoritarian Rule: Tentative Conclusions about Uncertain Democracies* (Johns Hopkins University Press, 2013) vii.

[18] See J.M. Colomer, 'Disequilibrium Institutions and Pluralist Democracy' (2001) 13 *Journal of Theoretical Politics* 235, 241; and 'Growth in United Nations Membership, 1945–Present' at www.un.org/en/members/growth.shtml#1980. Freedom House, *Discarding Democracy: Return to the Iron Fist. Freedom in the World 2015* https://freedom house.org/sites/default/files/01152015_FIW_2015_final.pdf. It is recognised here that other datasets, such as the Polity dataset, could be used. The Freedom House dataset is preferred here given that it bases its analysis on civil and political rights, whereas Polity focuses solely on political rights.

House's 2014 global list, for instance: Thailand, due to a *coup d'état* on 22 May 2014; and Libya, where initial movements toward democratic rule collapsed as the state descended into internal armed conflict.

3 Returning to Source: The Evolution of Democratisation Theory

In order to set out a useful framework for analysing the roles of courts in democratisation processes, it is necessary to understand the evolution of the concept in democratisation theory, a research field located in the discipline of political science. Democratisation theory encompasses three key fields: (i) transition to democracy; (ii) consolidation of democracy; and (iii) quality of democracy. Known by the unlovely terms 'transitology' and 'consolidology', the first two areas date from the 1970s and 1980s respectively,[19] while literature on the quality of democracy is of a much more recent vintage, dating to the late 1990s.

While this literature provides useful frameworks for understanding the overall trajectory and nature of democratisation in a post-authoritarian state, it also tends to highlight the difficulty of grasping democratisation. As a meta-concept that covers the initial concrete movement in a non-democratic regime to elections, and thereafter to the progressive realisation of a democratic order in the mould of a long-established liberal democracy of the Global North (or a 'reimagined' model of democracy[20]), democratisation is prismatic and expansive, referring to a system of processes which is almost unknowably complex, along a continuum of indefinite length, and with its ultimate horizon – the 'quintessentially contested'[21] concept of democracy – compounding and underpinning its problematic nature.

A Transition to Democracy

The literature on transitions to democracy was spurred by the third wave of democratisation in the 1970s, and developed alongside the global

---

[19] See e.g. P. Schmitter & J. Santiso, 'Three Temporal Dimensions to the Consolidation of Democracy' (1998) 19(1) *International Political Science Review* 69, 72, 77.

[20] It may be noted that some scholars contest the use of mature Western democracies as suitable democratic models for young democracies: see e.g. C.K. Lamont, J. van der Harst & F. Gaenssmantel (eds.), *Non-Western Encounters with Democratization: Imagining Democracy after the Arab Spring* (Ashgate, 2015).

[21] G. O'Donnell, 'The Perpetual Crises of Democracy' (2007) 18 *Journal of Democracy* 5, 6.

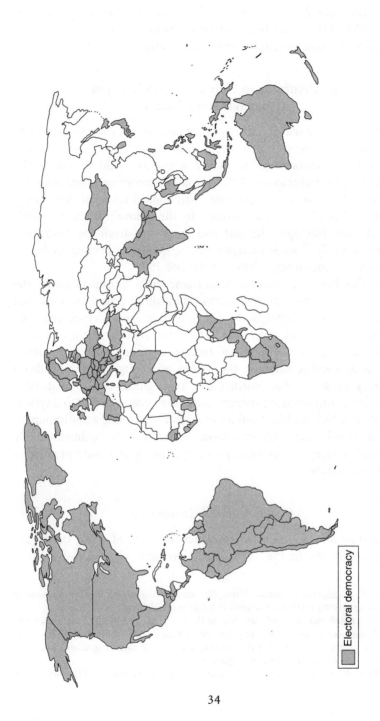

Electoral democracy

34

1. Albania
2. Andorra
3. Antigua & Barbuda
4. Argentina
5. Australia
6. Austria
7. Bahamas
8. Bangladesh
9. Barbados
10. Belgium
11. Belize
12. Benin
13. Bhutan
14. Bolivia
15. Bosnia-Herzegovina
16. Botswana
17. Brazil
18. Bulgaria
19. Canada
20. Cape Verde
21. Chile
22. Colombia
23. Comoros
24. Costa Rica
25. Croatia
26. Cyprus
27. Czech Rep.
28. Denmark
29. Dominica
30. Dominican Rep.
31. East Timor
32. Ecuador
33. El Salvador
34. Estonia
35. Finland
36. Fiji
37. France
38. Georgia
39. Germany
40. Ghana
41. Greece
42. Grenada
43. Guatemala
44. Guyana
45. Honduras
46. Hungary
47. Iceland
48. India
49. Indonesia
50. Ireland
51. Israel
52. Italy
53. Jamaica
54. Japan
55. Kenya
56. Kiribati
57. Kosovo
58. Latvia
59. Lesotho
60. Liberia
61. Liechtenstein
62. Lithuania
63. Luxembourg
64. Macedonia
65. Madagascar
66. Malawi
67. Maldives
68. Malta
69. Marshall Islands
70. Mauritius
71. Mexico
72. Micronesia
73. Moldova
74. Monaco
75. Mongolia
76. Montenegro
77. Namibia
78. Nauru
79. Nepal
80. Netherlands
81. New Zealand
82. Niger
83. Norway
84. Pakistan
85. Palau
86. Panama
87. Papua New Guinea
88. Paraguay
89. Peru
90. Philippines
91. Poland
92. Portugal
93. Romania
94. Samoa
95. San Marino
96. São Tomé & Príncipe
97. Senegal
98. Serbia
99. Seychelles
100. Sierra Leone
101. Slovakia
102. Slovenia
103. Solomon Islands
104. South Africa
105. South Korea
106. Spain
107. St Kitts & Nevis
108. St Lucia
109. St Vincent & Grenadines
110. Suriname
111. Sweden
112. Switzerland
113. Taiwan
114. Tanzania
115. Tonga
116. Trinidad & Tobago
117. Tunisia
118. Turkey
119. Tuvalu
120. Ukraine
121. United Kingdom
122. United States
123. Uruguay
124. Vanuatu
125. Zambia

Figure 1.1 Electoral Democracies Worldwide Today*

* *Source: Freedom House Freedom in the World 2015*

cresting, troughing, and eventual breaking of that wave in the 1990s. Building on pre-existing literature concerning definitions of democracy, this literature tended to adopt the minimalist definition of democracy proposed by Joseph Schumpeter in the 1940s,[22] requiring no more than free, fair, and regular elections.

Thus, the most common approach in the political science literature to delimiting this phase of democratisation is to chart its beginning and end on the basis of pivotal moments related to a democratic electoral process: the beginning marked, for example, by an official commitment by the authoritarian government to hold free and fair elections, or the sparking of a revolutionary insurrection; the end-point marked by the successful realisation of free and fair elections, the convening of a parliament with power to check the executive, or the election of a new president.[23] This 'transitology' literature is accordingly relatively unproblematic, as there is general consensus on where its temporal bounds lie and of what its nature consists, meaning that it is 'relatively simple to define, operationalize, and identify.'[24]

B   Consolidation of Democracy

By contrast, the concept of consolidation in the consolidology literature is highly contested. As the third wave polities continued to develop post-transition, political science scholars constructed increasingly elaborate frameworks of theoretical analysis to categorise the various regimes, to determine whether they could be considered to be consolidated, and to identify their nature vis-à-vis the long-established democracies of the Global North. The concept is 'double-barrelled',[25] incorporating both 'democracy' and 'consolidation of democracy'; thus, various conceptions are found in the literature and a fundamental line of division relates to the underlying definition of democracy itself, whether minimal ('thin') or substantive ('thick').

Based on the minimal Schumpeterian definition of democracy, Samuel Huntington in the early 1990s offered a 'two-party turnover' test to

---

[22] See J. Schumpeter, *Capitalism, Socialism, and Democracy* (Harper & Row, 1942).

[23] See e.g. J. Linz, 'Transitions to Democracy' (1990) 13 *The Washington Quarterly* 143, 157. Evidently, such events can only be identified as markers of transition retrospectively, given that promises of liberalisation can come to naught.

[24] B. Schneider, 'Democratic Consolidations: Some Broad Comparisons and Sweeping Arguments' (1995) 30 *Latin American Research Review* 215, 219.

[25] C. Schneider, *The Consolidation of Democracy: Comparing Europe and Latin America* (Routledge, 2008) 8.

assess whether a post-authoritarian democratic regime has become consolidated, that is, two successive peaceful transfers of power from one
party to the opposition was one indication that consolidation has been
achieved.[26] Juan Linz' more rounded conception views consolidation as
achieved when elections and related civil liberties have been institutionalised, all major political actors have renounced alternatives to democracy
and submit to operating within a democratic framework, 'and no political
institution or group has a claim to veto the actions of democratically
elected decision-makers'; in other words, when democracy has become
'the only game in town'.[27] This 'classical' conception of consolidation of
democracy is therefore limited in scope, seeking solely

> to describe the challenge of making new democracies secure, of extending
> their life expectancy beyond the long term [and] of making them immune
> against the threat of authoritarian regression[28]

More demanding conceptions of consolidation were subsequently elaborated in the 1990s. These, alongside elections, place a greater emphasis on
the rule of law and the protection of civil liberties and fundamental
rights,[29] due to concerns that the minimalist Schumpeterian definition of
democracy was over-inclusive. That definition allowed regimes with significant democratic deficits, but which hold regular and (relatively)
free and fair elections, to lay claim to the democracy label – variously
termed 'illiberal',[30] 'thin',[31] and 'façade' democracies.[32] Yet, these 'thicker'

---

[26] See Huntington, *The Third Wave* 266.   [27] Linz, 'Transitions'.
[28] A. Schedler, 'What is Democratic Consolidation?' (1998) 9(2) *Journal of Democracy*
91, 91.
[29] Philippe Schmitter, for instance, made use of a bipartite classification of procedural and
structural *minima*, encompassing 'civic rights of contestation and association, secret
ballots, universal suffrage and "the rule of law"' and 'regular elections, multiple political
parties, associational recognition and access, and an accountable executive.' See P.
Schmitter, 'The Consolidation of Political Democracies: Processes, Rhythms, Sequences
and Types' in G. Pridham (ed.), *Transitions to Democracy: Comparative Perspectives from
Southern Europe, Latin America and Eastern Europe* (Dartmouth, 1995) 550.
[30] See F. Zakaria, 'The Rise of Illiberal Democracy' (1997) *Foreign Affairs* 22, 43.
[31] See R. Munck, 'Introduction: A Thin Democracy' (1997) 24(6) *Latin American Perspectives* 5, 21.
[32] Guillermo O'Donnell used the terms 'façade democracy' and '*democradura*' to refer to a
post-transition regime that has suffered a 'slow death' of democratisation 'by the process
of successive authoritarian advances.' See G. O'Donnell, 'Transitions, Continuities, and
Paradoxes' in S. Mainwaring, G. O'Donnell & J. Valenzuela (eds.), *Issues in Democratic
Consolidation: The New South American Democracies in Comparative Perspective* (University of Notre Dame Press, 1992) 19, 33.

conceptions, based on normative and substantive definitions of democracy, rendered it considerably more difficult to ascertain whether a democracy could be said to be consolidated – a question to which the proponents of the substantive definition did not provide a satisfactory answer.

For instance, Robert Dahl's normative concept of democracy, 'poly-archy', ascribes seven essential attributes to a democratic regime: elected officials; free and fair elections; inclusive suffrage; the right to run for office; freedom of expression; alternative information; and associational autonomy.[33] Ascertaining whether such a regime has been achieved is more difficult than ascertaining when 'electoral democracy' has been achieved. This 'thicker' conception also renders it difficult to ascertain where a state lies on the consolidation spectrum, and elaborate models for assessment, which incorporate every possible element of a liberal democratic regime, have tended to be of limited use.[34]

The conceptual confusion has been compounded by the use of consoli-dation in both a negative and a positive sense in the literature. Viewed negatively, the objective is to identify signs of threatened backsliding from electoral democracy to authoritarianism, whether by the 'slow death' of successive authoritarian advances and a weakening of the existing democratic structures ('democratic decay' or 'deconsolidation'), resulting in a repressive façade democracy, or by the 'quick death' of a coup, invasion, or other crisis; and to ascertain with some confidence when a new democracy could be expected to persist into the future.[35] The common conception in the literature of consolidation as the absence of

---

[33] R.A. Dahl, *On Democracy* (Yale University Press, 2000) 90–9.

[34] Juan Linz and Alfred Stepan constructed perhaps the most complex formula for demo-cratic consolidation, as involving three separate but interrelated elements: (i) *behavioural* consolidation (the absence of any significant anti-democratic movements in a polity); (ii) *attitudinal* consolidation (requiring public support for democracy as the most legitimate form of government); and (iii) *constitutional* consolidation (entailing the submission by all political and other actors in the regime to a specific framework of laws, institutions and procedures; 'the rule of law'). Democratic consolidation was further subdivided into five 'arenas', each with its own guiding principles, provided in parentheses here: *civil society* (freedom of association and expression); *political society* (free, fair, and regular elections); *rule of law* (unconditional adherence to the constitution); *state apparatus* (usable and effective bureaucracy); and *economic society* (institutionalised market econ-omy). Linz and Stepan suggested that progress in these 'arenas' could be assessed against any or all of the three overarching sub-types of consolidation to provide a better picture of the overall consolidation process.

[35] See e.g. G. O'Donnell, 'Transitions' 33; and L. Diamond, *Developing Democracy: Toward Consolidation* (John Hopkins University Press, 1999).

breakdown suggested that consolidated democracies that broke down had never, in fact, been consolidated.[36]

Viewed positively, the concept in its classical sense can refer to the minimal process of the institutionalisation of the basic structures of a democratic regime, or more broadly to advances in the quality of democracy, or 'democratic deepening'; in other words, advancing from electoral democracy to liberal democracy (and thereafter to advanced democracy) by supplying the missing features of a full liberal democracy on the model of the established democracies of the West, a process which appears to have no clear terminus.[37]

Many criticisms of the concept of consolidation are found in the literature. It is ultimately meaningless; a congested 'cluster concept' without a true core, or at worst, no more than a label for the study of new democracies, which could be characterised as 'highly consolidated' or 'persistently unconsolidated' depending on the conception of democratic consolidation employed.[38] It is overly West-centric in using the long-established democracies as the standard model of democracy, while ignoring that these democracies developed at a slower pace and in wholly different historical, societal, and geo-political contexts to those of new democracies.[39] It is tainted by excessive teleology; evincing a tendency to view consolidation as a process that would progress unfettered were it not for certain obstacles, and an expectation in the 1980s onwards that the new third wave regimes would 'soon come to resemble the sort of democracy found in admired countries of the Northwest'[40] – an expectation that appears naïve to twenty-first century eyes.

The most damning criticism of consolidology as an intellectual project in the 1990s was that, while designed to explain the nature and development of the third wave regimes, it failed to provide a useful tool for analysing the numerous post-authoritarian regimes that had transitioned to democracy but which stubbornly continued to linger at various points on the spectrum of an ill-defined conceptual space between the two

---

[36] See Timothy Power's foreword to A. Nervo Codato (ed.), *Political Transition and Democratic Consolidation: Studies on Contemporary Brazil* (Nova Science, 2006).
[37] See Schedler, 'Democratic Consolidation' 94.   [38] Ibid. 101–2.
[39] In addition, Huntington's 'two-party turnover' test for consolidation, closely modelled on the tradition of strong two-party systems in Anglo-Saxon countries, was viewed as revealing an 'Anglo-Saxon bias'. See e.g. Schmitter, 'Consolidation' 543.
[40] G. O'Donnell, 'Illusions About Consolidation' (1996) 7(2) *Journal of Democracy* 34, 37, 46.

main referents of electoral democracy and liberal democracy.[41] Equally scathing criticisms are also found in more recent literature.[42]

In the late 1990s leading 'consolidologists' such as Guillermo O'Donnell turned their focus to other analytical frameworks, chiefly the concept of 'quality of democracy' (QoD),[43] designed to provide a means of analysing the true quality of a democracy – whether long-established democracy, third wave democracy, or otherwise – against a complex set of criteria. However, the problem with the QoD framework is that, in addressing *all* democratic regimes, it provides few pointers for achieving a better grasp of democratisation as a process, leaving us in a sort of analytical cul-de-sac. There are now any number of indices for rating democracy across the world, each weighted toward different measures, which simply highlights how contested the task of assessing democratic quality remains.[44]

Although transition and consolidation appear to constitute somewhat tarnished conceptual currencies, they are far from passé discourses. Indeed, the transitology and consolidology literatures continue to grow apace and the concept of quality of democracy has not supplanted the concepts of transition and consolidation as its proponents may have hoped. As Arnson and Lowenthal assert in their foreword to the 2013 edition of the 1986 *vade mecum* of democratisation theory, *Transitions from Authoritarian Rule: Tentative Conclusions and Uncertain Democracies*: 'The core insights developed by the project remain relevant today.'[45] We find recent high-quality comparative research on democratisation explicitly taking that book as its starting point, and other scholars continuing to find value in the conceptual framework of democratic

---

[41] See e.g. O'Donnell, ibid. 42–5. The four key regime types in the literature are authoritarian, electoral democracy, liberal democracy, and advanced democracy, with electoral and liberal democracy representing 'the empirical referents of all debate on democratic consolidation.'

[42] Stéphane Monclaire, for example, decries transitology for holding to a minimalist definition of democracy ('electoral' democracy) and describes consolidology as merely an attempt to remedy transitology's deficiencies by focusing on democratic survival in the medium term. See S. Monclaire, 'Democracy, Transition and Consolidation' in Nervo Codato (ed.), *Transition and Consolidation* 62, 73.

[43] Principal works on this concept include: G. O'Donnell, J. Vargas Cullell & O.M. Iazzetta (eds.), *The Quality of Democracy: Theory and Applications* (University of Notre Dame Press, 2004); and L. Diamond & L. Morlino (eds.), *Assessing the Quality of Democracy* (Johns Hopkins University Press, 2005).

[44] A useful list is provided at: www.democracybarometer.org/links_en.html.

[45] C.J. Arnson & A.F. Lowenthal, 'Foreword' in O'Donnell, Schmitter & Whitehead, *Transitions from Authoritarian Rule* ix.

consolidation.[46] Regime transformations across the Arab world have also driven a recent uptick in new scholarship using the framework of transition and consolidation.[47]

Significant aspects of the earlier consolidation literature are of particular utility for research on the role of courts in democratisation processes. In particular, Schmitter and O'Donnell's concept of 'disaggregation', which permits analysis of a democratic regime's component parts, suggests that democratic consolidation might be approached at different levels of analysis: at the level of a specific political institution ('group structuration'); the ways in which certain political institutions relate to one another ('(partial) regime structuration'); or as a process of linking the *Gestalt*, or network, of nascent political institutions to the economic and social groups on whose support or acquiescence such institutions depend.[48]

Indeed, the bulk of the literature conforms to this typology, tending to focus on the development and role of specific institutional types, institutions, and actors, such as presidentialism, parliament, and political parties;[49] on patterns of interaction between political institutions, such as executive-legislative relations;[50] and on the wider interaction between political institutions and other actors, such as elites, civil society, the military, and religious institutions, and including analysis of processes and values that provide a framework for interaction, such as human rights and labour politics.[51]

---

[46] See, in particular, K. Stoner & M. McFaul (eds.), *Transitions to Democracy: A Comparative Perspective* (Johns Hopkins University Press, 2013). See also, e.g., the works cited in note 15.

[47] See e.g. M. Hamad & K. Al-Anani (eds.), *Elections and Democratization in the Middle East: The Tenacious Search for Freedom, Justice, and Dignity* (Palgrave MacMillan, 2014).

[48] Schmitter, 'Consolidation' 551.

[49] See e.g. S. Mainwaring & M. Soberg Shugart (eds.), *Presidentialism and Democracy in Latin America* (Cambridge University Press, 1997); and G. Pridham (ed.), *Securing Democracy: Political Parties and Democratic Consolidation in Southern Europe* (Routledge, 1990).

[50] See e.g. R. Aiyede & V. Isumonah, *Towards Democratic Consolidation in Nigeria: Executive-Legislative Relations and the Budgetary Process* (Development Policy Centre, 2002).

[51] See e.g. J. Higley & R. Gunther (eds.), *Elites and Democratic Consolidation in Latin America and Southern Europe* (Cambridge University Press, 1991); J.S. Fitch & A. Fontana, *Military Policy and Democratic Consolidation in Latin America* (Centro de Estudos y Sociedad, 1990); J. Anderson, 'Catholicism and Democratic Consolidation in Spain and Poland' (2003) 26(1) *West European Politics* 137; and H.T. Sun, *The Political Economy of Democratic Consolidation: Dynamic Labour Politics in South Korea* (Chonnam National University Press, 2002).

4   Existing Frameworks: Conceptual Confusion
and Competition

Democratisation theorists have not tended to place much emphasis on law and courts in their work, and little effort has been expended to fully integrate the impact of courts and adjudication into their theoretical frameworks. This is despite the rule of law and the protection of fundamental rights being central to all but the most minimal conceptions of consolidation. As Juan Linz put it: 'No *Rechtsstaat*, no democracy.'[52] Schmitter suggests: 'If "electoralism" was the panacea of the transition stage, constitutionalism is probably that for democratic consolidation.'[53] However, there is a certain dismissiveness in the democratisation theory literature toward constitutional law and the process of constitutional adjudication, seemingly due to the ease with which many post-authoritarian regimes circumvented constitutional constraints and disregarded the judgments of constitutional courts.[54]

Other scholars in both political science and law have taken up the task, focusing in particular on so-called third wave democracies.[55] This may be viewed against the wider effort in the literature, especially since the 1990s, to assess the myriad connections between law, courts, and politics in both established liberal democracies and third wave democracies, addressing themes such as the global expansion of judicial power, at the domestic and international levels, and the 'judicialisation' of politics.[56] This literature, in the parlance of democratisation theory, tends to focus on group structuration (i.e. the development of the court itself) and partial regime structuration (primarily the relations between the constitutional court and the other branches of the state; or between the regional human rights court and the state).

The next two sections discuss the two principal ways in which democratisation is discussed in the literature on courts. First, scholars simply use terms such as 'democratisation', 'transition', 'consolidation', 'democratic improvement', and 'democratic deepening' as basic rubrics when analysing any state that has moved from authoritarian governance to

---

[52] J. Linz, 'Democracy Today: An Agenda for Students of Democracy' (1997) 20(2) *Scandinavian Political Studies* 115, 118.
[53] Schmitter, 'Consolidation' 555.
[54] Schmitter goes so far as to suggest that what appears to be of particular significance for democratic consolidation 'is less what is contained within the document than how it is drafted and ratified.' Ibid.
[55] See the works cited between (n. 24) and (n. 31) in the Introduction.
[56] See the works cited at (n. 55) and (n. 56) in the Introduction.

governance based on periodic free and fair elections. Second, scholarship on transitional justice and social justice is important for any understanding of democracy-building, but it will be argued that these concepts do not provide sufficiently precise analytical frameworks to address the questions at the heart of this study.

A   Confusion: (Mis)Use of Democratisation Theory Terminology

Democratisation theory terminology is widely used in the literature on courts in new democracies, by both political scientists and lawyers. However, there is striking conceptual and terminological confusion across (and even within) the majority of the literature. The principal problem is the failure to acknowledge the polysemic and contested nature of terms such as democratisation and democratic consolidation. Authors tend to refer to the concept as though its meaning is self-evident, without providing any definition of the term, or even a brief traversal of its various conceptual components. This is, in one sense, entirely understandable; given the charged and somewhat circular conceptual debates in democratisation theory, scholars working on courts have not wished to get bogged down in precise definitions. Presented with a landscape of conceptual quicksand, the temptation is to run as swiftly as possible across it lest the author lose all momentum.

For instance, in his introduction to the edited collection, *Democratic Consolidation in Eastern Europe: Institutional Engineering,* Jan Zielonka states: 'We try to avoid complex debates about definitions'.[57] References throughout the text to consolidation, consolidated democracy, and democratic consolidation – even contributions that include 'democratic consolidation' in the title – therefore leave the concept undefined and use the terms as broad rubrics.[58]

The same tendency is evident in many other works. Nancy Maveety and Anke Grosskopf's ground-breaking article on constitutional courts as 'conduits for democratic consolidation', despite making numerous references to democratic consolidation and including an entire section elaborating 'a theory of courts in democratic consolidation', adds little to the reader's understanding of the authors' conception of consolidation.[59] A further example is a relatively recent edited collection on the accountability function of courts in new democracies, which examines the political role of

---

[57] Zielonka (ed.), *Democratic Consolidation* v.   [58] Ibid. e.g. chs. 1, 2, 4, and 8.
[59] Maveety & Grosskopf, '"Constrained" Constitutional Courts' 463, 464, 466–9, and 485.

constitutional courts in new democracies in Latin America and Africa in holding political power-holders accountable when they act outside their constitutionally defined powers.[60] While it indicates that democratic consolidation is a central theme, little attempt is made to define the term.[61]

The distinction between the key concepts in democratisation theory – transition and consolidation – is also often under-appreciated. For instance, throughout the edited collection mentioned above, contributors refer to 'consolidated' and 'non-consolidated' democracies; the title of the book uses the umbrella term 'democratization', which incorporates both transition and consolidation, and certain authors appear to eschew any strict conceptual separation between 'transition' and 'consolidation', using the former term in a very broad sense which does not fit with the existing literature on democratic consolidation, or even using the terms interchangeably.[62] The unfortunate result is that the utility of otherwise highly valuable scholarship, and interesting observations and theses posited by the authors, is somewhat attenuated since we cannot be sure what the authors' conception of consolidation is: when it begins; what it consists of; and what they perceive its end-point to be.

Other analyses have attempted to engage more meaningfully with the literature on democratic consolidation. Christopher Walker, in his 2008 article on the Supreme Court of Argentina and democratic consolidation, provides a summary of much of the political science literature on the concept of democratic consolidation.[63] However, no mention is made

---

[60] Gloppen, Gargarella & Skaar (eds.), *Democratization and the Judiciary.*

[61] For example, the editors state at 1: 'Courts are important for the working and consolidation of democratic regimes. They facilitate government by contributing to the rule of law and by creating an environment conducive to economic growth. They also have a key role to play with regard to making power-holders accountable to the democratic rules of the game, and ensuring the protection of human rights as established in constitutions, conventions and laws.' Similar statements are found in, e.g., J. Couso, 'The Politics of Judicial Review in Chile in the Era of Domestic Transition, 1990–2002' 70; and R. Uprimny, 'The Constitutional Court and Control of Presidential Extraordinary Powers in Colombia' in Gloppen, Gargarella & Skaar (eds.), *Democratization and the Judiciary* 46–9.

[62] Javier Couso's title refers to 'The Era of Transition, 1990–2002' while Irwin Stotzky refers to 'the past three decades of democratic transition' at 202. Stotzky on 201 states: 'The transition or consolidation process is not always a progressive one.' In addition, Stotzky, in the concluding chapter acknowledges at 200: 'The complex question of when a democracy has been consolidated depends upon justificatory theories of democracy and is intimately connected with the stability of a specific political system.'

[63] C.J. Walker, 'Toward Democratic Consolidation - The Argentine Supreme Court, Judicial Independence, and the Rule of Law' (2008) 4 *High Court Quarterly Review* 54.

of the difficulties inherent in the concept, and one is left unsure as to precisely what characterisation of the concept Walker prefers. Some authors forego any use of democratisation theory terminology and concepts, even though their analyses are directly relevant. For instance, in their 2001 article on the role of constitutional courts in establishing and maintaining democratic government, which focuses on the Russian Constitutional Court of the 1990s, Lee Epstein and his co-authors do not make any use of consolidation as an overarching framework.[64]

However, precise terminology is important if we are to achieve even minimal clarity in discussing the roles of courts as democracy-builders. Consider, for instance, Tom Ginsburg's typology of various ways in which constitutional courts are said to impact on democracy-building, suggesting that they tend to play four possible roles: (i) triggering the transition to democracy (e.g. in Ukraine, where a Supreme Court judgment ordering Prime Minister Yanukovych to hold fresh elections triggered the Orange Revolution of 2004–2005); (ii) protecting the old regime after the democratic transition (e.g. in Turkey, where the Supreme Court after enactment of the 1982 Constitution acted to protect the previous, secular, regime from emerging Islamist democratic forces); (iii) inertia, where the court remains on the sidelines post-transition (e.g. in Chile, where the courts played a quiescent and muted role in governance for at least a decade after the return to democratic rule in 1990); and (iv) consolidation of the new democratic regime.[65] The first three roles listed are relatively rare. The fourth, consolidation, is generally viewed as the paradigmatic purpose of a constitutional court, and is generally the temporal phase scholars are investigating when analysing courts as democracy-builders. Yet, this is obscured by the variable use of terminology across the relevant scholarship.

B   Competition: The Use of Alternative or Competing Concepts

Two other concepts are particularly prominent in analysis of democracy-building: transitional justice and social justice. This section examines

---

[64] L. Epstein, J. Knight & O. Shvetsova, 'The Role of Constitutional Courts in the Establishment and Maintenance of Democratic Systems of Government' (2001) 35 *Law & Society Review* 117.

[65] T. Ginsburg, 'The Politics of Courts in Democratization: Four Junctures in Asia' in Kapiszewski, Silverstein & Kagan (eds.), *Consequential Courts*.

each concept in turn, and explains why the concept of democratisation is preferred as the governing concept for this study.

Transitional Justice

In the field of transitional justice, the concept of transition is the dominant focus, and it is used in a far more expansive manner than we have encountered in democratisation theory. The field is rooted in the attempt to understand the theoretical and practical implications of addressing past human rights violations in polities that have experienced violent conflict or the brunt of authoritarian government. Its core focus has been on accountability and justice mechanisms, such as truth commissions, and domestic and international criminal court proceedings, with a strong comparative bent.[66]

As such, the concept and field of transitional justice both dovetails with and transcends the concept of democratisation and democratisation literature. Like democratisation theory, the field has advanced in pace with real-world developments; focusing chiefly on the need to address past human rights abuses in two world regions (Latin America and CEE) where a majority of states transitioned to electoral democracy in the 1980s and 1990s, as well as the growing use and sophistication of peace negotiations and agreements in internal state conflicts across the world.[67] It is not a subset of democratisation, in that it encompasses scholarship on states that are not undergoing any form of democratisation, but which are undergoing other forms of transition, for instance, the transition from war to peace. However, there is significant overlap in the empirical contexts addressed by both fields, and some contexts – notably those of South Africa, Guatemala, and El Salvador in the 1990s – featured a clear fusing of the post-authoritarian context and emergence from armed conflict, in a context where all actors were at least agreed that the transition involved movement to democratic rule.

As the field has developed it has come to colonise an increasingly expansive conceptual territory, to focus on the overall role of law in such 'transitional' contexts (in the broad sense of 'transition' used in the literature), and the nature of the rule of law in such contexts. In particular, Ruti Teitel's concept of 'transitional jurisprudence' suggests that the notion of the rule of law in these unstable political contexts is

---

[66] See C. Bell, C. Campbell & F. Ní Aoláin, 'Transitional Justice: (Re)Conceptualising the Field' (2007) 3(2) *International Journal of Law in Context* 81.

[67] Ibid. 82.

contingent and operates both to maintain order and to facilitate the political transformation, which requires a lesser fidelity to ordinarily cardinal precepts such as consistency and predictability in the law.[68] Scholars have paid increasing attention to contextual factors affecting transitional justice processes, including not only the nature and reform of the constitutional order, through a focus on 'transitional constitutionalism' as inextricably entwined with transformative politics, but also the impact of international law and standards as exerting a 'pull', even on powerful states.[69] As Christine Bell and her co-authors note as regards post-conflict societies (which has clear resonance for post-authoritarian societies):

> This pull may be particularly strong in transitional societies where a context of conflict can no longer be invoked to justify departure from international standards. Equally, the intimate oversight relationship between international institutions and such societies creates powerful incentives for such state [sic] to 'play ball' (or be seen to) with international legal norms.[70]

In recent years the concept of transition itself in transitional justice, and its conceptual boundaries, have become increasingly blurred as scholars have re-framed justice issues originally outwith the bounds of the concept as transitional justice issues. We now see the term transitional justice applied to justice processes that are conducted in stable democracies far removed from any societal transition, conflict, or political regime change – for example, in reference to reparations for women incarcerated in a parallel prison system of laundries run by religious institutions in Ireland until the 1990s.[71] While this might be viewed as a helpful expansion of a field that has yielded significant insights in its traditional locus, it might also be viewed as degrading the concept to a loose, 'imperial' meta-concept, with reduced analytical

---

[68] R. Teitel, 'Transitional Jurisprudence: The Role of Law in Political Transformation' (1997) 106 *Yale Law Journal* 2035.

[69] See e.g. ch. 6 'Constitutional Justice' in R. Teitel, *Transitional Justice* (Oxford University Press, 2000) 191ff.

[70] Bell, Campbell & Ní Aoláin, 'Transitional Justice' 84.

[71] See e.g. K. O'Donnell, 'Thoughts on a New Ireland: Oral History and the Magdalene Laundries' *Human Rights in Ireland* 22 August 2011 www.humanrights.ie/law-culture-and-religion/thoughts-on-a-new-ireland-oral-history-and-the-magdalene-laundries/. See, more generally, S. Winter, *Transitional Justice in Established Democracies* (Palgrave, 2014).

utility; for every concept, there is a point at which elasticity degenerates into amorphousness.

Moreover, when we speak of the Constitution of South Sudan as a 'transitional constitution', and the UK Constitution as being 'in transition' there is ample scope for confusion.[72] In one sense, this is simply because it is at the same time both a word of ordinary English and a term of legal art, but where these uses are not clearly marked the capacity for the term to lack any clear meaning across the literature is obvious and the term of art can simply collapse into the ordinary usage. The conceptual confusion rife in other research areas is also a feature of transitional justice scholarship. For instance, in their introduction to the leading edited collection on the European Court of Human Rights, Michael Hamilton and Antoine Buyse refer to transition as a motif, to the aim to 'consolidate transitional gains', and to the 'transition from one legal system to another.'[73]

Transitional justice scholarship appears to recognise to some extent the limitations of the transition framework in capturing the challenges law and courts face in new democracies. Hamilton and Buyse expressly acknowledge that 'the line between transitional and non-transitional settings is evanescent'.[74] More importantly, both they and James Sweeney, in his monograph on the European Court's transitional jurisprudence, broaden their enquiry to encompass various matters that are not classic aspects of transitional justice; in particular, by examining the relationship between democracy and the protection of expressive, associative, and electoral rights.[75]

There is no attempt here to claim that the concepts of transitional justice and transition have lost all analytical utility. However, they are characterised by a degree of openness and imprecision that would tend to impede rather than assist the aim of this study.

Social Justice

To further complicate the picture, analyses of young and transitioning democracies tend to discuss democratisation and social justice in the same breath. To some extent this is unsurprising, after all, in practical

---

[72] See e.g. D. Oliver, 'The United Kingdom Constitution in Transition: From Where to Where?' in M. Andenas & D. Fairgrieve (eds.), *Tom Bingham and the Transformation of the Law: A Liber Amicorum* (Oxford University Press, 2009).

[73] Buyse & Hamilton (eds.), *Transitional Jurisprudence and the ECHR* 2, 4.   [74] Ibid. 8.

[75] Ibid. 11; and Sweeney, *Post-Cold War Era*.

and sociological terms, calls for democracy in authoritarian and newly democratic societies tend to be simultaneously calls for greater social justice – including demands for a more equitable and inclusive economic system, and the empowerment of minorities. As Widney Brown offers in relation to the Arab Spring:

> [T]he uprisings in the Middle East and North Africa ... were a cry for 'bread, freedom, social justice, and dignity' (*'aysh, hurriya, adala ijtima'ia, karama*'). There was no attempt to separate out the desire for economic security and opportunity from an end to repression and access to justice. People living at the intersection of repression and corruption know full well that the two go hand in hand.[76]

However, as with democratisation and transitional justice, defining social justice is a fraught exercise. With a conceptual pedigree almost equalling democratisation, 'social justice' was the rallying cry of the European uprisings and social movements of the 1840s onwards.[77] First expressed in the vernacular of the Italian Risorgimento as *giustizia soziale*, it was offered as an alternative to the laissez-faire and liberal theories of John Locke and Adam Smith – criticised by the philosopher Prospero Taparelli as embodying a 'tyrannous liberty'.[78] Significant developments elsewhere include the sixteenth-century writings of Bartolomé de las Casas railing against the unjust, unequal, and exploitative treatment of indigenous peoples in the Spanish New World; chiefly his *Very Brief Account of the Destruction of the Indies* presented to Charles V in 1542.[79]

Although it began as a formal concept (merely signifying justice in its ordinary meaning, extended to the social realm), since the Second World War it has become a material concept embodying a particular view of what is wrong and right with society – with social justice activists tending to view the world as 'deeply flawed'.[80] The socialist conception has gained greatest prominence in post-war thought, with the legacy that a focus on economic inequality lies at its core.[81] A UN report on

---

[76] W. Brown, 'Seeking Socioeconomic Justice' in D. Lettinga & L. van Troost (eds.), *Can Human Rights Bring Social Justice? Twelve Essays* (Amnesty International, 2015) 30.

[77] See M. Rapport, *1848: Year of Revolution* (Hachette, 2010) 406–7.

[78] T.P. Burke, 'The Origins of Social Justice: Taparelli d'Azeglio' (2010) 52(2) *Modern Age* 97, 104.

[79] See L. Hanke, *Bartolomé de las Casas: An Interpretation of his Life and Writings* (1951, H. Hanke edn, Springer, 2013).

[80] See D. Chong, 'How Human Rights Can Address Socioeconomic Inequality' in Lettinga & van Troost (eds.), *Twelve Essays* 20.

[81] Ibid. 104–6.

50   THE CORE CONCEPT: DEMOCRATISATION

social justice in 2006 follows this pattern by offering a basic definition
of social justice as 'the fair and compassionate distribution of the fruits
of economic growth'.[82]

However, as that report makes clear, social justice operates as a meta-
concept whose territory now encompasses not just distributive justice,
but a variety of dimensions including healthcare, minority empowerment, gender parity, environmental protection, and even intergenera-
tional justice.[83] As a result, it can be difficult to pin down what different
scholars mean by social justice, where they do not assay any definition.
A recent collection by Amnesty International, for instance, recognises
that it is not 'a neatly defined, uncontested concept. Actually, [it] means
different things even to people with relatively similar backgrounds.'[84]
Indeed, at times it is difficult to discern what added conceptual work the
word 'social' does in the term 'social justice' – when it can extend to
anything from agrarian reform to tax justice it can seem that we are back
to the original notion of social justice mentioned above, as simply 'justice'
applied to the social sphere.

As the earlier quote from Widney Brown suggests, for many social
justice and democratisation are simply twin goods to be pursued in
tandem; reference to one inescapably implies a reference to the other.
Certainly, both concepts seem to have a shared central meaning. They are
both animated by the same core values of equality, participation, and
inclusion (albeit themselves subject to differing interpretations), present
a counterpoint to the concentration of power in the hands of a self-
interested elite, and hold that the exercise of public power can only be
legitimate if exercised in the service of the wider political community.
Why not, then, simply fuse them when talking about wholesale transformation in post-authoritarian democracies – by subsuming the pursuit
of social justice within a concept of 'true' democratisation, or taking an
instrumental view of democratisation as primarily a vehicle for social
justice gains? Three key reasons caution against such an approach.

First, at an analytical level a failure to make some distinction could easily
cloud the assessment of progress in young democracies; for example, by

---

[82] The International Forum for Social Development, *Social Justice in an Open World:
The Role of the United Nations* (UN, 2006) 7 www.un.org/esa/socdev/documents/ifsd/
SocialJustice.pdf.
[83] Ibid. 1–7.
[84] D. Lettinga & L. van Troost, 'Introduction' in Lettinga & van Troost (eds.), *Twelve
Essays* 9.

allowing economic good news and stability to overshadow bad news concerning the trajectory of democratisation as a whole – as vividly underscored by a recent book decrying the end of free speech in Rwanda, a darling of the development community.[85] Certainly, while protection of core democratic rights is only possible in a minimally democratic society, social justice can, to some extent, be pursued with significant vigour in undemocratic regimes – the much-vaunted healthcare and education programmes of Communist Cuba being a high-profile example.[86]

Second, at an institutional level, for law and the courts democratisation appears to hinge largely on the vindication of core democratic civil and political rights, such as freedom of expression, information, and association, whereas the pursuit of social justice hinges on the vindication of social and economic rights, such as the rights to shelter and healthcare. As a voluminous scholarship discusses, these rights present different challenges for courts, and constitutional courts and human rights courts have different mandates in this regard. A lawyerly focus on rights adjudication, however, should not obscure the fact that both democratisation and social justice speak to struggles that are waged far beyond the courtroom. Indeed, the utility of rights litigation, and the entire human-rights edifice, remains hotly debated among social justice activists in particular: some see rights as a useful adjunct to political advocacy; others, seeking more radical change, see it as insufficient if transition to an economic model beyond neo-liberal free-market capitalism is the aim.[87]

Third, at a fundamental practical level for young democracies is whether democratisation gains facilitate the achievement of social justice gains, or vice versa. The UN's Copenhagen Declaration on Social Development, which stated that democracy and transparent government 'are indispensable foundations for the realization of social and people-centred sustainable development',[88] is echoed by its 2006 report on social justice, discussed above, which observes: 'Advancements in social justice ... require pressure from organized political forces.'[89] Evidently, political

---

[85] See A. Sundaram, *Bad News: Last Journalists in a Dictatorship* (Bloomsbury Publishing, 2016).

[86] See e.g. M. Serrano & V. Popovski (eds.), *Human Rights Regimes in the Americas* (United Nations University Press, 2010) 232.

[87] See generally Lettinga & van Troost (eds.), *Twelve Essays*.

[88] Y. Ghai, 'Human Rights and Social Development: Toward Democratization and Social Justice', Democracy, Governance and Human Rights Programme Paper Number 5 (October 2001), United Nations Research Institute for Social Development 9.

[89] The International Forum for Social Development, *Social Justice in an Open World* 6.

forces can only apply such pressure if they enjoy the freedom to organise, assemble, and express their positions freely. Similarly, the authors of *Why Nations Fail* argue that an 'extractive' (i.e. exclusionary and inequitable) economic system cannot be addressed without first transforming the extractive political system on which it is based. On this view, development of core democratic rights must take precedence in any attempt to transform a post-authoritarian order into a functioning democratic order and, in turn, a more socially just political community.[90]

That said, it is worth emphasising that the distinction between democratisation and social justice made here is not equated with any easy distinction between individual justice and structural reform, or between negative rights and positive rights. It is fully recognised, for instance, that attempts to vindicate 'classic' civil and political rights (e.g. associative rights) can require positive state action as readily as vindicating social and economic rights (e.g. the right to health). This point has been made by many scholars, and is worth keeping in mind.[91]

5   Toward a Workable Analytical Framework

For the above reasons, democratisation is preferred as the central concept for this book. To analyse the role of strong judicial review in the development of democratic governance, the framework of democratisation theory provides sharper, if far from perfect, tools. In particular, unlike transition in the sense used in transitional justice, it has at least clearer start and ultimate end-points, that is, a beginning in undemocratic rule and the end-point being, normatively, the achievement of a fully functioning democracy (often empirically represented by the political systems of the West, with all their imperfections). However, its relationship with these other concepts should be borne in mind.

This section attempts to set out a minimal conceptual framework for analysing the role of courts in democratisation processes. Due to the conceptual problems in existing literature, discussed above, it is often unclear how authors view or demarcate the start and end points of the

---

[90] D. Acemoğlu & J.A. Robinson, *Why Nations Fail* (Crown Business, 2012) 2. A contrary view is that the formal existence of channels for political participation in democratic decision-making is meaningless if acute economic constraints mean that individuals lack the time, capacity, or social capital to make use of such democratic freedoms: see e.g. Scheppele, 'Democracy by Judiciary'. This is discussed further in Chapter 7.

[91] See e.g. the discussion in Chapter 7 of Sadurski, *Rights Before Courts* 172ff.

democratisation process (at what point does a state become a 'normal' democracy?), and the extent to which their analysis appreciates and accommodates the differing contexts of adjudication in a new democracy as compared to a mature democracy. This renders it rather difficult to assess precisely what impact a court has had on the democratisation process, despite an embarrassment of riches in terms of raw data and qualitative analysis.

That said, this book does not seek to expend significant energy in interrogating the meaning of democratisation itself. It simply aims to derive an analytical framework from existing scholarship which is useful for the exploration of the key research questions, which avoids the terminological and conceptual confusion rife in the relevant literature, and which permits the sequence of events typical of democratisation to be more precisely located. This should assist in relating the activity of courts to the overall context of democratisation.

A   The Basic Framework: Between 'Too Much' and 'Not Enough'

As has been well established by now, the main challenge in analysing democratisation is in constructing a framework that achieves a balance between setting the standard at the empirical benchmark of existing mature liberal democracies found in the Global North or a deracinated ideal of fully-fledged democracy ('too much') and the minimal standard of electoral democracy ('not enough').

Beyond the problematic treatment of the concept in law and political science, one might resort to sociological analysis, for instance – focusing, perhaps, on what democracy, as the desired end-point of democratisation, means to people in a given polity – as holding out the potential to achieve a more organic and context-sensitive method of approaching a better understanding of democratisation. However, the danger with going too far down this route is that 'democracy' can so easily become freighted with meanings, expectations, and hopes that no political system could deliver – the promise of freedom, the promise of fairness, the promise of prosperity – that these all become cargo in democracy's hold, threatening to bring it down through the sheer weight of expectation. Democracy, in this vein, almost becomes conflated with *justice*; indeed, one sociological treatment of Brazil's legal development since return to democratic rule in 1988 hinges on the notion of travelling toward 'total justice'.[92] No contemporary democracy – no matter how well-regarded – has achieved this goal.

Moreover, as democratisation progresses, what people expect democracy to deliver tends to expand, not contract; thus tying our view of democratisation to *expectations of democracy* locks us into a recursive pattern, where the ultimate conceptual coordinates of democracy recede to an infinite horizon that cannot be reached. We cannot relentlessly expand what democracy is, or stuff it with every good imaginable, and expect it to retain any meaningful conceptual shape. There must be a point – not a bright line, but a foggy area of the continuum – where democracy ends and other concepts, such as justice, begin; otherwise, the latter is redundant and democracy becomes a sort of 'black hole' of meaning, swallowing everything (positive) in its path. Equally, there has to be some point at which democratisation ends and democracy begins; otherwise democratisation becomes an endless process, with no clear terminus; the shining city of democracy being always over the next hill, as an ideal rather than an empirical possibility.

Democratisation theory, for all its faults, provides the best prospect of achieving a useful analytical framework for addressing the democratisation context and toeing a line between democratisation as 'too much' and 'not enough'. This book draws on recent scholarship by Carsten Schneider, who, in an attempt to rehabilitate the consolidation concept, based on previous classic conceptions, opts for a more minimal 'negative and thin' conception centred on the 'expected persistence' of democratic governance, defining a consolidated regime as one that

> allows for the free formulation of political preferences, through the use of basic freedoms or associations, information and communication, for the purpose of free competition between leaders to validate at regular intervals by non-violent means their claims to rule ... without excluding any effective political office from that competition or prohibiting members of the political community from expressing their preference.[93]

This conception of consolidation, which echoes Dahl's polyarchy to some extent, tends to avoid an all or nothing approach by containing enough elements to exclude illiberal democracies, but not expecting a young democracy to contain every element present in a long-established

---

[92] See E. Botelho Junqueira, 'Brazil: The Road of Conflict Bound for Total Justice' in L.M. Friedman & R. Pérez-Perdomo (eds.), *Legal Culture in the Age of Globalization. Latin America and Latin Europe* (Stanford University Press, 2003).

[93] Schneider, *Consolidation of Democracy* 10.

democracy before it can be considered consolidated. As such, it evidently remains wedded to a relatively narrow concept of political democracy. It prioritises civil and political rights and the development of structural factors that serve the core needs of a functioning electoral system, with an inclusive and competitive electoral system being the main prize. Under this definition, a democracy can be considered consolidated even where serious economic inequality exists. Political inclusion, in a formal procedural sense, is what counts. Indeed, Dahl's polyarchy has been criticised as a conception of 'low-intensity' democracy that, unlike popular democracy, permits 'an anti-democratic social order punctured by sharp social inequalities and minority monopolization of society's material and cultural resources.'[94]

However, it should be emphasised that cleaving to a relatively minimal conception of consolidation does not necessarily suggest satisfaction with a minimal democracy; rather, it simply means that one sets a less demanding bar for achievement of a *core* functioning democratic order. Whatever one's conception of consolidation, it leaves further improvement, broadening, and deepening of democratic governance for what might be called a 'post-consolidation' phase.

A particular advantage of Schneider's definition, compared to older scholarship, is that it is based on a more comprehensive foundation of empirical research. Schneider's propositions are derived from a time-series, cross-sectional data set, which covers over thirty countries around the world across a twenty-five-year time period, on the basis of which Schneider sets out a Democratization Data Set, derived from other literature in the field, which incorporates twelve indicators of consolidation based on the behaviour of 'politically relevant actors'.[95]

These indicators are: (i) no significant political party denies the legitimacy of the existing constitution;[96] (ii) regular elections are held and

---

[94] W.I. Robinson, 'Global Capitalism and the Oromo Liberation Struggle: Theoretical Notes on US Policy Towards the Ethiopian Empire' in A. Jalata (ed.), *State Crises, Globalisation and National Movements in North-East Africa: The Horn's Dilemma* (Routledge, 2004) 49.

[95] Schneider, *Consolidation of Democracy* 18.

[96] Schneider's formulation is in fact 'No significant political party advocates changes in the existing constitution', which appears odd to a lawyer, but elsewhere in the text it is clear that this criterion refers to acceptance of the *legitimacy* of the constitution in place, with Schneider referring, for example, to the Chilean context where the constitution for the return to democratic rule contained many non-democratic elements imposed by the outgoing military rulers. Ibid. 35.

their outcomes are respected by those in positions of public authority and major opposition parties; (iii) the elections have been free and fair; (iv) no significant parties or groups reject previous electoral conditions; (v) electoral volatility has diminished significantly; (vi) elected officials and representatives are not constrained in their behaviour by non-elected veto groups within the country; (vii) a first rotation-in-power or significant shift in alliances of parties in power has occurred within the scope of the rules already established; (viii) a second rotation-in-power or significant shift in alliances of parties in power has occurred within the scope of the rules already established; (ix) agreement, formal and informal, has been reached on the rules governing the formation of associations and their behaviour; (x) executive format; (xi) territorial division of competence; and (xii) rules of ownership and access to mass media.[97]

Importantly, in this book the conception of consolidation is not used to assess precisely when consolidation has been achieved, but to guide our understanding of the courts' roles in achieving this level of democratic progress. Looking at these indicators with the eyes of a constitutional lawyer, the potential role of courts in the objective of arriving at such a state of affairs would appear to be focused on: ensuring that the electoral system is representative, fair, and inclusive; addressing constitutional challenges to electoral results; assisting in elaboration of the meaning and scope of the rights to association and assembly; interpreting constitutional ambiguities regarding the format of the executive; managing centre-periphery relations (which may not be as salient in a unitary state); and ensuring media plurality and freedom, as against both state intervention and private monopolies, and space for exercising the core democratic right to free speech more broadly. It appears clear that a court can play little role as regards items (iv); but it can play a certain role as regards item (vi), for example, by reducing the capacity of military actors to act as veto players in governance by reducing the scope for trials of civilians under military jurisdiction, or by striking down amnesty laws which shield military actors from prosecution for past rights abuses – which shows once again the overlap between democratisation theory and transitional justice. We will pick up this discussion again in Chapter 4, which more fully conceptualises the roles of courts as democracy-builders.

It may also be emphasised that there is no suggestion here of an artificially neat sequence whereby a minimal consolidated political

---

[97] Ibid. 18.

democracy is a precondition to the subsequent pursuit of social justice gains. Indeed, some social justice gains are generally necessary to ensure continued public 'buy in' to the democracy-building project as a whole, and the development of core democratic rights can be seen as facilitating the pursuit of social justice goals. However, this does not mean that courts must be the central actors in pursuing social justice. This point is picked up again in Chapters 2, 3, and 7.

We now have our initial steps toward elaborating a concept of 'democratisation jurisprudence'; namely, a distinct strain of jurisprudence aimed at democracy-building in post-authoritarian societies. This is fleshed out in Chapter 4. On the basis of the above, this book discusses democratisation according to a simple schema comprising two key phases: (i) transition to electoral democracy, as defined in the above section by reference to a key event integral to democracy (usually the achievement of a freely elected government), which provides an initial departure point that clearly demarcates the previous authoritarian regime from the democratic regime; and (ii) consolidation of democracy, as defined by Schneider. This leaves, at least by implication, a residual category of 'post-consolidation', which would be closer to a 'normal' mature democracy. However, it is a skeletal framework and, as regards the central concept of consolidation, requires significant fine-tuning.

B Bringing Law into the Framework

As stated in the Introduction, this book, focused as it is on constitutional and international adjudication, is centred on the consolidation phase of democratisation. More specifically, and importantly for lawyers, it focuses on what happens after the sublime moment of constituent power, in which the state is endowed with a new constitution (or alternatively, after substantial revision of the existing text); and after which, typically, a new constitutional court is established to guard the new constitution and help to make its paper promises a concrete reality. The position of regional human rights courts is entirely different; a state may have accepted the jurisdiction of such a court before the transition to electoral democracy, or after. This will have an effect on the relationship between that court and the domestic democratisation process; a factor considered in more depth in Chapter 4.

'New' has a broad meaning here: as regards constitutions, one can even include as a 'new' constitution an existing text that is interpreted and applied very differently in the new democratic era (e.g. in Chile).

Second, as the next chapter indicates, although the dominant focus in the literature has been on the establishment of new 'European'-style Kelsenian courts in new democracies, separate from the ordinary judiciary, a majority of new democracies in the post-war era have eschewed this option, choosing instead to endow the existing supreme court with new powers, reforming its jurisdiction, or creating a 'constitutional chamber' within the court. In rare instances, a Kelsenian court is already in place, the role of which changes significantly within the new democratic dispensation.

More importantly, the framework seeks to allow us to focus on the role of courts in the construction, not of a full liberal democracy, but of the *essentials* of a democratic order in which, as stated above, not only full, free, and fair elections are regularly held, but in which fundamental rights are respected, a commitment to democratic constitutionalism is present, state authority is subject to constraints, and public power is dispersed between different democratic actors. Construction of the *minima* of a democratic order is explored in depth in Chapter 4.

C Democratisation, Democracy, and Constitutionalism

In conceptualising the role of constitutional law and courts in democratisation processes we might speak of two enmeshed and mutually constitutive processes: 'democratic consolidation', which covers the process across the entire polity, at different levels, and 'constitutional consolidation', which covers one plane of the wider process, while simultaneously transcending it.

It is important to emphasise here the marked tension between democracy and constitutionalism – the latter being simply defined here as 'the commitment, on the part of any given political community, to accept the legitimacy of, and to be governed by, constitutional rules and principles.'[98] Though strongly linked in the contemporary constitutional imagination, they are not simply partner concepts which can develop together in seamless harmony. The 'antagonistic impulses' of each have been well canvassed by theorists including Neil Walker, Luigi Ferrajoli, James Tully, and Samuel Issacharoff.[99]

---

[98] Stone Sweet, 'Constitutions and Judicial Power' 152.

[99] S. Issacharoff, 'Constitutionalizing Democracy in Fractured Societies' (2004) 58 *Journal of International Affairs* 73. This is an abridged version of the article at (2004) 82 *Texas Law Review* 1861.

Ferrajoli, like many others, has observed that the normative paradigm of a post-war constitutional democracy does not fit with formal or procedural conceptions of democracy (i.e. conceptions based mainly on electoral criteria and a minimal sphere for meaningful participation by citizens in democratic governance). He argues that *constitutional* democracy cannot exist in the presence of powers unlimited by law; including the will of the majority. In this modern paradigm the law carves out a sphere of 'what cannot be decided'; in other words, there are certain issues that are not amenable to the decision-making process which channels the will of the people, as mediated by their representatives.[100] Thus, while the freedom of majority rule – the sphere of what *can* be decided – is broad, it is strictly limited by the sphere of what *cannot* be decided, as set out in substantive rules of law. Ferrajoli does not, however, view constitutionalism and democracy as existing in opposition, but rather, sees the constraints of constitutionalism as not only facilitating but also strengthening democracy in the fuller, post-war sense of governance by subordinating public powers and all individuals in the political community to the protection of fundamental rights, thereby broadening political democracy and the notion of popular sovereignty.[101]

Neil Walker departs from attempts to 'define up' democracy by imbuing it with constitutional elements, or 'defining down' constitutionalism to render it merely subservient to the aims of a thin procedural conception of democracy. Instead, he argues that the relationship between the two concepts presents a high level of complexity that is not always appreciated: democracy of itself is incomplete; and it is this incompleteness that both provides the justificatory basis for modern constitutionalism and which renders it inherently fragile.[102] Constitutionalism, in his view, provides a means of 'completing' democracy, but democracy in turn cannot supply constitutionalism with all of its vital components.

This tension, between democratic rule *qua* will of the majority, and constitutional democracy, which places constraints on the majority, and derives normative sustenance from sources outside democracy, is even more keenly felt in new democracies than in mature democracies. Effectively, elected representatives and the wider public, having just gained the

---

[100] L. Ferrajoli, 'The Normative Paradigm of Constitutional Democracy' (2011) 17 *Res Publica* 355, 358–61.
[101] Ibid. 361–3.
[102] N. Walker, 'Constitutionalism and the Incompleteness of Democracy: An Iterative Relationship' (2010) 39 *Rechtsfilosofie & Rechtstheorie* 206, 211.

power conferred by the ballot box, are immediately required to submit to constraints on that power, with domestic constitutional courts and regional human rights courts the core enforcers of those constraints. It must be a hard pill to swallow for those with newly-won political power.

The iterative relationship between democracy and constitutionalism is perhaps hardest to grasp in the democratisation setting, in comparison to stable authoritarian and full liberal democratic settings. Mark Tushnet, elaborating his conception of 'authoritarian constitutionalism',[103] suggests that, rather than understanding constitutionalism through a binary opposition of authoritarianism and democracy, it is best thought of as a spectrum, with authoritarianism at one end and liberal constitutionalism at the other, and various 'middle points' between the two extremes. While he applies this notion to analyse the stable 'authoritarian constitutionalism' of Singapore – which was previously viewed as a 'transitional' third wave regime, and is now considered a distinct regime type – it has a clear application to states which are undergoing an ongoing democratisation process.

Reflecting the truth that electoral democracy does not equate to full liberal democracy, fully-fledged liberal constitutionalism does not spring up overnight, but develops over time. It might be thought, then, that a new democracy in a successful ongoing democratisation process will move along the constitutionalism spectrum throughout the process, inching toward consolidation and, thereafter, toward the end-point of liberal constitutionalism. Less successful democratisation processes would find adherence to constitutionalism stalling at a certain point, or, in the case of authoritarian regression, sliding back down the spectrum. Indeed, Vicki Jackson, noting the tendency in third wave constitutional settlements underpinning the transition to democracy to leave difficult constitutional matters to the future, speaks of the result as an 'incremental constitutionalism', which requires extensive gap-filling usually to be resolved by a constitutional court.[104] As such, the root constitutive power of the documentary constitution is attenuated, with the court becoming a supplemental constituting force of sorts.

In the democratisation context we are therefore dealing, not with two relatively stable entities – democracy and constitutionalism – but rather, a context in which both are in flux, and where their iterative relationship

---

[103] M. Tushnet, 'Authoritarian Constitutionalism: Some Conceptual Issues' in T. Ginsburg & A. Simpser (eds.), *Constitutions in Authoritarian Regimes* (Cambridge University Press, 2014).

[104] V.C. Jackson, 'What's in a Name? Reflections on Timing, Naming, and Constitution-Making' (2008) 49 *William & Mary Law Review* 1249, 1265–8.

can be difficult to chart with ease. Rather than the terms 'constitutional democracy' or a 'constitutionalism of democracy',[105] we might speak of a 'democratisation constitutionalism'. The hallmark of this variant of constitutionalism is an inordinate pace of change, in an unstable sociopolitical setting, as compared to the relative stability of a long-established democracy or authoritarian regime. Chapter 4 elaborates on this point.

D Democratisation and Regional Governance

The above discussion, of course, relates solely to the domestic context. No discussion of democratisation in contemporary states can be complete without some appreciation of the role of governance systems beyond the state. The most remarkable development in the post-war era is the emergence of governance systems that transcend the long-held distinction between state-based governance and, outside the state, international law as the means to govern relations between states.

The global story – and the focus of an expanding literature – concerns the ongoing diminution of the nation-state as the privileged and core producer of law, to a reality featuring a variety of jurisgenerative processes that transcend the state, and in which numerous non-state centres of gravity exist for the elaboration of legal frameworks.[106] A 'cosmopolitan enthusiasm'[107] has taken hold, beginning in earnest in the post-war era but gathering pace alongside the democratisation processes of the third wave and beyond, with talk of the 'internationalisation' of constitutional law at the domestic level, and at the same time, the 'constitutionalisation' of international law.[108]

---

[105] This somewhat awkward phrasing is to avoid the term democratic constitutionalism, as employed by James Tully to mean something closer to political constitutionalism. See e.g. J. Tully, *Strange Multiplicity: Constitutionalism in the Age of Diversity* (Cambridge University Press, 1995).

[106] See e.g. J. Waldron, 'Foreign Law and the Modern *Ius Gentium*' (2005) 119 *Harvard Law Review* 129; R. Teitel, *Humanity's Law* (Oxford University Press, 2011); C. Bell, *On the Law of Peace: Peace Agreements and the Lex Pacificatoria* (Oxford University Press, 2008); and N. Walker, *Intimations of Global Law* (Cambridge University Press, 2014).

[107] G.W. Brown & D. Held, *The Cosmopolitanism Reader* (Polity, 2010) 50.

[108] See J. Klabbers, A. Peters & G. Ulfstein, *The Constitutionalization of International Law* (Oxford University Press, 2009); R. St John McDonald & D.M. Johnston (eds.), *Towards World Constitutionalism* (Martinus Nijhoff, 2005). Even classic international law matters are discussed in constitutional language. The United Nations Convention on the Law of the Sea (UNCLOS), for instance has been called 'a Constitution for the

Nowhere is this more obvious than in Europe, with a 'post-national constellation' comprising not only the regional order based on the European Convention on Human Rights, but also the EU.[109] The European experience has driven a particular scholarly narrative, which tends to emphasise the displacement of the state as the core site of governance power, and the 'salami slicing' of sovereignty across different arenas. The development of the EU and the European Convention system have, in general, tended to prise open the 'black box' of the domestic legal order to a much greater extent than traditional international law, with its limited tools of *ius cogens*, treaties, and conventions. Although these regional orders on rare occasions clash with overarching international law norms, the predominant effect has been to enhance the penetration of international law in the domestic context by building on existing international agreements, amplifying the binding effect of international norms, and requiring greater interaction with international courts.[110]

As far as courts are concerned, the development of meaningful regional governance may be viewed as tending to enhance 'cosmopolitan enthusiasm', by providing a bounded geographical space in which a sense of identification and connection, through shared norms or aspirations, can develop; not only through formal legal means such as treaties and inter-court co-operation, but also through regional judicial associations, conferences, and meetings.

Europe as a Global Outlier

However, it is important to avoid overstating the extent to which the European experience has been replicated in other world regions. This cosmopolitan enthusiasm is neither monolithic nor entirely linear; some states cling closer to the idea of state sovereignty than others, and for some scholars, such as Maarti Koskenniemi, international constitutionalism remains simply 'something of a game for intellectuals from the

---

Oceans.' See T.B. Koh, 'A Constitution for the Oceans', 6 December 2012 www.un.org/depts/los/convention_agreements/texts/koh_english.pdf.

[109] Kuhm uses the term to describe the global order, but it is an equally apt description of the European regional order. M. Kuhm, 'The Best of Times and the Worst of Times: Between Constitutional Triumphalism and Nostalgia' in P. Dobner & M. Loughlin (eds.), *The Twilight of Constitutionalism?* (Oxford University Press, 2010) 201.

[110] Rare clashes are epitomised by the *Kadi* saga that pitted EU law against binding UN Security Council resolutions: see Joined Cases C-584/10 P, C-593/10 P and C-595/10 P *European Commission and Others* v. *Yassin Abdullah Kadi* (Grand Chamber, 18 July 2013) (*Kadi II*).

middle powers'.[111] Despite a proliferation of regional integration projects in both Latin America and Africa, their development in both regions is often viewed as hampered by an enduring focus on state sovereignty, more jealously guarded than in Europe, and a tendency to stymie any effective pooling of sovereignty or action that would trammel the freedom of national governments to act.[112]

The pronounced diminution of the state in Europe is thus exceptional when set in the global context. In other world regions, while similar 'supranational' language is often used to describe regional integration projects such as MERCOSUR, the Andean Community, and the African Union, dilution of the state's centrality is far less evident, in the absence of any true equivalent of the supranational order of the EU. Although the principle of pooling sovereignty and creating a supranational legal order is conceded, the bodies in these regions still operate largely on intergovernmental lines – or even more narrowly in the case of MERCOSUR – along 'interpresidential' lines. This is even true of the East African Community (EAC), whose express *finalité politique* is a full political federation.[113] We see the form, but little of the substance, of a truly supranational legal order equivalent to that of the EU.[114]

The configurations of post-national governance differ from region to region. Instead of the twin regional pillars of a pan-regional economic community and a human rights system, seen in Europe, in Africa both pillars are fused in the African Union, albeit alongside a number of sub-regional orders such as the Southern African Development Community (SADC), the EAC, and the Economic Community of West African States (ECOWAS), as well as the Arab League to the north. In Latin America the closest equivalent to the Council of Europe is the Organization of American States (OAS), of which the Inter-American human rights system forms part. The OAS has, however, long been viewed in many

---

[111] M. Koskenniemi, *From Apology to Utopia: The Structure of Legal Argument* (Cambridge University Press, 1989) 54.

[112] See e.g. B.S. Levitt, 'A Desultory Defense of Democracy: OAS Resolution 1080 and the Inter-American Democratic Charter' (2006) 48(3) *Latin American Politics & Society* 93; and R.J.V. Cole, 'The African Court on Human and Peoples' Rights: Will Political Stereotypes Form an Obstacle to the Enforcement of its Decisions?' (2010) 43 *The Comparative and International Law Journal of Southern Africa* 23.

[113] See www.eac.int/integration-pillars/political-federation. See further, Chapter 3, Section 5.

[114] For extended discussion of the differences between regional orders, see T.G. Daly, 'Baby Steps Away from the State: Regional Judicial Interaction as a Gauge of Postnational Order in South America and Europe' (2014) (3)4 *Cambridge Journal of International and Comparative Law* 1011.

states as an instrument of US hegemony;[115] hence the proliferation of rival integration projects since the 1990s in particular, the leader being the Union of South American States (UNASUR). If successful, UNASUR, which is effectively an integration agreement between the Andean Community and MERCOSUR enshrined in a Constitutive Treaty of 2008, would integrate all hispanophone states and Brazil in South America.

Thus, in Latin America and Africa regional human rights regimes remain the core spheres in which anything like a supranational legal order – namely, one which tends to have a greater impact than international law more generally – has been shaped (or, in the case of Africa, is slowly emerging). Even then, the gulf between the EU and these other regimes gives one pause in ascribing the term supranational at all. This point is picked up again in Chapter 4.

Regional Constitutionalism and Democratisation

That said, it is clear that all regions display some form of pan-regional constitutionalism – or perhaps more accurately, a heterarchical plural legal order[116] – with the regional human rights court at its heart. As we will see in Chapter 3, the development of these courts, and the systems of which they are part, is intimately related to post-war democratisation processes. In Europe the development of a quasi-constitutional regional order formed part of the German redemocratisation project, with the 'European roof' of the European Community and Council of Europe providing added security against any reversion to authoritarian rule.[117] In Latin America, the regional human rights system came into its own due to the wave of democratisation that swept across the region in the 1980s, which created greater political space for assertive action by the Inter-American human rights organs. In Africa, the significant challenges to the development of the regional human rights system are rooted in the much more halting and problematic regional development of democratic rule, which remains a minority system of governance on that continent.

Walker observes that the incompleteness of both democracy and constitutionalism, and the resultant tensions in their iterative relationship, are even more acute in the case of constitutionalism transcending the state:

---

[115] H. de Zela Martínez, 'The Organization of American States and its Quest for Democracy in the Americas' (2013) 8 *Yale Journal of International Affairs* 23, 34.

[116] See the discussion in Chapter 4, Section 1.

[117] See e.g. R.H. Ginsberg, *Demystifying the European Union: The Enduring Logic of Regional Integration* (Rowman & Littlefield Publishers, 2010) Chapter 1.

Constitutionalism as a basic orientation and mobile set of techniques remains a necessary support for and supplement to democracy in the global age – and this supportive connection to democracy provides constitutionalism's abiding justification. Yet the emerging postnational constitutionalism, like state-centred constitutionalism before it, remains contingent upon non-democratic considerations . . . so reinforcing constitutionalism's abiding normative and sociological vulnerability.[118]

A sharp new distinction, he notes, has emerged between 'two opposing singular conceptions – between those who adhere to democracy's centrality to constitutionalism but doubt its viability in the postnational domain and those who would make a virtue out of constitutionalism's independence from democracy.'[119] Walker argues that both conceptions fail to acknowledge that democracy and constitutionalism lie in an inescapable state of 'mutual inextricability and mutual tension', which underlies ceaseless efforts to reconcile the two while simultaneously rendering such efforts futile.[120]

As we will see in Chapters 2 to 6, the distinction between these opposing conceptions comes to the fore in new democracies in somewhat different ways than it presents itself in mature democracies. The greater prominence of international law as a force shaping new democratic constitutions in the third wave of democratisation and the formal status accorded to international human rights law in these constitutions can blur what 'counts' as domestic or international law, or even what counts as constitutional or democratic. We see the strong influence of the European Convention on Human Rights and other international human-rights treaties on bills of rights in Central and Eastern Europe and in Africa and the Caribbean.[121] We see domestic constitutions and courts fusing international human rights law and constitutional law in a so-called 'block of constitutionality' (*bloque de constitucionalidad*)[122] in Latin America. We also see a 'creeping

---

[118] Walker, 'Constitutionalism and the Incompleteness of Democracy' 207.
[119] Ibid. 208.   [120] Ibid. 232.
[121] See e.g. A.E. Dick Howard, 'Constitution-Making in Central and Eastern Europe' (1994) 28 *Suffolk University Law Review* 5, 10–11; D. Galligan & M. Versteeg, 'Theoretical Perspectives on the Social and Political Foundations of Constitutions' in Galligan & Versteeg (eds.), *Social and Political Foundations of Constitutions* 3; and C.M. Fombad, 'Internationalization of Constitutional Law and Constitutionalism in Africa' (2012) 60 *American Journal of Comparative Law* 439, 445 ff.
[122] M.E. Góngora Mera, *Inter-American Judicial Constitutionalism: On the Constitutional Rank of Human Rights Treaties in Latin America Through National and Inter-American Adjudication* (Inter-American Institute of Human Rights, 2011) 169–98.

monism'[123] in various African common law courts, in formally dualist systems, through the use of human-rights treaties to interpret domestic constitutional law.

The perceived deficiencies of domestic legal orders in new democracies, and especially those of domestic courts, can create a greater functional role for international law – particularly, the case-law of regional human rights – to serve as an additional 'gap-filling' mechanism. As we will see in Chapters 4 and 5, in some cases this involves domestic courts invoking international law to bolster assertive decisions. In others, it involves regional human rights courts adopting unusually robust positions. We see such courts addressing systemic problems in a respondent state rather than merely addressing the individual case before it (as in Latin America and Europe). We see them adopting doctrines that seek to oblige domestic courts and other state actors to comply with the regional rights convention above all other law (as in Latin America). We also see them cutting across exercises of constituent power, not only by finding constitutional provisions incompatible with the regional human-rights instrument, and invalidating laws upheld by parliament and referendums, but also by intervening in constitutional amendment processes (with the latter two seen to greatest effect in Africa and Latin America). These developments are examined in more detail in Chapter 6.

6 Defining Key Terms

For the sake of clarity, in the coming chapters the following terminology is employed. The terms 'transition' and 'consolidation' are to be understood as defined earlier in this chapter. The terms 'new', 'young', and 'third wave' democracy are used to describe any polity that experienced a transition to electoral democracy after 1974. The term 'mature democracy' denotes any polity that achieved electoral democracy in the period before 1974, and which has not since suffered authoritarian reversal, or full rupture in democratic governance. Although, to some minds, the term 'young democracies' may appear incongruous for many states that transitioned to democracy over twenty years ago, it is used here in a relative sense, to distinguish them from the longer-established democracies in each region (e.g. Germany, Costa Rica).

[123] M.A. Waters, 'Creeping Monism: The Judicial Trend Toward Interpretive Incorporation of Human Rights Treaties' (2007) 107 *Columbia Law Review* 628.

2

The Rise and Limits of Constitutional Courts as Democracy-Builders

Since the Second World War, rights and review have been crucial to nearly all successful transitions from authoritarian regimes to constitutional democracy ... Indeed, it appears that the more successful any transition has been, the more likely one is to find an effective constitutional or supreme court at the heart of it

Alec Stone Sweet, 2012[1]

[E]specially in the past four or five years, it has become increasingly obvious that there is a need to establish specialised institutions to analyse and decide on compliance of laws with the Constitution. This is an indispensable requirement for the consolidation of a constitutional democracy.

President Vasile Gionea of the Romanian Constitutional Court, 1994[2]

Activist courts, such as the Colombian Constitutional Court, can play a key role in ushering in needed democratic transformations in transitional democracies.

Miguel Schor, 2009[3]

At the end of Chapter 1 we discussed the emergence in the post-war era of a new paradigm of constitutional democracy. This departs from a minimal procedural conception of democracy based on electoral arrangements alone, to embrace counter-majoritarian elements such as expansive rights protection, and with a court as the central enforcer of such elements. The previous

---

[1] A. Stone Sweet, 'Constitutional Courts' in M. Rosenfeld & A. Sajó (eds.), *The Oxford Handbook of Comparative Constitutional Law* (Oxford University Press, 2012) 827. Footnote omitted.

[2] Venice Commission, 'The Role of the Constitutional Court in the Consolidation of the Rule of Law', Bucharest, 8–10 June 1994. CDL-STD(1994)010 11.

[3] M. Schor, 'An Essay on the Emergence of Constitutional Courts: The Cases of Mexico and Columbia' (2009) 16 *Indiana Journal of Global Legal Studies* 173, 176.

chapter also noted the emergence of a post-national regional constitutional-ism, or at least a plural legal order, centred on the activity of regional human rights courts, which add an additional counter-majoritarian mech-anism to democratic governance in many new democracies. This chapter narrates the historical development of the domestic paradigm, and its allocation of a central role to constitutional courts at the national level.

It is argued here that the notion that any court, whether domestic or international, can play a central role in achieving a consolidated democratic order following authoritarian rule can be most clearly traced to the striking reassertion of democratic rule in West Germany after the Nazi era. Not-withstanding the totemic status of the US Supreme Court, it was in post-war Germany that a new form of constitutional democracy first emerged, with a novel constitutional court accorded a more explicit governance role than that of the US Court, and which witnessed a far swifter rise to prominence in the constitutional order than the latter's stately rise to constitutional centrality over the course of at least a century.[4] In his lively and absorbing account of this extraordinary ascent, Justin Collings argues that not only is the German Court widely regarded as the most successful and powerful court the world has ever seen, but also as a central engine of democratisa-tion.[5] For Collings it was the German Court, more than any other state institution, that transformed a political culture and society that was pre-democratic, if not anti-democratic, into a secure constitutional democracy.[6]

The German experience not only laid a template for adjudication at the domestic level in new democracies, but also helped to pave the way for assertive adjudication by courts at the regional level, with the Inter-American Court as the first true 'democratisation court' to emerge outside the state context. This is discussed in Chapter 3.

A more fundamental argument in this chapter is that the widespread perception of the capacity of courts to act as democracy-builders, or democratisation technology, rooted in the post-war German experience, is based to some extent on false premises. It tends to elide the particularly

---

[4] Although established in 1798 and arrogating to itself the power of strong judicial review in *Marbury* in 1803, the Court did not become a prominent actor in the US political system until the Lochner era (1897–1937), almost 100 years later (named after *Lochner v. New York* 198 US 45 (1905), in which it struck down scores of statutes aimed at social and economic reform).

[5] J. Collings, *Democracy's Guardians: A History of the German Federal Constitutional Court, 1951–2001* (Oxford University Press, 2015) xxix; indeed, democratisation is one of the central themes of the book, e.g. xxxii.

[6] Ibid. chs. 1–2.

propitious conditions for democratisation that prevailed in post-war Germany (and Western Europe more widely); conditions which, as we will see, have been largely absent in other world regions. This will come into stark relief as the chapter progresses.

1 Judicialised Democratisation: Rise of the Post-War Paradigm, 1945–1975

The year 1945 is a well-recognised historical marker between a world where strong judicial review was a niche governance mechanism and a world where it is dominant. Although such review had been introduced or adopted in various European and Latin American states in the nineteenth and early twentieth centuries, the courts had been reluctant to make use of the power (e.g. Norway, Portugal), never had the chance to use it (e.g. Spain, Frankfurt), saw the power suspended with the onset of authoritarian rule (e.g. Austria, Czechoslovakia), or had exercised it in a context of thin and testy acquiescence to judicial authority (e.g. Brazil, Costa Rica).[7] Even in the American 'cradle of constitutional adjudication',[8] where the Supreme Court's 1803 judgment in *Marbury* v. *Madison*[9] had established its power to invalidate laws incompatible with the constitution, the Court's role would not reach its current prominence until the 1960s.[10]

Today strong judicial review is found in some 150 of the UN's 194 Member States, across all world regions,[11] due to its exponential adoption after World War II, especially by newly democratic states.[12] As Law and Versteeg have noted:

---

[7] Strong judicial review was also established in Liechtenstein, Greece, Russia, and (by judicial arrogation) Romania. In Latin America such review powers were common, and used somewhat more frequently (e.g. in Brazil, Argentina, Costa Rica, and Colombia).

[8] D. Grimm, 'Address' in N. Dorsen & P. Gifford (eds.), *Democracy & The Rule of Law* (CQ Press, 2001) 7.

[9] See (n. 60) in the Introduction.   [10] See e.g. Schor, 'Mapping' 262.

[11] T. Ginsburg & M. Versteeg, 'Why Do Countries Adopt Constitutional Review?', (2014) 30(3) *Journal of Law, Economics and Organization* 587.

[12] It is worth noting that strong judicial review has also been adopted in undemocratic settings (e.g. Egypt, Armenia) to bolster the legal legitimacy of the regime and facilitate foreign investment, among other motives. Most unusually, the 'second' Constitutional Court of Chile, established in 1981 by the Pinochet regime, was designed to act as a parasitic twin in the democratic body, to safeguard the core of authoritarian values and privileges within the new Constitution of 1980 in the (by then) inevitable return to democratic rule. That said, in most non-democratic states where strong judicial review formally exists in the constitution it plays little part in the governance of the polity.

[S]ome 38% of all constitutional systems had constitutional review in 1951; by 2011, 83% of the world's constitutions had given courts the power to supervise implementation of the constitution and to set aside legislation for constitutional incompatibility.[13]

The idea that the Federal Constitutional Court of Germany provided the primary model for courts in new democracies of the post-war era is a commonplace, but the account usually begins and ends with the particular institutional innovations of that Court, and broad-brush reference to its case-law, with little sustained focus on how the Court's case-law was central to its being perceived as a model.[14] In addition, accounts tend to focus most often on the establishment of constitutional courts in post-Communist states after the collapse of the Soviet Union in 1989, and isolated examples such as the South African, Colombian, and Korean constitutional courts. This misses vital elements of the picture, such as how adoption of the German model in Southern Europe influenced its later adoption by Central and Eastern Europe (CEE) states, and the different approaches taken in Latin America, Africa, and parts of Asia.[15] This chapter attempts to provide a more holistic narrative.

A   Europe in 1945: Expectations of Tyranny in the 'Savage Continent'

Strong judicial review became increasingly common in the immediate post-war era, established in the constitutions of new democracies as diverse as Japan (1947), Italy (1948), Germany (1949), and India (1949), and amplified in other states (e.g. Costa Rica in 1949). However, it was most clearly in Europe that this led to the emergence of a new paradigm of 'constitutional democracy' and a 'new constitutionalism',[16] which places emphasis on the individual, trammels the power of democratic majorities, and places a constitutional court at the centre of governance. It is one of the most extraordinary aspects of our age. In May 1945, surveying the now 'savage continent' of violent restlessness, mob rule, shattered infrastructure, famine, communal revenge, and the collapse in many communities of any faith in institutions of law and

---

[13] Ginsburg & Versteeg, 'Why do Countries' 587. See also D.S. Law & M. Versteeg, 'The Declining Influence of the US Constitution' (2012) 87 New York University Law Review 762, 793.

[14] See e.g. Issacharoff, 'Democratic Risk' 13–15.   [15] e.g. ibid.

[16] Shapiro & Stone Sweet, Judicialization.

order,[17] Aldous Huxley could confidently predict the suspension of freedom across much of Europe:

> Personal liberty, presumably, will be gone from Continental Europe for at least a generation; for obviously the existing chaos cannot be controlled except by an iron tyranny[18]

Yet, while oppression was to be the lot of many of those east of the Iron Curtain, new constitutional means of countering tyranny were being crafted in the West amid the disorder. The judicial geography of the region quickly began to transform with the Austrian Constitutional Court resuscitated in 1945, followed in relatively quick succession by the establishment of Kelsenian courts in Germany (1951) and Italy (1956). The emergence of these constitutional courts did not merely signal a return to, or an attempt to revive, the failed experiments of the nineteenth and early twentieth centuries. As Richard Overy has observed, the German term for 'rebuilding' (*Wiederaufbau*) in the post-war setting was usurped by a concept of 'new construction' (*Neufbau*); the aim was not to restore Germany to its physical state before the devastation of the Second World War, but to create something different.[19] In perhaps a similar vein, these courts – especially those of Germany and Italy – represented a new construction, aimed at building a more effective and robust judicial power.

B A New Legal Technology: The Constitutional Court of Germany, 1951–1971[20]

A Democratic Experiment

The return of the defeated German power to electoral democracy in 1946 constitutes one of the most exceptional democratic transitions of the post-war era. In the decimated territory occupied by the Western Allies – whose aims were to achieve demilitarisation, denazification,

---

[17] See K. Lowe, *Savage Continent: Europe in the Aftermath of World War II* (Viking, 2012).

[18] G. Smith (ed.), *Letters of Aldous Huxley* (Chatto & Windus, 1969) 520, cited in R. Overy, 'Interwar, War, Postwar: Was there a Zero Hour in 1945?' in D. Stone (ed.), *The Oxford Handbook of Postwar European History* (Oxford University Press, 2012) 60.

[19] Overy, 'Interwar' 63.

[20] For a much more extensive treatment of the Court's first decades, see the prologue, introduction, and chs. 1–3 of Collings, *Democracy's Guardians*. By an odd quirk of circumstance this Section B A was written in early 2015, just before publication of Collings' book, but was revised in light of his in-depth analysis. For a more sceptical take on the Court, see another excellent work published in 2015: M. Hailbronner, *Traditions and Transformations: The Rise of German Constitutionalism* (Oxford University Press, 2015).

decentralisation, and democratisation – the drafting of the constitution of 1949 was pushed by exogenous forces, particularly the US government, in what has been called a 'revolution from the outside'.[21] It was an unusual text. Not only was it viewed by the German leadership as a provisional document, merely a 'Basic Law' in the absence of a unified Germany, it also counted as an anti-fascist document to chart a radical departure from Nazi rule – 'the counter-constitution to the unwritten one upon which the Nazi regime had been based'.[22] With the drafters viewing the Weimar polity as unworthy of recreation due to its weakness, disarray, and failure to prevent Nazi rule, 'new construction' was the only option.[23]

The hallmark of the text was the limits it placed on the exercise of democratic majoritarian decision-making, beyond what had been attempted in any previous or foreign constitution. Thus, we encounter a marked focus on human dignity, a generous raft of individual rights, a number of 'eternity clauses' (forbidding amendment of constitutional clauses enshrining the status of the new polity as a democratic federal republic based on the rule of law, fundamental rights, and the separation of powers), distaste for mechanisms of direct democracy, and specific mechanisms to allow for oversight of the political process, including not only impeachment of the president but also the outlawing of political parties. West Germany, unlike Weimar, was to be a 'militant democracy' fully equipped to address threats to democratic rule.[24]

Constitutionalism and the rule of law, conceived as separate from democratic governance under the Empire,[25] subservient to majority rule in Weimar, and wholly prostrate before political power under the Third Reich, were now employed to serve, underpin and protect a particular type of democratic system. Ferrajoli's sphere of 'what cannot be decided', discussed in Chapter 1, had expanded greatly, with majority rule constrained not only immediately but also intertemporally. In line with this innovative approach, a new judicial institution was inaugurated.

A Reconstructed Judicial Power

In contrast to the Basic Law as a whole, the Federal Constitutional Court, established in 1951 and based in Karlsruhe, was an endogenous creation

---

[21] V.R. Berghahn's preface to E.M. Hucko (ed.), *The Democratic Tradition. Four German Constitutions* (Berg Publishers Limited, 1987) 2. Collings states, however, that the Allied powers had little hand in the actual drafting of the text, see *Democracy's Guardians* xxi.
[22] Hucko, *The Democratic Tradition* 65, 68.   [23] Ibid.
[24] Collings, *Democracy's Guardians* xxiii.
[25] E. Blankenburg, 'Changes in Political Regimes and Continuity of the Law in Germany' in Jacob et al., *Courts, Law and Politics* 251.

with the roots of strong judicial review running deep into German constitutional history – although the US Supreme Court was also an influence.[26] To carry out its role as guardian of the new constitutional pact the Court was endowed with unprecedented powers to review legislation and state action, combining two powers previously kept separate: the 'political' power of the Weimar Republic's *Staatsgerichthof* to adjudicate on inter-branch and federal–state constitutional conflicts; and the 'judicial' power to review legislation for compatibility with the constitution.[27] In the West German constitutional convention of 1948–1949, Konrad Adenauer had argued:

> Tyranny by a single person is not the only form of dictatorship. Tyranny by a parliamentary majority is also possible. And we want to furnish protection against such tyranny in the form of a constitutional court.[28]

Thus, as well as adjudicating constitutional disputes between the principal organs of the federal state and between the federation and the states, the Court could be called on to settle constitutional questions in concrete cases and to perform abstract review of the constitutionality of federal or state law. It also held the exclusive power to ban, for unconstitutionality, political parties opposed to the 'free and democratic order'. Legislation in 1951 further enhanced the Court's position in the democratic dispensation by introducing a mechanism to allow direct petitions by individuals to claim infringement of basic rights by the state. It was 'a staggering conferral of judicial authority.'[29]

The Court was thrust into a prominent role from its first decision, ruling in 1951 on the constitutional validity of internal reshaping of the new German polity in a challenge to the merging of the *Länder* Baden and Württemburg.[30] Setting aside a federal law as unconstitutional, the Court strongly asserted the binding nature of its judgment on all organs of the state, including the parliament. At times likened to the US Supreme Court's foundational projection and articulation of constitutional supremacy in *Marbury*,[31] the German court had, it must be said, a

---

[26] For the development of strong review in Germany see ch. 2 in Kommers, *Judicial Politics in West Germany*.

[27] See D.P. Kommers & R.A. Miller, '*Das Bundesverfassungsgericht*: Procedure, Practice and Policy of the German Federal Constitutional Court' in Harding & Leyland (eds.), *Constitutional Courts* 104–5.

[28] G. Vanberg, 'Constitutional Courts in Comparative Perspective: A Theoretical Assessment' (2015) 18 *Annual Review of Political Science* 167, 170.

[29] Collings, *Democracy's Guardians* xxvi. [30] *Southwest State Case* 1 BVerfGE 14 (1951).

[31] See Kommers & Miller, '*Das Bundesverfassungsgericht*'.

stronger textual basis for adopting this stance than its American counterpart. This markedly different constitutional context precluded the Court from fully embracing 'passive virtues' – as advocated by the American theorist Alexander Bickel – to avoid certain political questions.[32] The Court viewed its duty as hearing all complaints brought before it, in order to achieve constitutional clarity and uphold the rule of law.[33]

That said, the Court generally exercised significant restraint, delaying judgments on difficult political questions in the hope that they would be resolved by other means, refraining from addressing tangential constitutional questions in cases before it, interpreting legislation in a manner conforming to the Basic Law where possible, and emphasising that it would not substitute its judgment on sound policy for that of the legislature.[34] The Court met and overcame its 'most dangerous and searching test' early on when it was required, between 1952 and 1954, to display nimble footwork, delaying tactics and remarkable solidarity in the face of significant manipulation and pressure placed on it to provide a constitutional imprimatur to the government's wish to ratify the European Defence Community (EDC) Treaty – a plan that was ultimately only quashed by the French parliament.[35]

Pioneering Post-Authoritarian Adjudication

Still being described as a 'democratic experiment' in 1964,[36] by 1976 the twenty-seven-year-old West German state was being described as an 'unshakeable democracy',[37] with the Court credited as having played a central part in this achievement through a succession of landmark judgments.

Since the very first analyses of the Court's case-law in the English language, the main aim has been to explain the Court's role to American audiences, with the institution presented first as an heir, and later as

---

[32] For an illuminating recent analysis of Bickel's theory, see E.F. Delaney, 'Analyzing Avoidance: Judicial Strategy in Comparative Perspective' (2016) 66(1) *Duke Law Journal* 1.

[33] D.P. Kommers, J.E. Finn & G.J. Jacobsohn, *American Constitutional Law: Essays, Cases, and Comparative Notes*, Vol. 1 (Rowman & Littlefield, 2009) 50.

[34] See E. McWhinney, 'Judicial Restraint and the West German Constitutional Court' (1961) 75 *Harvard Law Review* 5.

[35] Ibid. 13–18. See also Collings, *Democracy's Guardians* 15–26.

[36] T. Trombetas, 'The United States Supreme Court and the Federal Constitutional Court of Germany' (1964) 17 *Revue Hellenique de Droit International* 281, 297.

[37] Hucko, *The Democratic Tradition* 76.

a peer, of the more venerable US Supreme Court.[38] Donald Kommers' systematic English-language presentation of the Court's jurisprudence in 1989 revealed a wide-ranging case-law that addressed the nature of the new constitutional system, an interpretive framework based on the unity of the constitution, the nature of the separation of powers, and the federal design, the scope of the fundamental rights and economic liberties in the text, and the electoral system; mirroring whole swathes of US constitutional jurisprudence but also diverging from that jurisprudence in places.[39] However, presented thematically rather than chronologically, and at all times with the US audience in mind, this *vade mecum* can obscure the often stark dissimilarities between the Karslruhe court's early post-war case-law and US jurisprudence. If we focus on the first two decades of the Federal Constitutional Court's operation (1951–1971) these come to the fore.

The experience of the Nazi era hangs over many of the Court's key early decisions. In the *Civil Servants*[40] and *Gestapo*[41] judgments of 1953 and 1957 respectively, concerning measures to rehabilitate Nazi-era civil servants and agents removed in the earlier denazification process, the Court was required to address this legacy directly. It took care in its judgments to register an excoriating official history of administration and academe during the Nazi era, including naming names, at a time when the rest of officialdom preferred to embrace a policy of amnesty and amnesia.[42]

Perhaps the most vexed question – and one regarding which American jurisprudence was of little assistance – concerned the status of Nazi-era law. In 1968 the Court was confronted with a case concerning the legal effect on inheritance proceedings of an ordinance that had stripped the deceased of German citizenship, issued under the Reich Citizenship Act 1935, designed to deprive certain classes of persons (e.g. Jews) of citizenship.[43] In its judgment the Court made a clear distinction between

---

[38] As early as 1964 American scholars began observing that the US Supreme Court might learn something from its German counterpart: Trombetas (n. 35) at 281.
[39] D.P. Kommers, *The Constitutional Jurisprudence of the Federal Republic of Germany* (1st edn, Duke University Press, 1989): the current edition is D.P. Kommers & R.A. Miller, *The Constitutional Jurisprudence of the Federal Republic of Germany* (3rd edn, Duke University Press, 2012).
[40] *Civil Servants Case* 3 BVerfGE 58 (1953).
[41] *Gestapo Case* 6 BVerfGE 132 (1957). See McWhinney, 'Judicial Restraint' 10–11.
[42] See Collings, *Democracy's Guardians* 28ff.
[43] *Prior Laws Case* 23 BVerfGE 98 (1968). See A. Grabowski & M. Kieltyka, *Juristic Concept of the Validity of Statutory Law: A Critique of Contemporary Legal Nonpositivism* (Springer, 2013) 184–5.

unrecht ('false law') versus *recht* ('true law'): the former had to be expunged from the legal order; the latter remained valid and helped to maintain and nourish an image of German legal continuity in which arbitrary Nazi rule had been an aberration.[44] In the instant case, the Court held the ordinance to be such an intolerable contradiction to justice that it must be deemed retroactively invalid. The decision was an extreme instance of the Court's notable shift from the traditional German positivistic approach to constitutional interpretation in favour of a more 'American' pragmatic approach of reading the constitution 'against a background of social facts'.[45]

The recent experience of authoritarianism also informed the Court's highly protective approach to civil and political rights central to democratic governance. In the *Lüth* case of 1958,[46] concerning the prosecution of a Jewish official, Eric Lüth, for urging the public to boycott a new film by a Nazi-era director, the Court interpreted the free speech guarantee (Article 5) of the Basic Law in an expansive manner, setting down a general rule prohibiting content-based restrictions on the exercise of free speech if the freedom was to take its rightful place in the new democracy.[47] Although the significantly qualified constitutional provision itself, as Donald Kommers has noted, provided 'little basis for elevating speech into an absolute value capable of trumping other personal interests protected by the [Basic Law]',[48] the Court, by interpreting both the right and restrictions under the rubric of a principle of free speech, significantly attenuated the effect of the qualifications by identifying a constitutional 'restriction on restrictions'. In its judgment, the Court insisted that the values of the Basic Law, such as respect for human dignity and free speech, must permeate both state and society; a 'totalising' approach that enhanced the Court's own power.[49]

This expansive approach was mirrored in other judgments, such as the Court's invalidation in 1961 of a law seeking to establish a federal government-run television station;[50] a matter the government viewed as vital to counter the liberal nature of existing television services, and which the *Länder* viewed as federal meddling in cultural matters within their constitutional domain. With, as Witteman notes, 'the totalitarian

---

[44] Blankenburg, 'Changes in Political Regimes' 252–3.
[45] Trombetas, 'The United States Supreme Court' 295; and McWhinney, 'Judicial Restraint' 10, 12.
[46] *Lüth* 7 BVerfGE 198 (1958). See D.P. Kommers, *The Constitutional Jurisprudence of the Federal Republic of Germany* (2nd edn, Duke University Press, 1997) 364.
[47] Kommers, *Constitutional Jurisprudence* 1st edn 376.   [48] Ibid. 2nd edn 415.
[49] See Collings, *Democracy's Guardians* 54.   [50] *Fernseh* 12 BVerfGE 205 (1961).

misuse of German media for Nazi propaganda purposes still fresh in the national memory',[51] the Court delivered 'an extended lecture on political morality to the Adenauer regime',[52] emphasising the need to respect the competences of the *Länder* as well as free speech. Though perceived as the Court's entry into the arena of 'high politics', and received with consternation and bile in government circles, describing it as a 'false' decision amid warnings of 'Justitiar democracy', the Adenauer regime nevertheless submitted to it.[53] Collings tells us that many journalists at the time saw the decision as 'a kind of national civics lesson, an open essay in democratic ethics.'[54]

However, at every turn the Court also emphasised that the individual freedom enshrined in the Basic Law was subject to a certain conception of the community as resting on moral values and principles, such as fraternity, social discipline, and practical reasonableness; civilised behaviour, one might say. Principled limits on civil and political liberties included the concept of 'militant democracy', which restricted political advocacy in line with the Basic Law's numerous injunctions to uphold the 'free democratic basic order', the most extreme expression being the Court's power to ban political parties opposed to that order. The Court did so on only two occasions, banning the Socialist Reich Party in 1952 and the Communist Party in 1956. In these cases, the sensibilities of Allied Powers, Cold War divisions, and the desire to confirm West Germany's commitment to democracy are viewed as colouring the judgments; factors with which the US Supreme Court did not have to contend.[55]

The Court showed itself at its most active in shaping electoral rules with the aim of ensuring a genuinely representative political system, through what Kommers has called a 'jurisprudence of democracy'.[56] As well as insistently affirming the core democratic role of political opposition from the outset,[57] in key decisions the Court granted political parties the power to defend their institutional rights before the Court in a similar manner to other state organs,[58] struck down restrictive

---

[51] C. Witteman, 'West German Television Law: An Argument for Media as Instrument of Self-Government' (1983) 7 *Hastings International & Comparative Law Review* 145, 151.
[52] McWhinney, 'Judicial Restraint' 33.
[53] Ibid. 35; and Collings, *Democracy's Guardians* 78.   [54] Collings, ibid. 75.
[55] Kommers, *Constitutional Jurisprudence* 1st edn 227–8.
[56] D.P. Kommers, 'The Federal Constitutional Court: Guardian of German Democracy' (2006) 603 *Annals of the American Academy of Political & Social Science* 111, 111.
[57] Collings, *Democracy's Guardians* 9.
[58] *Danish Minority Case* 4 BVerfGE 27 (1954).

candidacy laws,[59] and upheld a law setting a five per cent threshold of votes cast for parties to sit in parliament,[60] to ensure 'orderly' governance in an electoral system characterised by diffuse voting patterns – the latter outcome informed by the instability inflicted on Weimar's parliamentary system by a 'chaotic carousel of shifting coalitions and collapsing governments, of immobile parliaments repeatedly dissolved.'[61] That said, Collings views the Court's shaping of the electoral system as a mixed success, with its empowerment of political parties as against party members (through judgments requiring state financing for smaller parties for instance) an enduring source of controversy.[62]

This is, of course, merely a flavour of the Court's early jurisprudence, which inescapably features a mixture of good and bad decisions. On the positive side we could talk about additional decisions helping to carve out a 'democratic public sphere', such as the *Public Assembly Law* judgment of 1966,[63] in which the Court robustly defended the freedom of assembly, striking down a Nazi-era law requiring police approval and supervision of public gatherings as stemming from 'the administrative thought of the totalitarian state', in which law was no more than a tool of those in power.[64] We could talk about the *Spiegel* judgment,[65] in which a split Court failed to take the state to task for aggressive government treatment of West Germany's leading *Der Spiegel* newspaper for an article decrying startling deficiencies in defence policy, but managed to register the discontent of the dissenters.[66] Least positively, we could talk about the *Emergency Laws* judgment of 1970,[67] in which a divided Court sustained emergency laws that accorded sweeping powers of surveillance to the state, provoking intense criticism that it had abandoned the constitutional principles it had painstakingly developed over its first two decades, and that the judgment marked a setback for the rule of law and democracy, and a retreat toward a deferential posture.[68]

We could delve deeper into the Court's case-law, but the point has been adequately made. As Collings so forcefully argues, the Court in its first decades – notwithstanding some negative decisions – came to be viewed as the central institution to: enforce strong respect for the Constitution; to vaunt respect for constitutional rights as an all-pervasive value of the West German

---

[59] McWhinney, 'Judicial Restraint' at 28.   [60] *Bavarian Party Case* 6 BVerfGE 84 (1957).
[61] Collings, *Democracy's Guardians* xxxiii.   [62] Ibid. 94–7.
[63] 20 BVerfGE 150 (1966). Collings, *Democracy's Guardians* 90.
[64] Collings, *Democracy's Guardians* 90.   [65] 20 BVerfGE 162 (1966).
[66] Collings, *Democracy's Guardians* 80–90.
[67] 30 BVerfGE 1 (1970). Collings, *Democracy's Guardians* 100–3.
[68] Collings, *Democracy's Guardians* 103.

state and a precondition for democratic rule; to address the past more forcefully than the representative branches of government; to educate the German public on the niceties and nuances of genuine democratic government; and to give teeth to the Basic Law's aspirations for a democracy capable of defending itself. Not only did the Court win its status as midwife and guardian of German democracy, Collings asserts, it also became itself 'an emblem of liberal-democratic stability'.[69] That the system its midwifery produced was an odd thing to many eyes – more *Rechtstaat* than democracy – only partially diminishes the achievement. Indeed, it is in Germany that we start to see the post-war trend of viewing a *Rechtstaat as* a democracy, with any clear boundary between the two increasingly difficult to discern despite their irresolvable tensions. As Collings notes, from the beginning, leading thinkers such as Jürgen Habermas questioned this development: 'Policy came from Bonn; values from Karlsruhe; but what came from the People?'[70]

That said, keeping in mind that the Court had few models for its role, it evinced a marked ability to judge the needs of the fledgling democratic order and not only to reconcile the countervailing tensions between majoritarian democracy and the enhanced constitutional constraints established to rein in anti-democratic forces, but also to mediate the recent past and the present. In its jurisprudence the Court created a new constitutional grammar and methodology for adjudication in the democratisation context – slowly developing its proportionality doctrine, for instance, to place greater constraints on government. It carved out a role that, though not without controversy, placed the Court as an accepted central actor in democratic governance. Perhaps the Court's most powerful achievement is that it expanded, in the post-war constitutional imagination, the limits of what a court could do and achieve, setting down a template for adjudication that has been replicated, to varying degrees and with varying success, by constitutional courts in new democracies.

C   The German Court as *Primus Inter Pares*

Although the Austrian and Italian constitutional courts also became fixtures in democratic governance in the early post-war period, the German constitutional court came to overshadow its sister courts.

---

[69] Ibid. xxix.
[70] Ibid. 61. See further, J. Habermas, 'Constitutional Democracy: A Paradoxical Union of Contradictory Principles?' (2001) 29 *Political Theory* 766.

The Italian court, for instance, enjoyed less expansive review powers and had no mechanism for receiving individual complaints; petitions were the sole preserve of the state, regional governments, and ordinary judges. It began operating in 1956, significantly later than the adoption of the new constitution in 1948, due to fears among political parties concerning its possible effect on politics, and was stymied by the opposition of the ordinary courts, jealous of the new institution.[71] It also operated in a very different political context. Unlike the 'zero hour' narrative of the return to democratic rule in West Germany, emphasising total rupture with the authoritarian period (although never fully reflecting reality), the dominant narrative in Italy was one of continuity. Italy had not lost the war; a 'legitimating fiction' aided by the Italian Constitutional Court's piecemeal invalidation of fascist laws.[72]

That said, the Court was viewed by the 1970s as having done more than parliament to rid the legal order of fascist elements, striking down laws as early as 1956, which allowed unlimited pre-trial detention, and vindicating the right to free speech. The Court also established from its first judgment the binding character of all constitutional norms, strengthening the normative force of constitutional law in a state with a tradition of 'legislative' constitutions that permitted easy amendment.[73] From 1970 the Court was also required to shape constitutional rules governing popular referendums, thereby overseeing the most naked expressions of majoritarian rule and, in various instances, blocking and circumscribing popular initiatives.[74]

The Austrian Constitutional Court's jurisprudence – particularly its fundamental rights jurisprudence – proved less expansive, with its main role focused on federal–state disputes,[75] while the model of judicial review in post-war France, restricted to abstract review of Bills, accorded a less central role to the courts and was emulated in only a small number of former French colonies.[76]

From the vantage point of the present it is, of course, tempting to settle into a Whig narrative of Germany's post-war experience as somehow

---

[71] M.E. de Franciscis & R. Zannini, 'Judicial Policy-Making in Italy: The Constitutional Court' in Volcansek (ed.), *Judicial Politics* 69–70.

[72] Ginsburg, 'Global Spread' 85.

[73] T. Groppi, 'The Italian Constitutional Court: Towards a 'Multilevel System' of Constitutional Review?' in Harding & Leyland (eds.), *Constitutional Courts* 139.

[74] De Franciscis & Zannini, 'Judicial Policy-Making in Italy' 76–7.

[75] See e.g. M. Stelzer, *The Constitution of the Republic of Austria* (Hart, 2011) 197–233.

[76] Mavčič, *Constitutional Review* 27.

pre-ordained, with the Federal Constitutional Court of Germany explicitly designed to guide the new polity from its disastrous past and to construct an enviably robust democratic system, laying a path for others to follow. However, as Kommers and Miller have observed, from the outset it could not have been predicted that the Court would come to occupy a central role in West Germany's project to create a new form of constitutional democracy:

> Few realized at the time that the Constitutional Court would play a vital role in shaping the politics and public philosophy of postwar Germany. Fewer still anticipated the Court's evolution into one of the world's most powerful and influential tribunals, serving as a model, alongside the U.S. Supreme Court, for other liberal democracies attracted by the prospect of placing fundamental law under the protection of independent courts of justice.[77]

While the Court had to work hard at the beginning to win full institutional independence from government oversight and a status co-equal to the representative branches,[78] and was the target of scholarly and governmental fulmination – even intimidation – in its earlier years, it is worth emphasising that democratisation in the new West German polity benefited from some remarkable factors: a 'rapid and robust economic revival';[79] direct oversight by Allied powers in the early years; the presence of significant numbers of US troops for decades, 'on hand to nip signs of radicalism in the bud';[80] a clear commitment to democratic governance by the main political forces; successive governments' strong desire to rehabilitate the state in the international arena and bind it to a coalition of Western liberal democracies;[81] a functioning competitive electoral system; a political project to build a European trading bloc with neighbouring democracies; strong public support for the Court at critical junctures (although a lot of its work went unnoticed);[82] and a legal tradition that had long placed binding law at the very centre of governance (the Nazi era excepted). All of this smoothed the path for the Federal Constitutional Court to assume an assertive role, helped along by astute judges with considerable political nous and the enactment of relatively few major laws that the Court felt compelled to strike down.

Yet, even with all of these advantages, the new West German state did not canter smoothly away from the Nazi past but slowly lurched free of it

---

[77] Kommers & Miller, *Constitutional Jurisprudence* 3rd edn xiii.
[78] See Collings, *Democracy's Guardians* ch. 1.
[79] Kommers, *Constitutional Jurisprudence* 1st edn 292.
[80] Collings, *Democracy's Guardians* xviii.   [81] Ibid. 3.   [82] Ibid. chs. 1–2.

in heaving lunges: like a strong hind mired in a bog, it made continual progress but at times threatened to go under. The success of the West German democratic experiment and the Court's accrual of such towering strength often had more to do with luck than law – not least the French National Assembly's quashing of the EDC Treaty in 1954 (preventing the risk of a headlong clash between the young Court and the government) and the fact that Adenauer's last-gasp effort in 1959 to cling to power as a more autocratic De Gaulle-style president failed to gain any political or popular traction.[83] It is all too easy, as Hailbronner argues, to indulge in exaggeration of the Court's role in shaping post-war West Germany.[84]

2   Global Diffusion of the Post-War Paradigm, 1974–2016

How, then, did the German model become a global model for court-centric democratisation? For the first three post-war decades the majority of continental Europe continued to labour under undemocratic rule; 1974 brought Portugal's Carnation Revolution, kickstarting the so-called third wave of democratisation, bringing transitions to electoral democracy from the late 1970s to the 1990s in other southern European states (Spain and Greece), CEE, Latin America and Asia, Russia, and various African states. After the fall of the Berlin Wall in 1989 the Federal Constitutional Court of Germany found itself again taking on a democratisation role; this time following the accession of the former GDR to the enlarged Federal Republic.

In each transition strong judicial review was introduced, revived, or strengthened, with the marked focus on human dignity and individual rights in Germany's Basic Law, one of the main referents as each state sought to achieve its own 'unshakeable' democracy. Indeed, one of the hallmarks of post-war constitutional law worldwide is the significant influence of the institutional form of Germany's Constitutional Court, which, as Ginsburg notes, is 'arguably the most influential court outside the US in terms of its institutional structure and jurisprudence.'[85] In many cases the institutional model of the Court was directly emulated (e.g. in Spain, South Korea, many CEE states, and Russia[86]) or indirectly replicated (e.g. Indonesia and Thailand, taking the South Korean Constitutional Court as a template[87]).

---

[83] Ibid. 68.   [84] Hailbronner, *Traditions and Transformations.*
[85] Ginsburg, 'Global Spread' 85–6.
[86] Kommers, Finn & Jacobsohn, *American Constitutional Law* 71.
[87] See Harding & Nicholson, *New Courts in Asia* chs. 7–8.

A The Logic of Diffusion

To the outsider's eye the logic of this diffusion appeared to assume that, if a strong constitutionalism capable of suppressing excesses of majoritarian power had led to successful democratisation in Germany, a similar or even more expansive approach would yield democratic dividends for the fragile new regimes. 'Thicker' constitutions and more powerful constitutional courts were simply equated with the achievement of a 'thicker' democracy, especially in climates where faith in political actors had curdled. Detailed rules for the operation of state organs and long bills of rights became common, often accompanied by eternity clauses and – resurrecting the stillborn 'social constitutionalism' of Mexico and Weimar Germany in the 1910s – social and economic rights (though such rights were not always fully justiciable). These all placed a greater interpretative and governance burden on the constitutional court.[88]

Scholarship has tended to focus on reasons for establishing Kelsenian courts in new democracies, with the reform of supreme courts largely ignored. Lawyers will offer functional reasons, such as the need for legal certainty and efficiency in a new constitutional order.[89] A 'powerful confluence of forces'[90] is presented as supporting the establishment of such a body. The need for a court untainted by links to the previous authoritarian regime. Concerns that existing supreme courts will not act to support nascent democratic institutions and values. The need for a more efficient method of ascertaining the constitutionality of laws and state action (by permitting such matters to be addressed at first instance rather than on appeal). A superior capacity to address political questions. The need to insulate the ordinary judiciary from politicisation. There is also the symbolic importance of more clearly indicating that the state is committed to the rule of law and rupture with the authoritarian past.[91] As a form of legal technology it has captured the imagination and esteem of scholars, constitution-makers, and policymakers like no other.

Others, such as Tom Ginsburg, speak more of fundamental drivers for the establishment of Kelsenian courts, with the dominant thesis being 'political insurance'.[92] Espoused by scholars from various fields,[93] it

---

[88] See e.g. Issacharoff, 'Democratic Hedging' 967.
[89] See e.g. ch. 2, V. Ferreres Comella, *Constitutional Courts and Democratic Values: A European Perspective* (Yale University Press, 2009).
[90] Horowitz, 'Constitutional Courts' 184.
[91] International IDEA, *Constitutional Courts* 19–20.   [92] See e.g. Ginsburg, *Asian Cases*.
[93] See Schneider, *Consolidation of Democracy* 15–16; Teitel, *Transnational Justice*; and Horowitz, 'Constitutional Courts' 184.

suggests that where the degree of power among political actors is uncertain they tend to pursue institutional configurations that disperse power and to construct bulwarks against the abuse of executive or state power in the new democratic regime, thereby insuring against the loss of power, both immediate (especially for authoritarian actors in the initial transition) and in the future (through electoral losses and rotations of power), by entrenching the constitutional bargain struck in the move from authoritarian to democratic rule.[94] Indeed, Issacharoff goes so far as to deem these courts as 'integral structural parts of the moment of original constitutional creation', which imposes a duty on such courts, not to simply 'guard' the original pact, but to 'reinforce the functioning of democracy more broadly'.[95] This, as discussed in Chapter 1, is an 'incremental constitutionalism', dependent on the court to resolve matters deliberately fudged in the initial pact.

As a global trend, Ginsburg and Versteeg assert that the insurance thesis has the most significant explanatory value when compared to other theories, which variously suggest a post-war rights-based popular demand for limiting majoritarian democracy (ideational theory), the need for such an institution in federal states (multi-level governance theory), and the emulation or adoption of constitutional models through the influence of foreign legal systems, the desire to attract foreign investment, or to gain acceptance or legitimacy on the international stage (diffusion theory).[96] However, the methodology of their analysis is debatable in places. Regarding diffusion theories, for instance, while they focus on shared colonisers, shared language, shared religion, and geographic proximity through shared borders,[97] it takes little effort to think of examples of diffusion where none of these factors are present; the influence of the German constitutional court on the establishment of a Kelsenian court in South Korea, for instance. Some research simply suggests that political actors believe that they will be able to control the new institution.[98] Under Galligan and Versteeg's view of a constitution as a useful co-ordinating mechanism to ensure effective

---

[94] Issacharoff provides a useful summary in 'Democratic Hedging' 985–6.

[95] Ibid. 986; see also his *Fragile Democracies* 225.

[96] Ginsburg & Versteeg, 'Why Do Countries Adopt Constitutional Review?'. The term 'multi-level governance theory', from the original working paper, is changed to 'coordination and commitment theory' in the published article.

[97] Ibid. 29.

[98] See, e.g. Hendrianto, 'Institutional Choice and the New Indonesian Constitutional Court' in Harding & Nicholson, *New Courts in Asia*.

government, a constitutional court may simply be viewed as central to its success in this regard.[99] In all likelihood it has been a complex admixture of all of the motives canvassed above, in differing proportions from state to state, which has led to the prevalence of constitutional courts worldwide in the new democracies of the post-war era. More widely, the global adoption of strong judicial review from the 1970s onward – and Kelsenian courts in particular – appears to have satisfied not only the specific objectives canvassed above, such as political insurance and legal certainty, but also sociocultural narratives of democratic rectitude or normality, justice, rights awareness, modernity, civilisation, liberalism, Europeanness, and Westernness. Until the late 1980s decisions to adopt such a legal technology were taken within the ideological battleground of the Cold War. By contrast, in the historical window after 1989, its adoption reflected the presentation of a suite of liberal democratic norms as not simply the *best*, but the *only* choice for polities emerging from authoritarian rule. As one group of scholars put it:

> Why have constitutional courts become so popular? The appeal is partly practical. Many countries have come to see judicial review as a mechanism for protecting democracy and human rights. The appeal is also political: In an era when appeals to many other forms of political legitimacy, such as communism and organic statism, have lost their attraction, the forms of constitutional democracy have become common currency.[100]

In CEE in particular, Lach and Sadurski suggest the dominant mood was to avoid experiments, with the slogan of a 'return to normalcy' indicating that 'a "normal" democratic system incorporates concentrated and centralised constitutional review best exemplified by German, Italian, Spanish and other (but not all) continental European constitutional courts.'[101] As one of the last regions to be swept by the third wave of democratisation, and with all states aspiring to membership of the EU, Kelsenian courts came to be viewed, not only as an *engine* of democratisation, but also as an *emblem* of democratic rule. As Lázló Sólyom observed in 2003, the 'very existence' of such courts 'obviously served as a "trade mark", or as a proof, of the democratic character of the respective country'.[102]

---

[99] See Galligan & Versteeg, 'Theoretical Perspectives' 23ff.
[100] Kommers, Finn & Jacobsohn, *American Constitutional Law* 24.
[101] K. Lach & W. Sadurski, 'Constitutional Courts of Central and Eastern Europe: Between Adolescence and Maturity' in Harding & Leyland (eds.), *Constitutional Courts* 69.
[102] L. Sólyom, 'The Role of Constitutional Courts in the Transition to Democracy: With Special Reference to Hungary' (2003) 18 *International Sociology* 133, 134.

New international bodies also took a leading role. In Europe the 1994 meeting organised by the Council of Europe's Venice Commission,[103] on 'the role of the constitutional court in the consolidation of the rule of law', encapsulated a conviction that strong courts were central to democracy-building,[104] as well as a view that judicialised, cosmopolitan, liberal democratic constitutionalism was the only option for new democracies. This is perhaps to be expected from an organisation whose official name is The Commission for Democracy Through Law. However, even here, an often overlooked factor in the CEE account is the strong influence of the Spanish experience. As Ackerman has noted: 'Spain's successful adaptation of the German constitutional model in its own transition from Francoism gave German solutions substantial influence in later transitions.'[105]

It is unsurprising that, with significant international guidance (from the Venice Commission and United Nations, among others), the drafters of Tunisia's 2014 Constitution opted to replace an existing advisory constitutional council with a constitutional court enjoying an expansive array of powers.

A mix of many of the above reasons will also be present in post-authoritarian states that eschew the establishment of a Kelsenian court but that nevertheless place a renewed focus on strong judicial review by an existing supreme court. Indeed, looking across post-authoritarian democracies outside Europe, despite rare geographical clusters of Kelsenian courts (e.g. in East Asia or West Africa), third wave democracies today contain far more supreme courts than Kelsenian courts (see Table 2.1).

3   Strong Judicial Review and Democratic Disappointment

A   Great Expectations

All these new and reformed courts have tended to be endowed with similar powers to the German and US courts, with the precise nature of those powers often dictated by institutional form (principally, whether a court is a Kelsenian constitutional court or a US-style supreme court).

---

[103] The Venice Commission is a form of official think tank on the rule of law, democracy, and human rights. See www.venice.coe.int.

[104] CDL-STD(1994)010.

[105] B. Ackerman, 'The New Separation of Powers' (2000) 113 *Harvard Law Review* 633, 637; citing L. López Guerra, 'The Application of the Spanish Model in the Constitutional Transitions in Central and Eastern Europe' (1998) 19 *Cardozo Law Review* 1937.

The German influence on the case-law of third wave courts is seen in everything from the virtually global adoption of some form of proportionality review, to the approach of the new constitutional courts in young European democracies to EU law,[106] to the principle of 'social minimum' in Colombian jurisprudence, which sets a baseline for a dignified existence in the framework of a social state, to the Brazilian Supreme Court's approach to authoritarian-era laws.[107]

Looking at the burgeoning scholarship on the operation of constitutional courts in new democracies across the world against Table 2.1,[108] and other sources, such as the Venice Commission CODICES constitutional case-law database,[109] we can at least say with confidence that courts worldwide (although displaying different emphases in their jurisprudence) appear to carry out similar roles to the German Constitutional Court, as previously outlined: vindicating fundamental rights; adjudicating on inter-branch (and often centre–periphery) disputes; monitoring the legislative process as virtual 'third chambers' of parliament; addressing transitional justice questions, such as the validity of trials of former regime officials; invalidating unconstitutional and authoritarian-era laws; and, in some cases, addressing the very constitutionality of constitutional amendments.

Although German and US jurisprudence has been the most influential, third wave courts have also been significantly influenced by British and Indian traditions, especially in the common law systems of Africa. We see, for instance, the influence of the Indian Supreme Court's 'basic structure' doctrine,[110] which asserts the Court's power to assess the validity of constitutional amendments, in the jurisprudence of the Colombian, Belizean, and Tanzanian courts[111] – although even that doctrine was inspired by the work of the German scholar Dietrich Conrad.[112]

However, as compared to the German Court, there has been a marked trend since the beginning of the third wave of democratisation to freight constitutional courts with an ever increasing adjudicative and governance

---

[106] See A.F. Tatham, *Central European Constitutional Courts in the Face of EU Membership: The Influence of the German Model in Hungary and Poland* (Martinus Nijhoff, 2013).
[107] Discussed in Chapter 5.
[108] See the works cited at (n. 24), (n. 25), and (n. 26) in the Introduction.
[109] www.codices.coe.int.
[110] Set out in *Kesavananda Bharati v. State of Kerala* (1973) 4 SCC 225.
[111] See e.g. Colón-Ríos, 'A New Typology' 145–6; and the Tanzanian High Court's judgment in *Mtikila v. Attorney General*, discussed in Chapter 6.
[112] Z. Hasan, E. Sridharan & R. Sudarshan (eds.), *India's Living Constitution: Ideas, Practices, Controversies* (Anthem Press, 2005) 166–7.

Table 2.1 *Constitutional Courts in New Democracies, 1974–2016*

State	Retained Supreme Court	Existing Kelsenian Court	New Kelsenian Court	New Constitutional Chamber
Southern Europe				
Portugal			X	
Spain			X	
Greece	X			
Central and Eastern Europe (and Russia)				
Bulgaria			X	
Croatia			X	
Czech Rep.			X	
Estonia	X			X
Hungary			X	
Latvia			X	
Lithuania			X	
Poland		X (1981)	X	
Romania			X	
Slovakia			X	
Slovenia			X	
Russia*			X	
South America				
Argentina	X			
Bolivia	X		X	
Brazil	X**			
Chile	X	X (1981)		
Colombia	X		X	
Ecuador	X		X	
Guyana	X			
Paraguay	X			X
Peru	X	X (1980)	X (1996)***	
Suriname			X	
Uruguay	X			
Venezuela*	X			X
Central America				
Belize	X			
Costa Rica	X			X
El Salvador	X			X
Guatemala			X	
Honduras	X			X
Mexico	X			
South and Southeast Asia				
Bangladesh	X			
East Timor	X			

Table 2.1 (*cont.*)

State	Retained Supreme Court	Existing Kelsenian Court	New Kelsenian Court	New Constitutional Chamber
India	X			
Nepal				X****
Philippines	X			
East Asia				
Indonesia			X	
Japan	X			
Mongolia			X	
South Korea			X	
Taiwan	X			
Thailand*	X			
Africa				
Benin			X	
Botswana	X			
Guinea-Bissau	X			
Kenya	X			
Lesotho	X			
Liberia	X			
Malawi	X			
Mauritius	X			
Namibia	X			
Niger			X	
Senegal			X	
Sierra Leone			X	
South Africa			X	
Middle East and North Africa				
Tunisia*****			X	

Note: This table excludes third wave democracies with very small populations, such as the island states of the Caribbean.

* Russia, Thailand, and Venezuela are no longer considered electoral democracies but are included here because they feature relatively prominently in the literature.

** The Brazilian Supreme Court was retained but reforms recast it as something much closer to a Kelsenian constitutional court; this is discussed in Chapter 5.

*** A 'new' constitutional court was established in Peru under the new Constitution of 1993.

**** Nepal chose to establish a constitutional chamber in its existing Supreme Court in its 2015 Constitution.

***** The Tunisian Constitutional Court has yet to be established under the 2014 Constitution due to political impediments to adoption of the necessary ordinary legislation.

burden: courts have been increasingly expected to carry out 'heavy lifting' in the process of consolidating democracy – which is to be achieved as quickly as possible. In many cases, third wave courts have been endowed with enhanced formal powers, compared to even the German constitutional court, such as the power: to address not only the validity of enacted legislation, but also 'legislative omission', where the legislature has left 'gaps' in the legal order by failing to enact legislation or adequate legislation (e.g. Hungary);[113] to act as first instance quasi-criminal trial courts for political corruption (e.g. Brazil); and to assess the constitutionality of international treaties (e.g. Tunisia). Courts have been increasingly required to adjudicate on social and economic rights (including fully justiciable rights in a growing number of states), with a wide range of such rights in the Portuguese Constitution of 1976, Latin American constitutions (e.g. Brazil and Colombia), most post-Communist states, the totemic South African Constitution of 1996, and, more recently, the ambitious 'transformational' constitutions adopted in states such as Kenya, Nepal, and Zimbabwe since 2010. Constitutional courts are also increasingly endowed with the power to issue advisory opinions as well as binding judgments (e.g. South Africa, Benin).[114] They have even been endowed with a 'quasi-parliamentary' role to hold public hearings concerning specific cases, at which political, civil society, and expert actors can deliberate (e.g. Brazil).[115] We increasingly see courts viewed not merely as 'negative' legislators but also as 'positive' legislators.[116]

In a similar manner to their counterparts in mature democracies, discussed in the Introduction, the range and nature of matters on which courts in post-authoritarian states are called to adjudicate has become increasingly vast, going beyond policy matters to matters of 'pure' politics,[117] encompassing the constitutionality of convictions for crimes against humanity, macroeconomic policy, foreign policy – and even, in

---

[113] A useful summary is found in K.B. Brown & D.V. Snyder, *General Reports of the XVIIIth Congress of the International Academy of Comparative Law* (Springer, 2011) 560ff.

[114] A.K. Abebe & C.M. Fombad, 'The Advisory Jurisdiction of Constitutional Courts in Sub-Sahara Africa' (2013) 46 *George Washington International Law Review* 55.

[115] See e.g. J. Massadas, 'Between Legal Authority and Epistemic Competence: A Case Study of the Brazilian Supreme Court' (2015) 9(6) *International Journal of Social, Behavioural, Educational, Economic, Business and Industrial Engineering* 2197.

[116] See generally, A.R. Brewer-Carías (ed.), *Constitutional Courts as Positive Legislators: A Comparative Law Study* (Cambridge University Press, 2013).

[117] See the discussion attached to (n. 65) and (n. 66) in the Introduction.

Kenya, the constitutionality of the trial of Jesus Christ.[118] Less tangible roles suggested by various scholars, which are specific to the democratisation context, include: delivering on the transformational promises of the new constitution;[119] fostering a new legal and political culture wedded to democratic constitutionalism;[120] providing a focal point for 'a new rhetoric of state legitimacy, one based on respect for democratic values and rights';[121] and educating the citizenry on ideals of representative democratic government, thereby ensuring the informed citizenry on which the principle of popular sovereignty rests.[122]

The sheer weight of expectation on a court at the dawn of the democratic project is underscored by the contemporary Tunisian experience. The first decision in May 2014 of an interim body established to provide limited *a priori* review of bills (pending the establishment, under the 2014 Constitution, of a new constitutional court with wider powers), in which it upheld a widely criticised Bill on electoral law, provoked a torrent of criticism. The body's refusal to decide on the constitutionality of a provision prohibiting members of the military and security forces from voting, thus leaving the provision intact, has been characterised as a denial of justice, a 'political decision', as missing a 'historic opportunity of paramount importance for law and civilization', and as already discrediting the new institution.[123] The Constitutional Court itself – whose establishment has been delayed due to political infighting[124] – faces even greater expectations, given that it is empowered not only to assess the validity of legislation against the Constitution, but also Bills, treaties, and proposed constitutional amendments, as well as deciding on

[118] See M. Murungi, 'Report from Kenya: Constitutional Court Considers the Legitimacy of the Trial of Jesus' *The Court* 28 September 2007 www.thecourt.ca/report-from-kenya-constitutional-court-considers-the-legitimacy-of-the-trial-of-jesus.

[119] See Vilhena Vilheira, Viljoen & Baxi, *Transformative Constitutionalism*.

[120] See, e.g. D. Grimm, 'Constitutional Adjudication and Democracy' in M. Andenas & D. Fairgrieve (eds.), *Judicial Review in International Perspective*, Vol. 2 (Kluwer Law International, 2000) 142: 'The independent judiciary may protect them by helping gradually to develop among citizens and legislators liberty-protecting habits based in part upon their expectation that liberty-infringing laws will turn out not to be laws.'

[121] A. Stone Sweet, 'Constitutional Courts' 827.

[122] See I. Stotzky, 'The Tradition of Constitutional Adjudication' in Stotzky (ed.), *Transition to Democracy* 349.

[123] See M. Ben Hamadi, 'Tunisie: Les "gardiens de la Constitution" essuient un flot de critiques' *HuffPost Maghreb* 27 May 2014 www.huffpostmaghreb.com/2014/05/27/tunisie-instance-controle-constitutionnalite_n_5395843.html.

[124] See e.g. T. Ginsburg & A. Huq (eds.), *Assessing Constitutional Performance* (Cambridge University Press, 2016) 219.

impeachment of the President, and acting as an arbiter in potential constitutional crises (e.g. disputes between the president and prime minister, states of emergency, or temporary vacancy of the presidency).[125]

B   The Reality of Third Wave Courts

When we consider the marked influence of the German experience on third wave systems of strong judicial review, what is most striking is the extent to which so few third wave courts have carried out their work in contexts similar to that of post-war West Germany.

Few other post-authoritarian states adopted a 'zero hour' narrative and commitment to democratic rule rivalling the Bonn republic, and a minority of third wave states at transition – chiefly those of Latin America – had, like post-war Germany, some prior experience of democratic rule and significant experience of constitutional review, or like Hungary at least a strong culture of legalism. Indeed, so alien is the constitutional court to Mongolian legal culture that its name (*Tsets*) was borrowed from the word for a judge in traditional wrestling.[126] In a significant number of African states, the legal inheritance from colonial rule included a focus on parliamentary, rather than judicial, supremacy and, by the time the third wave of democratisation had begun, most states had already experienced a failure of democratisation and constitutional renewal. As the editors of *Democratization and the Judiciary* note, African states, with the exception of South Africa,

> gained independence in the early 1960s, with similar constitutions that attempted – but failed – to curb the centralization of political power and the emergence of a single-party state.[127]

Thus, the perceived umbilical link between strong judicial review and democracy is different from region to region. Whereas such review represented a promise for the future in the third wave democracies of CEE, East Asia, and Africa, in the states of Southern Europe and South America (and indeed some CEE states) it often represented a promise

---

[125] See Articles 118–25 of the 2014 Constitution. Articles 80, 84, 88, and 144 set out additional functions.

[126] T. Ginsburg, 'Constitutional Courts in East Asia: Understanding Variation' in Harding & Leyland (eds.), *Constitutional Courts* 304.

[127] See the introduction to Gloppen et al., *Courts and Power* 5–6.

broken and made anew with the return to democratic rule. In many states, that promise, whether new or remade, is widely viewed as broken again. Although various third wave states have achieved consolidated democracy as defined in Chapter 1 – such as Southern European states (e.g. Spain, Portugal), numerous CEE states (e.g. Slovenia), South American states (e.g. Uruguay), and Asian states (e.g. South Korea) – in many cases democratic development has stalled, stagnated, or gone into reverse, with watchful eyes on democratic decay in states such as Brazil, Hungary, Poland, South Africa, and the Philippines, to name just a few.

The hoped-for result of judicialising the democratisation process in many third wave states – a democracy at least comparable to that of Germany in the 1970s – has not transpired in most contexts. Lach and Sadurski's observation that constitutional adjudication in the CEE region has been 'a mixed bag of undoubtedly courageous and democracy-strengthening decisions as well as of decisions which seem like a set-back to these values' can be applied to other regions.[128] In Latin America, although there is a sense that 'there have been remarkable advances in the consolidation of the rule of law and constitutionalism';[129] there remains a palpable air of disappointment that judges are not 'blazing the way to robust constitutional democracy in the way many hoped they might.'[130]

In some cases, the activity of the constitutional court has actively hindered democratisation. Take Ghana and Brazil, for instance. In Ghana the Supreme Court's upholding of a seditious libel statute, despite a strongly worded constitutional free speech guarantee, permitted criminal prosecutions against journalists and public figures for defamation of the government.[131] In Brazil, the Federal Supreme Court's active engagement in economic matters, due to the constitutionalisation of economic and fiscal policy under the 1988 Constitution, is viewed as having had a negative impact on economic development,[132] thereby adversely affecting democratisation itself. Other decisions of that Court, discussed in Chapter 5, are open to the same criticism.

---

[128] Lach & Sadurski, 'Constitutional Courts' 79.
[129] J. Couso, 'Models of Democracy and Models of Constitutionalism: The Case of Chile's Constitutional Court, 1970–2010' (2011) 89 *Texas Law Review* 1517, 1520.
[130] Kapiszewski, Silverstein & Kagan (eds.), *Consequential Courts* 1.
[131] See D.K. Linnan (ed.), *Legitimacy, Legal Development and Change: Law and Modernization Reconsidered* (Routledge, 2016) 64.
[132] See C. Santiso, 'Economic Reform and Judicial Governance in Brazil: Balancing Independence with Accountability' in Gloppen, Gargarella & Skaar (eds.), *Democratization and the Judiciary*.

However, deficient democratic progress is not, in general, a failure of most constitutional courts, which have had to contend with a mixture of diverse issues not faced by the Karlsruhe Court. These include: a lack of electoral competition; a highly deficient party system and/or enduring executive dominance; badly drafted or prolix constitutions; often difficult economic transitions (whether moving from the planned economies of post-Communist states, the import substitution model of Latin America, or the idiosyncratic socialism of many African states); and enduring military power into the democratic era. This has made for volatile politics and a more difficult institutional setting for courts to effect real change. The hand wringing and unsuccessful posturing of post-war German politicians in the face of judicial assertiveness is replaced by overt and sustained attacks in many states against strong review, such as threats to trammel the court's jurisdiction, or more subtle, but persistent, forms of resistance aimed at reducing public support for courts and even judges' psychological resilience.[133] It has been suggested that the incapacity of judges to constrain political actors in Tanzania and Zambia is tied to legal culture, the institutional framework and resource constraints within which courts operate, and a lack of public legitimacy.[134] Some courts, such as the Argentine Supreme Court, were cowed by successive purges in the democratic era, resulting in a 'captured court' with little willingness to defy an overweening executive until the electoral tide appeared to be turning.[135] In Russia it appears that only complete quiescence in the face of President Yeltsin's suspension of parliament by decree could have saved the Constitutional Court from dissolution in 1993.[136]

Moreover, despite the increasing tendency toward enshrinement of justiciable social and economic rights in new democratic constitutions – often urged by international actors[137] – many scholars now sound strong notes of

---

[133] See G. Helmke & J.K. Staton, 'The Puzzling Judicial Politics of Latin America: A Theory of Litigation, Judicial Decisions, and Interbranch Conflict' in Helmke & Rios-Figueroa (eds.), *Courts in Latin America*; and M. Safjan, 'Politics and Constitutional Courts (Judge's Personal Perspective)' (2009) 165 *Polish Sociological Review* 3.

[134] See the editors' introduction to Gloppen, Gargarella & Skaar (eds.), *Democratization and the Judiciary* 3–4.

[135] See G. Helmke, *Courts Under Constraints: Judges, Generals, and Presidents in Argentina* (Cambridge University Press, 2012).

[136] See Scheppele, 'Guardians' 1791ff.

[137] See, for instance, the International Commission of Jurists analysis of the draft Libyan Constitution in 2015: 'The Draft Constitution should ... be reformed to expand the provisions relating to economic, social and cultural rights.' International Commission of Jurists, *The Draft Libyan Constitution: Procedural Deficiencies, Substantive Flaws*

caution concerning the capacity of courts to deliver on the promises of social justice and social transformation that such rights embody. Octavio Ferraz argues that the recognition of justiciable social and economic rights places a court in an 'intractable dilemma': it can either robustly vindicate such rights when requested by applicants, and face accusations that it has 'illegitimately and incompetently overstepped the boundaries of judicial power', or take a more cautious approach and face the charge that it has failed to fulfil its role as 'guardian of the constitution'.[138] In state after state, the conclusion has been reached that, regardless of whether a court has taken a deferential or assertive approach, it cannot itself bring about social transformation – rather, it can achieve only modest improvements at the margins, and often at the high cost of antagonising political powers beyond the limits of their willingness to acquiesce to judicial authority.[139]

Of course, as discussed above, various scholars offer that constitutional courts can still contribute to democratic progress and social transformation by providing a forum for deliberation, requiring political powers to justify their policy choices, and educating the citizenry as to the proper functioning of democratic governance. However, adequately verifying success regarding such roles is difficult, and would require sophisticated sociological enquiry, beyond anything currently found in the literature.

That said, constitutional courts in young democracies worldwide often have a concrete positive impact on the trajectory of democratisation and on governance in a post-authoritarian state. They are, as Kapiszewski, Silverstein, and Kagan put it, 'consequential courts'.[140] Specific examples include: strong decisions of the Bulgarian and Czech constitutional courts upholding an expansive right to freedom of expression and setting strict limits on restrictions of the right – the Czech court, for instance, imposing an interpretation of a 'hate speech' law that precluded its abuse against mere expressions of sympathy with fascism and communism;[141]

(December 2015) http://icj.wpengine.netdna-cdn.com/wp-content/uploads/2015/12/Lybia-Draft-Constitution-Flaws-Deficiencies-Publications-Reports-2015-ENG.pdf.

[138] O.L.M. Ferraz, 'Between Usurpation and Abdication? The Right to Health in the Courts of Brazil and South Africa' in Vilheira, Viljoen & Baxi (eds.), *Transformative Constitutionalism* 378–9.

[139] See e.g. R. Gargarella, P. Domingo & T. Roux (eds.), *Courts and Social Transformation in New Democracies: An Institutional Voice for the Poor?* (Ashgate, 2006); Sadurski, *Rights Before Courts* 283–7; and R. Uprimny 'The Recent Transformation of Constitutional Law in Latin America: Trends and Challenges' (2011) 89 *Texas Law Review* 1587, 1604.

[140] See Kapiszewski, Silverstein & Kagan (eds.), *Consequential Courts*.

[141] See Sadurski, *Rights Before Courts* 231–2.

the continual oversight and limitation of presidential decree powers by the Chilean Constitutional Court;[142] successful blocking of government attempts to restrict freedom of association in Benin;[143] the Slovenian Constitutional Court's invalidation of a law permitting blanket secret surveillance of individuals by the state;[144] and the Colombian Constitutional Court's blocking of President Uribe's constitutional amendment seeking to extend presidential term-limits in 2010.[145]

Yet, when democratic decay gathers momentum, these courts have had less support to draw on than the German Constitutional Court during its first decades. International oversight and political pressure by organisations such as the Council of Europe, the OAS, and the UN – as well as regional human rights courts – have not provided a particularly strong bulwark against democratic backsliding in many states, and cannot compare to the post-war occupation of West Germany by US troops – when the German constitutional court issued its first judgment in 1951, some 75,000 US soldiers still remained on German soil and would stay in large numbers for the following decades.[146] This signal difference, and the additional factors discussed above, have significantly dented the capacity of many courts to meet the initial bullish expectation that they would underpin successful democratisation processes.

4   Pushing Courts Past Their Limits?: Hungary, Colombia, and South Africa

Perversely, it is often those contexts that render effective constitutional adjudication most difficult which have often led to even greater expectations of the courts to deliver on the democratic promises of the constitution where other state actors are deemed not equal (or committed) to the task. Courts have tended to approach their difficult institutional circumstances in different ways: through general quiescence, which prevents attacks; or restraint and strategic deference, which allows for progressive institution-building. In a small number of third wave states the political context of the democratisation process has led courts to

---

[142] See D.L. Scribner, 'Distributing Political Power: The Constitutional Tribunal in Post-Authoritarian Chile' in Kapiszewski, Silverstein & Kagan (eds.), *Consequential Courts*.

[143] Linnan (ed.), *Legitimacy, Legal Development and Change* 65 note 13.

[144] Sadurski, *Rights Before Courts* 201.

[145] The Colombian context is discussed in more detail below.

[146] See A. Baker, 'GIs in West Germany' in T. Adam (ed.), *Germany and the Americas: O-Z* (ABC-CLIO, 2005) 448.

assume adjudicative postures exceeding those of even the most assertive courts in mature democracies (the United States, Germany, and India).

A   Hungary: The Court as Both Democratic Opposition and Voice of the Constitution

The failure of modern parliaments to act as a check on government has been offered as a justification of the German Constitutional Court's role in post-war West Germany.[147] In Hungary, the Constitutional Court established under the wholesale revisions to the Communist-era constitution in 1989, adopted by the outgoing Communist parliament, found itself in a context where the competences of the executive and a unicameral parliament were intertwined, in a unitary state with a limited presidency, with the result that the Court came to act as the sole institutional check on government action.[148] Symbolising the new democratic order in the absence of a wholly new constitution,[149] and armed with greater powers and accessibility than most constitutional courts – including the ability to act of its own motion and an unusually open petition system[150] – the 'first' Court under President Lászlo Sólyom quickly became known in the 1990s for being 'one of the most activist in the world',[151] or less neutrally, as 'unusually aggressive' in dictating to the legislature and executive.[152]

Faced with sluggish action by the representative organs of government in dismantling the old Communist state and making good on the promises of the democratic era, the Court struck down almost one-third of the laws challenged before it between 1990 and 1996, including new laws as

---

[147] E. Benda, 'Constitutional Jurisdiction in Western Germany' (1981) 19 *Columbia Journal of Transnational Law* 1, 10.

[148] G.A. Toth, 'Historicism or Art Nouveau in Constitutional Interpretation; A Comment on Zoltan Szente's *The Interpretive Practice of the Hungarian Constitutional Court – A Critical View*' (2013) 14 *German Law Journal* 1615–16.

[149] See L. Sólyom, 'The Rise and Decline of Constitutional Culture in Hungary' in A. von Bogdandy & P. Sonnevend (eds.), *Constitutional Crisis in the European Constitutional Area: Theory, Law and Politics in Hungary and Romania* (Bloomsbury Publishing, 2015) 8.

[150] This unusually open system is viewed as having been 'well justified in the times of the change of the regime from dictatorship to democracy': P. Sonnevend, A. Jakab & L. Csink, 'The Constitution as an Instrument of Everyday Party Politics: The Basic Law of Hungary' in von Bogdandy & Sonnevend (eds.), *Constitutional Crisis*.

[151] Kommers, Finn & Jacobsohn, *American Constitutional Law* 71.

[152] Horowitz, 'Constitutional Courts' 187.

well as holdovers from the Communist era that allowed widespread state surveillance and government control of the judiciary (dwarfing the tally of the German constitutional court).[153] The Court also set out detailed instructions to the legislature for writing laws in cases of 'legislative omission', ordered parliament to pass new rules on its own procedures,[154] and generally, as Kim Lane Scheppele suggests, 'left relatively little room for politics'. With the Court 'for all intents and purposes running the country',[155] Justice Sólyom often spoke extrajudicially as though he were personally the 'mouthpiece' of the Constitution, not merely presiding over the Court as 'guardian of the Constitution'.[156] Scheppele asserts that the Court was the key bulwark against authoritarian backsliding:

> Whenever the new governments started to look like the communist-era government in the way they treated the citizenry (claiming laws should be applied retrospectively, tampering with the media, picking out favorites for special treatment, picking out enemies for deprivations of rights, breaking political promises), the Hungarian Constitutional Court sprung into action ... because Hungarians wrote petitions in droves[157]

This, Scheppele asserted approvingly, was 'democracy by judiciary'.[158] However, although it was the subject of much scholarly interest almost from its inception, the Court's remarkable power was short-lived. The Court's decision in 1995 holding major portions of a highly contentious austerity package to be unconstitutional, as breaching key social and economic rights in the revised 1989 Constitution, sufficiently angered the political branches that with renewal of its membership in 1998 the government (then under Viktor Orbán, the current Prime Minister) refused to renew President Sólyom for a second term and installed new judges with a far more sceptical view of judicial power.[159] The 'new' Court was, as a result, significantly less assertive. In addition, under the current conservative Fidesz government, the Court was packed and had

---

[153] G. Halmai & K. Scheppele, 'Living Well is the Best Revenge: The Hungarian Approach to Judging the Past' in A.J. McAdams (ed.), *Transitional Justice and the Rule of Law in New Democracies* (1997) 180.

[154] Horowitz, 'Constitutional Courts' 188.

[155] Scheppele, 'Democracy by Judiciary' 44.   [156] Scheppele, 'Guardians' 1758.

[157] Scheppele, 'Democracy by Judiciary' 51.

[158] Ibid. 3. Indeed, Scheppele went so far as to suggest: 'I think that democracy by judiciary may be an option that more deeply entrenched democracies may want to consider as well.'

[159] Ibid. 53–4.

its jurisdiction significantly narrowed under a new constitution (Basic
Law) of 2012, followed by a startling constitutional amendment of March
2013 that annulled all its decisions prior to that date.[160]

B Colombia: The Court as Sole Guarantor
of a Disowned Constitution

The Colombian Constitutional Court was established in 1992 under a
1991 Constitution that, as Uprimny recounts, was the product of a very
particular political and constitutional moment, with a constitutional
convention including many of the societal actors traditionally excluded
from the political process; former guerrillas, indigenous communities,
and religious minorities – as well as representatives of the traditionally
dominant Liberal and Conservative parties, who constituted just sixty
per cent of the convention members. The result was a text aimed at
broadening participation in political life, forming the basis for greater
social justice, and enhancing protection of human rights, with a rich
seam of both civil and political, and social and economic rights. The
Court was accorded a central role to put the new text into effect.[161]
    With the political system quickly shifting back to old habits of exclusion
and overweening presidential power, the Court was left as the sole state
institution committed to the Constitution and adopted an assertive stance
from the earliest days of its operation, aimed at remedying the defects of
Colombian society in a context where exclusionary politics and ordinary
political channels were unable to deliver many societal goods, including
peace, inclusion, equality, and fairness. Aided by a very open petition
system, the Court quickly amassed a voluminous jurisprudence curtailing
the presidential power to declare states of emergency, vindicating fundamental rights (including social and economic rights, indigenous peoples'
rights, and collective rights), defending congressional autonomy from the
encroachment of presidential power, blocking President Uribe's attempts to
overcome existing constitutional term-limits, and involving itself in economic governance, such as the implementation of the minimum wage.[162]

---

[160] See K.L. Scheppele. 'Understanding Hungary's Constitutional Revolution' in von Bogdandy & Sonnevend, *Constitutional Crisis.*
[161] Uprimny, 'Extraordinary Powers' 52.
[162] See M.J. Cepeda-Espinosa, 'Judicial Activism in a Violent Context: The Origin, Role, and
Impact of the Colombian Constitutional Court' (2004) 3 *Washington University Global
Studies Law Review* 529.

In particular, faced with a raft of justiciable social and economic rights, the Constitutional Court elaborated a particularly sophisticated, principled, and robust jurisprudence in this area. It has frequently ordered state agencies to help impoverished individuals, by providing medical treatment such as eye operations and AIDS medication, to provide state subsidies wrongfully denied by administrative actors, and occasionally extending its judgments to all persons in the same position as the claimant by recognising an 'unconstitutional state of affairs', with examples including ordering the state to adopt an action plan to address structural inadequacies in the prison system, and upholding the state's duty to guarantee access to education and adequate housing.[163]

As in Hungary, the Court's case-law prompted serious political backlash,[164] although threats against its jurisdiction and powers have not become a reality due to public support for the Court. Yet, it remains the case that the Court's unusual power is not so much evidence of democratic progress, as more akin to a sticking plaster for the deep-seated deficiencies in Colombia's democratic system. As one observer has noted:

> the activism of the Court has been prompted by the prevailing democratic deficit: the crisis in political representation and the weakness of the opposition and social movements.[165]

Indeed, notwithstanding the Court's highly assertive and far-reaching jurisprudence seeking the transformation of Colombian society, increasingly the view from grassroots level appears to be disappointment with the pace and nature of change.[166] In short, judicial action alone cannot transform society when the rest of the political order remains resistant to change.

---

[163] Ibid. 611–20.

[164] Every administration since 1991 has threatened constitutional reforms to overturn controversial judgments, or presented proposals for limiting the Court's jurisdiction. See R. Rodríguez-Raga, 'Strategic Deference in the Colombian Constitutional Court, 1992–2006' in Helmke & Ríos-Figueroa (eds.), *Courts in Latin America* 85–6.

[165] J. Faundez, 'Book Review: Roberto Gargarella, Pilar Domingo and Theunis Roux (eds.), Courts and Social Transformation in New Democracies: An Institutional Voice for the Poor? (Aldershot: Ashgate, 2006)' (2007) 39 *Journal of Latin American Studies* 419, 420.

[166] See a report compiled by the author for International IDEA, *The Judiciary and Constitutional Transitions*, conveying the discussions of a two-day workshop in The Hague on 14–15 November 2014: www.idea.int/sites/default/files/publications/the-judiciary-and-constitutional-transitions.pdf.

C   South Africa: The Court as Defender of the 'Deep Principle' of Democracy

Much ink has been spilled on the role of the South African Constitutional Court in that state's era-defining transition and democratisation process. The Court was integral to the political compromise that facilitated the democratic transition – as political insurance for the outgoing regime in particular, protection for the white minority more widely, and a check on dominance of the political system by the African National Congress (ANC) party – as well as indicating concrete commitment to the grand ideals in the new democratic constitution for a more just and equal society.[167] As Klug has observed, the Court 'has been called upon to address issues and to face challenges that would be considered extraordinary for any judiciary.'[168]

Its most remarkable role may have been that of reviewing the final constitution drafted by a constituent assembly as against the principles in the draft constitution, and its refusal to certify the original text without key revisions, despite its adoption by eighty-six per cent of the democratically elected Constitutional Assembly.[169] It quickly cemented its reputation for assertiveness in the 1990s with decisions that held the death penalty to be unconstitutional, ordered the enactment of laws on same-sex marriage in line with the Constitution, and upheld prisoners' voting rights.[170]

However, the Court has been required to strike an extremely difficult balance between attempting to deliver on the promises of democracy and social justice in the 1996 Constitution, and avoiding overstepping the bounds of possible (and democratically proper) action in South Africa's democratic system. Thus, despite its high profile internationally, the Court has been criticised at home, often strongly, not least for upholding the constitutionality of a constitutional amendment permitting 'floor-crossing' by politicians (i.e. defecting to another party while retaining one's seat) – characterised by some as a manipulation of the electoral system tending to strengthen the ANC's dominance and stymying meaningful multi-party competition by weakening smaller opposition parties[171] – and for taking a less robust

---

[167] Two books in the present Cambridge series alone address the South African Court: Roux, *Politics of Principle*; and J. Fowkes, *Building the Constitution: The Practice of Constitutional Interpretation in Post-Apartheid South Africa* (Cambridge University Press, 2016).
[168] H. Klug, 'Finding the Constitutional Court's Place in South Africa's Democracy: The Interaction of Principle and Institutional Pragmatism in the Court's Decision Making' (2010) 3 *Constitutional Court Review* 1.
[169] Choudhry, *Constitutional Courts* 27.   [170] Roux, *Politics of Principle* 235–364.
[171] Issacharoff, *Fragile Democracies* 351–64.

approach to upholding social and economic rights than other courts, such as the Colombian court discussed above.[172] The Court's 'reasonableness' approach to social rights adjudication, which accords significant deference to state organs concerning elaboration of policy on social justice matters, has polarised opinion. Some laud it as a way of giving meaning to the social and economic rights in the constitutional text, while others decry it as a great disappointment and a wasted opportunity in the quest for social justice in a state marred by extreme levels of socio-economic inequality and poverty.[173]

Despite its rather cautious approach in such contentious matters, the Court has nevertheless faced persistent complaints from political powers that it is breaching the separation of powers in the Constitution and acting as a force for 'minority tyranny' against the democratic majority.[174] Against this backdrop, the Court has explored in depth the meaning of constitutional democracy in light of the 1996 Constitution, which, as Theunis Roux suggests, explicitly envisages democracy not merely as a system of governance, but a value system based not only on 'the will of the people' but also the principle that 'every citizen is protected by law'. Human dignity, equality, freedom, and individual rights, repeatedly proclaimed within the text, are viewed not as subtracting from the democratic principle, but rather, lying in 'constructive tension' with majority rule.[175] The Court has indicated its rejection of any winner-takes-all conception of majority rule and has emphasised the need for a deliberative democracy where both minority and majority are included in public decision-making.

However, the elaboration of such principles has done little to forestall the ruling ANC's consolidation of its position as the dominant political force in South Africa, and in a climate of growing hostility toward the Court within the ANC, the government announced a review of the Court's powers in 2012.[176] Although this has not yet led to any concrete

---

[172] See U. Baxi, 'Preliminary Notes on Transformative Constitutionalism' in Vilheira, Viljoen & Baxi (eds.), *Transformative Constitutionalism* 46.

[173] J. Hohmann, *The Right to Housing: Law, Concepts, Possibilities* (Bloomsbury Publishing, 2013) 97.

[174] See Democratic Governance and Rights Unit, *Has the South African Constitutional Court Over-reached? A Study of the Court's Application of the Separation of Powers Doctrine between 2009 and 2013* (28 August 2014) 4–7 www.dgru.uct.ac.za/sites/default/files/image_tool/images/103/Separation%20of%20Powers%20Draft%20August%202014.pdf.

[175] T. Roux, 'The Principle of Democracy in South African Constitutional Law' in S. Woolman & M. Bishop (eds.), *Constitutional Conversations* (Pretoria University Law Press, 2008) 82.

[176] S. Gardbaum, 'Are Strong Constitutional Courts Always a Good Thing for New Democracies?' (2015) 53 *Columbia Journal of Transnational Law* 285, 288.

reforms, it has highlighted the Court's more precarious position in the contemporary political order in which the ANC seeks to free itself from standard forms of democratic and legal accountability.[177] Indeed, in a worrying echo of the Hungarian context, Issacharoff (among others) now speaks of the hope that South Africa once embodied turning to concern regarding 'the peril of constitutional retreat', and even the 'risk of descent into the excesses associated with strong-arm rule'.[178]

All is not lost, however. The electorate has emerged as the key power capable of countering the ANC's hegemony, delivering a bloody nose to the government in the 2016 municipal elections with an eleven per cent drop in support compared to the 2014 parliamentary elections;[179] spurred partly, it must be said, by the Constitutional Court's damning judgment in the *Nkandla* corruption case against President Jacob Zuma, which held that he had violated the Constitution by failing to repay government money spent on his private residence.[180]

5 Conclusion: Perception Versus Reality in Scholarship and Policymaking

It is clear from the above that, despite the global spread of courts as a legal technology to assist in the achievement of a functioning or consolidated democracy after authoritarian rule, in many states the expectations placed on courts have been unrealistic and impossible to meet. Instead of a global commonwealth of 'new Germanies' we see a starker picture. Compared to the perceived security of German democracy and its constitutional court some twenty-five years after transition in the late 1940s, courts in many third-wave democracies over two decades post-transition are under siege. 2012 was an *annus horribilis*, with the Hungarian and South African experiences joined by death threats against Romanian

---

[177] See a speech by the South African journalist Raymond Louw to the 2012 Rhodes University graduation, 'Meddling with Constitutional Court Powers a Threat to All', 22 April 2012 www.ru.ac.za/media/rhodesuniversity/content/communications/docu ments/Raymond_Louw%20Grad%20Address.pdf.

[178] Issacharoff, *Fragile Democracies* 242, 268.

[179] See e.g. S. Ryklief, 'South Africa's 2016 Municipal Elections – Why the Excitement?' *GroundUp* 23 August 2016 www.groundup.org.za/article/south-africas-2016-municipal-elections-why-excitement/.

[180] *Economic Freedom Fighters v. Speaker of the National Assembly and Others; Democratic Alliance v. Speaker of the National Assembly and Others* [2016] ZACC 11.

constitutional court judges in the midst of a political power struggle,[181] and at the regional level – as we will see in Chapter 3 – the Brighton Declaration (widely viewed as an attack on the European Court of Human Rights) and the dismantling of the South African Development Community (SADC) Tribunal in Africa. Recent years have seen the rot spread, with the irrefutable capture of Poland's Constitutional Tribunal between 2016 and 2017 at the hands of the Law and Justice Party (PiS) government a particularly alarming development.[182]

Indeed, when Stone Sweet, as quoted at the outset, opines that 'the more successful any transition has been, the more likely one is to find an effective constitutional or supreme court at the heart of it', there is a clear risk of mistaking *correlation* for *causality* (although this, of course, may not be his intended meaning). Most successful post-war democratisation processes have occurred in post-war Europe, where similarly propitious conditions existed for an accretion of judicial governance power.[183] One can easily invert Stone Sweet's statement to hold, correctly, that rights and review have also been central to most *unsuccessful* democratisation processes. Judicialisation – the ostensible transfer of governance power to courts – should therefore not be equated with democratisation; it can just as easily reflect a very problematic trajectory as democratic progress falters. Lawyers, in particular, can easily fall into the trap of exaggerating the importance of legal institutions. There has at times been a failure to distinguish what is legally and constitutionally innovative – of interest to lawyers – from the empirical question of whether courts have been as central to successful democratisation processes as they are often portrayed.

The limits of constitutional courts as democracy-builders have, of course, been noted by other scholars. Tom Ginsburg has cautioned that courts may 'play an essential role in structuring an environment of open political competition, free exchange of ideas, and limited government',

---

[181] Ibid.

[182] Tomas Tadeusz Koncewicz has chronicled this development in a series of blog posts and articles. See e.g. T.T. Koncewicz, 'Living under the Unconstitutional Capture and Hoping for the Constitutional Recapture' *Verfassungsblog* 3 January 2017 www.verfassungsblog.de/living-under-the-the-unconstitutional-capture-and-hoping-for-the-constitutional-recapture/.

[183] This is not to overlook states such as Costa Rica and Japan, although it is worth noting that the constitutional courts in these states are not perceived as central to their democratic success.

but do not lead the democratisation process itself.[184] A decade ago Irwin Stotzky opined:

> In the past three decades of democratic transition, the judiciary has had rather limited success in promoting democratic reform . . . [D]emocratic change cannot be created in a vacuum. All parts of the public and private sectors must work together on these problems. So far that has not happened.[185]

In short, it appears that constitutional courts are neither a guarantor of, nor a shortcut to, a functioning democratic system. Moreover, under-lying any analysis of the roles played by courts as democracy-builders is the core methodological challenge of discerning how and whether a court has an impact on *any* process, especially a process as multi-faceted and multi-causal as democratisation.

Yet, looking at the faith placed in courts in contemporary democracy-building projects, such as those in Tunisia, Kenya, and Nepal, one gets a strong sense that the dominant presentations of the virtues and effective-ness of such courts have overshadowed more nuanced presentations. This is not to say, of course, that these courts do not make a valuable contribution to consolidating democracy in a post-authoritarian society. It is simply to say that these roles appear to be more limited than is often claimed (or hoped). As we will see in the next chapter, the same can be said of regional human rights courts.

---

[184] Ginsburg, 'The Politics of Courts' 50.
[185] I.P. Stotzky, 'Lessons Learned and the Way Forward' in Gloppen, Gargarella & Skaar (eds.), *Democratization and the Judiciary* 202.

3

The Rise and Limits of Human Rights
Courts as Democracy-Builders

[The European Court of Human Rights] has been a vital part of European democratic consolidation and integration for over half a century

James Sweeney, 2013[1]

[T]he Inter-American Court's far-reaching exercise of authority in the field of amnesties and the broad interpretation of its own mandate seem to further democratization in various Latin American countries.

Nina Binder, 2011[2]

[The Inter-American Court of Human Rights] has turned out to be very important for the strengthening of democracy and the improvement of human rights in the Americas.

Diego García-Sayan, 2012[3]

It is clear from Chapter 2 that even the 'star' constitutional courts that have emerged in post-authoritarian states in recent decades have a very mixed record, and have tended to reveal the outer limits of what such courts can achieve as democracy-builders.

How do regional human rights courts fit into this picture? Like Germany's Federal Constitutional Court, both the European and Inter-American human rights courts are post-war creations, forming part of regional rights protection systems that stand as reactions to the depredations of undemocratic rule. The European Court of Human Rights was

---

[1] Sweeney, *Post-Cold War Era* 1.

[2] C. Binder, 'The Prohibition of Amnesties by the Inter-American Court of Human Rights' in A. Von Bogdandy & I. Venzke (eds.), *International Judicial Lawmaking: On Public Authority and Democratic Legitimation in Global Governance* (Springer, 2012) 324.

[3] Former president of the Inter-American Court: D. García-Sayan, 'The Role of the Inter-American Court of Human Rights in the Americas' (2012) 19 *UC Davis Journal of International Law & Policy* 103, 103. Similar statements are found in e.g. C. Grossman, 'The Inter-American System and Its Evolution' (2009) 2 *Inter-American and European Human Rights Journal* 49, 65.

established in 1959, a decade after the establishment of the Council of Europe in 1949 and adoption of the European Convention on Human Rights (ECHR) in 1950. The Inter-American Court of Human Rights was established in 1979, thirty years after the creation of the Organization of American States (OAS) in 1948 and proclamation of the American Declaration of Human Rights (ADHR) the same year.

The African Court on Human and Peoples' Rights, which is discussed toward the end of this chapter, is a more recent appearance. Established in 2006 (eight years after the adoption of its founding protocol), it is the judicial heart of the African Union (AU) system for the protection of human rights, mooted as early as 1961[4] but which only took root in 1981 with the adoption of the African Charter on Human and Peoples' Rights (ACHPR) by the Organisation of African Unity (OAU; now the AU) and the establishment of the African Commission on Human and Peoples' Rights in 1987.

1   Inflated Perceptions

In a similar manner to the inflated perception of domestic constitutional courts as democracy-builders, discussed in the previous chapter, the role of regional courts in supporting democratisation is easily overstated. For instance, James Sweeney's assertion that the European Court of Human Rights 'has been a vital part of European democratic consolidation and integration for over half a century',[5] could easily be understood as suggesting that this court was engaged in significant activity at the regional level parallel to the developing role of the Federal Constitutional Court of Germany at the domestic level. In reality, the European Court was virtually dormant until the 1970s; in terms of consolidation, as defined in Chapter 1, it was a peripheral actor in European democratisation processes until the 1990s, when Turkey and post-Communist states came under its jurisdiction. The only fully active regional court in any part of the world in the immediate post-war period was the EU's Court of Justice, which hit its stride in the early 1960s but which had, for instance, no hand in rights protection until the 1970s, and only a limited role thereafter.[6]

---

[4] Cole, 'The African Court' 24.   [5] Quoted at the start of this chapter.
[6] J.L. Murray, 'The Influence of the European Convention on Fundamental Rights on Community Law' (2011) 33 *Fordham International Law Journal* 1388, 1394.

As we will see, the Inter-American Court was the first regional human rights court to play a key part in any democratisation process, and remains the quintessential 'democratisation court' at the regional level worldwide. This chapter recounts the emergence of the European Court as a new form of legal technology and the slow development of its role, and contrasts this with the Inter-American Court, which, in a like manner to the German Court at the domestic level, rapidly pioneered a new form of jurisprudence in reaction to its political context, which built on the European approach but departs from it in significant ways. After assessing the roles of both courts as democracy-builders to date, the chapter finishes by briefly discussing the diffusion of this model to Africa and the Arab region, and the replication difficulties in those contexts.

2 The Slow Evolution of the European Court of Human Rights

The European Court of Human Rights constitutes one of the boldest new constructions of the immediate post-war era. With the exception of the defunct Central American Court of Justice[7] and the European Court of Justice, which had been established in 1952, it was an entirely new legal technology, with jurisdiction over sovereign states.

A A Contested Creation

As Ed Bates and others have recounted, the Court has been dogged by contestation since its genesis.[8] The non-governmental European Movement's early plans, from 1948 onwards, envisaged significant regional supervision of democratic states in Europe, including a right of individual petition to both a commission and a court of human rights, and with the commission empowered (but only by decision of a two-thirds majority) to conduct an enquiry into allegations of human rights abuses in the territory of the affected state.

---

[7] Established in 1907 to arbitrate in disagreements among Central American states, it was the first international court with jurisdiction over sovereign States, compulsory authority, and individual access. However, it only lasted until 1918. See R. Riquelme Cortado, 'Central American Court of Justice (1907–18)', *Oxford Public International Law* http://opil.ouplaw.com/view/10.1093/law:epil/9780199231690/law-9780199231690-e15.

[8] See E. Bates, *The Evolution of the European Convention on Human Rights. From its Inception to the Creation of a Permanent Court of Human Rights* (Oxford University Press, 2010).

However, these proposals were significantly attenuated in the final text of the ECHR, due to concerns among the Member States of the Council of Europe regarding judicial activism and the potential impact on state sovereignty. The right of individual petition to both organs, and state submission to the jurisdiction of the Court, were made optional; the commission's powers were reduced to a primary aim of seeking a friendly settlement between the parties to a disagreement and forwarding an opinion to the Committee of Ministers (the executive arm of the Council of Europe) where no settlement could be reached. Establishment of the Court itself was made subject to a declaration by a minimum of eight states (of ten original signatories) recognising its compulsory jurisdiction.[9]

The latter requirement was thought by many to postpone indefinitely the creation of a court for human rights, but it merely delayed it by nine years. Even then, the Court's role was entirely contingent on Commission activation, which, where it found a state violation of a Convention right, could refer the matter for a political decision by the Committee of Ministers, or a judicial decision by the Court – and the latter solely where the state(s) concerned had accepted the Court's jurisdiction.

B   Linking Rights Protection and Democratic Rule

Mirroring to some extent the constitutional developments in Germany and Italy, from the outset the linkage between rights protection and democratic rule was clear in the emerging regional framework. The 'Message to Europeans' drafted by the Swiss federalist, Denis de Rougemont, and adopted by some 800 participants at the final session of the Congress of Europe held in The Hague in May 1948, referred to what might be considered core elements of political democracy:

> We desire a Charter of Human Rights guaranteeing liberty of thought, assembly and expression as well as the right to form a political opposition[10]

From its creation in 1949 membership of the Council of Europe, and adherence to the ECHR, was predicated on democratic governance. All ten founding Member States were under democratic rule,[11] and the

---

[9] A.H. Robertson, 'The European Court of Human Rights' (1960) 9 *American Journal of Comparative Law* 1, 3–7.

[10] Robertson, ibid. 4.

[11] Belgium, Denmark, France, Ireland, Italy, Luxembourg, the Netherlands, Norway, Sweden, and the United Kingdom. Germany and Iceland joined the following year.

Statute of the Council of Europe strongly links respect for human rights
with democracy. For instance, its preamble states:

> [The signatory governments] ... Reaffirming their devotion to the spirit-
> ual and moral values which are the common heritage of their peoples and
> the true source of individual freedom, political liberty and the rule of law,
> *principles which form the basis of all genuine democracy*[12]

In the significant disagreement concerning the creation of a court (or
the need for any regional supervision organs more generally) both sides
invoked democratic arguments. Addressing opposition to the creation of
a court before a meeting of the Parliamentary Assembly of the Council of
Europe in 1949, former French minister Pierre-Henri Teitgen laid out the
fundamental need for such an institution:

> Many of our colleagues have pointed out that our countries are demo-
> cratic and are deeply impregnated with a sense of freedom; they believe in
> morality and in a natural law ... Why is it necessary to build such a
> system? ...
> Democracies do not become Nazi countries in one day. Evil progresses
> cunningly, with a minority operating, as it were, to remove the levers of
> control. One by one, freedoms are suppressed, in one sphere after
> another. Public opinion and the entire national conscience are asphyxi-
> ated. And then, when everything is in order, the 'Fuhrer' is installed and
> the evolution continues even to the oven of the crematorium.
> It is necessary to intervene before it is too late. A conscience must exist
> somewhere which will sound the alarm to the minds of a nation menaced
> by this progressive corruption, to warn them of the peril and to show
> them that they are progressing down a long road which leads far, some-
> times even to Buchenwald or Dachau.
> An international Court, within the Council of Europe, and a system of
> supervision and guarantees could be the conscience of which we all have
> need, and of which other countries have perhaps a special need.[13]

Teitgen not only viewed an international human rights convention
with a supervisory court as a 'canary in the mineshaft' regarding authoritarian degeneration, but also as a potential common 'bill of rights' for that
slim sickle-shaped slice of Western Europe where democratic rule per-
sisted; and as a beacon to those trapped behind the new Iron Curtain. Yet,
at the time of its adoption, the ECHR was apparently commonly viewed as
merely giving legal voice to a collective *political* pact against totalitarian-
ism, though the text reflected the ambivalence of its contested purpose.[14]

---

[12] Emphasis added.   [13] Quoted in Robertson, 'The European Court' 10.
[14] Bates, *Evolution of the European Convention* 8.

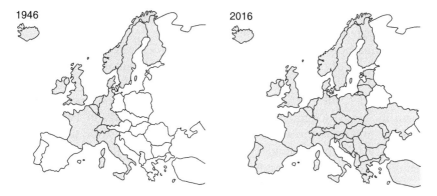

Figure 3.1 Electoral Democracies in Europe: 1946 and 2016

It is important to recall that, in 1950, robust judicial oversight even at the domestic level remained an odd proposition. The constitutional courts of Germany and Italy had yet to be established (and were not expected to assume as central a role in governance as they did), the revived Austrian constitutional court was creating few waves, the Irish Supreme Court had yet to reach its 1960s awakening, and the entire notion of strong judicial review of the German or US style was somewhat alien (if not repugnant) to the British and French.

C 1959–1998: From Underused Technology to Europe's Central Court

The perception of the ECHR as merely a political pact, and a strongly professed faith in domestic institutions for protecting rights, was reflected in the slow rate of submission to the Court's jurisdiction, dulling its impact for a generation. The Court was not established until 1959 and until recognition of the Court's jurisdiction by Italy and France in 1973 and 1974 respectively, West Germany and the United Kingdom were the only large Western European states subject to its oversight. Even then, strong British resistance to submitting to the Court was overcome in 1966 solely on policy advice that it would have little impact on British law.[15] The Convention system was often viewed from London as geared toward the continental states whose democratic processes had failed so

---

[15] Ibid. 10–12.

significantly in the inter-war period;[16] a perception that has continued in some quarters through subsequent decades.[17]

The European Court's democratisation burden was light for the first four decades of operation. In contrast to the voluminous jurisprudence produced by the domestic constitutional courts in Karlsruhe and Rome by the mid-1970s, the Court in Strasbourg had issued very few decisions, with its annual judgments only breaching single figures in 1981.[18] The Court, unlike the more active Commission, was an exotic technology; like a 1960s supercomputer, few knew how to use it, and even fewer could see its potential uses. In addition, cases before both organs tended to concern fine-tuning matters unrelated to constructing the essentials of a democratic order, such as linguistic parity between Belgium's two communities,[19] sex education,[20] legal aid,[21] and the rights of illegitimate children.[22] It was rare that the Strasbourg Court addressed transitional justice matters in a manner similar to the German Court in Karlsruhe. Even cases in the early 1960s, such as De Becker v. Belgium concerning forfeiture of free speech rights of a newspaper editor convicted as a Nazi collaborator, were resolved by friendly settlement and left a rather muted trace in the Court's case-law.[23]

It is only in the late 1970s, with the Court's foundational decisions on free speech in Sunday Times v. UK[24] and Handyside v. UK,[25] that something akin to a democracy-building jurisprudence addressing the essentials of democratic governance hove into view. Yet, even here, the respondent state concerned was a mature, stable democracy, rendering these judgments concerning democratic quality rather than consolidation of democracy; akin to the constitutional fine-tuning role played by constitutional courts in mature democracies. The Court's engagement

---

[16] See e.g. the observation that the European Convention was 'initially intended for defeated and conquered countries rather than the UK': P. Riddell, 'The Constitution and the Public – How Voters Forgot the Constitution' in M. Qvortrup (ed.), The British Constitution: Continuity and Change. A Festschrift for Vernon Bogdanor (Hart, 2013) 40.

[17] Sturgess & Chubb, Judging the World 115 quote Lord Wilberforce as stating that the ECHR 'was not devised for use by developed countries'.

[18] See www.strasbourgconsortium.org/docs/Chronological%20List%20of%20ECtHR%20 cases.pdf for a chronological list of the Court's judgments.

[19] 'Belgian Linguistics' case (No. 2) (1968) 1 EHRR 252.

[20] Kjeldsen, Busk Madsen and Pedersen v. Denmark (1976) 1 EHRR 711.

[21] Airey v. Ireland (1979) 2 EHRR 305.   [22] Marckx v. Belgium (1979) 2 EHRR 330.

[23] De Becker v. Belgium, ECtHR, App. No. 214/56 (27 March 1962). See Bates, Evolution of the European Convention on Human Rights 207ff.

[24] (No.1) (1979–80) 2 EHRR 245.   [25] (1976) 1 EHRR 737.

with the early third wave democracies of Spain, Portugal, and Greece was also minimal; seen in such rare cases as *Guincho* v. *Portugal*,[26] in which the Court held a firm line that it could not accept as a justification for excessively lengthy civil judicial proceedings the difficulties of overhauling a judicial system in the context of democratic restoration.

Indeed, it is arguable that prospective membership of the European Economic Community (EEC, now EU) did much more to keep democratisation on track in the new democracies than any intervention of the ECHR organs, given that both Spain and Portugal applied to join in the middle of, or shortly after, the transition to electoral democracy; finally acceding in 1986. It may also be argued that the integrative jurisprudence of the European Court of Justice in Luxembourg, its growing partnership with national courts from the 1960s onwards, and domestic acceptance (albeit qualified) of its assertion of the primacy and direct effect of Community law, did more to acclimatise European states and their constitutional courts to regional judicial power than the case-law of the Court in Strasbourg, by inaugurating a 'new normal' where sovereignty and judicial supremacy could increasingly be viewed as shared, rather than a *zero sum* game.[27]

In the Convention system, by the 1980s three key doctrines had been developed, which, as we will see in Chapter 6, would shape the Court's later approach to the new democracies of post-Soviet Europe. First, 'evolutive interpretation', by which the Court interprets the Convention dynamically 'in light of present-day conditions', allowed for progressively expansive readings of Convention rights. Second, the principle that Convention rights should be 'practical and effective', which precludes states from relying on the existence of purely formal rights guarantees in domestic law. Third is the 'margin of appreciation doctrine', by which the Court calibrates the extent to which a state is to be afforded discretion on a rights matter, with the determination often based on the extent to which there is European consensus on the matter (as divined by the Court) – an approach that, at the time of its elaboration, appeared to acknowledge the democratic maturity and generally high level of rights protection in the states under its purview. Increasing emphasis on the *res interpretata* authority of the Court's case-law, meaning that state obligations are based not only on the Convention, but on the Convention as

---

[26] (1985) 7 EHRR 223; discussed in Sweeney, *Post-Cold War Era* 3, 27.
[27] See Rosas, Levits & Bot (eds.), *The Court of Justice*.

interpreted by the Court, placed greater constraints on state organs to remain Convention-compliant.[28]

The European Court's jurisprudence also shows it, like many domestic constitutional courts, to be an heir of the Federal Constitutional Court of Germany. Its development of a proportionality test was influenced by the German proportionality doctrine.[29] Perhaps more strikingly, the European Court has also adopted its own version of the German doctrine of 'militant democracy' (discussed further below).[30]

While the Inter-American Court was slowly carving out its role in the 1990s – discussed in Section 3 – the European Court's role began to mutate. By 1990 the Court's prominence in European governance had increased significantly, with all Western European states recognising the right of individual petition and submitting to the Court's jurisdiction. The Commission's and Court's jurisprudential output from the 1980s onward increased markedly, touching on virtually any matter of policy or law in the contracting states. Corporal punishment in British schools, laws sanctioning homosexual acts in Northern Ireland, libel laws in Austria, and planning laws on expropriation in Sweden were all deemed violations of the Convention.[31] Increasingly confident characterisation of the Convention and Court as 'constitutional' entities in the 1990s, the long-diminished decision-making role of the Committee of Ministers, and the system's burgeoning caseload led to Protocol No.11 to the ECHR. This dissolved the European Commission, rendered the court as the sole adjudicative organ of the system, and rendered individual petition compulsory. The system had become a wholly judicial affair. Incorporation of the ECHR in national legal orders accelerated and the *res interpretata* effect of the Court's judgments was increasingly recognised, extending their application beyond the parties to any specific case and obliging states to comply with the Convention as interpreted by the Court.[32]

At the same time the Court's expanded geographical jurisdiction, as Turkey acceded in 1990 and states across the post-Communist world

---

[28] See J.H. Gerards & J. Fleuren (eds.), *Implementation of the European Convention on Human Rights and of the Judgments of the ECtHR in National Case Law* (Intersentia, 2014) chs. 1 and 2.

[29] D. Shelton (ed.), *The Oxford Handbook of International Human Rights Law* (Oxford University Press, 2013) 447.

[30] See Sweeney, *Post-Cold War Era* 192ff. This is discussed further at the end of Chapter 6.

[31] Bates, *Evolution of the European Convention* 18.

[32] See Gerards & Fleuren (eds.), *Implementation of the European Convention* chs. 1–2.

transitioned to democracy from the late 1980s and submitted to its jurisdiction between 1992 and 1998, moved it from a virtually exclusive focus on fine-tuning Western European democracies to engaging with democratisation processes in Central and Eastern Europe. As Peter Leuprecht observed in 1998 (in a highly critical vein), the democratic accession criteria of the Council of Europe were diluted to ease accession of these states after the fall of the Soviet Union,[33] thus transforming the Council's role – and, as a result, that of the European Court of Human Rights – from primarily the defence and fine-tuning of democracy to playing 'an active role in "democracy-building" in the post-communist countries'.[34]

The attendant 'Latin Americanization'[35] of the Court's docket required it to address much more severe human rights violations; in Russia's crushing of separatists in Chechnya, or torture in Turkey, for instance. The specific history of post-Communist states faced the Court with lustration measures of varying severity: the *Berlin Wall* cases concerning prosecution of East German senior officials for inciting homicide against 'border violators' attempting escape to West Germany; amnesty laws; restriction of electoral rights; and significant restrictions on the rights to free speech and freedom of assembly in censorious political systems accustomed to monopolies on public discourse.[36] All a far cry from the social and moral issues encountered by the Court during its first four decades.

3   The Inter-American Court as a Quintessential Democracy-Builder

The Inter-American Court of Human Rights presents a counterpoint to the experience of the European Court. Where the latter slowly grew into its role, focusing on fine-tuning the constitutional orders of stable democracies, the regional context of the former placed a greater demo-cratisation burden at its door. It was established in an entirely different historical and political setting where democratic rule had become an exception to almost universal authoritarian governance, where demo-cracy itself was a more contested currency, and where no functional

---

[33] Leuprecht, 'Innovations in the European System' 325–9.   [34] Ibid. 317.
[35] C.M. Cerna, 'The Inter-American System for the Protection of Human Rights' (2004) 16 *Florida Journal of International Law* 195.
[36] See Sweeney, *Post-Cold War Era*.

equivalent of the EU existed as a normative anchor for democratisation processes – which still remains the case, despite various pretenders to the 'supranational' crown in the region, including UNASUR's conjoining of MERCOSUR and the Andean Community, and the Pacific Alliance.[37]

A   A Post-War System Without a Post-War Narrative

While serious human rights violations are woven into the entire tapestry of American history, the Americas had not been affected by the Second World War in the same way as the Old World: the United States had lost many sons, but the Western Hemisphere as a whole was spared the killing fields, pogroms, and continent-wide savagery visited upon Europe. Establishment of the Inter-American system was therefore not – or at least, to a lesser extent than the European system – a red line in the sand, starting from zero with the promise 'never again'. Rather, it presented a comparatively moderate institutional advance, inspired in part by developments at the global level, drafted and adopted at the same time as the establishment of the United Nations and adoption of the Universal Declaration of Human Rights (UDHR), but largely building on a long history of incremental regional advances on human rights dating to the mid-nineteenth century.[38]

The development of post-war linkages between rights protection and democratic governance are rather less linear in Latin America than in Western Europe. Although the 1948 OAS Charter proclaimed that American solidarity is based on 'the effective exercise of representative democracy'[39] and made a rather fleeting textual reference to human rights,[40] as in the immediate post-war European context there were few stable or longstanding democracies among its founding twenty-one Member States; the United States being perhaps the only state which could convincingly claim the title.[41] The remaining twenty states, all located in Latin America, consisted of a mix of regimes, including starkly

---

[37] See Daly, 'Baby Steps'.

[38] These included the enactment of various instruments and resolutions on human rights at successive international conferences of the Americas from 1826 onwards. Shelton, *The Regional Protection* 68–70.

[39] Article 3, OAS Charter. For a useful overview of OAS endeavours to promote democracy in the Americas, see de Zela Martínez, 'The Organization of American States' 23.

[40] The original text of the OAS Charter contained a number of general declarations concerning human rights in Articles 3(j) (now 3(l)) and Article 13 (now 17).

[41] Canada was not among the founding members, and did not join the OAS until 1990.

non-democratic regimes (e.g. Paraguay), a variety of underdeveloped and new democracies (e.g. Argentina, Cuba), recently restored democracies (e.g. Brazil, Uruguay), a democracy emerging from civil war (Costa Rica), and two very precarious democracies (Peru and Venezuela suffered *coups* mere months after the Charter's adoption).

Unlike the ECHR system, which generally evolved in a context of progressive democratic development in the post-war period (with the signal exceptions of the *coups d'état* in Greece and Turkey between 1960 and 1980), for the first thirty years of the Inter-American system's development successful democratisation processes were in short supply, with Costa Rica being the rare exception among the Latin American states. As Gordon Mace puts it, the Inter-American system developed in fits and starts, mainly during 'windows of opportunity' afforded by periods of democratisation or redemocratisation in the region.[42]

The principal landmarks are: adoption of the American Declaration of Human Rights (ADHR) (1948), establishment of the Inter-American Commission on Human Rights (1959), conferral on the Commission of the power to receive individual complaints (1965), enhancement of the Commission's standing as guarantor of the ADHR, and recognition of the ADHR as a yardstick against which the activities of all OAS Members could be judged (1970);[43] adoption of the American Convention on Human Rights (ACHR, 'Pact of San José'), modelled on the ECHR and its institutional structure, as well as the ADHR and the International Covenant on Civil and Political Rights (ICCPR) (1969); entry into force of the ACHR (1978); and, finally, establishment of the Inter-American Court of Human Rights, as provided for by the ACHR (1979).

These institutional developments were often reactions to, or progress despite, authoritarian rule. The background to the Commission's establishment and the drafting of the ACHR and its institutional machinery in 1959 was political unrest in the Dominican Republic under the Trujillo dictatorship, which underscored the link between human rights violations and anti-democratic regimes, and encouraged the OAS Member States to 'shed their apathy towards human rights problems and ... to shape a regional system for their protection'.[44] Although most states had freely

---

[42] G. Mace, 'Sixty Years of Protecting Human Rights in the Americas' (2011) *Quebec Journal of International Law* 1, 2.
[43] Protocol of Buenos Aires of 1967, which entered into force in 1970.
[44] R.K. Goldman, 'History and Action: The Inter-American Human Rights System and the Role of the Inter-American Commission on Human Rights' (2009) 31 *Human Rights Quarterly* 856, 861.

elected governments and espoused a nominal commitment to constitutional democracy while the ACHR was under negotiation in the 1960s, at the time of the establishment of the Inter-American Court in 1979 almost every state in South America, bar Costa Rica, was under authoritarian rule or weak civilian governments under military tutelage.[45] In this light, the ACHR's emphasis on democratic government, and requirements that restrictions to certain rights must be 'necessary in a democratic society', did not fully reflect the reality of the Americas at that time.[46]

It was a particularly grim and systematic escalation of atrocities across Latin America in the 1970s – including torture and forced disappearances under Operation Condor,[47] an internationally co-ordinated clandestine campaign of political repression and terror aimed at eradicating Communist opposition, and massacres of indigenous peoples in various states – that lent a greater moral and political urgency to the Inter-American system. Later, it informed a firmer conviction that democratic governance, which had previously been viewed askance by left and right wing alike in the region, is the surest political system for the protection of human rights. In South America (but not Central America), 1978 is viewed as the year the succession of democratic transitions across the region began, with every state in the region having emerged from military rule by 1989.[48]

B   1978 Onward: The Court's Immediate Democratisation Burden

The strong, and largely sustained, wave of redemocratisation in South America in the 1980s opened a wider space for the OAS – and the Inter-American Commission and Court in particular – to take a more coherent and consistent stance on democratisation and the protection of human rights. As early as 1979 resolutions of the OAS not only condemned the human rights record of the Somoza regime in Nicaragua (based on a country report by the Commission) but also, for the very first time, declared the incumbent government to be illegitimate.[49] This political

---

[45] Ibid. 872.
[46] See e.g. Articles 15 (right of assembly), 16 (freedom of association), and 17 (freedom of movement and residence).
[47] The main participants were Argentina, Bolivia, Brazil, Chile, Paraguay, and Uruguay.
[48] A. Breuer, 'South America' in J. Haynes (ed.), *Routledge Handbook of Democratization* (Routledge, 2012) 46.
[49] M. Herz, 'The Organization of American States and Democratization' in Haynes (ed.), *Routledge Handbook* 339.

context transformed the Inter-American organs' role from mitigating the worst excesses of authoritarian regimes to providing a normative lodestar to fledgling democracies. However, armed conflict and accompanying atrocities in Central America required intensive engagement by the Inter-American system into the 1990s.[50]

Acceptance of the Court's jurisdiction was a relatively quicker process than the European experience: eight states had accepted its jurisdiction by 1985; twelve by 1990; and an additional eleven states by 2000, including the regional hegemons of Brazil and Mexico in 1998, which brought the total to twenty-three – virtually all states in Latin America, and mainly young democracies (long-democratic Costa Rica being the main exception).[51] However, the Court initially had very limited impact on democratisation processes throughout the 1980s, issuing solely advisory opinions until its first judgment in a contentious case in 1988.[52] From the late 1980s to the late 1990s, the Court handed down, at most, a handful of merits decisions in contentious cases each year, and, in many years during this period, no more than a single decision.[53] Indeed, the number of annual merits decisions did not hit double digits until as recently as 2004, and since then the annual number tends to vary between approximately ten and twenty decisions.[54]

That said, the Court quickly built up a significant jurisprudence at a much more rapid pace than its Strasbourg counterpart. Unlike the European Court, from its inception it faced a mixture of new democracies and authoritarian states, all featuring severe (and in the new democracies, often ongoing) human rights violations as it carved out its adjudicative role. The Court's assertive posture in its first merits

---

[50] de Zela Martínez, 'The Organization of American States' 26.
[51] The sequence of acceptance of the jurisdiction of the Inter-American Court by country is as follows: Costa Rica (1980), Honduras, Peru, Venezuela (1981), Argentina, Ecuador (1984), Colombia, Uruguay (1985), Guatemala, Suriname (1987), Chile, Panama (1990), Nicaragua, Trinidad and Tobago (1991), Bolivia, Paraguay (1993), El Salvador (1995), Brazil, Haiti, Mexico (1998), Dominican Republic (1999), and Barbados (2000). See www.cidh.oas.org/basicos/english/Basic4.Amer.Conv.Ratif.htm. Three states have since left the Court's jurisdiction: Trinidad and Tobago, Venezuela, and the Dominican Republic.
[52] *Velásquez-Rodríguez v. Honduras*, IACtHR (Ser. C) No.4 (29 July 1988).
[53] The highest number of decisions during this period was in 1997, with four decisions concerning Nicaragua, Peru (two), and Ecuador.
[54] The highest number of merits decisions in any one year to date is nineteen in 2012, which may be compared to 2011 (thirteen), 2010 (fourteen), 2009 (fifteen), 2008 (ten) and 2007 (ten). Source: 'Jurisprudence Finder' on the Inter-American Court's website www.corteidh.or.cr/cf/Jurisprudencia2/index.cfm?lang=en.

1978   2016

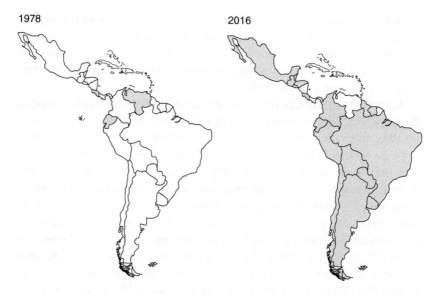

Figure 3.2   Electoral Democracies in Latin America: 1978 and 2016

judgment in 1988 –*Velásquez-Rodriguez* v. *Honduras*,[55] in which it found a violation of the ACHR in the lack of effective domestic remedies for forced disappearances and suggested (but did not order) measures to address these shortcomings – showed that it was not merely a paper tiger.[56] The Inter-American Commission, established in 1959, had laid the groundwork for an assertive role since the 1970s, ping-ponging across the region as a 'Hemispheric Grand Jury', shaming states such as Argentina and Nicaragua with reports detailing severe and widespread rights abuses.[57]

During the 1990s the Court grew in strength with judgments on matters such as violations of the right to life and physical integrity,[58] and, although it adopted European-style doctrines of 'evolutive interpretation' and 'practical effectiveness', it took a less deferential approach than

---

[55] IACtHR (Ser. C) No. 4 (29 July 1988).
[56] See e.g. J.F. Stack, 'Judicial Policy-Making and the Evolving Protection of Human Rights: The European Court of Human Rights in Comparative Perspective' in Volcansek (ed.), *Judicial Politics* 152.
[57] T. Farer, 'The Rise of the Inter-American Human Rights Regime: No Longer a Unicorn, Not Yet an Ox' (1997) 19 *Human Rights Quarterly* 510, 512.
[58] See V. Krsticevic, 'How Inter-American Human Rights Litigation Brings Free Speech to the Americas' (1997) 4 *Southwest Journal of Law & Trade in the Americas* 209.

the European Court. In particular, it eschewed any formal margin of appreciation doctrine due to the severity and scale of rights abuses in states under its jurisdiction. It also took an increasingly expansive approach to remedies beyond a Europe-style focus on monetary compensation; ordering investigations concerning acts underlying rights violations, for example, and leaving far less discretion to states regarding the manner of implementation than the Strasbourg Court was inclined to provide.[59] However, unlike the extraordinary volume of case-law and high compliance with judgments in Europe, the Court had still issued no more than thirty judgments by 1997 and compliance with judgments was underwhelming.[60] As Farer put it, the Court was 'no longer a unicorn, not yet an ox'.[61]

4   Pushing Review Past its Limits? Attempts at 'Structural Reform'

A   The Expansion of Review by Both Courts

As Alexandra Huneeus has recently recounted, by the early 2000s both the European and Inter-American courts, faced with significant deficiencies in the post-authoritarian democracies under their purview, began to realise the limits of individual-focused declaratory judgments. To stem systemic human rights abuses in these states, each court began to seek far-reaching transformations at the domestic level through deep incursions into the policy arena (e.g. ordering significant reform of prison and judicial systems) and monitoring implementation of their judgments.[62] These moves represented, as Huneeus has observed, an astonishing 'constitutional power grab'[63] – equalling even the most audacious expansions of judicial power at the domestic level.

The Inter-American Court was the pioneer of this new approach. By the late 1990s the exiguous capacity of individual-focused declaratory judgments to address the systemic roots of rights violations had become painfully apparent. In response, in 2000 the Court issued its first four judgments that expressly ordered state respondents to adopt specific bureaucratic or policy measures aimed at structural change in the domestic order (including the Court's landmark judgment in *Barrios Altos* v. *Peru* concerning the Peruvian criminal justice system's treatment of

---

[59] Huneeus, 'Reforming the State' 9–10.   [60] Krsticevic, 'Free Speech' 212.
[61] Farer, 'No Longer a Unicorn'.   [62] Huneeus, 'Reforming the State'.   [63] Ibid. 18.

authoritarian-era crimes).[64] It also began monitoring these judgments itself, in a context where the absence of any dedicated body for overseeing implementation of the Court's judgments had appeared to hinder implementation.[65]

In Europe the expansion of the Court's jurisdiction to highly deficient post-Communist democracies led to an unsustainable overloading of its docket as the same structural deficiencies gave rise to a high number of repetitive applications. At the urging of the Committee of Ministers of the Council of Europe, the Court, like its Inter-American counterpart, began efforts to address systemic deficiencies through 'structural reform' adjudication.[66] In *Broniowski* v. *Poland*[67] it crafted a 'pilot judgment' procedure in which it would take representative cases concerning a specific structural deficiency giving rise to repetitive rights violations in a respondent state, freeze all similar cases, issue a binding judgment ordering specific measures to address the problem, and monitor compliance (bolstering the monitoring role of the Council of Europe's Committee of Ministers). These have been joined by 'quasi-pilot judgments' in which the Court does not make its reform proposals binding by excluding them from the operative part of the judgment.[68] As Sadurski has noted, this has moved the Court to a 'quasi-constitutional' role,[69] or as Steven Greer puts it, a move from 'individual justice' to 'constitutional justice'.[70]

In the Inter-American context, the constitutional turn has been even more striking. In 2006 the Inter-American Court went a step further than the European Court by setting out its doctrine of 'conventionality control' in *Almonacid-Arellano* v. *Chile*,[71] which requested domestic courts to disapply rules, including constitutional provisions, deemed contrary to the Convention (as interpreted by the Court), even where the Convention lacks superior rank in domestic law, or where the court lacks the

---

[64] IACtHR (Ser. C) No. 87 (30 November 2001).
[65] Huneeus, 'Reforming the State' 8–11. Responsibility for ensuring compliance with the decisions of the Court lies with the governing bodies of the OAS: the Permanent Council and the General Assembly.
[66] Ibid. 11.   [67] ECtHR, App. No. 31443/96 (22 June 2004).
[68] Huneeus, 'Reforming the State' 11–12.
[69] W. Sadurski, *Constitutionalism and the Enlargement of Europe* (Oxford University Press, 2012) 1–2.
[70] See e.g. S. Greer & L. Wildhaber, 'Revisiting the Debate about 'Constitutionalising' the European Court of Human Rights' (2012) 12 *Human Rights Law Reports* 655.
[71] IACtHR (Ser. C) No. 154 (26 September 2006).

authority to override domestic law (a position since softened).[72] As Dulitzky observes, it marked a stark shift from the Strasbourg model, under which the Court allowed discretion to states in ensuring compatibility between the ACHR and domestic law, to something closer to the ECJ's assertion of the supremacy of Community law, which could not be overridden by domestic laws. As Dulitzky argues, the effect was to recast the Court itself as 'an Inter-American constitutional court',[73] an impression bolstered by the Court's subsequent extension of 'conventionality control' obligations to all state organs.[74] Coupled with the absence of a margin of appreciation doctrine, it accords much less leeway to domestic authorities in ensuring compliance with the American Convention.

B   The Impact and Limits of Human Rights Courts: Between Cassandra and Canute

The turn to structural reform adjudication by both courts has not, to date, been met with significant success. In fact, it appears to have left regional human rights courts in an impossible position. As Huneeus notes, had either court stuck to individual-focused declaratory judgments, leaving structural problems for resolution through political bodies, they could have been consigned to irrelevance.[75] A choice to act as an alarm system for gross rights violations, in particular, may well have condemned each court to a subsistence of continued functionality, but with severely reduced authority and influence; the Cassandras of international law.

Yet, the choice of each court to take the route of structural reform adjudication has scarcely been a better choice. Huneeus observes that the level of compliance with each court's structural reform judgments has been poor to date:

> For now, we know only that the European Court has declared as successful at least three of its twenty-nine pilot cases, and the Inter-American Court has closed only one of its roughly fifty-five structural cases. It is still too early to draw conclusions, comparative or otherwise, but the numbers are not encouraging.[76]

---

[72] See Dulitzky, 'An Inter-American Constitutional Court?' 60.   [73] Ibid. 47.
[74] *Gelman* v. *Uruguay* IACtHR (Ser. C.) No. 221 (24 February 2011). Discussed in Dulitzky, ibid. 51.
[75] Huneeus, 'Reforming the State' 18.   [76] Ibid. 40.

In other words, the combined figures for these courts are that four out of eighty-four judgments ordering structural reform have been deemed to be fully implemented. These also appear to be the ones that are easiest to implement – concerning compensation for loss of property due to loss of state territory, dysfunctional rent controls, state repayments of foreign currency savings, and procedures for demarcating indigenous lands.[77] While an optimist might suggest that compliance may improve over time, the low level of compliance with structural reform judgments must be viewed against the wider canvass of compliance with all kinds of judgments issued by these courts: in Europe partial compliance has become the 'new normal';[78] while in Latin America compliance with the Inter-American Court's decisions hovers at ten per cent, and is improving at a barely perceptible rate.[79] Compliance remains particularly lacking regarding the latter Court's orders for reparations beyond compensation, especially where a state is ordered to investigate or prosecute a rights violation.[80] Seemingly strong decisions, such as the Court's denunciation of illegitimate interference with the judiciary in Venezuela, have failed to achieve results on the ground.[81] Like the popular image of King Canute exposing the limits of his powers through futile attempts to command the tide, these discouraging figures suggest that the ambitious expansion of each court's remit to embrace structural transformation has starkly exposed the outer limits of its capacity to effect change.

This is not to say that these courts have achieved nothing as agents of democracy-building. Each has achieved significant victories. The

---

[77] The four judgments are: *Broniowski* v. *Poland*, ECtHR, App. No. 31443/96 (22 June 2004); *Hutten-Czapska* v. *Poland*, ECtHR, App. No. 35014/97 (19 June 2006); *Suljagic* v. *Bosnia and Herzegovina*, ECtHR, App. No. 27912/02 (3 November 2009); and *Awas Tingni Community* v. *Nicaragua*, IACtHR (Ser. C) No. 79 (31 Aug 2001).

[78] See M. Rask Madsen, 'The Challenging Authority of the European Court of Human Rights: From Cold War Legal Diplomacy to the Brighton Declaration and Backlash' (2016) 79(1) *Law and Contemporary Problems* 141, 172–3.

[79] D.A. González-Salzberg, 'Complying (Partially) with the Compulsory Judgments of the Inter-American Court of Human Rights' in P. Fortes, L. Boratti, A. Palacios Lleras & T.G. Daly (eds.), *Law and Policy in Latin America: Transforming Courts, Institutions, and Rights* (Palgrave Macmillan, 2017).

[80] Ibid.

[81] In *Apitz* v. *Venezuela* (Ser. C) No. 182 (5 August 2008) the Court ordered the reinstatement of three judges who had been fired, but this did not happen: see A. Huneeus, 'Rejecting the Inter-American Court: Judicialization, National Courts, and Regional Human Rights' in J. Couso, A. Huneeus & R. Sieder (eds.), *Cultures of Legality: Judicialization and Political Activism in Latin America* (Cambridge University Press, 2010) 128–9.

Inter-American Court's case-law has led to the repeal or restricted application of amnesty laws across the region, thus addressing impunity for authoritarian-era rights violations and allowing crimes such as forced disappearance to be investigated. It has successfully pushed reform of treason and anti-terrorism legislation, including diminution of military jurisdiction, in Peru and Ecuador.[82] Strict criminal defamation laws have also been repealed or amended,[83] and the right to freedom of information has been written into law across Latin America, spurred by jurisprudence from San José.[84] The European Court has also had a positive impact: invalidating the outlawing of a Communist party in Turkey as a disproportionate restriction of freedom of association;[85] softening the excesses of new democratic governments in property restitution and lustration programmes by emphasising rights protection and the need for adequate standards of procedural justice;[86] and, recently, its strong judgment against blanket state surveillance in Hungary (although the full impact of that decision is not yet clear).[87]

Taking a wider view, it is important to note that even partial compliance with structural reform decisions can have a significant impact – we will see in Chapter 6, for instance, how a judgment of the Inter-American Court led to the establishment of Brazil's National Truth Commission (*Commissão Nacional de Verdade*). We might also say that formal compliance is not everything; for instance, the courts in each region have provided a centre of gravity for the development of transnational civil society networks forming a regional epistemic community dedicated to democracy-building and social justice,[88] and various scholars argue that their judgments have important symbolic importance in setting standards and publicising violations.[89] However, signs suggest that it

---

[82] J. Pasqualucci, *Practice and Procedure of the Inter-American Court of Human Rights* (Cambridge University Press, 2012) 322.

[83] Krsticevic, 'Free Speech'.

[84] See e.g. García-Sayan, 'The Role of the Inter-American Court' 105ff.

[85] *United Communist Party of Turkey* v. *Turkey*, ECtHR, App. No. 19392/92 (30 January 1998). See Sweeney, *Post-Cold War Era* 195–6.

[86] Sweeney, *Post-Cold War Era* chs. 4 and 5.

[87] *Szabó and Vissy* v. *Hungary*, ECtHR, App. No. 37138/14 (12 January 2016).

[88] See e.g. M.N. Bernardes, 'Inter-American Human Rights System as a Transnational Public Sphere: Legal and Political Aspects of the Implementation of International Decisions' (2011) 15 *SUR – International Journal on Human Rights* 131.

[89] See e.g. A. Huneeus, 'Courts Resisting Courts: Lessons from the Inter-American Court's Struggle to Enforce Human Rights' (2011) 44 *Cornell International Law Journal* 49; and Buyse & Hamilton (eds.), *Transitional Jurisprudence and the ECHR*.

has proven difficult to catalyse wider public pressure on governments to effect difficult transformations through the often arid language of law, which is compounded by the lack of public visibility of human rights courts. Indeed, the Inter-American Court, in particular, appears to labour in relative obscurity; forthcoming research suggests that the Latin American public know little of its work.[90] Structural reform adjudication does not provide a solution to such problems.

In the Inter-American context, the Court faces stark challenges to building its authority and capacity to act as a democracy-builder. As well as institutional challenges – including a low budget, small caseload, and tense relationship with the Inter-American Commission[91] – states remain resistant to the notion that the Court's judgments have direct effect in national law (or are 'self-executing', in US parlance) and the Court faces significant hostility from numerous states, especially the neo-Bolivarian leftist governments in Venezuela, Ecuador, and Bolivia.[92] Democratic backsliding has also, at times, had a direct impact: the Court suffered significant setbacks in 2012 when Venezuela left its jurisdiction by denouncing the ACHR (a move spurred by the Supreme Court) and in 2014 when the Supreme Court of the Dominican Republic declared the instrument through which the Dominican State recognized the jurisdiction of the IACtHR to be unconstitutional.

The Court has also not been immune to missteps. For instance, it has been said that its categorical opposition to all forms of amnesty law had the effect of 'holding the Colombian peace process hostage' by limiting the room for manoeuvre in negotiations aimed at ending a half-century of violent conflict in that state.[93] In addition, the attenuation of its strong position against criminal defamation in a recent case against Argentina,

---

[90] D. Gil, R. Garcia & L.M. Friedman, 'Media Representations of the Inter-American System of Human Rights' in Fortes, Boratti, Palacios Lleras & Daly (eds.), *Law and Policy in Latin America*.

[91] Huneeus, 'Rejecting the Inter-American Court' 118.

[92] Recent attempts to weaken the Inter-American system for human rights protection have focused on the Inter-American Commission and special rapporteur on freedom of expression, but would have a clear knock-on effect on the Court's role given its institutional link with the Commission as the referral organ to the Court. See *International Justice Resource Center*, 'OAS Concludes Formal Inter-American Human Rights 'Strengthening' Process, but Dialogue Continues on Contentious Reforms' 24 March 2013 www.ijrcenter.org/2013/03/24/oas-concludes-formal-inter-american-human-rights-strengthening-process-but-dialogue-continues-on-contentious-reforms.

[93] G. Alvira, 'Toward a New Amnesty: The Colombian Peace Process and the Inter-American Court of Human Rights' (2013) 22 *Tulane Journal of International & Comparative Law* 119, 144.

for which little reason is provided in the judgment, is viewed as a sign of internal tensions in the Court – the decision was the result of a bare majority of four of the seven justices.[94] As Eduardo Bertoni, a former special rapporteur on freedom of expression at the Inter-American Commission, has observed:

> The Mémoli decision is undoubtedly a setback and a wake up call about the divisions within the Court. It also shows the need of the Court to regain its legitimacy and reputation as a protector of freedom of expression, so necessary in our region today.[95]

In Europe, overall, the verdict on the European Court's contribution to the consolidation of post-Communist democracies is mixed. Despite positive judgments, discussed above, its vindication of free speech has been inconsistent – at times placing undue emphasis on the social sting of statements implying collaboration with the Communist-era regime, for instance.[96] Case-law on access to the electoral system is also viewed as uneven, with the Court's methodology for approaching the balance between the alleged threat posed by parties to the democratic order and the openness of the electoral arena seeming rather opaque.[97] Most strikingly, the Court's refusal to find the dissolution of the four million member Refah Partisi (Welfare Party) by the Turkish Constitutional Court to constitute a violation of the right to associate in Article 11 ECHR, on the basis that the party aimed to replace the democratic order with a sharia-based order, has been described as 'the largest single interference with freedom of association in European jurisprudence.'[98]

As Sweeney observes, the challenges presented by the new states have left the Court in a difficult position, and constrained by the doctrinal legacy of its earlier case-law. It seeks to maintain the human rights standards built since the 1970s and to pay homage to the principle of the universality of human rights. However, it increasingly finds itself according states a margin of appreciation to allow greater restrictions of rights in service of democratisation aims (what Sweeney would view as 'transitional justice' aims) – such as the dismantling of Communist

---

[94] *Mémoli v. Argentina*, IACtHR (Ser. C) No. 265 (22 August 2013).
[95] E. Bertoni, 'Setbacks and Tension in the Inter-American Court of Human Rights' *Media Legal Defence Initiative* 17 December 2013 www.mediadefence.org/blog/setbacks-and-tension-inter-american-court-human-rights#.VUvAQ_lVjDV.
[96] Sweeney, *Post-Cold War Era* ch. 6.   [97] Ibid. ch. 8.
[98] P. Harvey, 'Militant Democracy and the European Court of Human Rights' (2004) 29 *European Law Review* 407, 417 as cited in Sweeney, *Post-Cold War Era* 196.

governance structures and diminishing the power of political actors from the old order.[99] This lies in stark contrast to its less flexible approach toward earlier third wave democracies in Southern Europe. Yet, the Court, like its counterpart in San José, has also been strongly criticised for adopting inflexible positions in certain cases. In particular, its judgment in *Sejdić and Finci* v. *Bosnia and Herzegovina*, which held aspects of the consociational democratic arrangements in Bosnia and Herzegovina to violate the right to equality under the European Convention, has been decried as misguided and badly reasoned, and as potentially threatening not just the democratisation process, but even the fragile peace which had been in place for little over a decade.[100]

Like the Inter-American Court, the Strasbourg Court faces significant challenges as a democracy-builder. Some challenges are institutional. In the context of its impossible caseload, the overall quality of the Court's judgments has been viewed by some as decreasing.[101] An ongoing reduction in the Court's caseload since 2012, partly due to the significant impact of introduction of individual applications to Turkey's Constitutional Court, had started to raise hopes that the worst was over.[102] However, fresh figures for 2016 show a sharp uptick in applications from Hungary, Romania, and Turkey – the latter alone seeing over 5,000 new applications since July 2016 in relation to the government's response to the 15 July *coup* attempt.[103]

The wider political threats facing the Court have multiplied. The backlash against the Court, culminating in the 2012 Brighton Declaration's reassertion of the importance of subsidiarity and the margin of appreciation doctrine, had already left the Court somewhat diminished in its capacity to pursue assertive decision-making,[104] yet the Court's

---

[99] Sweeney, *Post-Cold War Era.*   [100] McCrudden & O'Leary, *Courts & Consociations.*

[101] See in particular chs. 26–28 of N. Huls, M. Adams & J. Bomhoff (eds.), *The Legitimacy of Highest Courts' Rulings. Judicial Deliberations and Beyond* (TMC Asser Press, 2009).

[102] By the start of 2014 the number of pending applications before the Strasbourg regarding Turkey had fallen to 11,000, and as of January 2016 stood at 8,648. See European Court of Human Rights Press Country Profile: Turkey www.echr.coe.int/Documents/CP_Turkey_ENG.pdf.

[103] European Court of Human Rights press release, 'President Raimondi Presents the Court's Results for 2016', ECHR 037 (2017) 26 January 2017.

[104] The Declaration led to adoption of Protocols 15 and 16, which re-emphasise the principle of subsidiarity and permit national courts to seek advisory opinions from the Strasbourg Court on the application and interpretation of Convention rights. See N. O'Meara, 'Reforming the ECtHR: The Impacts of Protocols 15 and 16 to the ECHR'. iCourts Working Paper Series, No. 31, 2015.

attempts to appease its political critics risk damaging its hard-won moral authority and legitimacy in the eyes of civil society actors.[105] In Turkey, President Erdoğan has not only declared that his government will no longer comply with the Court's judgments,[106] but has also talked of plans to remove the system of individual applications to the Turkish Constitutional Court, introduced in 2012,[107] which would sharpen the already acute caseload crisis. Ongoing democratic decay in other states such as Hungary, Poland, and Croatia may not only present further challenges to the Court's authority, but also reveal the failure of regional adjudication to stem this decay.[108] Worst of all, renewed calls for withdrawal from the Court from the UK Prime Minister[109] threaten to collapse the entire European Convention system by encouraging a rush for the exit among other states (e.g. Russia).[110]

5   The Difficulties of Diffusion: The African and Arab Human Rights Courts

The past decade has seen the African Union (AU) establish a regional human rights court, which began operating in 2006, and the announcement in late 2014 that a regional human rights court will be established for the

---

[105] D.T. Björgvinsson, 'The Role of Judges of the European Court of Human Rights as Guardians of Fundamental Rights of the Individual.' in M. Scheinin & M. Aksenova (eds.), *Judges as Guardians of Constitutionalism and Human Rights* (Edward Elgar Publishing, 2016).

[106] M. Akyol, 'The Rage against the Constitutional Court' *Hürriyet Daily News* 12 March 2016 www.hurriyetdailynews.com/the-rage-against-the-constitutional-court.aspx?page ID=238&nid=96345.

[107] See S. Demirtaş, 'New Turkish Constitution to Redefine Powers of Constitutional Court and Judiciary' *ConstitutionNet* 29 March 2016 www.constitutionnet.org/news/new-turk ish-constitution-redefine-powers-constitutional-court-and-judiciary.

[108] See e.g. T.G. Daly, 'The Democratic Recession and the "New" Public Law: Toward Systematic Analysis' *International Journal of Constitutional Law Blog* 22 April 2016 www.iconnectblog.com/2016/04/the-democratic-recession-and-the-new-public-law-toward-systematic-analysis.

[109] See W. Worley, 'Theresa May "Will Campaign to Leave the European Convention on Human Rights in 2020 Election"' *The Independent* 30 December 2016 www.inde pendent.co.uk/news/uk/politics/theresa-may-campaign-leave-european-convention-on-human-rights-2020-general-election-brexit-a7499951.html.

[110] See a policy paper by the author and Tobias Lock, *Brexit and the British Bill of Rights* (Edinburgh Law School and Bingham Centre for the Rule of Law, February 2017), which is the outcome of a high-level meeting held at Edinburgh Law School on 27 October 2016.

twenty-one member states of the Arab League.[111] The full motives for installing these courts are not always easy to discern. However, in these developments we see a move from the contestation in 1940s Europe regarding the democratisation role of a regional court, and the considered ambivalence to such a court in 1970s Latin America, to an even more problematic scenario where a commitment to regional supervision, at the political level, often appears wafer-thin, if not entirely driven by pragmatic motives to present a veneer of democratisation. Of course, one can also characterise the development of the European and Inter-American human rights systems as propelled by similar motivations: a European desire to reclaim global moral superiority after the degradation of World War II, and a Latin American desire to project a more democratic regional image, each supported by a tutelary stable democracy (the United Kingdom and United States respectively) and vocal civil society campaigns. Yet, in Africa and the Arab world the gap between rhetoric and reality often appears wider.[112]

A   The African Court's First Decade in a Hostile Climate, 2006–2016

As Makua wa Mutua has emphasised, the African human rights system emerged at a time when, having fought colonial rule partly on the basis of rights arguments, African states found themselves under increasing scrutiny as human-rights discourse was universalised in the 1970s, due to the emergence of brutal dictatorships across the region in the 1960s:

> The [African] leadership had to reclaim international legitimacy and salvage its image. In 1979, shaken by these perceptions, the OAU Summit in Monrovia, Liberia, appointed a committee of experts to prepare a draft of an African human rights charter. It was ironic that virtually none of the men, the Heads of State and Government, were freely and fairly elected. Without exception, they presided over highly repressive states. It was virtually the same club of dictators who adopted the African Charter in Nairobi, Kenya in 1981. Thus was born the African human rights system.[113]

---

[111] Algeria, Bahrain, Comoros, Djibouti, Egypt, Iraq, Jordan, Kuwait, Lebanon, Libya, Mauritania, Morocco, Oman, Palestine, Qatar, Saudi Arabia, Somalia, Sudan, Tunisia, United Arab Emirates (UAE), and Yemen. Syria's membership of the League was suspended in 2011 in response to its brutal response to pro-democracy protests.

[112] For a comprehensive account of the development of the African regional human rights protection system until 2011 see Kiwinda Mbondenyi, *International Human Rights*.

[113] M. wa Mutua, 'The African Human Rights System in a Comparative Perspective' (1993) 3 *Review of the African Commission on Human and Peoples' Rights* 5, 7.

The African Commission, created as a stand-alone institution in 1987, and faced with almost universally undemocratic regimes, found little room to manoeuvre following its establishment.[114] It adopted a more deferential posture than its counterparts in other regions, through a focus on 'positive dialogue', inconsistent use of provisional measures, and a reluctance to follow up its decisions.[115] That said, it has at times adopted assertive postures concerning matters such as the use of secret military trials, free speech, the right to fair trial and due process, and the ousting of judicial jurisdiction, although it has not addressed gross and systematic violations with any vigour.[116]

Largely at the urging of academics and NGOs, the AU adopted a protocol in 1998 to establish an African Court on Human and Peoples' Rights, ratified six years later, and with the Court finally established in 2006.[117] Although the Court came into being in a rather more democratic climate, with a number of new electoral democracies having emerged in the 1990s (including Benin, Namibia, Malawi, Mali, South Africa, and Tanzania), its operation is more restricted than the other two regional human rights courts. Cases can be brought before the Court by the Commission, a state, or an African inter-governmental organisation. However, there has been seemingly little appetite to do so.[118] The Court has the power to allow individuals and NGOs to petition it directly, where a state has made an optional declaration recognising such petitions. However, only eight of the thirty states under the Court's jurisdiction have done so; a factor viewed as significantly limiting the scope of the Court's material jurisdiction, and leading to a six-year wait for its first merits decision in a contentious case.[119] Thus, unlike the European Court's impact in the CEE region or the Inter-American Court in Latin America, the African Court has had no hand in the first fifteen years of democratisation processes in Africa.

---

[114] The only electoral democracies in the region in the late 1980s were Botswana, The Gambia, and Mauritius.
[115] See G. Bekker, 'The African Commission on Human and Peoples' Rights and Remedies for Human Rights Violations' (2013) 13 Human Rights Law Review 499.
[116] Ibid. 504.   [117] Cole, 'The African Court' 26.
[118] M. Ssenyonjo, 'Direct Access to the African Court on Human and Peoples' Rights by Individuals and Non Governmental Organisations: An Overview of the Emerging Jurisprudence of the African Court 2008–2012' (2013) 2(1) International Human Rights Law Review 17, 51–4.
[119] To date, only Benin, Burkina Faso, Côte d'Ivoire, Ghana, Malawi, Mali, Rwanda, and Tanzania have made such declarations. Rwanda has since withdrawn its declaration, discussed below.

1989   2016

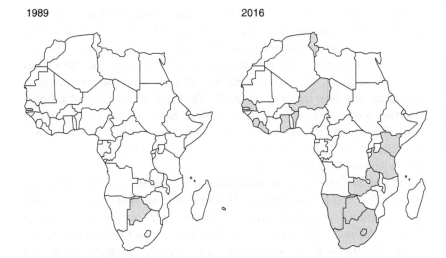

Figure 3.3   Electoral Democracies in Africa: 1989 and 2016

Unlike the African Commission, which has been viewed as a quiescent organ, the African Court – drawing significant inspiration from the case-law of its European and Inter-American counterparts – has adopted a strident tone in its judgments to date, although it has encountered difficulties in ensuring enforcement.

In the Court's first merits judgment, *Mtikila* v. *Tanzania*, the Court unanimously found the state's constitutional ban on independent candidacy in elections a violation of the African Charter, having adopted the same general interpretive approach as the European and Inter-American Courts – and like the latter, having eschewed any margin of appreciation doctrine.[120] However, the Court's judgment has been met with considerable resistance by the Tanzanian authorities.[121] In March and December

---

[120] ACtHPR, App. 009/2011 and 011/2011 (14 June 2013).

[121] See O. Windridge, 'Guest Post: 2014 at The African Court on Human and Peoples Rights–a Year in Review' *Opinio Juris* 10 January 2015 www.opiniojuris.org/2015/01/10/guest-post-2014-african-court-human-peoples-rights-year-review; and Legal and Human Rights Centre (LHRC) & Tanzania Civil Society Consortium for Election Observation (TACCEO), *Report on the United Republic of Tanzania General Elections of 2015* (March 2016), urging government action to remedy the defects identified by the Court: www.humanrights.or.tz/userfiles/file/Report%20on%20the%20Observation%20of%20the%202015%20General%20Elections%20in%20Tanzania.pdf. The judgment is discussed in more detail in Chapter 6.

2014, the Court found two violations of the Charter in cases against Burkina Faso. In *Zongo* v. *Burkina Faso*[122] the Court found the state in violation of rights to judicial protection and free speech for failing to investigate and prosecute the killers of a journalist and his companions in 1998. In *Konaté* v. *Burkina Faso*[123] the Court unanimously ruled a twelve-month sentence of imprisonment for criminal defamation imposed on the applicant journalist in 2012 (for having accused a public prosecutor of corruption) to be a violation of the right to freedom of expression in the African Charter. The judgment has raised hopes for reform of criminal defamation laws across Africa,[124] and has at least led to law reform in Burkina Faso.[125] In *Thomas* v. *Tanzania*,[126] *Onyango* v. *Tanzania*,[127] and *Abubakari* v. *Tanzania*,[128] decided in 2015 and 2016, the Court took robust stances, finding the state in violation of the right to a fair trial in Article 7 of the African Charter in each case.

Significantly, the Court is operating in a region where a number of other assertive regional adjudicative bodies have suffered very significant political backlash. This is starkly underscored by the fate of the Tribunal of the fifteen-member Southern African Development Community (SADC).[129] Established in 1992, it was effectively 'dismantled' in 2012 due to opposition to its strong stances on human rights – spearheaded by undemocratic Zimbabwe and democratic Tanzania;[130] a fate reminiscent of the Hungarian constitutional court discussed above. Initially suspended, the Tribunal was reanimated in 2014 with its jurisdiction reduced to inter-state disputes.[131] Other sub-regional courts,

---

[122] ACtHPR, App. No. 013/2011 (28 March 2014).
[123] ACtHPR, App. No. 004/2013 (5 December 2014).
[124] See International Federation of Journalists, 'IFJ and FAJ Welcomes African Court's Landmark Decision in Favour of Freedom of Expression' 10 December 2014 www.ifj .org/nc/news-single-view/backpid/1/article/ifj-lauds-african-courts-landmark-decision-in-favor-of-freedom-of-expression-in-africa.
[125] O. Windridge, 'Protecting the Safety of Journalists: the Role of the African Court' *ACtHPR Monitor* 20 September 2016 www.acthprmonitor.org/protecting-the-safety-of-journalists-the-role-of-the-african-court.
[126] ACtHPR, App. No. 005/2013 (20 November 2015).
[127] ACtHPR, App. No. 006/2013 (18 March 2016).
[128] ACtHPR, App. No. 007/2013 (3 June 2016).
[129] Angola, Botswana, Democratic Republic of Congo, Lesotho, Madagascar, Malawi, Mauritius, Mozambique, Namibia, Seychelles, South Africa, Swaziland, Tanzania, Zambia, and Zimbabwe.
[130] Føllesdal, Peters, Karlsson Schaffer & Ulfstein (eds.), *Legitimacy* 8.
[131] R. Ndlovu, 'SADC Tribunal Back with Mandate Reduced to Interstate Cases' *BDLive* 20 August 2014 www.bdlive.co.za/africa/africannews/2014/08/20/sadc-tribunal-back-with-mandate-reduced-to-interstate-cases.

namely the East African Court of Justice (EACJ) and the ECOWAS Court, have met similar resistance when they have attempted to address human rights violations and electoral matters.[132]

There are also dubious AU plans (though as yet unlikely to be realised[133]) to merge the Court with the AU's Court of Justice (as yet not established) to create an African Court of Justice and Human Rights; with talk of further expanding the new court's remit to international criminal jurisdiction.[134] We also see backtracking in acceptance of the Court's full jurisdiction; in February 2016 Rwanda communicated its intention to withdraw its acceptance of direct individual applications to the Court (apparently in reaction to applications being made by individuals connected to the 1994 genocide), a move that may embolden others.[135] In sum, we encounter an increasing rhetoric of rights review and judicialisation without any accompanying willingness to submit to such review.

B   The New Arab Human Rights Court: A Potemkin Tribunal?

None of this augurs well for the Arab Court of Human Rights, which is in the final stages of planning. Condemned by the Egyptian international lawyer Mahmoud Cherif Bassiouni as a 'Potemkin Tribunal,'[136] the Court would be based in Bahrain – a state, it has been noted, 'where the ruling family commands seriously abusive security forces and dominates a highly politicized justice system' – allegedly part of a public relations

---

[132] See K.J. Alter, J.T. Gathli & L. Helfer, 'Backlash against International Courts in West, East and Southern Africa: Causes and Consequences' (2016) 27(2) *European Journal of International Law* 293.

[133] Protocol on the Statute of the African Court on Justice and Human Rights, adopted at the AU Summit in Sharm El-Sheikh, Egypt, on 1 July 2008. To date only five of the fifteen ratifications necessary to enter into force have been made, by Libya, Mali, Burkina Faso, Benin, and Congo.

[134] See V. O. Nmehielle, 'Saddling the New African Regional Human Rights Court with International Criminal Jurisdiction: Innovative, Obstructive, Expedient' (2014) 7 *African Journal of Legal Studies* 7.

[135] See Centre for Human Rights University of Pretoria, 'Report: Rwanda's Withdrawal of its Acceptance of Direct Individual Access to the African Human Rights Court' 22 March 2016 www.chr.up.ac.za/index.php/centre-news-a-events-2016/1604-report-rwandas-withdrawal-of-its-acceptance-of-direct-individual-access-to-the-african-human-rights-court.html.

[136] R. Lowe, 'Bassiouni: New Arab Court for Human Rights Is Fake "Potemkin Tribunal"' *International Bar Association* 1 October 2014 www.ibanet.org/Article/Detail.aspx?Arti cleUid=c64f 9646-15a5-4624–8c07-bae9d9ac42df.

exercise by that state to convince the international community that it is committed to political reform.[137] The Court is envisaged as operating largely on a state-to-state basis, with no provision made for petitions by individuals or NGOs. There is also potential for government interference with judicial appointments, insufficient protections for applicants and witnesses, and an absence of enforcement mechanisms. The International Commission of Jurists (ICJ) has opined that the Court's Statute does not establish a 'genuine human rights court'[138] and in its Tunis Declaration of 2015 set out significant revisions required for an effective institution.[139]

The Court would be tasked with interpreting the League's Arab Charter on Human Rights, adopted in 2004, which is not only problematic in content, but whose reported manner of adoption alone gives cause for considerable pessimism.[140] As Rebecca Lowe recounts:

> Indeed, it was only due to misbehaviour by former Libyan leader Muammar Gaddafi at the 2005 LAS summit in Tunis that the statute got passed at all, he [Bassiouni] reveals.
>
> 'The Saudi King, chairing, said it was a no smoking room, and Gaddafi promptly leaned back in his chair and continued to puff arrogantly on his cigarette like a child and a madman. Mubarak leaned over and said something to him, and he just blew smoke over his head in response. The meeting then broke up – and in the end we only had five minutes to discuss the Charter. So it was swiftly approved, despite nobody knowing anything about it.'[141]

The prospects of such a court are further undermined by recent research. Cesare Romano, in a survey of 'international judicialization' in the Arab world, argues that there are simply too many factors hindering international judicial power for it to take root, including:

---

[137] J. Stork, 'New Arab Human Rights Court is Doomed from the Start' *International Business Times* 26 November 2014 www.ibtimes.co.uk/new-arab-human-rights-court-protects-rulers-doomed-fail-1476728.

[138] Lowe, 'New Arab Court'.

[139] See 'The Tunis Declaration on the Arab Court of Human Rights' http://icj.wpengine.netdna-cdn.com/wp-content/uploads/2015/05/MENA-Arab-Court-Tunis-Declaration-Advocacy-2015-ENG.pdf. See also ICJ, *The Arab Court of Human Rights: A Flawed Statute for an Ineffective Court* (8 April 2015) http://icj.wpengine.netdna-cdn.com/wp-content/uploads/2015/04/MENA-Arab-Court-of-Human-Rights-Publications-Report-2015-ENG.pdf.

[140] Regarding the Charter, see generally M. Rishmawi, 'The Arab Charter on Human Rights and the League of Arab States: An Update' (2010) 10 *Human Rights Law Review* 169.

[141] Lowe, 'New Arab Court'.

1989   2016

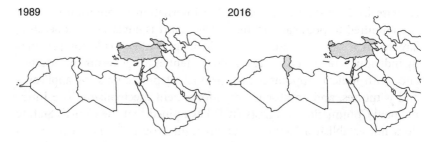

Figure 3.4   Electoral Democracies in the MENA Region: 1989 and 2016

internecine struggles and rivalries and the intentional ineffectiveness of the Arab League; a 'personalization' of states and autocratic power structures; an insufficient rule of law culture; and very limited economic integration due to minimal intra-regional trade.[142] Add Alshehri's observations on the universally undemocratic nature of regimes in the region, a very low level of ratification of human rights treaties in general, distrust toward empowerment of regional human rights organs, and characterisation of international human rights as vectors of a Western 'imperialist' agenda, virtually 'non-existent' judicial independence and separation of powers, and denial of even basic human rights at the domestic level, and the outlook for the Court is not encouraging.[143]

Yet, despite this reality, Alshehri speaks of the Court as a 'dream come true' for citizens of Arab states, which 'will go a long way towards ensuring that the rights of the Arab people are respected'.[144] This, regrettably, appears to be misplaced hope. If the perception of the European Court as a key actor in democratisation is somewhat mistaken, the impact of the Inter-American Court is easily overstated, and the African Court has struggled so far to make itself heard in a region with a high proportion of non-democratic regimes, what hope is there for a similar court in the Arab region, dominated by non-democratic regimes, riven by enmities and, in a number of states, engaged in armed conflict?[145]

[142] C.P. Romano, 'International Judicialization in the Arab World: An Initial Assessment', (2016) iCourts Working Paper Series, No. 49 47–54.
[143] S. Alshehri, 'An Arab Court of Human Rights: The Dream Desired' (2016) 30 Arab Law Quarterly 34.
[144] Ibid. 34, 50
[145] See also T.G. Daly, 'Repression in Bahrain: The End of Any Hope for an Effective Arab Court of Human Rights?' International Journal of Constitutional Law Blog 22 July 2016 www.iconnectblog.com/2016/07/repression-in-bahrain-the-end-of-any-hope-for-an-effective-arab-court-of-human-rights/.

6   Conclusion: Embracing Both Reality and Hope
   Concerning Courts' Roles

As we encountered in Chapter 2, there often appears to be a significant gap in contemporary scholarship and policymaking between perception and reality concerning the capacities of human rights courts as democracy-builders. Even the most prominent and assertive human rights courts, in Europe and the Americas, have encountered stark limits to their abilities to shape young democracies and influence the trajectory of democratisation. Moreover, the 'back-up' supervisory role of regional human rights courts has not prevented significant democratic decay in states such as Hungary, Poland, Argentina, and Venezuela. These rapid developments (although less surprising with the benefit of hindsight) have rather punctured the positive view forwarded by Buyse and Hamilton only five years ago:

> With all its flaws and limitations, the work of the European Court ... engenders a renewed belief in legal processes as opposed to violent armed struggle or revolution, while at the same time binding down the Gulliver of authoritarianism with strong ropes so that society does not revert to dictatorship.[146]

Of course, mirroring scholarship on constitutional courts, we find statements that recognise the limits of these courts. James Sweeney, for instance, notes:

> It is ... worth remembering that, as only one element of the Council of Europe, itself an external factor in each state's transitional process, the impact of the European Court of Human Rights' jurisprudence on the ultimate success or otherwise of the Contracting Parties' transition should be kept in perspective.[147]

However, in a similar manner to the often excessive faith placed in constitutional courts as democracy-builders in contemporary scholarship and policymaking, there is a strong impression that an unrealistic view of these courts' democracy-building capacities remains common. We see it in everything from contemporary calls for the Strasbourg Court to even assume additional duties,[148] to arguments for the establishment of an

---

[146] Buyse & Hamilton (eds.), *Transitional Jurisprudence and the ECHR* 295.
[147] Sweeney, *Post-Cold War Era* 22.
[148] For instance, in a recent talk Eyal Benvenisti proposed that the Court could take on a more expansive role in pushing for participation by citizens in decision-making processes in other states, which have transborder effects on them: E. Benvenisti, 'The Margin of Appreciation and the Facilitation of Democratic Deliberation', at the conference 'Margin of Appreciation and Democracy: Conference on Human Rights and Deference to Political Bodies', iCourts, University of Copenhagen, 13 April 2016.

International Constitutional Court and World Court of Human Rights, to Alshehri's seemingly vain hope in the promise of the Arab Court of Human Rights, as discussed above.

However, although tending to paint a somewhat pessimistic picture, there is a message of hope hidden in the past two chapters; namely, that courts at both levels can often achieve concrete, albeit limited, results in supporting democratisation, and that they can perhaps function more effectively as democracy-builders if we recognise their limits. The next chapter attempts to conceptualise more clearly the different roles that courts at both levels play in constructing the essentials of a democratic order, how both levels interact, and how they impact on other actors in the democratisation context.

4

'Democratisation Jurisprudence': Framing Courts' Democracy-Building Roles

The times were difficult, there were gangsters, poverty, crisis . . . Yet there was an odd phenomenon, which is perhaps fully comprehensible only to the lucky ones who have personal experience of that era. It was this extraordinary expectation, zeal, anxiety mixed with enthusiasm, coupled with quests, scruples and a desire to act. A singular and unique atmosphere. Decisions had to be taken promptly, no one had been properly prepared for such a job. Despite the vacuum of experience and knowledge, defying the atmosphere of tangible political tensions, everyone was still trying to do his or her best.

Chief Justice of Estonia Rait Maruste, 2009[1]

Judges in the international arena are, in some senses, freer to make law, and . . . are not obliged to follow their earlier decisions. National law, particularly in a common law system that has been around for seven hundred years, is highly detailed, complex and well developed. There is an enormous body of precedent to call on and a great deal of written material. In national law there are also huge and complex statutes that make it relatively difficult to argue that there are any gaps in the law.

Garry Sturgess & Philip Chubb, 1988[2]

What do courts actually do to 'build' democracy in a post-authoritarian state? In Chapters 2 and 3 we examined the perception of courts as drivers of, or even indispensable to, successful democratisation, arguing that this perception can be easily overstated. It is nevertheless clear that the courts at each level do play a role in buttressing democratic consolidation in post-authoritarian states. Part of the perception problem analysed in the previous two chapters stems from the fact that the roles carried out by constitutional courts and regional human rights courts in

---

[1] R. Maruste, 'The Outset of Constitutional Judicial Review' in G. Suumann (ed.), *15 Years of Constitutional Review in the Supreme Court of Estonia* (Supreme Court of Estonia, 2009) 13.
[2] Sturgess & Chubb, *Judging the World* 91.

new democracies have been under-conceptualised, with the result that it is difficult to frame their adjudicative role in supporting (or, in some cases, hindering) the democratisation process. Leading scholars such as Tom Ginsburg have blazed a trail in conceptualising the roles played by constitutional courts at the domestic level as democracy-builders, as discussed in Chapter 1, and scholars such as James Sweeney and Alexandra Huneeus have significantly enhanced our understanding of the roles played by regional human rights courts. However, there remains a need for a fuller theorisation and conceptualisation of the roles played by both courts, which also integrates analysis of the courts at both levels, and their interaction.

This chapter therefore seeks to conceptualise the roles that both constitutional courts and regional human rights courts play in respect to democratisation processes, through an organising concept of 'democratisation jurisprudence'. The aim is to carve out a clear framework for analysing the courts' roles, and how they interact, intertwine, and impact on one another. Notwithstanding the use of the term democratisation, the main focus here is on democratic consolidation, as defined in Chapter 1. Section 1 sets out the overall context of the enquiry, Sections 2 and 3 conceptualise the roles of constitutional courts and regional human rights courts respectively, Section 4 explores the interrelationship between the courts at each level, and Section 5 briefly considers the overall systemic complexity in which inter-court interaction takes place.

The term jurisprudence is used advisedly here. Like political jurisprudence or transitional jurisprudence, democratisation jurisprudence is not a full-blown theory of law, but something closer to what Conrado Hübner Mendes calls a 'middle-level' approach. It rests a number of rungs below legal theory on Sartori's 'ladder of abstraction', but a number of rungs above scholarship that analyses the most important decisions of a specific court in a new democracy without elaborating any overarching analytical framework.[3] However, unlike Mendes' normative theory concerning the deliberative role of constitutional courts, this is a theoretical framework grounded in analysis of the empirical reality, presented in Chapters 2 and 3 and the comparative case-studies in Chapters 5 and 6.

1   Democracy-Building: A Unique Judicial Task

The vista facing courts in a new democracy is a challenging one. Paraphrasing Chief Justice Maruste, quoted at the outset, the times are always

---

[3] Hübner Mendes, *Constitutional Courts* 11–14.

difficult, there are always hostile forces and often economic uncertainty. Evidently, his description of the Estonian Supreme Court tackling their task in the early 1990s is not universal. As we saw in Chapter 2, not all courts set out on their democracy-building journey with vim; not all courts begin with a vacuum of experience; nor do all judges do their best. However, this quotation captures, to some extent, the very different context of constitutional adjudication in a state that has just transitioned to electoral democracy, compared to a mature democracy.

Looking at the second introductory quotation, referring to the centuries-old English common law system, we see the stark difference between the context of a mature democracy and a new democracy; in the latter there is usually a new or revised constitution, with which significant elements of the pre-existing law is inconsistent, often in a legal order that has been distorted, stultified, or shrunken during authoritarian rule. In a sense, it places constitutional courts in a position akin to their international counterparts, as Sturgess and Chubb put it: 'freer to make law, and ... not obliged to follow their earlier decisions.' In some cases, the position is reversed: the regional human rights court pre-dates the state's transition to democracy, and has a significant corpus of jurisprudence compared to a newly established, or reformed, constitutional court – especially the *tabula rasa* faced by a Kelsenian court. The position could not be further from what Stephen Tierney has called 'the resilient gradualism of British constitutional change'.[4]

A   *The 'New Normal': Adjudication in a*
Cluttered Legal Landscape

It is important to emphasise that states that have transitioned to democracy during the third wave of democratisation have faced a far more cluttered normative landscape than the Federal Constitutional Court did when it began operating in 1951 (or, for that matter, the Italian or Austrian constitutional courts). Notwithstanding the presence of a foreign power on German soil, the German court had significant autonomy to elaborate its own lines of jurisprudence and to seek tailor-made solutions to the new state's post-war challenges. Competing sources of law and jurisprudence outside the state had yet to develop. The international human rights architecture was in its infancy: the Universal Declaration of Human Rights (UDHR) was only three years old when the German Court issued its

---

[4] S. Tierney, "The Three Hundred and Seven Year Itch': Scotland and the 2014 Independence Referendum' in Qvortrup (ed.), *The British Constitution* 146.

ground-breaking first judgment; while the UN's two international covenants on human rights did not enter into force until 1976,[5] by which time West German democracy had become viewed as 'unshakeable'.[6] The European Court of Human Rights had yet to hit its stride – and did not deliver a judgment in a case against Germany until 1975 (some six other applications having been ruled inadmissible).[7] The highest domestic courts in postcolonial Africa of the 1960s similarly operated in a context where the state remained the privileged producer of law and where domestic jurisprudence had scant international competition – the African Commission on Human Rights, for instance, was not established until 1987. As discussed in Chapter 3, the European Court played a peripheral part in the democratisation processes of Spain and Portugal from the mid-1970s onwards.

Constitutional courts in later democratisation processes have faced a more complex configuration, consisting of multiple sites of constitutional authority at the state, regional, and global levels, in which regional human rights in particular have become core producers of case-law. Decision-making by global bodies, such as the UN's Human Rights Committee, charged with supervision of compliance with the ICCPR, has also become more prominent. Although this complexity is faced by courts in all democracies – new, developing, and mature alike – it gains particular prominence in the democratisation context. As discussed in Chapter 1, international law and jurisprudence tends to provide a way of filling gaps in the new domestic legal order, by aiding courts in the interpretation of the domestic constitution and offering solutions to distinctive legal problems faced in new democracies. At times, international organs – especially regional human rights courts – seek to impose their preferred solutions on new democracies, seemingly on the basis that such states (and their courts) cannot be trusted to find their own solutions.

B   Monism, Dualism, and the Core Role of Courts

Domestic courts are not, however, merely passive recipients of international norms. Rather, they play a central role in mediating the extent to

---

[5] The International Covenant on Civil and Political Rights (ICCPR) entered into force on 23 March 1976. The International Covenant on Economic, Social and Cultural Rights (ICESCR) entered into force on 3 January 1976.

[6] See Chapter 2.

[7] *Klass* v. *Germany* (1979–80) 2 EHRR 214. Source: the European Court's HUDOC database, www.hudoc.echr.coe.int/eng.

which the new democratic legal order is constructed from international and foreign materials. The concepts of monism, which conceives of domestic and international law as fused and accords hierarchical superiority to the latter, and dualism, which conceives of domestic and international law as occupying separate, if interacting, spheres, remain central to any conceptualisation of the interface between national and international legal orders. However, they require some finessing here.

Various scholars emphasise that domestic courts are core mechanisms for co-ordinating relationships between state and international sites of legal authority. Nijman and Nollkaemper, for instance, though accepting that various factors cut across the explanatory power of either monism or dualism in today's world, such as the development of 'common values' and the 'de-formalization of international law', nonetheless conclude that the impact of international law remains subject to the actions of domestic actors.[8] While national legislatures were once the primary fulcrum in this process, they note that executives and courts have come to play increasingly prominent roles as 'gatekeepers' for the reception of international law.[9] Rather than a radical new monism, they argue, like others,[10] for the existence of a 'global legal pluralism', referring to

> diverse State and non-State and mixed legal regimes created by a diversity of communities [and] embedded in a community of principles, [which] allow co-existence and co-operation between multiple legal systems.[11]

Evidently, the co-existence of these legal systems is not always entirely harmonious, and much depends on the manner in which courts at both the domestic and regional contexts navigate their roles. Nico Krisch, for instance, has explored the manner in which constitutional courts and regional courts in Western Europe interact, not as a 'constitutional' order with a clear hierarchy, but as a plural legal order characterised by heterarchy, in which judicial strategy and judicial politics across the system divide allow the overall system to function without undue friction.[12]

---

[8] J. Nijman & A. Nollkaemper, 'Beyond the Divide' in Nijman & Nollkaemper (eds.), *New Perspectives on the Divide between National and International Law* (Oxford University Press, 2007) 341, 342, 359.

[9] Ibid. 359. This is borne out by other scholars. See e.g. C. Hillebrecht, 'The Domestic Mechanisms of Compliance with International Human Rights Law: Case Studies from the Inter-American Human Rights System' (2012) 34(4) *Human Rights Quarterly* 959, 966.

[10] See, in particular, Krisch, *Beyond Constitutionalism*.

[11] Nijman & Nollkaemper, 'Beyond the Divide' 359–60.

[12] Krisch, *Beyond Constitutionalism* ch. 4.

We return to this in considering interaction between constitutional courts and regional human rights courts toward the end of this chapter. First, the differing roles of the courts at each level will be sketched out. To orient ourselves through the discussion that follows, it is useful to keep in mind the fundamental dividing line between the courts at each level is that constitutional courts are inescapably embedded within a single democratisation process, whereas a regional human rights court is external to any one democratisation process. This factor strongly shapes their diverging roles.

2   Constitutional Courts: Building Democracy from Within the State

We clearly have a wealth of raw data and viewpoints about the roles of constitutional courts in new democracies. We saw in Chapter 2 that these courts are empowered to carry out a wide range of functions, from adjudicating separation of powers disputes to addressing legislative omission. We have seen that, empirically, the roles of constitutional courts in new democracies worldwide run the gamut from peripheral actors to central, even dominant, actors in governance. Notwithstanding this diversity, Ginsburg, in a descriptive summary of the central role played to date by courts as 'downstream democratic consolidators', identifies the core of this role:

> [Th]e courts can become important sites of contestation between elements of the old regime and new, devices for facilitating transitional justice, allies of the new order, or systematic dismantlers of the legal infrastructure of the old regime . . . [C]ourts play an essential role in structuring an environment of open political competition, free exchange of ideas, and limited government.[13]

In addition, in Chapter 7 we discuss at some length a number of normative arguments concerning the role courts should play in supporting democratisation. Wojciech Sadurski and Alec Stone Sweet suggest that rights protection is one of the main roles a court can play. Roberto Gargarella and Samuel Issacharoff add a second role of constraining the state. Gargarella's concept of 'democratic justice' suggests, more specifically, two key roles of guarding against, first, the gradual establishment of restrictions on basic civil and political rights, such as the rights

---

[13] Ginsburg, 'The Politics of Courts' 50.

to freedom of expression and fair trial, and second, the executive's tendency to amplify its powers and distort or overcome democratic controls.[14] Issacharoff, noting the distinctive central role played by courts in 'sculpting democratic politics' in many third wave democracies,[15] suggests that the court's role should be 'to reinforce the functioning of democracy more broadly' by filling gaps in the governance structure – for example, by adjudicating on impeachment processes and the openness of electoral competition,[16] and by curbing the excessive concentration of power at any one site.[17] Others, such as Daniel Bonilla Maldonado and Manuel Cepeda-Espinosa appear to see courts as capable of an even broader governance role that addresses economic governance, socio-economic inequality, and even constraining state violence.[18]

However, none of these scholars quite captures the peculiar nature and context of adjudication in states undergoing democratisation processes, nor do they provide a full framework for better understanding the role of constitutional courts in constructing the *minima* of a democratic constitutional order. This section, therefore, aims to take a step back from the existing scholarship to sketch the outlines of democratisation jurisprudence as an organising concept for an analytical framework applicable to a wide variety of constitutional courts, across geographical regions, based on key insights in the literature. In line with the initial analytical framework sketched in Chapter 1, and taking Ginsburg's description of the core role of courts as democratic consolidators as a starting point, the conceptual framework here focuses on a relatively narrow concept of democratic consolidation, which prioritises the establishment of a functioning political democracy, while incorporating transitional justice elements.

A The Distinct Context of Democratisation

In attempting to capture what is distinct about the context of democratisation compared to that of a mature democracy, it is worthwhile

---

[14] R. Gargarella, 'In Search of a Democratic Justice – What Courts Should Not Do: Argentina, 1983–2002' in Gloppen, Gargarella & Skaar (eds.), *Democratization and the Judiciary.*

[15] Issacharoff, *Fragile Democracies* 9.　　[16] Issacharoff's 'Democratic Hedging' 986–7.

[17] Issacharoff, *Fragile Democracies.*

[18] See Chapter 7. See also J. Ríos-Figueroa, *Constitutional Courts as Mediators: Armed Conflict, Civil-Military Relations, and the Rule of Law in Latin America* (Cambridge University Press, 2016).

considering the constitutional, political, and institutional contexts in which a constitutional court in a new democracy operates.

Constitutional Context

Scholarship in transitional justice, comparative constitutional law, and democratisation studies underlines that, in stark contrast to the evolutionary constitutions of polities such as the United Kingdom and New Zealand, new constitutions in states transitioning from authoritarian rule inevitably refer to the legacy of the past. They therefore aim not only at 'entrenching' new rules but also at 'disentrenching' the previous order, with a particular focus on constraining state power and illiberal tendencies.[19] That said, the extent to which a true constitutional break from the past is achieved depends on the *manner* of transition (e.g. whether managed by authoritarian powers; as the result of revolution; whether short or protracted) and the constitutional drafting *process*, both of which shape the *product* – the constitution itself.[20]

A key insight from the judicial politics literature is of relevance here:

> Policy-making by courts ... occurs when the case involves choice and judgement, when judges are called upon to select from among competing rules, interpret new ones, or act in the absence of clearly articulated executive, legislative or constitutional norms ... Of necessity, judges ... make policy when they 'write on a clean slate', in addressing a new legal question or interpreting a new rule.[21]

This observation gains added force in the context of democratisation, when constitutional courts are typically required to interpret new constitutions and to put flesh on the bare skeleton of the constitutional text. Faced with the 'silences, gaps and abeyances'[22] of the new constitutional text, constitutional courts in new democracies must make fundamental choices regarding constitutional meaning. As mentioned above, unlike their counterparts in long-established democracies, courts in new democracies are usually much less constrained by any pre-existing corpus of jurisprudence and have a freer hand not only to interpret the constitution, but also to shape the constitutional regime as a whole. The requirement placed on courts in new democracies to engage in wholesale

---

[19] See e.g. C. Sunstein, 'The Negative Constitution: Transition in Latin America' in Stotzky (ed.), *Transition to Democracy* 367–8.

[20] R. Teitel, *Transitional Justice* (Oxford University Press, 2000) 197ff.

[21] Volcansek (ed.), *Judicial Politics* 1–2.

[22] M. Loughlin, *The Idea of Public Law* (Oxford University Press, 2003) 50.

constitutional construction and interpretation is therefore a far cry from the general role of constitutional fine-tuning carried out by courts in long-established democracies, on the basis of substantial pre-existing jurisprudence.

In addition, the constitutional settlement often contains features that are not found in a mature democracy. It has been observed that most third wave democratic transitions contain countermajoritarian elements designed to calibrate a balance of power between the old and new regimes. As discussed in Chapter 2, constitutional courts can be one such element, alongside bills of rights, eternity clauses, and other mechanisms. Others, which are more peculiar to post-authoritarian polities, include restrictions on electoral competition (e.g. by preserving legislative seats for members of the old regime, or providing for legislative appointments more generally), power-sharing mechanisms (e.g. providing for a multi-member executive presidency), and restrictions on the prosecution of former regime members for rights abuses (e.g. amnesty laws).[23] These elements need not be part of the formal constitutional text. As we will see in Chapter 5, the constitutional pact underpinning Brazil's transition from military to civilian rule included not only the constitution of 1988, but also a meta-constitutional amnesty law of 1979, which formed the basis for a negotiated relinquishment of power by the military government. Here, we get a sense of constitutions, not simply as statements of democratic values or co-ordinating mechanisms, but, in Galligan and Versteeg's words, as at least partly the product of 'haphazard bargains, raw power play, and the political agenda of self-interested elites.'[24]

Political Context

Evidently, courts in the democratisation setting operate in an entirely different political context to a long-established, stable democracy of the kind now found in regions such as Western Europe, North America, and Australasia. A new democracy is a democracy only in the relatively minimal sense of elected government, a democratic constitution, and state institutions organised along liberal democratic principles (e.g. the separation of powers), but which do not necessarily all espouse a strong commitment to those principles. New democracies often contain

---

[23] See S. Alberts, C. Warshaw & B.R. Weingast, 'Democratization and Countermajoritarian Institutions' in T Ginsburg (ed.), *Comparative Constitutional Design* (Cambridge University Press, 2012).

[24] Galligan & Versteeg, 'Theoretical Perspectives' 19.

significant political actors (e.g. an ousted communist party, military forces), which are opposed, whether expressly or not, to the new democratic order. In addition, as Denis Galligan notes, the state's administrative machinery may be wedded to authoritarian modes of governance, prioritising efficiency, effectiveness, and secrecy over rights protection and transparency, and, as a self-contained autonomous normative order, may evince resistance to legal efforts to render it more mindful of such values.[25] The continuing prevalence of torture by police authorities in Tunisia, five years after the state's first democratic elections, is a particularly stark illustration of this point.[26] Even political actors ostensibly committed to democratic rule have different conceptions of what is permissible in a system of democratic governance; the tension between thin and thick conceptions of democracy once again plays a central part. In many cases, the balance of power between the old regime and the new regime is not always clear, which can exert a significant constraint on the new regime's freedom to manoeuvre. Overall, authoritarian governance practices cast a long shadow and can continue to subvert the rule of law even decades after the initial transition to democracy.[27]

Concerns regarding the separation of powers – i.e. a functional division of state power; what Martinez terms a 'horizontal structuring'[28] – are also often heightened in new democracies. While there is no one model, and certainly no 'perfect' model, for a separation of powers,[29] some have argued that greater activity by constitutional courts in mature democracies is warranted given the increasing imbalance of power between parliaments and executives since the mid-twentieth century,[30] not only in presidential systems but also in parliamentary systems. In new

---

[25] D. Galligan 'Authoritarianism in Government and Administration: The Promise of Administrative Justice' (2001) 54(1) *Current Legal Problems* 79.

[26] See, for example, S. Lutyens & H. Tlili, 'Torture and Police Abuse Still a Reality, Five Years after Tunisia's Revolution' *France 24* 14 January 2016 www.france24.com/en/20160114-focus-tunisia-police-abuse-torture-violence-security-forces-revolution-ben-ali.

[27] For an illuminating account, see D. Dolenec, *Democratic Institutions and Authoritarian Rule in Southeast Europe* (ECPR Press, 2013).

[28] J.S. Martinez, 'Horizontal Structuring' in Rosenfeld & Sajó (eds.), *Comparative Constitutional Law*.

[29] Different systems worldwide lie on a spectrum from a strong separation (e.g. United States, Brazil) to more fused powers (e.g. United Kingdom), while the 'new constitutionalism' in Latin American countries such as Bolivia and Ecuador has involved experiments with more elaborate formal constitutional divisions of power. See e.g. R. Uprimny, 'Recent Transformation'.

[30] Discussed in S. Tierney, *Constitutional Referendums. The Theory and Practice of Republican Deliberation* (Oxford University Press, 2012) 24–5.

democracies the justification often gains added currency where the challenge is to rebalance a system that previously hoarded political power at one site. Whether power was wielded by a markedly strong 'hyperpresidential' executive, a Communist politburo, a military junta, or one-party rule, such systems tend to leave strong traces in the political organisation and culture of the new democratic order; or even continue into the new order, with hyperpresidential systems and the domination of single parties a common feature in the new democracies of the third wave.

It is important to emphasise here that, in the contemporary world, those seeking to subvert democracy are often not wearing jackboots. They come wearing business suits, speaking the language of constitutionalism and democracy. Many elected leaders in third wave democracies have attempted (and sometimes succeeded in achieving) a sophisticated hollowing out of constitutional structures which aim at constraining power, holding it to account, and preventing its misuse – what David Landau calls 'abusive constitutionalism.'[31] The subjugation of the Hungarian constitutional court by technically constitutional means in 2012, discussed in Chapter 2, has become the paradigmatic example.

Abusive constitutionalism brings to the fore the critical problem of constraining constituent power, and the challenge this poses for courts. Regarding constitutional amendment, Landau, Issacharoff, and others have observed that attempts by regimes from Colombia to India to change the constitutional rules in their favour have been struck down by courts. The clearest doctrinal approach is the Indian Supreme Court's 'basic structure' doctrine, asserting the power to assess the compatibility of amendments with the basic structure of Indian democracy.[32] Moves by regimes to craft new constitutions in order to entrench their power (as seen in Venezuela) are much harder to address: the constitutional court, as a 'constituted' organ under the existing constitution, has little power to constrain such activity; or can justify refusal to intervene on the basis that the matter concerns an exercise of constituent power.[33]

Institutional Context

As Chapter 2 made clear, constitutional courts are not simply agents of democratisation, but are also *subjects* of democratisation. They are expected to carry out a very extensive role when they are, typically, at their weakest. The court not only has to engage in the construction of a

---

[31] Landau, 'Abusive Constitutionalism'. [32] See Chapter 2.
[33] See Landau, 'Abusive Constitutionalism' 205.

new constitutional order, often negotiating a hostile political matrix as it does so, but must also in a sense construct *itself*, by deciding on key matters such as the acceptable scope of constitutional review, procedure before the court, and the binding nature of its decisions. This is especially true of a new Kelsenian court established under the democratic constitution, but even supreme courts which transcend the old and new order face the challenge of re-making their role in the new dispensation (as seen in the Brazilian context, discussed in Chapter 5). A complicating factor is that courts are often also subject to institutional shaping by the other governmental branches (not always with malicious intent). The successive amplification of the Brazilian Supreme Court's powers in the 1990s and the diminution of the Hungarian Constitutional Court in 2012 are two clear examples of a relatively benign and a hostile institutional intervention respectively.

The reality is that unusually assertive courts, such as the Hungarian, South African, and Colombian courts discussed in Chapter 2, are a minority. The majority of constitutional courts in the post-war era have evinced an initial timidity in carrying out their role, but have gradually found their feet, building their authority in increments and slowly finding a niche in the democratic order, whether central or peripheral. Judicial politics scholars, using game theory and other behavioural models, indicate the strategies employed by such courts to pursue both institution-building and capacity-building in the early years of a new democracy – from Latvia to South Africa to South Korea we get a sense of similar tactics being employed and similar challenges faced. Courts, faced with a hostile institutional matrix and often weak public support, pick their battles very carefully.[34]

No matter how they develop, it is worth emphasising that these courts, embedded as they are in the domestic constitutional context, cannot work outside that context, and this shapes their approach to their role. It is also worth stressing that, unlike the other branches of government, they are generally reactive institutions in the sense that they can only address matters that are brought before them. Only a minority can address certain constitutional matters *sua sponte*. This, of course, also applies to regional human rights courts. Nevertheless, as Shapiro has observed, all

---

[34] See, in particular, Harding & Leyland (eds.), *Constitutional Courts*; Zielonka (ed.), *Democratic Consolidation*; Epstein, Knight & Shvetsova, 'The Role of Constitutional Courts' 149ff; and Roux, *Politics of Principle*.

courts through their jurisprudence can signal to their constituencies what they are willing to adjudicate on, and how they might adjudicate.[35]

B Distinguishing Features of Domestic Democratisation Jurisprudence

It is necessary to admit from the outset that any attempt to identify the core role of a constitutional court in achieving the essentials of a constitutional democracy will be at least minimally normative, involving selections as to what is considered most important. Nevertheless, perhaps a defensible approach is to seek what distinguishes democratisation jurisprudence from constitutional jurisprudence in a mature democracy, by conceiving of it as a creature of *time, tempo, context, content,* and *methodology.*

Time

It may appear evident, but it is worth stating that the heartland of domestic democratisation jurisprudence will be found in the earlier years following the transition to electoral democracy; a rough estimate might be the first twenty years. It might be likened to an irregularly spaced chromatic scale, with a flurry of notes played at one end, tapering off to a point where the pitches are spaced wide apart, and used to play an occasional note.

Tempo

The concept of democratisation jurisprudence in no way denies the fact that constitutional courts in mature democracies hand down decisions of fundamental importance to the polity, concerning the electoral system, separation of powers issues, and so on. For instance, the US Supreme Court's recent judgment in *Evenwel* v. *Abbott*[36] concerned the constitutional meaning of 'one man, one vote', which had the potential to transform the political power of different voting districts (although the Court's judgment ultimately pursued a line more compatible with the *status quo*).[37] However, these tend to be rare decisions, punctuating the general role of the court in fine-tuning the constitutional order.

---

[35] See e.g. M. Shapiro, 'The Mighty Problem Continues' in Kapiszewski, Silverstein & Kagan (eds.), *Consequential Courts* 385–6.
[36] 578 US ___ (2016).
[37] See e.g. L. Denniston, 'Opinion Analysis: Leaving a Constitutional Ideal Still Undefined' *SCOTUS blog* 4 April 2016 www.scotusblog.com/2016/04/opinion-analysis-leaving-a-con stitutional-ideal-still-undefined.

This is in stark contrast to constitutional courts in new democracies, where, due to the presence of a new constitutional text, decisions concerning the very fundamentals of the constitutional order are made on a frequent basis. To use a metaphor common to democratisation theory and transitional justice scholarship, the court in a new democracy is required to simultaneously build and navigate the ship, whereas its counterpart in an established democracy is generally required to simply navigate the ship, making minor, and occasionally major, modifications as it sails.[38] It is important to stress that institutional design can play a part in the immediacy with which the court can act to address deficiencies in the legal order: a system with a supreme court may require matters to wend their way through the appeals process before final adjudication by that court; a Kelsenian court, by contrast, is usually able to address matters relatively quickly.

Context

We canvassed above the main differences between the context of a mature democracy and a new democracy by reference to the constitutional, political, and institutional contexts. It is worth recalling from Chapter 1 the more basic point that the context of a new democracy is paradigmatically characterised by an inordinate pace of change, relative to a mature democracy, across multiple planes: political, economic, social, and – most importantly for our purposes – constitutional and legal. This period of intense flux differs from state to state, but persists for many years, even in what are commonly perceived as the shortest periods of consolidation (in the CEE states). Thus, whereas constitutional courts in long-established democracies are faced infrequently with issues of fundamental importance to the constitutional order, in an overall context of stability, constitutional courts in new democracies are faced *frequently* with questions that cut to the foundations of the constitutional order, in a context of overall *instability*.

The level of transformation required in the new democracy depends, to a significant extent, on the regime that preceded it. Building democracy from the ashes of a short-lived military dictatorship that suspends the constitution and carries out its policies without writing them into law will require less intensive transformation than a longer-lived military regime that leaves a significant legacy of authoritarian law, including an

---

[38] See e.g. J. Elster, C. Offe & U.K. Preuss, *Institutional Design in Post-Communist Societies: Rebuilding the Ship at Sea* (Cambridge University Press, 1998).

authoritarian constitution. Building democracy in the aftermath of long-term totalitarian rule requires perhaps the most effort, requiring a drastic change not only in governance modalities, but in the entire economic, political, and social ordering of society, the nature of the state, and its relationship with the people.

Content

When one surveys the breadth of matters decided upon by constitutional courts in new democracies, it is clear that not all their decisions concern matters central to the construction of the *essentials* of a democratic constitutional order. A useful approach is to proceed from the insight that constitutions in new democracies have both an entrenchment and a disentrenchment function, discussed above, and the observation in Chapter 1 that constitutional courts are increasingly designed to supplement the 'constituting' function of the constitution as a feature of what Vicki Jackson calls 'incremental constitutionalism'.[39] The court is, in this way, required not only to entrench the new constitution and construct a new constitutional order, but also to disentrench the pre-existing constitutional order. Its role therefore has both constructive and destructive aspects.

Recalling that a court's democracy-building task lies in constructing the essentials of a democratic order, a number of points are clear as regards entrenchment of the new constitution. Not everything a court does in entrenching the new order is central to that task. It is important to emphasise here the distinction made in Chapter 1 between democracy and justice, and that the framework for consolidation of democracy elaborated in that chapter requires relatively minimal democratic structures to be in place for a democracy to be considered consolidated. A democracy is consolidated if it provides basic protection to expressive, associative, and information rights, undergirding a functioning and inclusive system of electoral competition. These rights are counted, time and again, across scholarship, legal instruments, and policy documents, as core democratic rights.[40] Of course, as Walker notes, 'even within these core categories, hard questions arise about how far we should go.'[41]

---

[39] Jackson, 'What's in a Name?' 1265–8.
[40] See e.g. J. Vidmar, 'Judicial Interpretations of Democracy in Human Rights Treaties' (2014) 3 *Cambridge Journal of International and Comparative Law* 532.
[41] N. Walker, 'Constitutionalism and the Incompleteness of Democracy' 219.

It is not possible here to resolve that question. It is perhaps more helpful to approach the matter in a negative sense. The court will not succeed in its task as democracy-builder if it fails to vindicate core democratic rights and to elaborate expansive interpretations of their scope; subject to their delimitation where used as a means to subvert others' rights or with the aim of threatening, in a real sense, the existence of the democratic order. The court will fail in its task if it allows arbitrary or disproportionate restrictions on access to the electoral arena; such as an unjustifiably high electoral threshold to gain representation in parliament. The court will fail in its task if it does not robustly address the potential re-emergence of authoritarianism, including, in particular, attempts to accrete power at one site and to subvert the functional division of state power.

Taken together with the protection of core democratic rights, the court's task might be characterised as assisting in the construction of a democratic public sphere; that is, a significant zone of freedom for individual citizens, civil society organisations, and political actors to engage in meaningful deliberation concerning key questions and challenges for the democratic community. This includes the ability to hold those in power accountable for their decisions, without fear of reprisal. Evidently, this framework excludes many other rights; including social and economic rights. Recalling from Chapter 1 again the distinction between democracy and justice, and between democratisation and social justice more specifically, while protection of core democratic rights is incompatible with authoritarian government, historical and contemporary states show that social and economic rights can be accorded extensive protection in undemocratic regimes (e.g. the right to health in Cuba).

As regards disentrenchment of the prior regime, four key functions might be suggested. First, the court must articulate the relationship, and the extent of rupture, between the new constitutional order and the old. A focus on legal continuity with the authoritarian regime can diminish the impact of the new constitution, while a focus on rupture tends to permit the court to take more robust stances to protect and develop the new democratic order. This will become clearer when discussing the Brazilian case-study in Chapter 5.

Second, the court must address the validity of law carried over from the previous regime. With the adoption of a new democratic constitution in a post-authoritarian state the legal system becomes a normative chimera overnight. The new or revised constitution sets out a framework that, typically, asserts the democratic nature of the state, affirms a separation of powers, and enshrines fundamental rights guarantees; a sort of blueprint for the new democratic order which the court must somehow bring to life. Yet, invariably, a significant *residuum* of repressive laws remains in place from the previous regime, which are antithetical to any democratic system, accompanied often by repressive attitudes among democratically elected actors, who may – and often do – view such laws as useful. Representing a particularly problematic example of Luigi Ferrajoli's conflict between 'the constitutional *ought* and the legislative *is*', the status to be accorded to such laws and, in particular, the way in which incompatible pre-constitutional laws might be addressed, is a central question which has to be faced early in the life of a post-authoritarian regime; one which is not faced by courts in mature democracies.[42] Addressing authoritarian-era law evidently does not imply its wholesale deracination or extirpation, or a rejection of *all* prior law. Such an approach would be impossible without bringing the ship of state to a halt. Rather, it necessitates a reordering, a reevaluation and, occasionally, a rejection of certain elements. The use of presidential decrees to legislate, or emergency powers, for example, might still be allowed, but subjected to much stricter parameters than under the previous authoritarian regime.

Third, the court must address transitional justice questions, which often focus on the constitutionality of prosecutions against actors from the previous regime and 'legacy' cases concerning fundamental rights violations committed under the previous regime. This, in particular, places a court in the precarious position of judging the balance of power between the old and new orders.

Finally, while engaging in entrenchment and disentrenchment, the court must mediate its own role and place in the new democratic order, in a context where a true division of state power is nascent and fragile. Landmark decisions delineating the court's jurisdiction would be included – for example, the elaboration of a 'political questions' doctrine (whether explicit or not). Case-law concerning constitutional crises, such as impeachment or an impasse between political powers, would also be key.

Methodology

There has been much discussion in recent years of the global citation by constitutional courts of their peers' jurisprudence in other states, as well as the decisions of international courts and adjudicative bodies. Courts

---

[42] Ferrajoli, 'Constitutional Democracy' 363.

will look outside their own system to discover common principles of law, address gaps and ambiguities, to refer to solutions that have worked in other states, to dispel local fears concerning the consequences of a particular solution to a legal problem, or when the law before the court finds its roots in international law.[43] In new democracies the characteristic deficiencies and innovations in the new legal system drive courts toward greater reliance on external case-law.

First, Johanna Kalb argues that constitutional courts in new democracies engage in 'strategic' citation of the case-law of foreign constitutional courts and international courts (especially regional human rights courts) to bolster their adjudicative role.[44] This is seen in the comparative case-studies presented in Chapters 5 and 6, with references to both foreign and international jurisprudence in key case-law of the Brazilian Supreme Court and the Tanzanian superior courts, for instance. Cosmopolitan 'enthusiasm', viewed in this way, is underpinned by highly instrumentalist motives. Drawing on external jurisprudence allows the court to place its decisions in a wider context and, to some extent, transcend its *problématique* of 'embeddedness' in the domestic order, by tethering itself to transnational norms and perspectives, and emphasising that its decisions are neither arbitrary nor self-serving.

Second, such citation serves the functional purpose of seeking solutions in the absence of a pre-existing corpus of case-law. Compared to the constitutional courts of post-war Western Europe, the courts of the third wave of democratisation have been able to draw on a considerable '*acquis jurisprudentiel*' from courts operating in previous (or ongoing) democratisation processes. This is seen, for instance, in Brazilian judges' reference to German, Italian, and Spanish case-law in addressing the status of authoritarian-era law in the new constitutional order, in the case-study presented in Chapter 5. Institutional form can be key in this regard. Unlike Kelsenian courts, which are generally limited to 'space travel' through comparative analysis of foreign and international jurisprudence, supreme courts retained into the democratic era can also engage in 'time travel' by drawing on previous decisions of the court. This can have a significant impact on the mode and robustness of 'democratisation jurisprudence'; as seen in the Brazilian case-study in Chapter 5.

---

[43] See B. Markesinis & J. Fedtke, *Judicial Recourse to Foreign Law: A New Source of Inspiration?* (Routledge, 2012) ch. 3.

[44] J. Kalb, 'The Judicial Role in New Democracies: A Strategic Account of Comparative Citation' (2013) 38 *Yale Journal of International Law* 423.

Third, the strong influence of international law on the content of third wave constitutions, and the status attached to international law in those constitutions, tends toward a reflexive reliance on international law when interpreting the new constitution, producing a type of constitutional *mischsprache*. This is particularly evident where international law is invoked in order to legitimise controversial decisions, examples include: the Argentine Supreme Court's reliance on Inter-American case-law to strike down the amnesty law adopted after the military regime collapsed;[45] and the South African Constitutional Court's reliance on international treaties to strike down legal provisions offering inadequate structural safeguards for specialised anti-corruption prosecutors.[46]

C The Shape of Domestic Democratisation Jurisprudence

On the basis of the literature as a whole, democratisation jurisprudence might therefore be viewed as involving eight core strains of activity, which may be characterised as falling within three interrelated dimensions:

(i) Facilitating the creation of a democratic public sphere
    1. Upholding core democratic rights
    2. Shaping an inclusive electoral system
    3. Curbing the re-emergence of authoritarianism
(ii) Mediating the shift from an undemocratic to democratic order
    4. Articulating the relationship between the old and new constitutional order
    5. Addressing/eliminating authoritarian legislation
    6. Addressing key transitional justice questions
(iii) Carving out a role for the court in the new democratic order
    7. Delineating the Court's jurisdiction
    8. Addressing crises.

A number of clarifications are required here. First, these tasks are not viewed as autonomous and hermetically sealed categories. For example, within the first dimension, striking down a law seeking to repress public protests would not only fall under category (1) concerning core democratic rights, but also under category (3) by curbing the emergence of

---

[45] See J.S. Elias, 'Constitutional Changes, Transitional Justice, and Legitimacy: The Life and Death of Argentina's "Amnesty" Laws' (2008) 31 *Hastings International and Comparative Law Review* 587.
[46] See Issacharoff, *Fragile Democracies* ch. 11.

authoritarianism. There is also no strict separation across the dimensions, broadly reflecting the fact that the roles of entrenchment and disentrenchment are intertwined. As we will see in Chapter 5, for instance, addressing violations of the separation of powers can entail the entrenchment function of articulating the nature of that separation in the democratic constitution, alongside the disentrenchment function of articulating the relationship between the old and the new constitutional order.

Second, this is a maximal list. Not all constitutional courts in new democracies would fulfil all of these tasks; and, certainly, the jurisprudence of different courts would contain different emphases on different categories. For instance, where the new democratic government moves to repeal the worst authoritarian laws, this saves the court from having to address challenges to those laws. In addition, the presence and openness of an individual complaint procedure would tend to affect the number of rights challenges. The presence of a supreme electoral court will reduce the constitutional court's ability to shape the rules of the electoral system. However, the framework appears sufficiently flexible to accommodate such differences.

Third, there is no suggestion here that the constitutional court in a new democracy is entirely self-aware in the elaboration of its democratisation jurisprudence. However, an awareness of the particular context of democratisation may be discerned in some decisions, based on close textual analysis.

Fourth, as indicated in Chapter 2, democratisation jurisprudence can both hamper and help democratisation, and the framework permits such instances to be more clearly identified.

Fifth, there is no suggestion that the framework elaborated above can be considered definitive. Indeed, given the problematic and prismatic nature of democratisation and democracy, as discussed in Chapter 1, no doubt the framework is open on all flanks to criticism: its exclusion of social and economic rights, for example; or its inability to precisely assess when a constitutional order can be considered consolidated.

Finally, in selecting the democratisation jurisprudence of any given constitutional court, a strong tension between what can be generalised and what is context-specific has to be accommodated: veering unduly toward the former would lead to an excessively stylised, ahistorical account of the democratisation case-law of a given court, sacrificing resonance with reality for analytical clarity or neatness; veering too far toward the latter would leave simply a single-state account, of limited application to other states.

D The Impact of Design

As discussed briefly in the Introduction, constitutional courts in new democracies exhibit considerable diversity. Key factors affecting a constitutional court's effectiveness include: (i) the nature of the constitutional text (e.g. length, indeterminacy, legitimacy); (ii) the structure of the court, its membership, even its location; (iii) guarantees of judicial independence; (iv) the mechanisms of review (abstract, concrete, *a priori* and/or *a posteriori*); (v) the effect of constitutional court decisions (whether advisory, *inter partes* or *erga omnes*); and (vi) the court's ability to control its docket.[47] These can all have powerful path dependent effects on the court's ability to positively impact on the democratisation process.

The nature of the powers and jurisdiction granted to a court appear to be particularly important. Lach and Sadurski, for example, count the competence to review legislation as the most crucial power of the courts[48] and also identify 'a clear correlation between the existence of an activist and powerful constitutional court and the availability of a direct complaint procedure',[49] with the very open access to the Hungarian and Colombian constitutional courts viewed as a factor in their unusually assertive jurisprudence.[50] Certain powers are viewed as having undesirable results; for example, the power of abstract review of the constitutionality of Bills can tend to 'politicise' the court's work, requiring it to effectively act as a third legislative chamber when opposition politicians seek review to frustrate the government's legislative agenda – as seen in Romania, among other states.[51] By contrast, the range of powers accorded to a court does not appear to be a particularly important factor.[52]

---

[47] See generally Zielonka (ed.), *Democratic Consolidation*; Harding & Leyland (eds.), *Constitutional Courts*; and J. Ríos-Figueroa, 'Institutions for Constitutional Justice in Latin America' in Helmke & Rios-Figueroa (eds.), *Courts in Latin America*.

[48] Lach & Sadurski, 'Constitutional Courts' 53.

[49] Ibid. 63. Conversely, Couso identifies the lack of an individual complaint procedure as one of the explanatory factors for the submissive nature of the Constitutional Court of Chile: 'The Politics of Judicial Review' 86–7.

[50] See A. Jakab & P. Sonnevend, 'Continuity with Deficiencies: The New Basic Law of Hungary' (2013) 1 *European Constitutional Law Review* 102, 122; and Cepeda-Espinosa, 'Judicial Activism' 553.

[51] Lach & Sadurski, 'Constitutional Courts' 69.

[52] Some courts with a large number of powers on paper, such as those in Ecuador and Venezuela, are perceived as having been less effective than those with comparatively few powers, such as the Council of Grand Justices in Taiwan. See generally Harding & Leyland (eds.), *Constitutional Courts*.

Although Kelsenian courts may carry certain advantages, it is not possible to state simply that they are superior to supreme courts as a form of democratisation technology. Supreme courts often avail of procedural rules to give priority to constitutional issues, and many Kelsenian courts have no direct complaint procedure for individuals. Matters such as tenure affect the shape of jurisprudence in a new democracy. Supreme court judges tend to enjoy life tenure, whereas Kelsenian court judges often have fixed term-limits, leading to more frequent changes in court membership and a heightened capacity for jurisprudential shifts.[53] Ultimately, even with the best selection methods, guarantees of judicial independence, and funding, there is no predicting what a court will do in the new democratic setting.

3   Regional Human Rights Courts: Building Democracy from Outside

Regional human rights evidently approach the deficiencies of a new democracy from an entirely different perspective and institutional setting, as compared to domestic constitutional courts. The most fundamental is, of course, that such courts are external to the state and do not derive their claim to power from the constitution. This section attempts to capture the key differences.

A   Regional Human Rights Courts: Kelsenian Courts Writ Large?

Since the 1990s regional human rights courts have increasingly been likened by scholars to domestic constitutional courts, differentiating them from classic international courts, which operate solely within the realm of international law, such as the International Court of Justice (ICJ).[54] Alec Stone Sweet, for instance, has vigorously argued the case for viewing the European Court of Human Rights as a 'constitutional court' of sorts, on the basis that the scope of the Court's authority is comparable to that of domestic constitutional courts as is its use of similar techniques

---

[53] See e.g. Scheppele's treatment of the less activist Hungarian constitutional court after the departure of President Sólyom: 'The New Hungarian'.

[54] Although even that court is discussed in constitutional terms: see e.g. M.S.M. Amr, *The Role of the International Court of Justice as the Principal Judicial Organ of the United Nations* (Martinus Nijhoff, 2003) 317.

and methodologies. This is in a context where the European Convention has been 'constitutionalised' through the combined effect of Protocol 11 and the incorporation of the Convention in the legal orders of the Contracting Parties, with the Strasbourg Court accorded dominance of the Convention system.[55] Stone Sweet sums up his argument as, 'if a duck-like creature looks, walks and quacks like a duck, then . . . even if it is not really a duck, I am going to call it one.'[56] He is not alone. Actors within the Court have described it as a 'quasi-constitutional court for the whole of Europe',[57] and the same language is used in reference to the Inter-American and African human rights courts; Néstor Pedro Sagües, for instance, describes the Court in San José as 'a supranational human rights constitutional court.'[58]

It is true that regional human rights courts resemble domestic constitutional courts (particularly Kelsenian courts) in many ways: they are the final interpreters of a text that forms the foundation of a normative order; they adjudicate on a wide range of matters key to domestic social and political systems; order relief for wronged parties; and in doing so constrain the exercise of political power – the very essence of constitutional law. They can also perform symbolic functions. Buyse and Hamilton, for instance, assert in the European context that accession to regional organisations and ratification of treaties such as the European Convention system serve 'symbolic and legal markers which reflect key steps in a transition process' (which they use in the 'loose' sense of transitional justice).[59]

Indeed, the likeness to constitutional courts is in some ways most striking as regards the Inter-American Court, given: its seven-member membership structure (compared to the European Court's sprawling membership); its more developed advisory role compared to the European Court; its power to engage in abstract *a priori* review of national

---

[55] A. Stone Sweet, 'On the Constitutionalisation of the Convention: The European Court of Human Rights as a Constitutional Court', Yale Law School Faculty Scholarship Series. Paper 71, 2009.
[56] Ibid. 5.
[57] See e.g. L. Garlicki, 'Judicial Deliberations: The Strasbourg Perspective' in Huls, Adams & Bomhoff (eds.), *The Legitimacy of Highest Courts' Rulings* 390–1.
[58] N.P. Sagües, 'Obligaciones Internacionales y Control de Convencionalidad' (2010) 8 *Estudios Constitucionales* 117, 126; cited in O. Ruiz-Chiriboga, 'The Conventionality Control: Examples of (Un)Successful Experiences in Latin America' (2010) 3 *Inter-American & European Human Rights Journal* 200, 205.
[59] Buyse & Hamilton (eds.), *Transitional Jurisprudence and the ECHR* 287.

laws (albeit rarely used); and the absence of any 'margin of appreciation' doctrine, which allows the European Court to accord states a measure of discretion regarding rights protection. It also evinces a tendency toward a monist approach concerning serious rights violations; and a more general tendency to order states to take specific remedial steps, unlike the European Court, which tends to leave a freer hand to states outside the 'pilot judgment' and 'quasi-pilot judgment' procedures. The European Court's approach has led some, such as Andreas Føllesdal, to argue that its review function constitutes 'weak' review.[60] This does capture in many ways the reality of the Court's authority, in that its judgments do open up a form of dialogue between the errant state and the Court as regards implementation. However, in principle the Court retains the 'final say' as to the validity of laws as against the European Convention, which is the hallmark of strong judicial review, as defined in the Introduction to this book.

Ultimately, as observed by Roel de Lange, any international human rights court in truth occupies an odd half-way house between a standard international court and a domestic constitutional court. It certainly has some of the functions and attributes of the latter, but has 'a totally different jurisdiction [and] a totally different "mission"'.[61] Regional human rights courts are not simply constitutional courts covering a larger territorial area. As discussed in Chapter 1, the Council of Europe, the OAS, and the African Union cannot be likened to federal states, unlike the quasi-federal nature of the European Union. As even Stone Sweet acknowledges, the European Court does not possess the formal power to invalidate legal acts;[62] nor do the other two regional courts – despite the Inter-American Court's pretensions to do so under the conventionality control doctrine.

More crucially, the remit of such courts extends to the protection of human rights alone. While this positions them at the centre of many disputes at the domestic level, and is a function of the utmost importance, it does not fully mirror the wider remit of domestic constitutional courts, which are tasked also with addressing, *inter alia*, separation of powers disputes (both inter-branch and centre-periphery) and ensuring the coherence of the entire constitutional order, often by striking difficult

---

[60] Føllesdal, 'Much Ado'.
[61] R. de Lange, 'Judicial Deliberations, Legitimacy and Human Rights Adjudication' in Huls, Adams & Bomhoff (eds.), *Legitimacy of Highest Courts' Rulings* 451, 463.
[62] Stone Sweet, 'Constitutionalisation' 1.

balances between constitutional principles and rights, or the exigencies of the overall political setting and rights protection. An international convention on human rights, no matter how much we squint, is not equivalent to a domestic constitution.

Rather than focusing on Stone Sweet's ducks, then, it might be more useful to conceive of constitutional courts and regional human rights courts as resembling the related Lapiths and centaurs of Greek mythology; while both look the same when viewed from certain angles, a fuller view reveals many glaring dissimilarities.

B   Distinguishing Characteristics of Regional Democratisation Jurisprudence

In considering the distinguishing features of regional democratisation jurisprudence in light of the discussion in Chapter 3, it is evident that it differs significantly from domestic democratisation jurisprudence.

Time

Unlike a domestic constitutional court, which ordinarily can only begin its democratisation jurisprudence after the transition to electoral democracy, a regional human rights court's democratisation jurisprudence will often transcend multiple transition processes and the court will often be required to adjudicate in a regional context containing both democratic and non-democratic states (see Figure 4.1). Unlike the domestic context, a regional court's democratisation jurisprudence is potentially not time-barred; if even one state in the system is under authoritarian rule or in the early decades of a democratisation process, this will affect the court's case-law.

Tempo

Allied to the above, the frequency of a regional human rights court's democratisation jurisprudence will depend on the regional context; in particular, the democratisation trajectories of the states subject to the Court's jurisdiction. For instance, a preponderance of mature democracies, or at least consolidated democracies, in the region subject to the court would lead to a reduced frequency; with the converse also true. It is worthwhile emphasising here, too, that the mission of a regional human rights court and access rules – particularly the requirement to exhaust domestic remedies – mean that there is a considerable time lag in its interventions. It is unlike a human rights commission, for instance, which can address matters almost contemporaneously. An example is

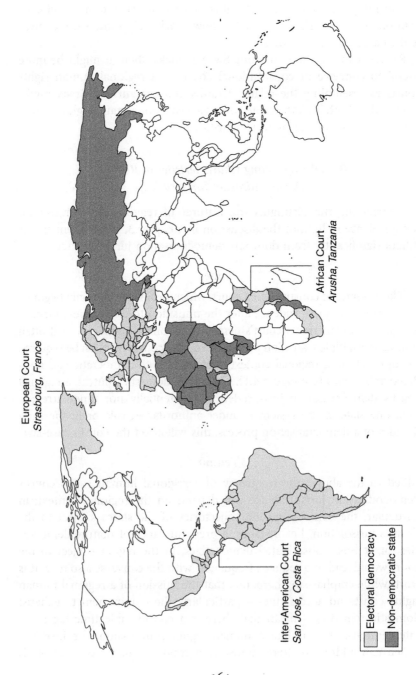

European Court
Strasbourg, France

African Court
Arusha, Tanzania

Inter-American Court
San José, Costa Rica

Electoral democracy

Non-democratic state

European System

Electoral democracies*

1. Albania
2. Andorra
3. Austria
4. Belgium
5. Bosnia-Herzegovina
6. Bulgaria
7. Croatia
8. Cyprus
9. Czech Rep.
10. Denmark
11. Estonia
12. Finland
13. France
14. Georgia
15. Germany
16. Greece
17. Hungary
18. Iceland
19. Ireland
20. Italy
21. Latvia
22. Liechtenstein
23. Lithuania
24. Luxembourg
25. Macedonia
26. Malta
27. Moldova
28. Monaco
29. Montenegro
30. Netherlands
31. Norway
32. Poland
33. Portugal
34. Romania
35. San-Marino
36. Serbia
37. Slovakia
38. Slovenia
39. Spain
40. Sweden
41. Switzerland
42. Turkey
43. Ukraine
44. United Kingdom

Non-democratic states

45. Armenia
46. Azerbaijan
47. Russia

Inter-American System

Electoral democracies

1. Argentina
2. Barbados
3. Bolivia
4. Brazil
5. Chile
6. Colombia
7. Costa Rica
8. Dominican Rep.
9. Ecuador
10. El Salvador
11. Guatemala
12. Honduras
13. Mexico
14. Nicaragua
15. Panama
16. Paraguay
17. Peru
18. Suriname
19. Uruguay

Non-democratic state

20. Haiti

African System

Electoral democracies

1. Benin
2. Comoros
3. Ghana
4. Kenya
5. Lesotho
6. Malawi
7. Mauritius
8. Niger
9. Senegal
10. South Africa
11. Tanzania
12. Tunisia

Non-democratic states

13. Algeria
14. Burkina Faso
15. Burundi
16. Cameroon
17. Chad
18. Congo
19. Côte d'Ivoire
20. Gabon
21. Gambia
22. Libya
23. Mali
24. Mauritania
25. Mozambique
26. Nigeria
27. Rwanda
28. Sahrawi Arab Dem. Rep.*
29. Togo
30. Uganda

* 'Electoral democracies' here are those recognised as such by Freedom House in its 2015 *Freedom in the World* report. See Chapter One.

** As stated in the Introduction, the Sahrawi Arab Democratic Republic (SADR) is not a fully recognised state by the UN and is claimed by Morocco, but is listed as a separate entity in AU statistics.

Figure 4.1 Jurisdictional Territory of Human Rights Courts in 2016

the Inter-American Commission's report on rights protection in Peru, following an on-site visit in 1998, which played a part in Alberto Fujimori's decision to resign as president, having seized power through an *auto-golpe* or self-coup in 1992.[63]

Context

Recalling previous discussion of the constitutional, political, and institutional contexts in which domestic constitutional courts operate, the context faced by a regional human rights court is arguably more complex. The political context involves not only overlapping planes of transformation (e.g. economic, political, legal) at the domestic level, but varying levels and paces of change, across multiple states. Each of the regional human rights courts has jurisdiction over both democratic and non-democratic states (see Figure 4.1). This strongly influences the types of cases that come before each court and, in turn, the shape of its jurisprudence. The mix of regimes drives jurisprudence in certain directions: a preponderance of new democracies in Latin America tends toward closer supervision by the regional court; a mix of mature and new democracies in Europe requires a difficult balancing act; and a majority of undemocratic regimes coupled with a minority of new democracies in Africa places the African Court in a difficult position.

The territorial jurisdiction of the court and the cultural homogeneity of the region is also a factor. The European Court has the most extensive geographic spread, stretching across an extremely diverse set of nations from Iceland to Russia, and with all young democracies in the region party to the system. The Inter-American Court operates in the most homogenous region, being, in essence, a human rights tribunal for Central and South America, with only one non-democratic state (Haiti) under its purview.[64] The African Court has the least contiguous jurisdictional territory. There are essentially two 'state party regions': one comprising a high number of states in the west; the second comprised of a smaller number of states in the south and east of the continent. Together these 'regions' contain young democracies as diverse as South Africa and

---

[63] Rodríguez-Pinzón, 'Inter-American Human Rights System' 256; and Buyse & Hamilton (eds.), *Transitional Jurisprudence and the ECHR* 19.
[64] The Court currently has jurisdiction over twenty of the thirty-five OAS Member States. Some states have ratified the ACHR but not accepted the Court's jurisdiction (e.g. Jamaica), and an important minority, including the United States, Canada, and many Caribbean states, have not ratified the Convention at all. The only Caribbean adherent is Barbados.

Ghana, and a variety of troubled non-democracies, including Burundi and Mali. Between these two regions lies a thick strip of states that have not, to date, accepted the Court's jurisdiction.

Unlike a constitutional court, which is involved in the wholesale construction of the constitutional order, a regional human rights court's role is at once both narrower and broader; addressing solely rights issues in each domestic order, but in the process shaping a region-wide normative system regarding common problems. A constitutional court can tailor its decisions to the domestic context, and can modify its approach as democratisation progresses (or otherwise). By contrast, a regional human rights court must, in its case-law, speak first to the respondent state, but also more widely to a community of twenty or more states. It has, in this way, less room to manoeuvre for taking a deferential approach to the particularities of a given state, lest this set a precedent that would hamper the Court in addressing other states in the future. As Sturgess and Chubb so aptly put it: '[International courts] have to tread a much thinner line through many more places.'[65]

In addition, whereas a domestic constitutional court builds its democratisation jurisprudence in relation to one bounded political community, a regional court has a differential impact across its region, depending on the point at which a new democracy submits to its jurisdiction, the number of cases brought before the court, and the capacity and inclination of civil society actors to use petitions as an avenue for pursuing political reform and justice. The independence and quality of the domestic constitutional court's case-law will also affect the number of petitions brought to the regional level.

In the Latin American context, for instance, a quantitative analysis of the Inter-American Court's case-law reveals that some states have appeared much more regularly before the Court than others. While Peru and Venezuela have had many appearances before the Court (although even Peru's high tally only numbers in the thirties), most states have been before the Court less frequently, with many the subject of a mere handful of merits judgments. While the 'top five' states (Peru, Venezuela, Guatemala, Colombia, and Ecuador) have had cases before the Court fairly consistently over the past two decades or so, a number of states have experienced long periods between appearances (e.g. Haiti, Suriname). The two hegemons of Latin America, Brazil and Mexico, were latecomers

[65] Sturgess & Chubb, *Judging the World* 81.

to the Court, with decisions against them only appearing in the past ten to fifteen years (Brazil in 2002; Mexico in 2008).[66]

At the institutional level, regional human rights courts face both advantages and disadvantages in comparison to domestic constitutional courts. On the one hand, they tend to encounter, if anything, more intense accusations concerning a lack of democratic legitimacy and their separation from any single democratisation process renders it difficult for the court to assess the 'democratisation needs' and particularities of a given state – to 'judge' democratisation, in other words.[67]

On the other hand, being an external actor brings distinct advantages. It allows the court to remain separate from the upheaval found in a new democracy. Unlike a supreme court retained after a democratic transition it is not tainted by prior operation within the non-democratic regime. Also, unlike a domestic court, its externality allows it to transcend the normative straitjacket of a constitutional court, as guardian and constituted power of the constitution. It thus has a freer hand to recommend amendments to the domestic constitution and, crucially, to address dubious constitutional amendment processes under the practice of 'abusive constitutionalism'.

Externality is evidently not immunity from hostile reactions. Regional human rights courts can be vulnerable to damaging institutional shaping, with recurrent challenges to the African and Inter-American courts and the fate of the SADC Tribunal, discussed in Chapter 3, redolent of similar attacks at the domestic level.

Content

Earlier in this chapter we conceptualised the content of domestic democratisation jurisprudence as relating to eight core interrelated strains of activity, across three broad dimensions: development of a democratic public sphere; mediating the shift from an undemocratic to a democratic regime; and the court's carving out a role for itself in the new democratic order. The democratisation jurisprudence of regional human rights courts may also be viewed within these three dimensions.

However, the institutional setting of a regional court fundamentally changes the way in which it approaches these tasks, its capacity to effect

---

[66] This quantitative analysis is based on all decisions of the Court in contentious cases since 1988, listed on its website at www.corteidh.or.cr/index.php/en/jurisprudencia.

[67] See Føllesdal, Peters, Karlsson Schaffer & Ulfstein, Legitimacy; and Huls, Bomhoff & Adams (eds.), Legitimacy of Highest Courts' Rulings.

change on the ground, and the justifications it provides for its role. It does not operate to entrench an entirely new constitutional order, or to act as a central mediator between the old and the new constitutional order in any given state as a domestic court does, but rather to elaborate a pan-regional minimum standard of rights protection. There is no one constitutional order that must be disentrenched, and so the court must mediate a relationship between its international 'bill of rights' and multiple pre-existing authoritarian constitutional orders, which have no direct relationship to the international bill of rights. Unlike a new democratic constitution in a post-authoritarian setting, the human rights convention is not a successor to the old constitution but an external and alternative normative source.

Regarding institution-building, the Court (depending on its vintage) will have to delineate its jurisdiction, decide on its procedure, and negotiate how it views its role in the system, which is dependent on how it views the claims of state sovereignty, its relationship with other bodies (if any) in the system, and its institutional security in the region. Certain doctrinal developments, such as the European Court's margin of appreciation doctrine, can have a significant impact on the Court's jurisprudence, providing greater flexibility as well as inconsistency. The eschewal of such a doctrine by the other courts, in turn, renders it more difficult to provide tailor-made solutions for the various states subject to their jurisdiction.

How a regional court addresses crises – institutional, political, or constitutional – is also important. The European Court's unmanageable workload has been one factor driving its move to 'constitutional' rather than 'individual' justice through the pilot judgment procedure, discussed in Chapter 3. It has also been required to bring considerable political delicacy to bear on the political attacks against its jurisdiction, from states such as the United Kingdom and the Netherlands, in order to retain the authority to tackle problems in young democracies. The Inter-American Court has had to navigate: attempts to escape its jurisdiction in cases before it for judgment (e.g. by Peru in the 1990s[68]); explicit and indirect challenges against its authority by domestic courts (e.g. Vene-zuelan and Brazilian courts); and attempts by political actors to subor-dinate the Inter-American human rights protection system through ostensible reform – a regional variant of the abusive constitutionalism

---

[68] *Ivcher-Bronstein* v. *Peru*, IACtHR (Ser. C) No. 54 (6 February 2001).

seen at the state level.[69] The African Court's unexpectedly strident tone in its first merits judgment in 2013 may be related to the political cowing of the SADC Tribunal and the East African Court of Justice in 2012 – as a more prominent court, there would be a higher political cost in dismantling it.

Methodology

In a similar manner to the drivers of a particular adjudicative methodology at the domestic level, at the regional level human rights courts refer to the jurisprudence of other regional human rights courts and international adjudicative bodies (e.g. the Human Rights Committee, the International Labour Committee) as a 'gap-filling' mechanism to bolster the force of their decisions and as a way of interacting with the wider normative order of international law.[70] As well as space travel, human rights courts in the Inter-American and African systems can also engage in time travel to a limited extent, by drawing on what is often a considerable corpus of decisions by the regional commission on human rights. For example, the Inter-American Court's approach to calibrating deference to national courts might be said to draw from the Inter-American Commission's development of a 'Fourth Instance Formula', which takes into account the independence and impartiality of domestic courts, and the severity and nature of the rights violation, in according some measure of deference.[71]

Regional human rights courts can also refer to international law as a way of reconciling domestic law and the exigencies of international human rights law, and mediating the shift between the old and new legal order while maintaining a thread of legal continuity. An example is *Korbely* v. *Hungary*[72] concerning the prosecution of military officers who took part in quelling the Hungarian uprising of 1956 under a new law passed after the democratic transition. The law was held to be valid only insofar as prosecutions would be based on violation of the prohibition of crimes against humanity in the 1949 Geneva Conventions, which form the core of international humanitarian law, and held to be invalid in

---

[69] See the discussion in Chapter 2.

[70] This is not to suggest that they always agree: Sweeney, *Post-Cold War Era* 108, for example, notes a divergence between the European Court and the Human Rights Committee concerning property restitution schemes in post-Communist Europe.

[71] See Rodríguez-Pinzón, 'Inter-American Human Rights System'.

[72] (2010) 50 EHRR 48.

respect of any prosecutions beyond this limit, which would constitute a law with retroactive effect.[73] Regional human rights courts also draw on domestic constitutional law, sometimes explicitly, such as the European Court's development of a German-style doctrine of 'militant democracy', mentioned in Chapter 3; sometimes more obliquely, such as the Inter-American Court's move toward a US-style doctrine of 'actual malice', which sets a high standard for successful prosecutions for criminal defamation, without citing any US jurisprudence.[74]

C Impact of Design

Like constitutional courts, a number of design factors affect the operation and effectiveness of regional human rights courts.

Membership and Powers

The European Court's forty-seven judges and its institutional configuration of multiple chambers renders its jurisprudence less stable and predictable than the much smaller panels in the Inter-American and African Court (although the institution of the Juriconsult now assists in achieving consistency).[75] The Inter-American Court has made much more significant use of its advisory powers than the other two courts (which are wider than those found in the European system), and has employed its more generously worded reparations power expansively to encompass not just compensation and the amending of domestic law, but also the investigation of crime and symbolic acts such as the erection of monuments (although, as noted in Chapter 3, compliance with orders for investigation is low). In addition, the European Court is the only court fully open to direct individual petitions; individuals may not petition the Inter-American Court directly and such petitions require a state declaration in the African system, which only a small minority of courts have made to date.

---

[73] Sweeney, *Post-Cold War Era* 60–1.
[74] See E. Carter, 'Actual Malice in the Inter-American Court of Human Rights' (2013) 18 *Communication Law and Policy* 395.
[75] J. Fraser, 'Conclusion: The European Convention on Human Rights as a common European endeavour' in S.I. Flogaïtes, T. Zwart & J. Fraser (eds.), *The European Court of Human Rights and its Discontents: Turning Criticism into Strength* (Edward Elgar Publishing, 2013) 199.

The Nature of the Regional Bill of Rights

The human rights conventions in each region also betray significant differences of relevance here. The European Convention on Human Rights, as a creature of its time, focuses almost exclusively on civil and political rights and limits the grounds upon which specific rights can be restricted. Article 17 ECHR, which prohibits abuse of Convention rights to attack or destroy the rights of others, has also proven useful to the Court in a number of cases, allowing it to deny protection to extreme right-wing views, for instance.[76] The American Convention on Human Rights is drafted in the light of bitter experience, for instance, Article 13 not only guarantees freedom of expression and prohibits censorship but also prohibits 'indirect' means of restricting the right; akin to an international echo of the German constitutional court's principle of a 'restriction on restrictions', discussed in Chapter 2. The central African text, the African Charter of Human and Peoples' Rights, contains open-ended 'clawback' clauses (e.g. 'subject to law and order', 'within the law'), which allow states to restrict the Convention rights to the maximum extent permitted by domestic law.

Each text also protects core democratic rights differently. The ECHR (Article 15) permits derogation from *all* rights (except the right to life, prohibition on torture, slavery, and unlawful punishment) and protects a basic right to regular elections in Protocol 1 to the Convention. Article 23 ACHR, by contrast, enshrines a non-derogable broader right to participate in government, including the right to take part in the conduct of public affairs and vote, and emphasises that the Convention does not preclude the recognition of any right 'inherent in the human personality or derived from representative democracy as a form of government' (Article 29). The African Charter (Article 13) similarly guarantees the right of individuals to 'participate freely in the government' of their country. In addition, both the OAS and the AU adopted separate democratic charters in 2001 and 2007 respectively – cited at the start of Chapter 1 – that commit states to a 'thick' form of democracy, including respect for rights, free and fair elections, the separation of powers, and citizen participation in public affairs; the Inter-American Democratic Charter goes as far as recognising a 'right to democracy' (Article 1) and a state obligation to 'promote and defend' democracy.[77]

---

[76] See Sweeney, *Post-Cold War Era* 151.
[77] Inter-American Democratic Charter, 2001; and African Charter on Democracy, Elections and Governance, 2007.

To a certain extent, the institutional differences among these three courts and the lynchpin instruments they interpret are smoothed out by significant cross-fertilisation in their case-law, with each court cherry-picking from the jurisprudence of the other. The Inter-American and African courts' free speech jurisprudence, for instance, draws heavily on European case-law,[78] while the European Court invokes Inter-American case-law on forced disappearances, torture threats, and interim measures,[79] and the African Court has mitigated the impact of 'clawback' clauses by adopting European-style proportionality analysis. In a similar manner to the domestic context, we see the elaboration of another form of *acquis jurisprudentiel*, elaborated and mutually enriched by the court in each region.

We now have a better sense of the different ways in which domestic and regional courts engage in democracy-building through democratisation jurisprudence. How, then, do the courts at both levels interact?

4 How Courts at Each Level Interact

Thus far, we have examined the democracy-building roles of the courts at each level separately. However, it is important to emphasise here that the different strains of democratisation jurisprudence at the domestic and regional levels are inter-linked. The case-law of domestic constitutional courts may be thought to act as a primary source of normativity in the democratisation process, while the jurisprudence of regional human rights courts presents a secondary site of normativity. The latter impacts on the democratisation process and constitutional regime construction in a very different manner, depending on the openness of a given state, legal system, and its constitutional court to regional oversight. In some cases, however, the regional human rights court assumes the place of primary site of normativity; chiefly, where recourse to the domestic constitutional court concerning an alleged violation has been blocked or is not open.

In other words, the majority of the new democratic constitutional order will generally be hammered out on the anvil of domestic court decisions; with the regional human rights court playing a subsidiary and supportive role. However, where domestic reliance on regional case-law

---

[78] See e.g. A. Úbeda de Torres, 'Freedom of Expression under the European Convention on Human Rights: A Comparison with the Inter-American System of Protection of Human Rights' (2003) 10 *Human Rights Brief* 6; and *Konaté* v. *Burkina Faso*.

[79] See European Court of Human Rights, *References to the Inter-American Court of Human Rights in the Case-law of the European Court of Human Rights* (Council of Europe, 2012).

in interpreting the constitutional text is pronounced, or where the domestic court is inaccessible or lacks independence, we see a more intense blurring of the boundaries between the two. As discussed in Chapter 1, at times it can be hard to distinguish international law from constitutional law. Indeed, we might say that, in some domestic decisions we see international law *as* domestic constitutional law.

There is, then, no strict separation of the two bodies of jurisprudence. In contrast to domestic democratisation jurisprudence, regional democratisation jurisprudence might be viewed as impacting in three ways, and is by turns alternative, internal, and external to the core site of domestic case-law (these categories will become clearer in Chapters 5 and 6):

(i) *reception*, whereby the constitutional court, voluntarily, in its own jurisprudence, affirms and applies norms elaborated by the international human rights court in its case-law;

(ii) *imposition*, whereby the regional human rights court holds that a constitutional court decision, which is key to the democratisation process, has failed to vindicate one of the rights in the regional human rights convention, or where it enjoins domestic courts to adhere to its jurisprudence more broadly; and

(iii) *interaction*, whereby divergence in the case-law of a constitutional court and the international human rights court opens a space, a critical arena, of dialogic interaction in which the courts tussle for normative supremacy, or, if possible, seek to reconcile their positions.

A   Inter-Level Interaction as a Coherent System

In existing scholarship the dominant portrayal of the relationship between constitutional courts and regional and human rights courts in new democracies is one based on partnership: a mixture of 'reception' and 'interaction' in the schema above. In Europe, Peter Leuprecht has suggested: 'A fruitful dialogue has developed between the Strasbourg institutions and domestic courts whose respective case law mutually support and enrich each other.'[80]

Scholars in Latin America have begun to go beyond the language of mere 'dialogue' by speaking of constitutional courts and regional human rights courts as a 'structural coupling' transcending their respective spheres

---

[80] Leuprecht, 'Innovations in the European System of Human Rights Protection' 317.

and creating a transnational legal space.[81] Diego Rodríguez-Pinzón sees a 'harmonic resonance' between national courts and the Inter-American Court.[82] Diego García-Sayan, similarly, suggests that the Inter-American Court's jurisprudence has revitalised national judiciaries, strengthened the rule of law in various states, and (implicitly) democracy:

> By accepting international standards and substantive criteria that place the rights of the individual at the forefront, domestic judicial systems are legitimizing and revitalizing their role and, thereby, that of the rule of law as a core value.
>
> . . .
>
> Increasingly, the highest courts of several countries of the region are taking inspiration from the Inter-American Court's jurisprudence and supplementing, in a conceptual manner, their national circumstances with certain developments of the Inter-American Court.[83]

Abramovich notes that 'decisions made by the organs of the [Inter-American] system in a particular case, in interpreting the treaties applicable to the conflict, have a heuristic value that transcends the victims affected in this process'.[84] Certainly, it appears that, since the 1990s, the Court's case-law has provided not only a normative pathway for national courts to follow, legitimising bold decisions which they might otherwise be too timid to hand down, but also a particular adjudicative framework which can be adopted in domestic cases that never reach the Inter-American system. We might characterise this aspect of the Court's case-law as a sort of 'normative ellipsis', as it provides a starting point for national courts but leaves them to fill in the blanks that appear in cases before them. In doing so, it would appear to strengthen the national courts' roles in the consolidation of the democratic constitutional order.

B   Resistance, Inconsistency, and Differential Deference

However, some scholars are more careful in their characterisation. In Europe, Sadurski speaks of CEE courts and the European Court forming

---

[81] See M. Torelly, 'Transnational Legal Process and Constitutional Engagement in Latin America: How do Domestic Constitutional Regimes deal with International Human Rights Law?', Society of Legal Scholars (SLS) Second Graduate Conference on Latin American Law and Policy, St Antony's College, Oxford, 7 March 2014.

[82] Rodríguez-Pinzón, 'Inter-American Human Rights System' 257.

[83] García-Sayan, 'Constitutionalism' 1836–7, 1839.

[84] V. Abramovich, 'From Massive Violations to Structural Patterns: New Approaches and Classic Tensions in the Inter-American Human Rights System' (2009) 11 *SUR – International Journal on Human Rights* 7, 12.

'de facto alliances' to pierce the veil of the state – suggesting that partnership is context- and case-specific.[85] The role of domestic courts in acting as 'gatekeepers' in the reception of international and regional law, and Krisch's presentation of a heterarchical plural legal order in Europe's regional human rights system, discussed at the start of this chapter, come to the fore here. Whereas talk of regional orders as constitutional orders and structural couplings tends to reconceptualise regional judicial communities as something closer to a monist (geographically bounded) 'international law-as-federal order', this picture of frictionless partnership hides much nuance.

Despite a prevailing presentation of harmonious partnership in Latin America, as discussed in Chapter 5, we see significant resistance to the Inter-American Court's jurisprudence in national courts. Alexandra Huneeus has led the way in theorising instances of domestic courts 'rejecting' and 'resisting' the Inter-American Court, suggesting as core explanatory factors: judicial culture and domestic courts' self-perception of the scope of their role; judicial attitudes to regional oversight and a wish to retain the 'final say' in constitutional matters; executive influence (e.g. the case of Venezuela); the overall ideological leanings of the state; the formal status of international law under the constitution; and even familiarity with regional jurisprudence and international law.[86]

Although resistance has at times a highly negative and overt tone – the highest courts of Venezuela and the Dominican Republic calling on their governments to leave the Inter-American Court's jurisdiction being the most alarming examples[87] – it is often subtler. Even in one of the core examples of a 'structural coupling', between the Inter-American Court and the Argentine Supreme Court, which is 'one of its greatest allies in the region',[88] a rhetoric of submission is in fact accompanied by a praxis of inconsistent reception of the Court's case-law.[89] In Chapter 5 we will see that judges at the Federal Supreme Court of Brazil appear to jealously guard their constitutional supremacy, generally avoiding any citation of Inter-American case-law.

---

[85] Sadurski, *Constitutionalism* 1.
[86] See Huneeus, 'Rejecting the Inter-American Court'; and Huneeus, 'Courts Resisting Courts'.
[87] See e.g. Huneeus, 'Courts Resisting Courts' 500.
[88] Huneeus, 'Rejecting the Inter-American Court' 114.
[89] D.A. Gonzalez-Salzberg, 'The Implementation of Decisions from the Inter-American Court of Human Rights in Argentina: An Analysis of the Jurisprudential Swings of the Supreme Court' (2011) 15 *SUR – International Journal of Human Rights* 113.

In the European context, although overt resistance is rare,[90] harmony is also easily overstated. In particular, 'dialogue' between the European Court of Human Rights and domestic constitutional courts appears to be confined to a small number of cases, and is limited to the courts of Germany and the United Kingdom having the confidence to question Strasbourg case-law. These are merely two of the forty-seven constitutional courts subject to the European Court's jurisdiction, and are both located in mature democracies.[91]

Even in Europe's clearest example of a 'structural coupling' between the regional and domestic court it does not appear possible to ensure absolute harmony between regional and national jurisprudence. Turkish constitutional reforms of 2010 introduced a procedure for individual applications to the Turkish Constitutional Court expressly modelled on that of the Strasbourg Court, with the twin aims of the procedure being to ensure effective human-rights protection at the national level and to reduce individual applications to the Strasbourg Court – effectively recasting the Constitutional Court as a form of domestic arm of the Strasbourg system (although one should not push this point too far).

This reform has led to much greater efforts by the Constitutional Court to bring its case-law in line with Strasbourg jurisprudence, on matters such as free speech, military jurisdiction, and fair trial. Yet here also the national court has departed from Strasbourg jurisprudence in matters that have tested the limits of its new liberalism.[92] This is epitomised in its recent judgment refusing, on entirely procedural (and criticised as unconvincing[93]) grounds, to hear an appeal by the families of

---

[90] The starkest expression of resistance in Europe has come from the Federal Constitutional Court of Germany in its *Görgülü* judgment of 14 October 2004 111 BVerfGE 307 (2004), in which the Court indicated that constitutional courts should disregard Strasbourg jurisprudence where it contravenes central elements of the domestic legal order, legislative intent, or the Basic Law, provoking a strong reaction from Strasbourg: See Krisch, *Beyond Constitutionalism* ch. 4.

[91] Gerards & Fleuren (eds.), *Implementation of the European Convention* 71–82.

[92] See e.g. an early analysis of the Court's new approach: Z. Arslan, 'Constitutional Complaint in Turkey: A Cursory Analysis of Essential Decisions', Conference on 'Best Individual Complaint Practices to the Constitutional Courts in Europe', Strasbourg 7 July 2014 www.coe.int/t/dgi/hr-natimplement/Source/echr/Conference_07072014_Speech_Arslan.pdf.

[93] See e.g. *Hürriyet Daily News* 'Top Court Refuses Appeal by Families of Uludere Victims' 26 February 2016 www.hurriyetdailynews.com/top-court-refuses-appeal-by-families-of-uludere-victims-.aspx?pageID=238&nID=95773&NewsCatID=509.

thirty-four individuals wrongfully killed in 2011 by military airstrikes in Uludere (Roboski in the Kurdish language) against the Military Prosecutor's decision not to pursue prosecutions, seemingly in contravention of Strasbourg case-law requiring adequate state action under the Article 2 ECHR right to life.[94]

In Africa, although various constitutions refer to international human rights treaties and the Banjul Charter,[95] reference to African Charter norms by domestic constitutional courts is rare.[96] The African Court has not been in operation long enough, nor has it had the opportunity to issue enough decisions, to allow it to foster a significant relationship with courts at the national level. That said, various African courts (and the Brazilian Supreme Court) evince a certain openness to international jurisprudence *in general*, including an increasing tendency to cite decisions of the European Court of Human Rights.[97]

Differential Deference Based on Democratic Quality

There is an emerging argument from various quarters for differential deference from regional human rights courts to constitutional courts, depending on their democratic credentials. Başak Çalı, for instance, argues that deference is warranted by the European Court of Human Rights to domestic courts, using the margin of appreciation doctrine, where there is more than one reasonable interpretation of Convention rights. However, she suggests that the Court should only accord such deference to 'responsible' domestic constitutional courts with a strong respect for the rule of law and international human-rights norms, and which take Strasbourg jurisprudence seriously in interpreting fundamental rights. She cites by way of support the Strasbourg Court's willingness to accord interpretive discretion to the Federal Constitutional Court of Germany in one case, but not to the Azeri domestic courts in another (although it has to be said the gravity of rights infringement in these cases

---

[94] In particular *McCann* v. *UK* (1996) 21 EHRR (6 October 1995); and *Dink* v. *Turkey*, ECtHR, App. No. 2668/07 (14 September 2010).

[95] Fombad, 'Internationalization' 445ff.   [96] Cole, 'The African Court'.

[97] See M. Killander & H. Adjolohoun, 'International Law and Domestic Human Rights' in Killander (ed.), *International Law*; and T.G. Daly, 'The Differential Openness of Brazil's Supreme Federal Court to External Jurisprudence', International Association of Constitutional Law (IACL) World Congress 2014, Oslo, Norway, 16–20 June 2014 www.jus.uio.no/english/research/news-and-events/events/conferences/2014/wccl-cmdc/wccl/papers/ws5/w5-daly.pdf.

is very different).[98] It is unclear, in her analysis, where other young European democracies and their courts may lie.

Similarly, certain scholars have begun making the case for the adoption of a margin of appreciation doctrine by the Inter-American Court, on the basis that its jurisdictional territory contains some states (e.g. Costa Rica) which have sufficient democratic credentials to be accorded a level of deference in how they order their affairs.[99] It appears to be, like Çali's argument, a case for 'differential deference' from the regional human rights court. Of course, from a regional court's perspective, such an approach would have to be very carefully handled to avoid a hollowing out of its function, or unjustifiable inconsistency in its approach to different states.

It is striking how these emerging positions, focusing on the democratic credentials of states, echo the debates in Europe in 1949 concerning the establishment of a regional human rights court. As discussed in Chapter 3, the argument against such an institution then, as Pierre-Henri Teitgen observed, was that the states to be supervised were 'democratic and ... deeply impregnated with a sense of freedom; they believe in morality and in a natural law' – with the signal difference that the newer debate focuses on institutional interaction between the regional court and domestic courts, and not with the state as a whole. To a certain extent, conflict between the domestic and regional orders is built into the very nature of regional oversight, and the democratic nature of the state will always play a part in calibrating the extent of regional oversight; an approach that, evidently, departs from international law's traditional agnosticism concerning the internal political system of states.[100]

---

[98] B. Çali, 'Domestic Courts and the European Court of Human Rights: Towards Developing Standards of Weak International Judicial Review.' *Opinio Juris* 11 January 2013 www.opiniojuris.org/2013/01/11/domestic-courts-and-the-european-court-of-human-rights-towards-developing-standards-of-weak-international-judicial-review.

[99] Two papers presented at a conference in 2014 devoted themselves to this argument: X. Soley Echeverría, 'The Legitimatory Discourse of Inter-American Constitutional Adjudication'; and S. Hentrei, 'The Conventionality Control of the Inter-American Court of Human Rights as a Manifestation of Complementarity', 'Latin American Constitutionalism: Between Law and Politics', University of Glasgow, 2 July 2014. Both will be published in A. von Bogdandy, E. Ferrer, M. Morales & F. Piovesan (eds.), *Transformative Constitutionalism in Latin America: A New Latin American Ius Commune* (Oxford University Press, forthcoming).

[100] For a general account of how international law has shed this agnosticism, see Thomas Franck's seminal article 'The Emerging Right to Democratic Governance' (1992) 86(1) *Journal of International Law* 46.

Regional jurisprudence finding a violation of the regional bill of rights is often, though not always, an indirect criticism of the failings of the domestic constitutional court, or a recognition of its incapacity to adjudicate. Where the domestic court is unable to assert itself in the democratic order, due to political pressure for instance, the regional court can justify performing a 'back-up' function. It is where the domestic constitutional court enjoys sufficient independence and quality of decision-making that the picture is more problematic; where the regional court might see a hierarchical relationship, the domestic court may see a heterarchical relationship. Indeed, as the Brazilian context in Chapter 5 demonstrates, increasing centrality for the domestic court in a newly democratic political order can render it less, not more, receptive to the sharing of judicial space and constitutional supremacy. The choice between assertive and deferential adjudication at the domestic level has ramifications for case-law at the regional level, and vice versa. Assertive adjudication at both sites can become somewhat of a *zero sum* game, with debate centring on which level should have the final say. However, it may be recalled that in this book the focus is on how this affects the overall effectiveness of courts as democracy-builders.

5   The Wider Context: Adjudication in Three-Dimensional Political Space

The above focus on the binary relationship between the courts at the regional and domestic levels should not blind us to the reality that, even at only the judicial level, the level of interaction between courts is complex. We see domestic courts, in elaborating democratisation jurisprudence, referring to the case-law of not only foreign constitutional courts and the human rights court for their region, but also that of human rights courts in other regions. We see regional human rights courts referring to one another's case-law, and drawing on domestic constitutional case-law. We might therefore characterise democratisation jurisprudence as the product of an epistemic community where norms emanating from courts in both mature and new democracies, as well as those elaborated by regional human rights courts, directly and indirectly influence case-law production at each judicial site.

More widely, as noted in the introduction to this chapter, the elaboration of democratisation jurisprudence does not merely concern the relationships between judicial actors, but also an array of systemic actors at the domestic, regional, and global levels, all of which have an impact on one another's roles. The judicial epistemic community discussed above is thus merely one universe in a relational multiverse, where each judicial actor manages relationships with, and whose action is affected by, non-judicial actors. Kim Lane Scheppele talks of adjudication taking place in a 'three-dimensional political space'.[101] She uses the metaphor to capture a more complex reality than the presentation of domestic and transnational courts' relationships with one another as vertical, and relationships between domestic courts in different states as horizontal:

> Imagine playing chess on a three-dimensional chessboard where a piece from one level can knock out a piece from another or where a particularly important player can escape to another level for safety. Sometimes, moves on one level of the chessboard can be duplicated at other levels only after time passes. Sometimes moves on one level speed the moves on another. Transnational and national courts are both players in the game of transnational constitutionalism, but they do not exist simply in a hierarchical relationship to each other. They are somewhat differently positioned in this three-dimensional space with different sorts of opportunities for maneuver.[102]

While Scheppele employs the metaphor to analyse the shifting and context-specific interrelationship between courts, political actors, and law in the domestic, regional, and global arenas concerning anti-terrorism law, it is useful here as a way of avoiding false binaries (i.e. representing relationships as simply court–court, parliament–court, state–court, and so on).

It is evidently impossible to do justice to the full complexity of the systemic context in which courts operate. However, three basic points may be made, which are of relevance to the role of courts as democracy-builders. First, the potential for clashing interpretations of law at the domestic and regional levels creates a certain opening for national governments to cherry-pick between adherence to international and national law, while claiming fidelity to the rule of law. Second, openness in the domestic court to international law does not always stem from entirely pure motives; in Argentina, for instance, reference to Inter-American jurisprudence has been used as a way to circumvent constitutional provisions impeding government policy preferences, in a context

---

[101] K.L. Scheppele, 'The Constitutional Role of Transnational Courts: Principled Legal ideas in Three-Dimensional Political Space' (2010) 28 *Penn State International Law Review* 451.
[102] Ibid. 452.

where the Supreme Court has yet to shed its experience of successive purges by post-transition presidents.[103] Third, the number of actors on the chessboard, and their relationships to one another, has changed greatly in recent decades. Key here are the shift in governance power from legislatures to executives, and the growing governance role of 'the people'; not as a theoretical entity, but as a living entity endowed with constitutional agency, through mechanisms of direct democracy such as referendums.[104]

The relationship between judicial power, political power, and constituent power has therefore changed dramatically, compared to the post-war context in which the German Constitutional Court carved out its role.

6   Conclusion: Different Roles, Different Impacts

In the Introduction to this book the judicial stand-off between the Supreme Court of Brazil and the Inter-American Court of Human Rights was briefly discussed. This chapter has made the first step toward a deeper understanding of the overall context of that stand-off by conceptualising the divergent roles that constitutional courts and regional human rights courts play in new democracies, the differing levels of impact they tend to have on domestic democratisation processes, the nature of their interaction, and the complexity of the overall systemic context in which they interact. It has sought to underscore the signal difference between the courts at each level, of embeddedness and externality regarding the democratisation process. This fundamentally shapes the courts' roles at each level, their capacity to act as democracy-builders, and their capacity to work in harmony toward that goal. In Chapters 5 and 6 these observations are applied to Brazil as a case-study, which is 'thickened' by introducing comparative material from other jurisdictions in Latin America, Europe, and Africa.

---

[103] Elias, 'Argentina's "Amnesty" Laws' 628–44.
[104] See Tierney, *Constitutional Referendums* ch. 1.

5

Domestic Democratisation Jurisprudence in Action: Brazil Since 1988

In Chapter 4 a conceptual framework was sketched out for analysing the roles of constitutional courts and regional human rights courts as democracy-builders. This chapter and Chapter 6 utilise that framework to analyse the differing impacts of the Federal Supreme Court of Brazil and the Inter-American Court of Human Rights on Brazil's democratisation process, with their divergence concerning Brazil's Amnesty Law of 1979 as a central point of focus. The aim is to provide concrete examples of how courts at each level operate as democracy-builders, how they interact, and how their interaction impacts on the democratisation process. This is then situated within the wider context of the post-war global model for court-centric democratisation. This chapter therefore presents the Brazilian experience as a case-study of domestic democratisation jurisprudence, while Chapter 6 provides a comparison to other states in the regional, Latin American context, and also comparison to the inter-regional context, by reference to developments in Europe and Africa. Together, these two chapters show us how distinct patterns of judicial interaction recur across states and regions, and the involvement of different sites of constitutional authority in key cases before the courts.

1 Purpose and Structure of this Case-Study

This chapter explores domestic democratisation jurisprudence by analysing the Federal Supreme Court of Brazil (hereinafter, the Supreme Court/ the Court) following Brazil's return to democratic rule in 1985. The conceptual framework set out in Chapter 4 should enable us to home in on what it is about the democratisation context that has made jurisprudence in Brazil's new democracy distinctive, as compared to the jurisprudence of a court in a mature democracy. First, the impact of the constitutional, political, and institutional contexts on the court's role as a democracy-builder are discussed. Highlighted here are the path-dependent effects of Brazil's democratic constitution of 1988; a political context since 1988 marked by a difficult economic transition, a constitutional crisis, and a desire for efficient governance; and the Court's evolving view of its role in the new order, partly in reaction to institutional shaping by the political branches. Second, core examples from the Court's democratisation jurisprudence since 1988 are analysed, to reveal its nature as a creature of time, tempo, context, content, and methodology. The overall aim is to illuminate the way in which a constitutional court acts as a democracy-builder from within the state, before moving to discussion of external regional adjudication in Chapter 6.

2 Constitutional, Political, and Institutional Contexts

The constitutional, political, and institutional contexts in which a court in a new democracy operates, discussed separately in Chapter 4, are addressed together here, revealing the ways in which they impact one another and have combined effects on the court's role.[1]

First, a word about the overall context of Brazil's transition to democracy in 1985. Brazil, like other new democracies of the third wave era, across world regions, defies neat post-war narratives of total rupture between the old and new orders. The state has a complex relationship with democracy and constitutionalism, having oscillated between democratic and authoritarian rule throughout the twentieth century. Oligarchic government during the First Republic (1889–1930) was displaced by revolution ushering in the Second Republic (1930–1937) and a new Constitution of 1934, followed by a *coup d'état* leading to President Getúlio Vargas' semi-fascist 'New State' (*Estado Nôvo*) (1930–1945) and his personal 'grant' of a new Constitution of 1937. The political trajectory of the state blurred the lines between democratic government and authoritarianism. Vargas was initially accorded the presidency by the military following the *coup*, ruling as dictator from 1937–1945, but governed again as a constitutionally elected president in the early 1950s (1951–1954)[2] during the fragile democratic period of 1945–1964, which brought another Constitution in 1946.

---

[1] I am grateful, in completing this section, to Virgílio Afonso da Silva, who gave me advance sight of the first two chapters of his forthcoming book, *The Constitution of Brazil: A Contextual Analysis* (Hart Publishing, forthcoming).

[2] See E. Bradford Burns, *A History of Brazil* (3rd edn, Columbia University Press, 1993) 346–7.

A further *coup* by the military in 1964, to combat what was viewed as encroaching Communist subversion, led to two decades of direct military rule and systematic repression that left 10,000 Brazilian citizens in a form of exile, over 500,000 individuals 'arrested, banished, exiled, removed from public office, forced into retirement, prosecuted or indicted,'[3] almost 500 killed,[4] and hundreds 'disappeared' by the regime.[5] Two authoritarian constitutions, adopted in 1967 and 1969, wrote repression into the supreme law while seeking to maintain an outward appearance of democratic rule.[6] Political 'opening' (*abertura*), beginning in 1974, initiated a markedly slow transition to civilian rule managed at all times by the military,[7] and underpinned in particular by a broad amnesty in the spirit of reconciliation – the Amnesty Law of 1979. With the adoption of the new democratic Constitution of 1988, the Brazilian republic had enacted no less than seven constitutions during its history.[8]

A   New Democratic Constitution of 1988

The democratic constitution of 1988 was a new departure for Brazilian constitutional law, and would have profound effects on the Supreme Court's democracy-building function. Representing a strong reaction against the historical and immediate experience of authoritarian rule, entrenched inequality, and social injustice, the text lies squarely in the slipstream of the post-war 'new constitutionalism' discussed in Chapter 2, with a strong emphasis on human dignity (one of the constitution's fundamental principles), democratic rule, and a vast raft of fundamental rights, including a range of social and economic rights (although the text is silent as to whether they are justiciable). In addition, a number of 'eternity clauses' (*cláusulas pétreas*) prohibit amendment of constitutional

---

[3] G. Mezarobba, 'Between Reparations, Half Truths and Impunity: The Difficult Break with the Legacy of the Dictatorship in Brazil' (2010) 13 *SUR – International Journal on Human Rights* 7, 10.

[4] D. Politi, 'Uncomfortable Truths' *New York Times* 28 September 2012 http://latitude .blogs.nytimes.com/2012/09/28/brazils-truth-commission-gets-to-work/?_r=0.

[5] Mezarobba, 'Between Reparations' 14.

[6] The 1969 Constitution, although technically an amendment significantly enhancing the repressive character of the 1967 Constitution, was a new constitution in all but name.

[7] See, for example, N. Schneider, 'Impunity in Post-Authoritarian Brazil: The Supreme Court's Recent Verdict on the Amnesty Law' (2011) 90 *European Review of Latin American and Caribbean Studies* 39, 40–1.

[8] 1891, 1934, 1937, 1946, 1967, 1969, and 1988.

provisions on rights, the federative form of the state, direct, secret, universal, and periodic voting, and the separation of powers.

Due to various factors, including a maximalist drafting approach by Congress, a political context in which constitutional negotiations lacked 'any sort of political trust and credibility', and the radically different ideological backgrounds of the framers (especially concerning economic and fiscal matters), the text constitutionalises a vast array of matters that ordinarily would be left to legislation, 'hard-wires' certain policy preferences into the Constitution to remove them from the political arena, and contains significant internal contradictions.[9] The resulting text, with its 'open texture, programmatic norms and indeterminate provisions',[10] 'trivial details and unaffordable promises',[11] and dependence on ordinary legislation to put many of its provisions into effect, not only constitutionalised politics, but also set the scene for the 'judicialisation of politics'.[12] It is a good example of the 'incremental constitutionalism' discussed in Chapters 1 and 3. The constitutional pact, while seeking to bind all negotiators into the future with thick constraints, fudged a range of matters and left difficult issues to be resolved by the Supreme Court, as a secondary 'constituting' force of the new democratic order.

B   Tensions Generated by Institutional Continuity

Despite the language of rupture surrounding the Constitution's drafting, there was significant political and institutional continuity between the old and new orders: the presidential system was retained; the first president after the 1985 elections was elected by the same electoral college that had installed previous military presidents;[13] and the option of a new

---

[9] See L.J. Alston, M.A. Melo, B. Mueller & C. Pereira, 'On the Road to Good Governance: Recovering from Economic and Political Shocks in Brazil' in E. Stein, M. Tommasi, C.G. Scartascini & P.T. Spiller (eds.), *Policymaking in Latin America: How Politics Shapes Policies* (Inter-American Development Bank, 2008) 119.

[10] L. Prado Verbicaro, 'Um Estudo Sobre as Condições Facilitadoras da Judicialização da Política no Brasil' (2008) 4 *Revista Direito GV* 389, 390.

[11] A. Zimmermann, 'Constitutions without Constitutionalism: The Failure of Constitutionalism in Brazil' in M. Sellers & T. Tomaszewski (eds.), *The Rule of Law in Comparative Perspective* (Springer, 2010) 137.

[12] Prado Verbicaro, 'Um Estudo'.

[13] The first president elected from the opposition in 1985, Tancredo Neves, died before taking office and the presidency was assumed by Jose Sarney, the vice-president and previously head of one of the two approved military parties, who had formed a dissident political party during the democratic transition. Nervo Codato (ed.), *Transition and Consolidation* 1.

Kelsenian constitutional court was eschewed in favour of retaining the existing Supreme Court. That said, the Court's institutional place and powers were transformed. Its previously broad jurisdiction was reduced to mainly constitutional matters.[14] Its review powers were enhanced by expanding access to an existing abstract review mechanism (the direct action of unconstitutionality, or ADI) from the Attorney General alone to a broad range of actors, including the President, Congress, state legislative assemblies, governors, political parties with congressional representation, and the federal Bar Association. Having been an American-style supreme court for almost a century, the Court was remade as something that looked much closer to a Kelsenian court. However, its work remained dominated by its appellate function and, for individuals, the only access to the Court remained by appeal from the lower courts.

The Court's overall role under the new dispensation was a characteristically onerous one, emblematic of the expectations placed on constitutional courts in new democracies of the third wave era. The Court was expected to protect the gains of the new democratic order

> against any possible re-emergence of authoritarianism by upholding the Constitution and its principles [and to] embody this democratic reaction against the authoritarian past by strengthening and enforcing the democratic Constitution.[15]

The Court had never enjoyed such centrality in the constitutional order. It had previously enjoyed some 'political prominence' and periods of fertile jurisprudence during the First Republic (1889–1930), and a minority of judges had displayed 'moral courage' during the military dictatorship of the 1960s before being brought to heel through a concerted campaign of intimidation, forced retirement of critical judges and court packing.[16] However, it had been reduced to a peripheral state organ by the mid-1980s before the 1988 Constitution pushed it firmly into the limelight, amplifying its role at the centre of the constitutional order as 'guardian of the Constitution'.[17]

The retention of the basic presidential framework that had existed under the old constitution (and all constitutions since the republican

---

[14] A Superior Court of Justice was also established by the 1988 Constitution to operate alongside a top tier of pre-existing military, labour, and electoral courts.
[15] J. Zaiden Benvindo, *On the Limits of Constitutional Adjudication: Deconstructing Balancing and Judicial Activism* (Springer, 2010) 92
[16] K. Rosenn, 'Separation of Powers in Brazil' (2009) 7 *Duquesne Law Review* 839, 845.
[17] Article 102, Federal Constitution of 1988.

constitution of 1891) tended toward a continuity of modalities of governance and of institutional form, which, coupled with the new powers granted to the Court, had the clear potential to bring the executive and judicial powers into conflict. The constitutions enacted under military rule had maintained the appearance of a separation of powers while heavily centralising power in the executive, allowing the military executive a free rein to pursue policy preferences and to shape the social and economic orders through decree-laws.[18] In a similar manner to the 'authoritarian' tendencies of administrative organs, discussed in Chapter 4, governance in Brazil under military rule prized efficiency and effectiveness over competing values that would render governance more difficult; such as rights protection, deliberation among the representative organs, transparency, and constitutional control by the judiciary. At root, the military had based their claims to rule on their being the sole state organ with the capacity to achieve progress in an ungovernable state; making much, for instance, of the 'economic miracle' (milagre econômico) their policies had produced in Brazil in the period 1969–1973.[19]

The new civilian governments after the transition to democracy in 1985 were faced with difficult economic straits and high expectations among the population for greater prosperity as well as greater freedom. Yet, the unwieldy 1988 Constitution quickly came to be viewed, in political circles, as a poor co-ordinating device for effective governance, with amendment of the long provisions on economic and fiscal matters becoming a 'major orientation' in order to achieve the aim of effecting a full transition to a free market economy.[20] In this context of economic, political, and social transformation, and the pressing need for clarification of the outsized and rights-heavy constitutional text and the constitutional boundaries between the branches of government, political actors were strongly incentivised to bring actions before the Court, although it took considerable time for civil society to 'discover' the Court – the Court's public profile was rather low for its first fifteen years in particular.[21]

---

[18] See Rosenn, 'Separation' 849.

[19] See e.g. T.E. Skidmore, The Politics of Military Rule in Brazil, 1964–85 (Ebsco Publishing, 1988) 110.

[20] C. Hübner Mendes, 'Judicial Review of Constitutional Amendments in the Brazilian Supreme Court' (2005) 17 Florida Journal of International Law 449, 453.

[21] See V.A. da Silva, 'Discovering the Court: Or How Rights Awareness Puts the Brazilian Supreme Court in the Spotlight' (2012) 1 This Century's Review 16.

From the outset the Court evinced caution and restraint concerning its new status and powers, stuck between its previous identity as a 'judicial' supreme court and its new form modelled on the more 'political' Kelsenian courts of Europe. It therefore generally avoided actions that might bring it into major conflict with the other branches. Characterising constitutional norms as having differing levels of 'efficacy', the Court was often able to transfer constitutional disputes back to the legislature.[22] Unlike the Hungarian Constitutional Court's energetic and expansive use in the early 1990s of its power to addressed legislative omission (before it fell out of favour with the judges),[23] the Brazilian Supreme Court took a relatively cautious approach to its new power to address legislative omission, keeping to simple declarations that legislation was required to give effect to a constitutional provision.[24] Overall, it played a 'limited' role in rights adjudication until the late 1990s.[25]

Kapiszewski attributes the Court's general restraint to its institutional security and stability: a long history; no judicial purges since well before democratisation; meaningful guarantees of tenure and judicial independence; autonomy regarding budgetary matters; procedural continuity through the change of regime; and a sense of the institution as separate from individual judges.[26] Others have suggested that the legacy of its suppression under military rule simply left the Court ill-equipped to fulfil its much more expansive role under the new Constitution.[27] The Court's unmanageable docket, due largely to the absence of *stare decisis* and docket-control powers, must have also played a part – it exploded from under 10,000 annual cases before 1988 to approximately 100,000 cases a

---

[22] See A. Reis Freire, 'Evolution of Constitutional Interpretation in Brazil and the Employment of a Balancing "Method" by Brazilian Supreme Court in Judicial Review', VIIth IACL World Congress, Athens, Greece, 2007 www.academia.edu/8306512/Evolution_of_Constitutional_Interpretation_in_Brazil_and_the_Employment_of_Balancing_Method_by_Brazilian_Supreme_Court_in_Judicial_Review.

[23] Sadurski, *Rights Before Courts* 19.

[24] D. Kapiszewski, 'How Courts Work: Institutions, Culture and the Brazilian *Supremo Tribunal Federal*' in J. Couso, A. Huneeus & R. Sieder (eds.), *Cultures of Legality* 72–3. This is not a criticism of the Court, whose approach appeared faithful to Article 103 § 2: 'Whenever there is a declaration of unconstitutionality because measures to make a constitutional rule effective are lacking, the appropriate Branch shall be notified to adopt the necessary measures.'

[25] Ibid. 171–2.

[26] Ibid 61ff. Kapiszewski also adds a professional ethos of collegiality as a significant factor, but this is strongly disputed by Virgílio Afonso da Silva, see e.g. 'Deciding without Deliberating'.

[27] Zaiden Benvindo, *On the Limits* 92ff.

year by the mid-1990s. The Court even had, for a time, a drive-through window in the basement to process case filing.[28]

C 'Judicial Activation': How the Court was Pushed into a More Central Role

In many ways, the inflated constitution appeared to impede, rather than facilitate, the Court's capacity to act as a democracy-builder. Vilhena Vieira, for instance, suggests that after an initial period of harmonising the pre-existing legal order with the standards in the new Constitution, from the early 1990s to the early 2000s the Court expended significant energy tackling questions concerning economic governance and reform.[29] It was forced to squander precious institutional capital on assertive decisions that did little to address the key pathologies of the nascent democratic order. For instance, the Court's suspension of various aspects of pension reform legislation in 1999, due to the law's negative impact on the pension entitlements of retired public servants, was a 'serious blow' to the government's compliance with budget targets agreed with the International Monetary Fund (IMF).[30]

However, such upsets were rare. Due to a perception of the Supreme Court as a safer pair of hands, successive executives sought to quell activism in the lower courts by diminishing the importance of diffuse review and amplifying the Supreme Court's review powers.[31] Changes to the Court's institutional machinery introduced by constitutional reform in 1993, legislation in 1999, and further constitutional reform in 2004, progressively expanded the competences of the Court: adding two new mechanisms for abstract review to expand the Court's oversight role; permitting the Court to hold public hearings where clarification is required concerning complex matters, and to modulate the effect of findings of unconstitutionality;[32] as well as amplifying the binding nature of the Court's decisions. Along with a significant change in membership in the early 2000s, the general effect was to push the Court to assume a

---

[28] Kapiszewski, 'How Courts Work' 58.

[29] O. Vilhena Vieira, 'Descriptive Overview of the Brazilian Constitution and Supreme Court' in Vilhena Vilheira, Viljoen & Baxi, *Transformative Constitutionalism* 98–100.

[30] D. Kapiszewski, 'Power Broker, Policy Maker, or Rights Adjudicator? The Brazilian *Supremo Tribunal Federal* in Transition' in Helmke & Ríos-Figueroa (eds.), *Courts in Latin America* 159.

[31] Zaiden Benvindo, *On the Limits* 95–108.   [32] Law 9.868/99.

more generally assertive role.[33] In recent years Brazilian scholars such as Oscar Vilhena Vieira have begun warning of the perils of 'supremocracy', with the Court enjoying supremacy vis-à-vis not only other courts, but also against other branches of government.[34]

This is a far cry from the common discussion of the judicialisation of politics through a simple narrative of self-empowerment, discussed in the Introduction to this book. In place of so-called judicial activism, we see what might be termed judicial *activation*. As we will see in the case-law analysis below, significant conflict within the Court surrounded the precise role the Court should play in the new order, and whether its new institutional form as a quasi-Kelsenian court changed its role. This clearly impacted not only on the Court's role in supporting democratisation, but also on the connected task of mediating its own place in the democratising order.

3   The Supreme Court's Democratisation Jurisprudence

A   *Key Points for Navigating the Case-Law*

Examining Brazilian Supreme Court jurisprudence in terms of time, tempo, context, content, and methodology, it is clear that the first twenty years of the Court's operation (1988–2008) constitute a fertile ground for the sort of democratisation jurisprudence we would expect to find – although, as we will see, the Supreme Court, for a number of reasons, is still grappling with issues related to the democratisation process close to the thirty-year mark. Indeed, the Court's case-law since 1988 mirrors, in many ways, the German Constitutional Court's post-war case-law explored in Chapter 2, with the constitutional status and validity of authoritarian-era laws, vindication of core civil liberties, fundamental separation of powers issues, and shaping of the electoral system all relating to the creation of a democratic public sphere and mediating the shift from the old to the new democratic order. Recalling Sadurski's conclusion, cited in Chapter 2, that the case-law of constitutional courts in the CEE region has been a mixture of democracy-enhancing and democracy-hindering decisions, we will see that the same can be said of the Brazilian Court.

---

[33] Zaiden Benvindo, *On the Limits* 95–108.
[34] See O. Vilhena Vieira, 'Supremocracia' (2009) 8 *Revista Direito GV* 441 (2009).

The context and content of each decision are inescapably intertwined. With the overall context faced by the Court, sketched above, in mind, the case-law analysis below focuses on the specific context of each case discussed, in order to divine more clearly the fundamental drivers of assertive and deferential decisions. The democratisation context tends to recalibrate how a court approaches certain questions, and how it views its role at different points. We also get a sense from the case-law below of the way in which democratisation cases drive particular methodologies, to fill gaps and provide a justificatory basis for assertive decisions by situating decisions within a transnational *acquis jurisprudentiel*, as discussed in Chapter 4.

As considered in the Introduction, a number of features make the Supreme Court a useful case-study: the Court's odd position after 1988 between a traditional 'American-style' supreme court and a Kelsenian constitutional court; the way in which it reveals the greater burden placed on the court as a democracy-builder under the global post-war model of court-centric democratisation; and the Supreme Court's *seriatim* decision-making procedure, where one judge prepares an initial 'report' and the other judges vote individually in a public session without prior consultation or knowledge of the rapporteur-judge's opinion, which provides insights into contestation within the Court as to its role as a democracy-builder. We will see below that it is not possible to talk of a majority judgment, or *per curiam* decision, beyond majority votes for the specific decision in the case.

Reinforcing the observations above regarding the role of political branches in pushing the Court to assume a more central role, the case-study below further underscores the limited explanatory power of the language of judicial activism and judicial restraint. By contrast, scholars of the Brazilian Supreme Court make a fundamental distinction between *consequencialista* and *legalista* judges. The former, often with more experience in politics, tend to be more open to factoring in the political or economic consequences of their decisions, and can be more supportive of the Court's role in addressing political questions. The latter evince a tendency to focus on narrower legal-constitutional considerations in their judgments but, by holding firmer to the constitutional text, can show a greater willingness to invalidate legislation.[35]

---

[35] See Kapiszewski, 'How Courts Work' 64; and F. Luci Oliveira, 'Justice, Professionalism, and Politics in the Exercise of Judicial Review by Brazil's Supreme Court' (2008) 2(2) *Brazilian Political Science Review* 93, 107–8.

For reasons of narrative coherence, the sections below address the Court's mediation of the shift from an undemocratic to a democratic order first, before considering its shaping of a democratic public sphere, while acknowledging that these dimensions are interlinked. The section ends with discussion of the *Amnesty Law Case* of 2010, and finally a discussion of the key insights we can draw from the way in which the Court has carved out a role for itself since 1988. This will provide a good basis for comparison with the Inter-American Court's engagement with Brazil's democratisation process in Chapter 6.

B   Mediating the Shift from an Undemocratic to a Democratic Order

Mediating the shift from the old to the new order is a complex task for any constitutional court in a new democracy. The new democratic constitution may add new rights, innovations such as eternity clauses, and stronger review powers for a court as a central organ. However, in other respects the constitutional text may not depart radically from its predecessor. Elements of continuity are seen in the shift from authoritarian to democratic regimes across the world; even the shift from totalitarian rule in post-Communist Eurasia. In this sense, formal legal rupture with the previous regime is never total. This challenge is discussed with reference to two key judgments: the *Provisional Measures Case*, decided in 1990,[36] and the *Prior Laws Case*,[37] decided in 1992.

Provisional Measures Case

The *Provisional Measures Case* concerned new rules in the 1988 Constitution aimed at restricting presidential law-making to exceptional cases. As discussed above, a key pathology of Brazilian governance under authoritarian rule had been the use of presidential decree-laws as the central law-making process.[38] The new text therefore concentrated virtually all legislative power in Congress. The president's power to issue 'delegated laws' (something akin to a decree-law) was subjected to congressional permission, and the issuance of 'provisional measures' by the president was permitted solely in cases of 'relevance and urgency'. While the use of delegated laws quickly fell away under the new constitutional regime, they were simply replaced by use of the provisional measures, in

---

[36] ADI 293 (6 June 1990).   [37] ADI 2-1 (6 February 1992).
[38] Rosenn, 'Separation' 848–9.

a context where the new constitutional arrangements appeared to render governance significantly more difficult,[39] and the ordinary legislative process in Congress proved unduly ponderous.[40] The president was required to submit such measures immediately to Congress, which had to decide on their conversion into law within thirty days, failing which the measure was to be deemed null and void *ab initio*.[41] This inverted the rules under the authoritarian constitution of 1969, which had characterised congressional silence as approval of the president's law-making power. However, the Constitution did not address whether the reissuance of a provisional measure, which had not been converted into law, was permitted.

In 1990 the Prosecutor General mounted a constitutional challenge against President Collor's issuance of a provisional measure that differed little in substance from a previous measure, one day after its explicit rejection by Congress. The president's action, he contended, struck not only at the separation of powers principle at the heart of the Constitution, essential to a democratic state based on the rule of law and 'democratic normality',[42] but also at respect for the Supreme Court's decisions, given that the Court had already asserted in 1989 the power to review use of the mechanism for manifest abuse.[43] The stakes were high: the provisional measure formed part of President Collor's plan to address an acute economic crisis.

Despite the pressing political context, in a unanimous decision the Supreme Court, having confirmed that there was little material difference between the two measures, held that the reissuance of a provisional measure rejected by Congress was impermissible. The rapporteur-judge Justice Celso de Mello emphasised that the formal controls on the president's powers in this area had been established to prevent the indiscriminate use, and possible abuse, of this 'exceptional power' from usurping the ordinary legislative process, in a new constitutional environment where the principle of separation of powers formed one of the 'nuclei' of the Constitution and in which the executive's powers were 'defined and limited'.[44] To allow the reissuance of rejected provisional measures, with cosmetic modifications, would 'rupture' the harmonious relationship between the powers envisaged in the Constitution.[45] Various judges pointed to the unappealing

---

[39] Ibid. 856.   [40] da Silva, *Constitution of Brazil*, ch 2.   [41] Ibid. 857.
[42] ADI 293 (6 June 1990). Report of the rapporteur-judge (*relatório*) 14.
[43] ADI/MC 162 (14 December 1989); see Rosenn, 'Separation' 858.
[44] ADI 293 (6 June 1990) 44–5.   [45] Ibid. 45.

vista presented by allowing the executive to disregard the legislature's clear role in policing the validity of provisional measures. It would, they opined, entail substitution of the plural organisation of political power for the 'monocracy of the sole legislator, long banned by the free society that has emerged from modern civilization', and even suspension of the Constitution itself.[46] As the President of the Court put it:

> The understanding that the executive power . . . can instantly reissue an interim measure rejected by Congress, would have the consequence of maintaining indefinitely a norm with the force of law, even against the will of the majority of Congress, expressed in its deliberations which rejected the previous interim measure. Such an understanding is in open conflict with the precepts of the Constitution that define the exercise of legislative power . . . and which call for the independence and harmony of the Powers of the Union, of the fundamental principles of the Republic and the basis of the democratic order.[47]

The decision is thus marked by strong entrenchment language, emphasising the exalted status of the constitution in the new democratic order. In their opinions the judges repeatedly affirmed the supremacy of the Constitution and the necessity to 'unconditionally respect'[48] the constitutional framework for exercising state power. Alluding to the context of economic crisis in which the case had arisen, Justice Brossard stated 'the Constitution is not merely an ornament to be displayed on quiet and mild days', refuting the 'false dilemma' between allowing the president to freely issue provisional measures, or 'chaos'. Insisting that the president had many other means to address the crisis, he denied that the 'routine' action of requiring the president to respect the constitutional framework could be painted as an institutional crisis.[49]

Prior Laws Case

In the *Provisional Measures* case, the Court was faced with a relatively neat question and a clear constitutional provision. In the *Prior Laws Case*, decided two years later, the Court was required to address the much more difficult question of how to address laws enacted before promulgation of the 1988 Constitution – a question with special significance for the status of authoritarian-era laws in the new constitutional order.[50] As suggested

---

[46] Ibid., Justice Borja, 69, 62.   [47] Ibid. Justice da Silveira, 82.   [48] Ibid 43.
[49] Ibid. 63–4.
[50] Of course, the question also related to the status of laws from more democratic periods, such as 1946–1964.

in Chapter 4, the elimination of such laws, which are incompatible with the new democratic constitution, appears central to a successful democratisation process. Where the other branches of government are sluggish in repealing such laws – as discussed in the Italian and Hungarian contexts in Chapter 2 – the role of the constitutional court takes centre stage.

The question came before the Supreme Court when a teachers' union challenged by a Direct Action of Unconstitutionality (ADI) various regulations on school fees contained in two decree-laws dating from 1969 and 1988, as inapplicable due to their incompatibility with the new Constitution. Effectively, the Court was being asked to use the new ADI mechanism for constitutional control under the 1988 Constitution to address the constitutionality of laws enacted under a previous constitutional text. This question was of particularly acute significance in the Brazilian context. The military juntas that had ruled from 1964 to 1985 had never outwardly discarded their fidelity to constitutionalism, seeking at all times to achieve their ends through constitutional and ordinary enactments:

> In this respect, the methods of military rule in Brazil more closely resembled those of South Africa's apartheid than of Argentina's Dirty War, in the singular degree to which the rulers' most repressive policies were publicly promulgated as positive law.[51]

With the 1988 Constitution silent regarding the status of such laws, the State argued, on the basis of longstanding academic and judicial doctrine in Brazil, based on the views of Hans Kelsen, that the ADI mechanism was not an appropriate avenue to challenge such laws given that 'unconstitutionality' refers solely to laws enacted after promulgation of the contemporary Constitution. Laws enacted prior to the new constitution could be subject solely to 'revocation'.[52]

The implications of each position were clear. Allowing the ADI mechanism to be used to challenge pre-1988 laws would facilitate a quick bonfire of the military regime's legislative legacy, especially given that decisions in ADI actions were binding *erga omnes*, unlike appeal decisions, which had solely *inter partes* effects. Denying use of ADI actions would require applicants to first challenge laws before the ordinary

---

[51] See M.J. Osiel, 'Dialogue with Dictators: Judicial Resistance in Argentina and Brazil' (1995) 20 *Law and Social Inquiry* 481, 528.

[52] ADI 293 (6 June 1990) 6.

courts, with a slow appeals process to the Supreme Court to obtain a definitive judgment on the matter. The votes presented two diametrically opposed approaches: that of the rapporteur-judge, Justice Paulo Brossard; and that of Justice Sepúlveda Pertence.[53]

Justice Brossard, siding with the State's argument, and placing heavy reliance on the Court's established case-law on the subject and key Brazilian scholarship, argued that because the ADI mechanism is directed at unconstitutionality it could not be used to challenge legislation enacted under the military government.[54] His judgment, throughout, appeared to emphasise continuity: continuity with the established case-law of the Court; and legal continuity, as far as possible, with the previous regime. As in previous periods of constitutional transformation in Brazil's history – the 1930s, 1940s, and 1960s – the Court could only assess old laws on appeal from the lower courts, and would revoke them only where incompatibility with the new constitution was manifest.

Justice Pertence's analysis provided a striking counterpoint, going to great lengths to argue for a departure from the Court's previous jurisprudence. The methodology pursued by each judge comes to the fore here. Where Justice Brossard's judgment looked backwards, mining the Court's previous jurisprudence for the solution to the question, Justice Pertence looked outwards, with a far-reaching comparative review of post-war European thought on how best to address the legislative legacy of authoritarian, fascist, and Nazi rule.[55] Focusing in particular on the post-war democracies of Italy and Germany, and Brazil's sister-democracies of the third wave of democratisation, Spain and Portugal, his brief *tour d'horizon* stressed that the newly established constitutional courts in each country had adopted a pragmatic, systematic, and effective approach to addressing authoritarian laws, relying mainly on concentrated constitutional control.[56]

While recognising that the mixed Brazilian system of diffuse and concentrated constitutional control (which allows ordinary judges to address the constitutionality of laws) complicated the task, Justice Pertence proffered an alternative solution to allow the ADI mechanism to be employed to challenge a pre-1988 law. The Court could follow a doctrine

---

[53] The other judges, almost without exception, simply voted with Justice Brossard or Justice Pertence.

[54] ADI 293 (6 June 1990) 9–21.   [55] Ibid. See 84–108 in particular.

[56] See e.g. his reference to the 'markedly pragmatic solution of Spanish constitutional jurisprudence', 89.

of 'qualified revocation', permitting such a law to be invalidated from the date of the Constitution's promulgation. His opinion squarely addressed the fact that Justice Brossard's approach would impede the entrenchment of the new Constitution and the disentrenchment of the previous constitutional-legal order:

> [This] leaves, in consequence, the disentangling of controversies to fluctuate, for years, based on disagreements between judges and courts throughout the country, until they come, if they come, before [the Supreme Court], after a long trek through the often tortuous system of appeals. Moreover, nor will the decision of the Supreme Court, devoid of binding force *erga omnes* [in appeals cases under diffuse review], settle these contradictions. With all of this, inevitably, not only the speed, but the uniformity of the judicial task of ensuring conformity of the old law to the new guidelines of the Basic Law will be lost, with patent damage to jurisdictional effectiveness and legal certainty ... [And] would unnecessarily delay the imposition of the superior norm.[57]

He underlined the nature of the new constitution and the break it presented from the previous order through the exercise of constituent power:

> the 1988 Constitution is the result of a rupture from the previous order, effected by [law] EC/85 which, by altering the constitutional revision procedure of the 1969 Constitution, invested the National Congress with the powers of a constituent assembly to vote on a *new* constitution, which could hardly be legally reduced to a simple reform of the previous constitution.[58]

This focus on discontinuity rather than continuity is perhaps the touchstone of the entire judgment. Emphasising the rupture effected by the new constitution, he cast aside the fig-leaf of constitutional adjudication as apolitical in arguing for an approach that would ensure the 'effectiveness' of the Constitution, a watchword throughout the judgment:

> I am aware ... that the option, which the problem imposes, is not only technical. It is high constitutional politics: accepting the reasonableness of the various legal solutions presented, the choice among them by a court like this is to guide oneself towards that which appears to be the most appropriate to ensure the effectiveness of the Constitution, which is the fundamental commitment of this House.

[57] Ibid. 83   [58] Ibid. 98–9.

> Moreover, nor is it new to recognise straightforwardly that the disentangling of the matter cannot dispense with consideration of the consequences of each alternative as regards the efficiency and quality of the control of the legitimacy of laws.[59]

The majority of the Court, however, voted in favour of Justice Brossard's traditional technical approach. As two Brazilian scholars have noted: 'Because of this technicality, a large set of laws enacted prior to the Constitution of 1988 are immune from direct constitutional review'.[60] The Court's decision led to growing calls in subsequent years for a new constitutional action to be established for challenging pre-1988 laws before the Court, culminating in the introduction, in 1999, of the Petition for Non-compliance with a Fundamental Precept (*Arguição de descumprimento de preceito fundamental*; or ADPF), which permits review of the constitutionality of public acts and laws that could not be addressed through existing review mechanisms.

Although the Court's approach tended to bat the ball back to the other branches, no immediate move was made to systematically repeal the worst remnants of military-era laws. It was not until 2009 that the government proposed the establishment of a working group to discuss bills to revoke the remaining laws from the military regime deemed contrary to human rights or that had supported serious human-rights violations.[61] This led to long delays in various laws coming before the Court, including the Press Law of 1969 and the Amnesty Law of 1979, both of which are discussed in the following sections. The former wended its way through the ordinary courts, finally appearing before the Supreme Court by way of extraordinary appeal (*recurso extraordinário*), while the latter was finally challenged by way of an ADPF action.

We see here the negative side of the Court's role. This decision, merely four years after promulgation of the new constitution, divested the Court of one of its main disentrenchment functions, the elimination of authoritarian laws. By departing from the focus in European constitutional courts on effective disentrenchment of such laws, the effect was to extend the heartland of democratisation jurisprudence beyond its usual confines,

---

[59] Ibid. 113.

[60] T. Bustamante & E. de Godoi Bustamante, 'Constitutional Courts as "Positive/Negative Legislators": The Brazilian Case' (2011) 3 *Revista Forumul Judecatorilor* 89, 95.

[61] B. Konder Comparato & C. Sarti, 'Amnesty, Memory, and Reconciliation in Brazil: Dilemmas of an Unfinished Political Transition', paper presented at the International Studies Association Annual Convention, San Diego, 1–4 April, 2012 http://files.isanet .org/ConferenceArchive/f2ecc7f25f6147f9ac79067fb7142135.pdf.

requiring the Court to address such laws twenty-five years after the transition to democracy in 1985.

C   Facilitating the Creation of a Democratic Public Sphere

In Chapter 4, key aspects of a court's role in facilitating the creation of a democratic public sphere were discussed: the protection of core democratic rights; the shaping of inclusive electoral rules; the calibration of a functioning division of state power; and guarding against a re-emergence of authoritarianism in the new order. These roles are analysed here through reference to three cases before the Court in the 1990s and 2000s: the *Right to Protest Case* in 1999;[62] the *Electoral Thresholds Case* in 2006;[63] and the *Press Law Case* of 2009.[64] Together, these cases demonstrate the considerable challenges faced by a court in a new democracy in constructing a meaningful sphere of autonomy for politicians, civil society, and individuals to engage in deliberation, and to ensure that law-making is subject to democratic constraints so that such a sphere is protected.

They also reflect the cross-cutting nature of the dimensions of democratisation jurisprudence discussed in Chapter 4. In the *Right to Protest Case*, for instance, we can discern the Court's curbing of authoritarian governance modalities, already seen in the *Provisional Measures Case*. In addition, the cases discussed here all feature, to some extent, a mediation of the shift between the old and new orders. Whereas courts in long-established democracies such as the United States tend to frame threats to the democratic order in hypotheticals, this demonstrates once again one of the hallmarks of adjudication in a new democracy compared to an old democracy; it is difficult for courts in new democracies to say what democratic law is without referring to the undemocratic experiences of the recent past.

Right to Protest Case

The *Right to Protest Case* concerned a decree issued in March 1999 by the Governor of the Federal District of Brasília under the legislative powers accorded to him by an Organic Law enacted under the authoritarian 1969 Constitution.[65] The decree placed a blanket ban on public

---

[62] ADI 1969 MC (24 March 1999).   [63] ADI 1.351 (7 December 2006).
[64] RE 511.961 (17 June 2009).
[65] The Federal District of Brasília is the capital district, modelled on the federal district of Columbia in the United States.

protests using sound-producing vehicles, radios, and other devices in Brasília's government district – comprising three main squares and adjacent roads in which the seats of the three apex federal powers are located (the President, Congress, and the Supreme Court) – ostensibly aimed at preventing the disturbance of civil servants during working hours.

A number of workers' unions and the Workers' Party (PT) filed an ADI action against the decree, on the basis that it violated the constitutional right to freedom of assembly.[66] We get echoes of the *Provisional Measures Case* here. The dispute had become a flash point between the Court and the Governor; the decree in question was the third issued by the Governor on this matter, after two previous, almost identical, decrees issued in January 1999 had been struck down by the Court for unconstitutionality. However, unlike the *Provisional Measures Case*, here was an open attack on the Court as an institution, challenging its authority to control the actions of a political organ. The Governor's exasperation had been openly expressed in a decision accompanying publication of the third decree, the first line of which bemoaned the necessity to issue the decree again due to a 'veritable vicious circle involving the judicial machinery'.[67]

Perhaps in light of the Governor's intransigence, the rapporteur-judge Justice Marco Aurélio appeared to take the opportunity to draw a clear line in the sand, emphasising not only the importance of the right at hand to democratic deliberation, but also the repression of the right in Brazil's past. His judgment first set about dismantling any justification for the enacted decree. Noting that it did not apply to activities of a 'civico-military, religious or cultural nature', Justice Aurélio emphasised that this nevertheless left the control of protests within the hands of the district, and as such, represented an attempt to censure alternative ideologies and political outlooks, presented as going to the heart of citizenship itself. How could a decree, he asked, impede Brazilians from celebrating, hypothetically, the nation winning a fifth World Cup?[68] How could a decree prevent citizens from protesting for community improvement, or commemorating victims of the struggle to achieve democratic

---

[66] Article 5.XVI: 'All persons may hold peaceful meetings, without weapons, in places open to the public, regardless of authorization, provided that they do not frustrate another meeting previously called for the same place, subject only to prior notice to the competent authority.' Official translation: www.codices.coe.int.
[67] ADI 1969 MC (24 March 1999). Page 293 of the judgment.   [68] Ibid. 297.

transition?[69] His judgment denounced not only the authoritarian past, but also authoritarian tendencies in the new democracy:

> the injustice is of those who shame the citizens who wish to live in a democratic homeland, and who dishonour the heroes, many anonymous, who fought, some to death, for a country free from the disgrace of authoritarianism, the craven shackles of dictatorial despotism. Brazilians cannot bear more false protectionism whose sole result is the backwardness, the ignominy of a nation. It is commonplace to say that democracy is learned every day and continuously, and that restrictions are not placed on one of the most important constitutional guarantees – the freedom of expression of thought, closely linked to the right of assembly – which will give force and sustenance to an organism that wishes to be democratic . . . especially the Brazilian state, which aspires to the respect of other nations at the auspicious occasion of being definitively placed on the roll-call of politically consolidated countries, for which one of the basic presuppositions is the certainty, in no instance rebuttable, that the people are assured the full and unrestricted right to demonstrate. It will not be in the capital of the country that we, Brazilians, will retreat from that proposition . . .
>
> To repeat: the freedom of assembly . . . is inextricably associated with another of greater importance in societies which call themselves democratic: [it is] attached to the expression of thought. The freedom of assembly envisaged in the constitutional provision is not limited to those who demonstrate silently. On the contrary, the rationale of the provision is the airing of ideas, regardless of their religious, cultural or political aspects.[70]

Like Justice Pertence in the decision discussed above, Justice Aurélio emphasised the significance of the new Constitution's break with the past:

> One might think, that the act emanated from the competent legislative authority, in accordance with the Charter [Constitution]. . . of 1969, which permitted ordinary legislation to regulate the locations and conditions for holding meetings. However it is no longer that Constitution, enacted by a military junta, which is in force, but the people's Constitution of 1988.[71]

By layering longstanding Brazilian and American case-law stressing the wide scope of the right, and its negative and positive dimensions, Justice Aurélio concluded that the freedoms of assembly and expression could not be subject to preventative restriction, but solely to constraints

---

[69] Ibid.   [70] Ibid. 298–9.   [71] Ibid. 299.

where their exercise is 'unreasonable', harming property or people.[72] A majority of the Court voted with him for suspension of the decree.

Electoral Thresholds Case

Almost a decade later, and some twenty years distant from the transition to democracy, we find the Court still carving out the essentials of a democratic public sphere, and still preoccupied by the experience of authoritarian rule. Having ruled in the early 1990s on matters such as the regulation of free airtime for political parties in 1994 (holding it to be a matter for Congress),[73] in the Electoral Thresholds case in 2007 the Court was obliged to consider the nature of representative democracy in the Brazilian constitutional order, its relationship with the 1988 Constitution, and the tension between an effectively functioning political system and maximal representation of the people.

The return to electoral democracy in 1985 had brought a liberalisation of the regime for the creation of new political parties, and the re-establishment of parties abolished by the military regime, which had tightly controlled a two-party system in a 'show democracy' until 1979. Article 17 of the 1988 Constitution enshrined the liberal regime for the creation of national parties, stating:

> The creation, amalgamation, merger and dissolution of political parties is free, with due regard for national sovereignty, the democratic regime, the plurality of political parties and the fundamental rights of the individual

The democratic period witnessed a proliferation of parties, rising to some twenty-nine in total, although five parties dominated the electoral landscape. With the stated aim of enhancing the functioning of parliament by avoiding the operation of excessively small parties, the 1995 Law on Political Parties set an electoral threshold, requiring political parties to obtain at minimum five per cent of all valid votes (i.e. excluding void and spoiled votes) and at least two per cent of the total votes in a third of the states of the federation in order to operate in the National Congress, and to gain access to funding from the Parties' Fund, and significant publicly funded air time on radio and television stations.[74] In the 2007 general election, only seven parties met the required threshold.

Facing removal from Congress and a significant reduction in publicly funded air time, nine political parties, including the Communist Party of

---

[72] ADI 1.351 (7 December 2006) 302–3.   [73] ADI 956, 958 and 966 (1 July 1994).
[74] Law 9.096/95.

Brazil (PC do B) and the Green Party (PV), challenged these provisions, arguing that they violated not only the liberal system envisaged in Article 17, but also the principle of equal treatment before the law and equality of arms for all political parties, as well as representing flagrant disrespect of minorities and a blatant attempt by the dominant parties to preserve their power.[75]

In a unanimous decision, the Court held the challenged legal provisions to be unconstitutional. The rapporteur-judge, Justice Aurélio, reasoned that the threshold requirements struck at two basic functions of the Constitution: to ensure political pluralism; and to guard against the tyranny of the majority. Underlining the need to safeguard fundamental constitutional principles – including the democratic regime, a plurality of parties and fundamental rights[76] – he offered the view that even a single representative in either House of Congress could perform the constitutional function of countering majoritarian excesses:

> Ultimately, the constitutional provisions envisage neutralisation of the tyranny of the majority, keeping hegemonic, and therefore totalitarian, views out of the national arena.[77]

The legislature's competence to address the functioning of parliament, he stressed, could not permit unreasonable and excessive measures.[78] Not only would the thresholds bar a significant number of political parties from Congress, but they would also reduce their public funding by over ninety-nine per cent, while apportioning virtually all available funds to the seven parties meeting the threshold; an 'unacceptable' result under the requirement of reasonableness.[79] The judgment unequivocally linked the countermajoritarian purpose of the Constitution with the exigencies of the principle of representative democracy at the heart of the constitutional text:

> Let it be noted ... that lying behind all this discussion is the critical point concerning protection of individual and minority rights, which does not conflict with the principles of majority government – whose purpose is the broad well-being of the people, from the will of the majority, provided that they respect the rights of minority groups ...
>
> In a Democratic State based on the Rule of Law, no majority organized around any ideology or purpose – however laudable it appears – may take away or restrict the fundamental rights and freedoms of minority groups,

---

[75] ADI 1.351 (7 December 2006) 21–2.   [76] Ibid. 46–7.   [77] Ibid. 50.   [78] Ibid. 53.
[79] Ibid. 58.

including the freedom to express themselves, to organise themselves, to denounce, to dissent and to be represented in decisions that affect the fate of society as a whole, in short, to participate fully in public life, including overseeing the actions determined by the majority.[80]

Press Law Case

Similar reasoning, and a doctrinal shift from reasonableness to proportionality, is found in the final case to be considered in this section: the *Press Law Case*, decided in 2009. The case concerned a challenge brought by the Public Prosecutor against a key authoritarian-era law requiring journalists to hold a government-approved degree to practice their profession, arguing that the 1988 Constitution did not permit excessive or unreasonable restrictions on professional activity, and that the restrictions in place not only violated the Constitution's generous free speech guarantees but also the free speech guarantees in Article 13 of the American Convention on Human Rights, which Brazil had ratified in 1992.[81]

A lower court had upheld the validity of the law on the basis of the State's arguments that 'incalculable damage' could be caused by an unqualified journalist, in the same manner as an unqualified lawyer, doctor, or engineer. Before the Supreme Court the same arguments were made. While accepting that freedom of the press was umbilically linked to liberty, freedom of expression, and information, the State insisted that regulation was required to curb the danger of poor journalism damaging public order, and that the practice of journalism required a broad knowledge of cultural, social, legislative, and economic matters, as well as technical and ethical training concerning the conduct of interviews, research, reporting, and publishing.[82] Denying any incompatibility with the American Convention, the State argued that the law protected

---

[80] RE 511.961 (17 June 2009) 60.

[81] The free speech guarantees of the Constitution of Brazil are:
Article 5.IX: '[T]he expression of intellectual, artistic, scientific, and communications activities is free, independently of censorship or license'.
Article 220: 'The manifestation of thought, the creation, the expression and the information, in any form, process or medium shall not be subject to any restriction, with due regard to the provisions of this Constitution.
Paragraph 1. No law shall contain any provision which may represent a hindrance to full freedom of press in any medium of social communication, with due regard to the provisions of article 5, IV, V, X, XIII and XIV.
Paragraph 2. Any and all censorship of a political, ideological and artistic nature is forbidden.' (Paragraphs 3 and 4 concern, inter alia, the State's competence to regulate public entertainment and commercial advertising.)

[82] RE 511.961 (17 June 2009) 706–8.

rights and ensured a more effective right to information, as well as protecting all of society:

> What exists is simply ordinary legislation which ensures the regular exercise of this right, in order that society can continue to progress in a secure manner toward the strengthening of democratic institutions.[83]

The Supreme Court found for the appellant, holding by an eight to one majority that the challenged provision was invalid under the 1988 Constitution as a direct violation of the guarantee of professional liberty, read in conjunction with the constitutional free speech guarantees. In an extensive judgment – ranging across German proportionality doctrine, side glances at Spanish and Portuguese law, previous decisions of the Supreme Court, Brazilian and American scholarship dating back to the nineteenth century, and placing heavy reliance on an Advisory Opinion of the Inter-American Court of Justice[84] – the rapporteur-judge, Justice Gilmar Mendes, stressed that the legislature must have regard to standards of reasonableness and proportionality in establishing restrictions by law, with the final assessment falling to the courts as to whether a restriction is justified.[85] He held the challenged provision to be disproportionate, on the basis that the requirement of technical training did nothing to avoid unethical or abusive journalism.[86]

Justice Mendes emphasised three fundamental points: the express prohibition against prior control of free speech in the Constitution; the distinction between journalism and other public services, such as the practice of law or medicine, due to the 'umbilical link' between journalism and the rights to expression and information;[87] and the key value of journalism to a democratic and plural society.[88] In his concluding remarks, he noted the original authoritarian purpose of the decree at issue:

> It is clear that the requirement of a college degree in journalism to pursue the profession had a clear purpose: to cut off from the means of communication intellectuals, politicians and artists who opposed the military regime. It is clear, therefore, that the said normative act serves other values that are no longer valid in our democratic state ... Decree-Law n.° 972/1969 would not pass under the scrutiny of the National Congress

---

[83] Ibid. 710.
[84] IACtHR, *Compulsory Membership in an Association Prescribed by Law for the Practice of Journalism (Arts. 13 and 29 American Convention on Human Rights)*, Advisory Opinion OC-5/85 (Ser. A) No. 5 (13 November 1985).
[85] RE 511.961 (17 June 2009) 739–49.   [86] Ibid. 755–7.   [87] Ibid. 761.   [88] Ibid. 761

in the context of the current constitutional state, in which fundamental rights and guarantees are guaranteed to all citizens.[89]

This decision, closely following three other decisions in which the Court had declared authoritarian laws concerning the press and imprisonment for civil debt as invalid under the 1988 Constitution, appeared to signal that the bonfire of the military dictatorship's laws was now being kindled.[90]

D Revisiting the Democratic Transition: The Amnesty Law of 1979

The discussion thus far provides some very useful context for finally analysing the Court's judgment in the Amnesty Law Case.[91] In the latter half of 2008, the National Bar Association, joined by various other human rights organisations, took an ADPF action to challenge the validity of the Law's application to state agents who had committed crimes during the dictatorship of 1964–1985. With the Supreme Court evincing greater assertiveness regarding rights protection and an increased propensity to strike down authoritarian-era laws, it appeared a propitious time for a challenge. In addition, in the wider regional context, various constitutional courts in Chile, Argentina, and Uruguay had already reinterpreted or invalidated amnesty laws, in line with the jurisprudence of the Inter-American Court of Human Rights.[92]

The 1979 Amnesty Law had granted a 'broad, general and unrestricted' amnesty to all individuals, from both the military regime and the opposition, involved in politically motivated crimes committed between 2 September 1961 and 15 August 1979. The established interpretation of its scope was extremely wide, including torture, kidnapping, and homicide, even where such crimes were merely 'connected' with political crimes. Coupled with a requirement that prosecutions for torture and murder could be taken solely on the initiative of the Public Prosecutor's Office, few criminal prosecutions had taken place, even after the return to electoral democracy – fostering, it has been suggested, a 'climate of forgetfulness and impunity'.[93]

---

[89] Ibid. 784.
[90] See ADPF 130 (30 April 2009); RE 349.703 (3 December 2008); and RE 466.343 (3 December 2008).
[91] ADPF 153 (29 April 2010).   [92] Schneider, 'Impunity' 44.
[93] Mezarobba, 'Between Reparations' 17.

This was in marked contrast to neighbouring states such as Argentina and Chile, where trials of high-ranking military leaders were pursued shortly after the return to democratic rule, even where amnesty laws had been enacted. As democratisation progressed and human-rights concerns became more central to successive governments' agendas, the state had become more open to acknowledging responsibility for serious past human-rights abuses and the provision of financial compensation to victims of political persecution.[94] However, as regards the issue of the disappeared, it continued to avoid the twin issues of investigation and prosecution at every turn.[95]

In this context the applicants requested either a holding that the law was invalid under the 1988 Constitution, or in the alternative, for a reinterpretation of Article 1 of that Law in conformity with the Constitution, to hold that the amnesty granted to the perpetrators of 'political and connected crimes' does not apply to 'common crimes', such as rape, forced disappearance, and murder committed by state agents against the political opposition.[96] They not only argued that the law violated constitutional rights by hindering victims of the military regime and their family members from identifying persons responsible for committing acts of torture and murder, but also challenged the very democratic foundations of its enactment.[97] In particular, it was argued that the law violated democratic and republican precepts enshrined in the Constitution given that it had not been enacted by the people but, rather, sanctioned by a president who was an army general under a military regime, and enacted by a Congress elected at the pleasure of the regime, before the elaboration of the 1988 Constitution by a freely elected Congress.[98]

For the State, the Prosecutor General argued that the case could not be divorced from its historical context:

> Amnesty, in Brazil, we all know, resulted from a long national debate, with the participation of various sectors of civil society, in order to facilitate the transition between the authoritarian regime and the present democratic regime. Brazilian civil society, beyond a simple participation in this process, articulated itself and marked in the history of the country a struggle for democracy and peaceful and harmonic transition, capable of avoiding further conflicts.[99]

---

[94] The State enacted a law in 1995 and established various commissions to compile reports and manage reparations to victims of political persecution. Mezarobba, 'Between Reparations' 13ff.

[95] Ibid. 16.   [96] Ibid. 17–18.   [97] Ibid. 18.   [98] Ibid. 19.

[99] ADPF 153 (29 April 2010). Report of the rapporteur-judge (*relatório*) 9.

The Court, by a seven to two majority, voted to uphold the law. The rapporteur-judge, Justice Eros Grau – who had himself been tortured by state agents in the 1970s – strongly argued not only for the constitutionality of the law, but for its social value as the catalyst for the democratic transition. He challenged the action as ignoring the historical fact that the amnesty was not simply imposed by the regime, but fought for by opponents of the regime in a climate of increasing public opposition to military rule after the oil crisis of 1974 and the ensuing economic recession, forming the centre of a public campaign 'expressive of the most vibrant page of resistance and democratic activity in our History', and one that the Bar Association itself (now challenging the law) had supported at the time.[100]

Stressing that the democratic movement in that era had been obliged to accept certain limits to the accountability of regime agents, the 'bilateral' character of the amnesty, the dangers of focusing on human dignity at the cost of other values, and the Court's clear historical jurisprudence from the 1900s, 1950s, and 1980s, which had consistently upheld a broad interpretation of successive amnesty laws, he insisted that the amnesty law '[h]as to be interpreted in light of the reality of the time in which it was enacted.'[101] Essentially, he argued, the applicants were attempting to rewrite history itself and, more importantly, that the Court had no role in rewriting laws in a democratic state:

> In a Democratic State based on the rule of law the Judiciary is not permitted to alter, or to provide a re-wording, different to what [the law] contemplated. It can, from [a law], produce various standards. But not even the Federal Supreme Court is authorised to rewrite amnesty laws . . .
>   Since that agreement resulted in a legal text, it is exclusively the Legislature which can revise it.[102]

If we look closely at the reasoning in the majority votes, we can discern a core concern regarding the law's place in Brazil's new democratic order, which seemed crucial in staying the Court's hand. The Court appeared to view the law, certainly not as an ordinary law, and not quite as an exercise of constituent power, but as a form of meta-constitutional act transcending the old and new constitutional orders, and the facilitating condition for the constituent act of founding a new constitutional order, perhaps somewhat similar to a popular referendum that forms the basis for a new constitution – what Tierney calls a 'constitution-framing'

---

[100] Ibid. 21–2.   [101] Ibid. 25–34.   [102] Ibid. 38–39.

referendum.[103] Conceived in this way, it appeared immune to judicial review. Beyond the Supreme Court's general disregard for Inter-American case-law, this may provide an additional explanation as to why, despite the clear relevance of the Inter-American Court's significant jurisprudence on amnesty laws, and the conferral of 'infraconstitutional' status on the American Convention in a recent Supreme Court judgment (i.e. below the Constitution, but above ordinary law),[104] the votes for the majority all cast the case as entirely a domestic matter, to be decided within the parameters of domestic constitutional law.[105]

4   Carving Out a Role for the Court: Six Key Lessons

What do these cases tell us about the Court's task of carving out a role for itself in the new democratic order? Six fundamental lessons come into focus, all of which underscore the observation in Chapter 4 that we have no way of predicting how a court will act as a democracy-builder in the new order.

The first is that, within the overall democratisation context, a constitutional court's role as a democracy-builder is fundamentally based on a complex dialectic between the constitutional text and the institutional setting of the court. In the Brazilian context the breadth of the 1988 Constitution, coupled with the lack of any direct access to the Court for individuals, appeared to diminish the Supreme Court's ability to focus on constructing the essentials of a democratic order. The institutional setting of the Court, in turn, affected the capacity of the constitutional text to effect rupture with the old order. In the *Prior Laws Case*, in particular, the strong disentrenchment aims of the constitutional text were diluted in a cocktail of legal-technical reasoning within the Court.

Second is the effect of contestation regarding the Court's role in the new order. This is seen in the limits set by the Court on its role in policing the proper exercise of the president's law-making powers in the *Provisional Measures Case*. While accepting the Court's 'American-style' role as a 'balancing wheel' to ensure the 'proper functioning of the

---

[103] Tierney, *Constitutional Referendums* 11.

[104] *Civil Imprisonment of Debtors Case* RE 349.703 & RE 466.343 (3 December 2008).

[105] See Torelly, 'Transnational Legal Process' 21–2. For further discussion of the Supreme Court's relationship with the Inter-American Court, see T.G. Daly, 'Brazilian Supremocracy and the Inter-American Court of Human Rights: Unpicking an Unclear Relationship' in Fortes, Boratti, Palacios Lleras & Daly (eds.), *Law and Policy in Latin America*.

democratic institutions' enshrined in the Constitution,[106] judges repeatedly emphasised that the control of provisional measures was a matter for Congress, and the Court could have no role in exercising 'preventive' constitutional review of such measures by reviewing the reasons for their issuance, or their substantive content.[107] Justice Pertence's unsuccessful argument in the *Prior Laws Case* for a more central role for the Court as a transformational institution, capable of remaking the law in the democratic image of the new order, also underscores this contestation:

> to refuse to allow invocation of the direct action of unconstitutionality to purge old laws incompatible with the new constitutional order, the Supreme Court would shirk a mission and a responsibility that are its alone. Inalienably the Court's.[108]

Third, even when the Court speaks as one, and seeks to positively impact on the democratisation process, it can have little immediate effect. For instance, in the *Provisional Measures Case*, although the Court unanimously and clearly stated its position on the exceptional nature of such measures and the need to respect the separation of powers set out in the constitutional text, the judgment did little to prevent their abuse. As Rosenn observes, concerning the reissuance of provisional measures not rejected by Congress (a different matter to the specific issue addressed in the *Provisional Measures* judgment): 'Until 2001, there is little doubt that Brazilian presidents seriously misused the provisional measure in a way that seriously threatened the separation of powers.'[109] In reality it required a constitutional amendment to reduce use of the power by placing additional constraints on its use.[110] Even then, as recently as 2007, the Court was required to strike down an attempt to reissue a provisional measure rejected by Congress in the same legislative session,[111] and continues to assert that it will only 'exceptionally' review whether the requirements of urgency and relevance have been met.[112]

Fourth, even where a judgment is effective, it is not always the case that it has a positive impact on democratisation. In the *Electoral Thresholds Case*, for instance, the Court's protection of minority political persuasions in the democratic community may have harmed democratic governance. In Brazil, the fragmentation and clientelism generated by the

---

[106] ADI 293 (6 June 1990). Justice de Mello, 84.
[107] See e.g. Justice Pertence's vote, ibid. 50.   [108] Ibid. 79.
[109] Rosenn, 'Separation' 857.   [110] Ibid. 859–60.   [111] Ibid. 859.
[112] See e.g. ADI 4.029 (27 June 2012).

presence of such a large number of political parties in parliament has been offered as a key reason for the ongoing post-1988 crisis of legitimacy affecting the National Congress and its inability to meet social demands.[113] The chronic crisis has culminated in the perceived 'implosion' of Brazil's democratic system in 2016 with the impeachment of President Rousseff in the context of a nosediving economy and bribery scandal.[114] This provides a contemporary example of the concerns motivating other courts to uphold electoral thresholds. As Issacharoff notes, the German constitutional court upheld a similar five per cent threshold in 1957 to ensure good governance, in a context where political fragmentation in the Weimar Republic was viewed as a factor leading to Nazi rule. The Czech and Romanian constitutional courts, following the German example, have done the same to avoid 'excessive splintering of the political spectrum'.[115]

Fifth, democratisation jurisprudence is not all about the exercise of the strong judicial review power to invalidate laws. In the *Provisional Measures Case*, for instance, the Court's firm line on use of provisional measures ultimately played a part in the passing of a constitutional amendment to curb their use. In other cases, the Court has had the opportunity to clearly articulate the difference between democratic and undemocratic governance, the value of countermajoritarian constraints on democratic decisionmaking, and the relationship between the old and new constitutional orders. However, in a democratic system unused to detailed analysis of the content of Court judgments, it would be quite a stretch to suggest that political actors, and Brazilian society more widely, have paid particular heed to these open discussions of democratic ethics.

The final lesson, which provides a useful link to the next chapter, is the significant but fluctuating role of external law in the Supreme Court's democratisation jurisprudence. As with other constitutional courts of the third wave, the Court has tended to refer to the case-law of foreign constitutional courts to bolster robust decisions. Reference to the Court's own past jurisprudence is more mixed: it can be used to cleave to a

---

[113] See da Silva, *Constitution of Brazil*, ch 2.
[114] See U. Friedman, 'The Slow Implosion of Brazilian Politics' *The Atlantic* 19 April 2016 www.theatlantic.com/international/archive/2016/04/brazil-impeachment-dilma-rousseff/478677; and J. Watts & D. Bowater, 'Brazil's Dilma Rousseff Impeached by Senate in Crushing Defeat' *The Guardian* 1 September 2016 www.theguardian.com/world/2016/aug/31/dilma-rousseff-impeached-president-brazilian-senate-michel-temer.
[115] Issacharoff, 'Democratic Hedging' 976.

more deferential role, as seen in the *Prior Laws Case*, or to underscore continuity in upholding core democratic rights, as seen in the *Right to Protest Case*. Importantly, reference to the jurisprudence of the Inter-American Court's case-law has been rare. We see it in the *Amnesty Law Case*, where Justice Lewandowski, departing from the majority, concluded that agents of the state are not 'automatically covered' by the 1979 amnesty law and argued for a case-by-case approach to its application. Most exceptional is the significant emphasis placed by Justice Mendes on Inter-American jurisprudence in the *Press Law Case*, citing an Inter-American advisory opinion which held that diploma requirements for journalists constituted a violation of the American Convention, and the need to provide expansive protection of free speech as the cornerstone of a democratic society.

5   Conclusion: The Stark Limits of a Court in a Dysfunctional Democracy

The case-law analysed above ends at the 2010 mark, with the Supreme Court's judgment in the Amnesty Law case. In the intervening years, Brazilian democracy has come under severe pressure, with declining economic fortunes and the twin evils of inflation and recession exposing and exacerbating deep structural problems that render Brazil's system of democratic governance deeply dysfunctional. Already in mid-2012 the Supreme Court was thrust into the middle of the so-called *mensalão* political scandal concerning illegal vote-buying in Congress (which almost toppled President da Silva's government), due to its constitutional role as a first-instance criminal trial court for holders of high office. The Court's raft of guilty verdicts represented for some a positive sign of judicial independence; for others, a negative politicisation of the Court and an unwarranted increase in its powers.[116]

During July and August 2013, I was in Brazil as mass protests erupted nationwide, starkly revealing public dissatisfaction with the progress of Brazil's democratisation process, encompassing left-wing claims against enduring socio-economic inequality, middle-class and élite unhappiness

---

[116] See e.g. C.M. Barbosa, 'The Brazilian Supreme Court: Between Activism and Judicial Responsibility' *International Journal of Constitutional Law Blog* 25 December 2012 www.iconnectblog.com/2012/12/the-brazilian-supreme-court-between-activism-and-judicial-responsibility.

with the democratisation of public power, and a perceived 'radicalism' of the left-wing government, and all bemoaning entrenched and widespread corruption.[117] By 2016 this had culminated in the current acute crisis of Brazil's democratic institutions, with the political impeachment of President Rousseff on charges of irregular accounting in managing the federal budget. Many claimed this was a *coup* by other means, restoring the old élites to power and thrusting the Supreme Court into the political fray again by requiring it to settle the 'rules of the game' for the impeachment process and requiring the Chief Justice to preside over the process.[118]

Juliano Zaiden Benvindo, writing in December 2016, captured the problem well:

> If the Supreme Court has been dubbed the institutional arbiter of the current political turmoil by trying to pacify conflicts, which might justify its activism, it has nonetheless been engulfed by the same political dynamics in which it is supposed to be intervening. Daniel Vargas, Professor at the Getúlio Vargas Foundation in Rio de Janeiro, has argued, for instance, that the Brazilian Supreme Court is not the medicine but rather a symptom of a disease that has spread throughout Brazilian democracy: We, Brazilians, always resort to the Supreme Court whenever we need a political or economic decision, which shows that 'Brazilian democracy bleeds more and more.'[119]

Whether the 'quasi-coup' perception of Rousseff's impeachment is true or not, it is undeniable that Brazilian democracy has reached an impasse, which at its core is related to the dysfunctional design of its democratic system.[120] While it would be absurd and unfair to lay the crisis of Brazilian democracy at the Supreme Court's door, it has at times exacerbated rather than ameliorated deficiencies in the democratic system, with its frustration of the much-needed political reform

---

[117] See e.g. A. Saad Filho, 'The Mass Protests in Brazil in June–July 2013' *Global Research Project* 15 July 2013 www.globalresearch.ca/the-mass-protests-in-brazil-in-june-july-2013/5342736.

[118] J. Zaiden Benvindo, 'Abusive Impeachment? Brazilian Political Turmoil and the Judicialization of Mega-Politics' *International Journal of Constitutional Law Blog* 23 April 2016 www.iconnectblog.com/2016/04/abusive-impeachment-brazilian-political-turmoil-and-the-judicialization-of-mega-politics.

[119] J. Zaiden Benvindo, 'Abusive Judicial Activism and Judicial Independence in Brazil' *International Journal of Constitutional Law Blog* 22 December 2016 www.iconnect blog.com/2016/12/abusive-judicial-activism-and-judicial-independence-in-brazil.

[120] See contra, C. Pio, 'The Impeachment Vote in Brazil Is Definitely Not a Coup' *New York Times* 19 April 2016 www.nytimes.com/roomfordebate/2016/04/18/in-brazil-a-house-cleaning-or-a-coup/the-impeachment-vote-in-brazil-is-definitely-not-a-coup.

to address excessively fragmented political representation in Congress a particularly jarring example.

Four simple lessons can be gleaned from the Brazilian experience. First, incremental constitutionalism has its limits, and deep design flaws in the constitutional and political order of a new democracy cannot be fully mitigated by any constitutional court. Second, there is in fact no guarantee that a constitutional court will act to mitigate, rather than exacerbate, those design flaws. Third, an overly inclusive constitution-drafting process, an excessive focus on judicial review and rights in a new democratic constitution, and a failure to address key structural issues, can leave a new democracy hobbled from the beginning. Fourth is the point, emphasised in Chapter 2, that judicialisation should not glibly be taken as a sign of a positive democratisation trajectory; it can just as easily signal deep-rooted problems in a state's democratic development.

Overall, the Brazilian experience, echoing the discussion in Chapter 2, once again suggests that serious caution is warranted in placing undue focus on a constitutional court, and constitutional law more broadly, in any democracy-building project. The next chapter moves to comparative analysis of the Inter-American Court's democratisation jurisprudence concerning Brazil, highlighting the key differences between domestic and regional courts as democracy-builders.

6

Regional Democratisation Jurisprudence:
Shaping Democracy from Outside

Analysis of the Brazilian Supreme Court's case-law in Chapter 5 has served to highlight the hallmarks of domestic democratisation jurisprudence: the Court's symbolic and governance power as guardian of the new constitution; its embeddedness in the process as both agent and subject of democratisation; its position as a constituted power of the democratic constitution and how this informs its role; and the differing impact of its decisions, ranging from the invalidation of laws to an inability to constrain certain unconstitutional patterns of governance. We have seen how the Supreme Court's situation within the state context means its democratisation jurisprudence is inextricably bound to the past experience of undemocratic rule; entrenchment of the new constitution, in this way, cannot be fully decoupled from disentrenchment of the previous constitutional order.

In this chapter we move to consideration of regional democratisation jurisprudence through a comparative analysis of the Inter-American Court's engagement with Brazil's democratisation process. The aim is, again, to apply the insights of the conceptual framework elaborated in Chapter 4 to concrete empirical contexts. We will see that the Court's impact on Brazilian democratisation was muted until its decision invalidating the Amnesty Law in 2010, some months after the Supreme Court had upheld the law's constitutionality. Our main points of orientation here are how the Court's institutional setting and its externality to any domestic constitutional context affects its decision-making and its capacity to impact on the democratisation process from without. The case-study presented here is considerably shorter than the first case-study. The main purpose is simply to tease out some of the key differences and similarities between regional democratisation jurisprudence and its domestic variant, before turning to a comparison with regional adjudication in Africa and Europe.

1   Distinct Nature of the Regional Setting

The content of key decisions of the Inter-American Court is discussed later in this chapter. This section, on the basis of the analytical framework elaborated in Chapter 4, briefly addresses the distinct nature of regional democratisation jurisprudence as a creature of time, tempo, context, and methodology, through an analysis of the Inter-American Court.

As discussed in Chapter 3, although it was established in 1979 the Inter-American Court's first decision in a contentious case was not issued until 1988 – the year the Supreme Court was revived under Brazil's new democratic constitution. Yet, their institutional experiences have exhibited stark differences. For instance, by the mid-1990s, when the Supreme Court's docket had become unmanageable, the Inter-American Court was still issuing, at most, a handful of merits decisions in contentious cases each year, and, in various years during this period, no more than a single decision.[1]

The impact of the Inter-American Court on democratisation in Brazil was negligible for the first decade or so, given that Brazil was one of the last states in Latin America to submit to the Court's jurisdiction, in 1998. This, coupled with the Supreme Court's general aversion to citing Inter-American jurisprudence in the democratic era, considerably dulled the penetration of such case-law in the domestic order. However, this does not make Brazil an entirely exceptional case; the Inter-American Court's impact on any state has generally been modest, with only a handful of states being subject to more than ten judgments since 1988. It is only when we look at its effects across the region as a whole that we see its notable influence. As we will see later in the chapter, even the Court's most significant decision against Brazil – declaring the invalidity of the 1979 Amnesty Law – has had only a limited impact on Brazil's democratisation process.

In the next section we discuss the Inter-American Court's democratisation jurisprudence concerning Brazil, which began in 2002 with its first decision against Brazil. First, it is useful to recall from Chapter 3 that, despite its underwhelming docket, by 2002 the Inter-American Court had already established a reputation for forthright decision-making concerning: the crime of forced disappearance; the invalidation of amnesty and criminal defamation laws; the importance of the right to information

---

[1] See Chapter 3.

placing a clear obligation on all organs to abide by the ACHR, including domestic courts; and it had begun to move toward its doctrine of 'conventionality control'. What drove this assertiveness?

In Chapter 3 we saw how the Inter-American Court began operating as transitions to democracy were sweeping South America, which required it to address a mix of new democracies alongside stubbornly authoritarian regimes in Central America. Telling details reveal the precarious position of the Court as it set about its task in the 1980s. For instance, compared to the post-war modernist splendour of the Supreme Court in Brazil, the proceedings of the Inter-American Court in its early years 'took place in a make-shift courtroom which consisted of four tables and the equivalent of lawn chairs.'[2] The Court was then, and remains, a part-time institution: judges had to take time off from their day jobs to attend to cases.[3] Thus, unlike the Supreme Court of Brazil, the Inter-American Court had to carve out its role from rather modest materials.

Taking a closer look at the cases in which the Court's landmark decisions were issued, we get a sense of certain particularities of regional democratisation jurisprudence and the very different institutional setting of a regional human rights court, compared to a domestic constitutional court. In its very first judgment, *Velásquez-Rodriguez* v. *Honduras* in 1988,[4] the respondent State's active opposition to the hearing of the matter appeared to incentivise the Court to adopt an assertive posture, to address the case on the basis of legal principle, and to show that it was not merely a paper tiger.[5] In assessing the evidence in the case it stressed that, as an international tribunal, the standards of proof would be less formal than in a domestic criminal proceeding. More importantly, in addressing the State's preliminary objection that the applicant had failed to exhaust domestic remedies, the Court used the opportunity to assess whether domestic remedies for the rights violation were available, adequate, and effective, allowing it to assess the quality of the justice system in Honduras under authoritarian rule.

---

[2] J. Allain, 'Laurence Burgorgue-Larsen & Amaya Úbeda de Torres, 'The Inter-American Court of Human Rights: Case-Law and Commentary' (2013) 17 *Edinburgh Law Review* 115.

[3] See e.g. Grossman, 'Inter-American System' 64.

[4] IACtHR (Ser. C) No.4 (29 July 1988).

[5] See e.g. J.F. Stack, 'Judicial Policy-Making and the Evolving Protection of Human Rights: The European Court of Human Rights in Comparative Perspective' in Volcansek (ed.), *Judicial Politics* 152.

The Court found for the applicant, noting that domestic remedies for forced disappearance were: ineffective given that the detention complained of was clandestine; inapplicable in practice due to formal procedural requirements; ignored by the authorities; or unavailable due to intimidation of lawyers and judges involved.[6] By laying bare the systemic failure of the Honduran judicial system to investigate, prosecute, or adjudicate on cases of disappearance, and the fact that the rights violations by public actors were not authorised by domestic law, in a context where the Honduran Supreme Court had played no role, the Court's externality to the domestic context appeared to be an advantage, permitting it to perform the quasi-constitutional function of identifying structural defects in the legal order, in the course of dispensing 'individual' justice (although this is not, strictly speaking, a structural reform judgment, given that the reforms needed were not placed in the operative part of the judgment).

We see the particular challenges raised by the regional setting time and again in the Court's jurisprudence. Notable examples among the new democracies in the region are the tactical use of *allanamientos* by states, by which they offer reparation to victims of rights violations as a way of 'playing the system' to prevent the issuance of a full binding judgment of the Court;[7] and the persistence of arguments claiming that domestic remedies have not been exhausted, sometimes made on misleading presentations of the workings of domestic law.[8] More particularities will come to the fore as the chapter progresses. These are all ways in which the Court's capacity to pursue not only individual justice is hampered, but also, more widely, its ability to elaborate a form of pan-regional 'constitutional' justice.

It is unsurprising, given this context, that the Court tends to draw on external normative sources to bolster its decisions. Its decision concerning Brazil's Amnesty Law, *Gomes Lund (Guerrilha do Araguaia)* v. *Brazil,*[9] is indicative of its broad approach, with the Court citing decisions of the Human Rights Committee, the OAS Special Rapporteur on Freedom of Expression, various Special Rapporteurs at the UN, the

---

[6] IACtHR (Ser. C) No.4 (29 July 1988) para. 80.

[7] See J. Cavallaro & S.E. Brewer, 'Reevaluating Regional Human Rights Litigation in the Twenty-First Century: The Case of the Inter-American Court' (2008) 102 *American Journal of International Law* 768.

[8] See e.g. the Brazilian State's arguments in *Escher* v. *Brazil*, IACtHR (Ser. C) No. 200 (6 July 2009).

[9] IACtHR (Ser. C) No. 219 (24 November 2010).

Secretary General of the UN, the European Court of Human Rights, the African Commission on Human Rights, and the constitutional courts of Argentina, Chile, Peru, Colombia, and Uruguay.

2   The Inter-American Court's Key Decisions Concerning Brazil

Like domestic democratisation jurisprudence, the Inter-American Court's democratisation jurisprudence concerning Brazil may be identified as relating to the three dimensions set out in Chapter 4: facilitating construction of a democratic public sphere; mediating the shift from an undemocratic to a democratic order; and carving out the Court's own role in shaping the democratisation process. However, as we will see, the manner in which the Inter-American Court approaches these tasks, and the ways in which its impact is registered, differs significantly from adjudication at the domestic level.

A   A Norm Cascade or a Bare Trickle?

Compared to the continuous stream of case-law from the Brazilian Supreme Court, between 2002 and 2016 the Inter-American Court handed down no more than seven decisions in actions taken against Brazil. However, it has found violations of the Convention in every case bar one – a remarkable strike rate by any standards. No systematic study of these decisions exists in the literature, but the majority address a mixture of authoritarian practices that bled into the democratic era and the legislative legacy of authoritarian rule. Four of the seven cases are of particular importance here.[10]

In *Nogueira de Carvalho* v. *Brazil*[11] in 2006 the Court found no violation of the Convention in the State's investigation into the 1996 murder of a human-rights activist and journalist who had denounced the activities of 'the Golden Boys', a death squad in which civil police officers and

---

[10] *Matter of Urso Branco Prison regarding Brazil*, IACtHR, Provisional Measures Order (18 June 2002); and *Ximenes Lopes* v. *Brazil*, IACtHR (Ser. C) No. 149 (4 July 2006), concerning ill-treatment of mentally ill persons, are not discussed here. Nor is the Court's latest decision in *Case of the Hacienda Brasil Verde Workers* v. *Brazil*, IACtHR (Ser. C) No. 318 (20 October 2016), which concerned the right not to be subjected to slavery and trafficking in persons.

[11] IACtHR (Ser. C) No. 161 (28 November 2006).

other government officials had allegedly taken part. In *Escher* v. *Brazil*[12] in 2009 the Court found a violation of the Convention right to privacy (Article 11) due to police wiretapping, and subsequent broadcast, of phone conversations of members of the Landless Rural Workers Movement. The judgment held that the wiretapping had been conducted in breach of Brazilian law and that the State had provided no satisfactory explanation as to how the recordings had made their way into the public domain.[13] In *Garibaldi* v. *Brazil*,[14] also in 2009, the Court found the State in violation of the Convention rights to judicial guarantees and judicial protection (Articles 8 and 25) due to the State's lack of due diligence in investigating the death of an activist during an extrajudicial operation to evict the families of landless rural workers in the south of Brazil. Finally, *Gomes Lund* in 2010, discussed in the next section, addressed the State's failure to investigate the disappearance of guerrilla fighters in the Araguaia region of the Amazon in the 1970s in the course of a military operation.

The facts of the *Nogueira*, *Escher*, and *Garibaldi* cases are complex and need not detain us here. What is important is that, although the State in the latter two cases was ordered to conduct an effective investigation, it has been unable to fully comply for various reasons. To a certain extent, this stems from the federal structure of the state and the weakness of any mechanism to co-ordinate portions of the federal government to pursue compliance, or between federal and state entities.

> [C]lassic institutional difficulties still have not been resolved. Repeated non-compliance with obligations to investigate, present in all of the rulings [of the Inter-American Court against Brazil], indicates an ineffective police and investigative apparatus, as well as a lagging judiciary and deficient training program for State human rights agents.[15]

We get a sense here, similar to the Supreme Court's decisions in cases such as the *Provisional Measures Case*, that what can look at first glance like successful democratisation jurisprudence can prove to have very little effect on the ground. A 'norm cascade' at the Inter-American source can all too easily turn into a bare trickle at its Brazilian destination.

---

[12] IACtHR (Ser. C) No. 200 (6 July 2009). See also the Court's interpretation of the judgment, IACtHR (Ser. C) No. 208 (20 November 2009).
[13] para. 162. [14] IACtHR (Ser. C) No. 2013 (23 September 2009).
[15] E.M. Coimbra, 'Inter-American System of Human Rights: Challenges to Compliance with the Court's Decisions in Brazil' (2013) 19 *SUR – International Journal on Human Rights* 57, 69.

It has also been repeatedly observed in recent years that 'control of conventionality' – concerning the role of domestic organs in ensuring compliance with the American Convention on Human Rights – is simply not a reality in any of Brazil's state organs, including the police, judiciary, and military.[16] This tends to lead to pessimistic conclusions concerning the Court's quasi-advisory rulings in contentious cases where it finds no Convention violation. In *Nogueira de Carvalho*, for instance, while the Court emphasised the importance of protecting human-rights defenders engaged in revealing the truth of past rights violations, which may be seen as a core aspect of the construction of a democratic public sphere, it is hard to tell whether this had any concrete effect on Brazil's state machinery.[17] The Court's intervention regarding the Amnesty Law, by contrast, has had a clear impact.

B   An External Take on Brazil's 1979 Amnesty Law

The Amnesty Law of 1979 came before the Inter-American Court as the end-point of a separate legal battle to that which had brought the law before the Supreme Court. It had begun in the lower courts of Brazil in 1982, seeking a state investigation into the disappearances of seventy people, including local civilians and members of a Communist guerrilla movement, by the military authorities between 1972 and 1974 in covert military action to eliminate the movement.

Political solutions offered to the applicants, including the Law of the Disappeared of 1995, which provided for compensation to be paid to the relatives of the Araguaia guerrillas, all stopped short of investigation. In 2003 President da Silva, spurred by the acceptance of a petition against the State to the Inter-American Commission on Human Rights, had made the further move of establishing a governmental Inter-Ministerial Commission, charged with obtaining information on the remains of the Araguaia victims. However, that commission solely included state representatives and appeared to have submitted to onerous conditions imposed by the military regarding the sought information – crucially, that it would not be used to revise the Amnesty Law. The Commission's final report in 2007 accepted the military authorities' claims that all

---

[16] M.N. Bernardes, 'Inter-American Human Rights System as a Transnational Public Sphere: Legal and Political Aspects of the Implementation of International Decisions' (2011) 15 *SUR – International Journal on Human Rights* 131, 144–6.

[17] See the Court's comments at para. 76.

documents concerning the Araguaia guerrilla massacre had been des-troyed.[18] Thus, no movement was made to repeal the Amnesty Law or to investigate the Araguaia massacre and pursue prosecution of those responsible. The military appeared to still wield considerable power as a veto actor in Brazil's democratic order.

In November 2010, mere months after the Supreme Court had upheld the Amnesty Law, the Inter-American Court handed down its decision, holding that certain provisions of the Law, in precluding the investigation and punishment of severe human-rights violations, were incompatible with the American Convention and had no legal basis. Although it recognised the efforts the State had made to address past human-rights violations of this nature, the Court held that that the law was no longer to be invoked as an obstacle to a full investigation of the facts in the case, or the identification and punishment of those responsible for the guerrillas' deaths.

The Inter-American Court was not amenable to State arguments that the Amnesty Law's validity had been upheld by the Supreme Court, and, unlike that court, was not swayed by the contention that the law had implemented a political decision, agreed by actors across the political spectrum, which had facilitated 'the transition to a State of law'.[19] Without engaging with this argument the Court simply reiterated its established position that all amnesties for serious violations of human rights, however enacted, are invalid under the Convention.[20] Trans-ported to the regional setting, the 'quasi-constituent power' arguments before the Supreme Court appeared to lose all traction in the proceedings before the Inter-American Court. External to the Constitution of 1988, external to the state, and tasked with upholding a separate normative instrument, the Court had no institutional connection to, and felt in no way bound by, a domestic meta-constitutional agreement made over thirty years previously.

Having observed that courts in Argentina, Chile, Peru, Uruguay, and Colombia had adhered to its jurisprudence in divesting amnesty laws of legal effect,[21] the Court expressly, though tersely, noted that the Brazilian authorities, including the Supreme Court, had failed to carry out any

---

[18] C. MacDowell Santos, 'Transnational Legal Activism and the State: Reflections on Cases Against Brazil in the Inter-American Commission on Human Rights' (2007) 7 *SUR – International Journal on Human Rights* 29, 44.

[19] IACtHR (Ser. C) No. 219 (24 November 2010) para. 136.   [20] Ibid. para. 175.

[21] Ibid. paras. 163–70.

'conventionality control' to assess the Amnesty Law against Brazil's obligations as a party to the American Convention, as required under its 2006 decision in *Almonacid-Arellano* v. *Chile*[22] (which concerned the application of Chile's 1978 Amnesty Decree to block the prosecution of military officials for the Pinochet-era disappearance of Arellano Almonacid, a school teacher, union leader, and anti-government activist in the Chilean Communist Party):

> [W]hen a State is a Party to an international treaty such as the American Convention, all of its organs, including its judges, are also subject to it, wherein they are obligated to ensure that the effects of the provisions of the Convention are not reduced by the application of norms that are contrary to the purpose and end goal and that from the onset lack legal effect. The Judicial Power, in this sense, is internationally obligated to exercise 'control of conventionality' ex officio between the domestic norms and the American Convention, evidently in the framework of its respective jurisdiction and the appropriate procedural regulations. In this task, the Judicial Power must take into account not only the treaty, but also the interpretation that the Inter-American Court, as the final interpreter of the American Convention, has given it.[23]

Beyond reparations for the individual applicants, the State was ordered to, *inter alia*: investigate and prosecute those responsible and to determine the whereabouts of the victims; to guarantee to avoid any repetition of the violations, including human-rights training for the armed forces; to recognise a stand-alone crime of forced disappearance in domestic law; to provide access to, collation of, and publication of relevant documents in the State's possession; and to create a truth commission.

C   The Decision's Impact on Brazil's Democratisation Process

The Amnesty Law decision is notable for its direct impact on Brazil's democratisation process, unlike the negligible impact of the judgments in *Escher* and *Garibaldi*. Although the State has not been willing to repeal the Amnesty Law in line with the Inter-American Court's judgment, the Court's decision had the signal effect of bolstering pre-existing civil society demands for a truth commission to address the abuses of the military rule.[24]

---

[22] IACtHR (Ser. C) No. 154 (26 September 2006).
[23] IACtHR (Ser. C) No. 219 (24 November 2010) para. 176.
[24] Marcelo Torelly lays out other effects of the judgment, including adding to moves toward adopting a law (Law No. 12.527) to give effect to the extensive constitutional right to personal information held by the state or public agencies, which had lain dormant since

In November 2011, at the initiative of President Rousseff, a National Truth Commission (*Commissão Nacional de Verdade*) was established, charged with producing a report on human-rights abuses committed from 1946 to 1988. Over a period of two years the Commission conducted hearings and gathered expert testimony concerning the military juntas of 1964–1985 in particular. Its final report, issued in December 2014: found that torture, summary executions, and forced disappearances had constituted official state policy under the military governments of 1964–1985; documented a raft of politically motivated killings; called for the military to recognise their responsibility for the 'grave' rights violations perpetrated under their rule; identified by name 377 people as responsible for such abuses; recommended that those still alive should be brought to trial; and called for amendment of the Amnesty Law to preclude its application to such cases in light of their gravity.[25] A proliferation of truth commissions in individual states, and even universities, has been said to reflect 'growing civil society demand for accountability', in a historical context of weak civil society mobilisation to address impunity in Brazil.[26]

The Court's decision, and the domestic constitutional and political changes it set in train, also appears to have bolstered a sea-change in the perception of the Amnesty Law. While it remains in force, there are increasing questions surrounding its legitimacy;[27] and moves to challenge or circumvent its application in the context of prosecutions against government officials and members of the police and military forces for authoritarian-era crimes.[28] This has all occurred in the teeth of

the Constitution's enactment in 1988. See M. Torelly, 'Gomes Lund vs. Brasil Cinco anos Depois: Histórico, impacto, evolução jurisprudencial e críticas' in F. Piovesan & I.V. Prado Soares, Impacto das Decisões da Corte Interamericana de Direitos Humanos na Jurisprudência do STF (Editora Juspodium, 2016) 548–55.

[25] National Truth Commission (Brazil), *Relatório da Comissão Nacional da Verdade*, 10 December 2014 www.cnv.gov.br.

[26] F. Lessa, T.D. Olsen, L.A. Payne & G. Pereira, 'Persistent or Eroding Impunity; The Divergent Effects of Legal Challenges to Amnesty Laws for Past Human Rights Violations' (2014) 47 *Israel Law Review* 105, 124.

[27] See e.g. S. Monteiro de Matos, 'Anístia Democrática? Sobre a (I)legitimade da Lei da Anistia Brasileira' (2012) 7 *Revista Anistia Política e Justiça de Transição* 136.

[28] See H. Stone, 'Brazil Prosecutes Retired Colonel Over Disappearances in Challenge to Amnesty Law' *The Pan-American Post* 14 March 2012 www.panamericanpost.blog spot.com/2012/03/brazil-prosecutes-retired-colonel-over.html. See also Amnesty International 'Brazil: Historic Efforts by Federal Prosecutors to Challenge Decades of Impunity for Military Regime' *Amnesty International* 25 April 2012 www.amnesty.org/en/latest/news/2012/04/brazil-historic-efforts-federal-prosecutors-challenge-decades-impunity-military-regime.

significant military opposition.[29] Therefore, not only has the work of the Truth Commission facilitated at least some political discussion of the experience of military dictatorship; it has also confirmed full civilian control of the government apparatus and the clear limits of the military as an unconstitutional veto power. While this is a highly positive achievement, which can ultimately be credited to the Inter-American Court, it appears that this key insight has not yet been widely appreciated,[30] and it is important not to exaggerate the wider impact of the decision; it has not sparked a society-wide conversation about the authoritarian era, for instance.[31] Section 3 places the Brazilian experience in the wider regional context.

3   Brazil in the Wider Regional Context of Latin America

The discussion in Chapter 5 and this chapter so far have revealed stark differences between the democratisation jurisprudence of the Brazilian Supreme Court and the Inter-American Court, in terms of volume, content, motivation, and impact. They have also revealed a lack of engagement by the Brazilian Court with the Inter-American Court of Human Rights in the elaboration of such jurisprudence, which has dulled the latter's capacity to impact on the democratisation process. How does the Brazilian scenario fit within its wider regional context? The following section focuses on judicial interaction between the Inter-American Court and other constitutional courts in Latin America, as a central aspect of the way in which the Inter-American Court seeks to impact on democratisation processes, before considering in more depth the way in which the Inter-American Court's externality to the state affects its adjudication within a three-dimensional political space.

A   The Brazilian Supreme Court: A Regional Outlier?

It is tempting to characterise the Supreme Court's refusal to genuflect before the Inter-American Court as anomalous, given that other constitutional courts have tended to engage in a 'lively interaction' with their

---

[29] See e.g. G. Duffy, 'Brazil Truth Commission Arouses Military Opposition' BBC News 11 January 2010 http://news.bbc.co.uk/1/hi/8451109.stm.

[30] I am grateful to Marcelo Torelly for this observation.

[31] I am grateful to Virgílio Afonso da Silva for this insight.

regional counterpart.[32] We have seen above, for instance, that the constitutional courts in five of Brazil's neighbouring countries have shown a marked willingness to invalidate or curb application of domestic amnesty laws in line with the Inter-American Court's case-law.

Various constitutional courts (e.g. Colombia and Peru), inspired by the French doctrine of 'bloc de constitutionnalité', have through their case-law elevated international human-rights norms to constitutional status; conceiving constitutional law and certain international human-rights norms – particularly Inter-American norms – as forming a coherent and combined set of standards for judicial review.[33] Even the Chilean Constitutional Court, which eschews the formal doctrine of a constitutional block, 'reflexively' uses Inter-American jurisprudence to reinterpret domestic law.[34] Inter-American jurisprudence has thus tended to influence their democratisation jurisprudence to a greater extent than its peripheral role in Brazilian jurisprudence.[35] That said, as Huneeus has observed, the Court has 'variable authority' across the region, which depends on the particular strain of domestic constitutionalism, the legal profession's approach to the Court, and the ability of the Court's supporters to influence those in power.[36]

The Inter-American Court's elaboration of a doctrine of 'control of conventionality', discussed in Chapter 3, has sought to build on domestic moves, due to a growing realisation in the Court since the early 2000s that its jurisprudence will have little effect without the active assistance of state organs, especially domestic courts. In 2001 Justice Trindade (then President of the Court), in a concurring opinion in the Court's landmark free speech judgment in *The Last Temptation of Jesus Christ* case against Chile,[37] emphasised that a continuing violation of the Convention could arise from the content not only of national legislation but also the '*jurisprudence constante*' of national courts.[38] Speaking of the

---

[32] D. García-Sayán, 'Una Viva Interacción: Corte Interamericana y Tribunales Internos' in *La Corte Interamericana de Derechos Humanos: Un Cuarto de Siglo: 1979–2004* (Inter-American Court of Human Rights, 2005) www.corteidh.or.cr/docs/libros/cuarto%20de %20siglo.pdf.
[33] See Góngora Mera, *Inter-American Judicial Constitutionalism* 171ff.   [34] Ibid. 139.
[35] See further, C. Ayala, 'The Judicial Dialogue between International and National Courts in the Inter-American Human Rights System' in Scheinin & Aksenova (eds.), *Judges as Guardians*.
[36] A. Huneeus, 'Constitutional Lawyers and the Inter-American Court's Varied Authority' (2016) 79 *Law and Contemporary Problems* 179.
[37] *Olmedo-Bustos et al. v. Chile*, IACtHR (Ser. C) No. 73 (5 February 2001).
[38] Ibid. Concurring Opinion of Judge Cançado Trindade, 3.

'ideal of the full compatibilization of the domestic legal order with the norms of the international protection of human rights', he urged the need for 'a true change of mentality, in the high courts of almost all countries of Latin America':

> A new mentality will emerge, with regard to the Judiciary, as from the understanding that the direct application of the international norms of human rights protection is beneficial to the inhabitants of all countries, and that, instead of the adherence to juridico-formal constructions and syllogisms and to a hermetic normativism, what is truly required is to proceed to the correct interpretation of the applicable norms, whether of international or national origin, so as to secure the full protection of the human being . . .
>
> [T]here exists no legal obstacle or impossibility at all for the direct application at domestic law level of the international norms of protection, but what is rather required is the will (animus) of the public power (above all the Judiciary) to apply them, amidst the understanding that one will thereby be giving concrete expression to common superior values, consubstantiated in the effective safeguard of human rights[39]

In place of the German Federal Constitutional Court's lecture on political morality to the Adenauer regime in 1961, discussed in Chapter 2, we see here a lecture on *judicial* morality, exhorting constitutional courts to act as the domestic enforcers of the Inter-American Court's jurisprudence. Justice Trindade's approach was reformulated by the Court five years later as the 'control of conventionality' doctrine in *Almonacid-Arellano* v. *Chile*:

> [W]hen the Legislative Power fails to set aside and/or adopts laws which are contrary to the American Convention, the Judiciary is bound to honor the obligation to respect rights as stated in Article 1(1) of the said Convention, and consequently, it must refrain from enforcing any laws contrary to such Convention . . .
>
> 124. The Court is aware that domestic judges and courts are bound to respect the rule of law, and therefore, they are bound to apply the provisions in force within the legal system. But when a State has ratified an international treaty such as the American Convention, its judges, as part of the State, are also bound by such Convention. This forces them to see that all the effects of the provisions embodied in the Convention are not adversely affected by the enforcement of laws which are contrary to its purpose and *that have not had any legal effects since their inception*. In other words, the Judiciary must exercise a sort of 'conventionality control'

---

[39] Ibid. para. 37, para. 40.

between the domestic legal provisions which are applied to specific cases and the American Convention on Human Rights. To perform this task, the Judiciary has to take into account not only the treaty, but also the interpretation thereof made by the Inter-American Court, which is the ultimate interpreter of the American Convention.[40]

It is notable that the doctrine is expressed in 'constitutional' language reminiscent of the discussion of 'revocation' in the Brazilian Supreme Court's *Prior Laws* judgment, in the Court's reference to Convention-incompatible laws having had no legal effects since the Convention's adoption. Rather than an abstract monism, the particular care taken to address domestic courts suggests a conception of 'international law-as-federal-order', as discussed in Chapter 4.

However, also as discussed in Chapter 4, despite a rather harmonious pan-regional picture from afar, a closer inspection reveals that the Brazilian Supreme Court is merely at one end of a spectrum of differential adherence to the Inter-American Court's decisions.[41] The Argentine Supreme Court, for instance, was a regional front runner in affirming the interpretive guidance value of Inter-American jurisprudence in its *Giroldi*[42] judgment of 1995. This was seen to full effect in the *Simón*[43] decision of 2005, in which it invalidated Argentina's amnesty laws in line with Inter-American jurisprudence, stating that the status accorded to international human rights law by constitutional reforms in 1994 would require, at times, exceptions to the Constitution to be recognised; or 'bubbles' in the Constitution into which the Court would insert external norms.[44] Yet, as Damián González-Salzberg has observed, the Court's case-law on the binding nature of Inter-American Court decisions has been quite inconsistent, evincing significant 'jurisprudential swings', and ignoring the Inter-American Court's case-law in some judgments after *Simón*.[45] It has been noted that the *Simón* decision dovetailed with the policies of the new Kirchner administration elected in 2003, and that Court's annulment in 2007 of pardons granted to the top tier of junta generals after the transition to be unconstitutional was strongly

---

[40] IACtHR (Ser. C) No. 154 (26 September 2006) paras. 123–4. Emphasis added.
[41] See, in particular, Huneeus, 'Rejecting the Inter-American Court'.
[42] *Giroldi, Horacio y otro*, Causa No. 32/93 (7 April 1995). See García-Sayan, 'Constitution-alism' 1839.
[43] *Simón, Julio Héctor y otros*, Causa No. 17.768 (14 June 2005).
[44] Elias, 'Argentina's "Amnesty Laws"'.
[45] González-Salzberg, 'Implementation of Decisions' 121–4.

pushed by President Kirchner.[46] This tends to suggest less wholesome drivers for the Argentine Court's engagement with Inter-American jurisprudence than a sense of judicial partnership. In other states, such as Chile, judicial acceptance of 'control of conventionality', explicitly using Inter-American case-law as an inescapable standard for constitutional adjudication, is partial at best.[47]

For all the talk of transnational judicial community and a pan-regional constitutional order, then, the national context and the domestic court's role as a gate-keeper regarding the reception of international norms remain central. Beyond domestic court resistance, wider institutional obstacles to compliance with Inter-American decisions discussed above in the Brazilian context are also mirrored across the region. As Huneeus notes, Inter-American orders that target the executive alone achieve much higher rates of compliance than those that target multiple state actors, which achieve abysmal compliance rates.[48] Institutional actors, including executives, judiciaries, prosecutors, and legislatures, have varying incentives to comply and partner with the Inter-American Court, and in many cases the incentives are predominantly negative, in the sense that compliance cuts across their own hard-won power and autonomy.[49]

B   Oddities of Adjudication in Three-Dimensional Political Space

The discussion thus far has focused mainly on the relationship between domestic courts and the Inter-American Court, and how this affects their roles as democracy-builders. In this section, we broaden the canvas to get a picture of the interaction of courts and non-judicial actors in a three-dimensional political space, to use Scheppele's chess board metaphor from Chapter 4. We have already seen, for instance, the Brazilian State flitting between different levels of the chess board in cherry picking its implementation of the Inter-American Court's orders in *Gomes Lund*. Here, we look at two other examples, offered by two Inter-American Court judgments: *The Last Temptation of Christ* case against Chile in 2001;[50] and *Gelman v. Uruguay* in 2011.[51]

---

[46] S. Levitsky, 'Argentina: From Kirchner to Kirchner' (2008) 19 *Journal of Democracy* 16, 21.
[47] G. Aguilar Cavallo, 'El Control de Convencionalidad: Análisis en Derecho Comparado' (2013) 9 *Revista Direito GV* 721, 743.
[48] Huneeus, 'Courts Resisting Courts' 508–11.   [49] Ibid. 511–18.
[50] *Olmedo-Bustos et al.* v. *Chile*, IACtHR (Ser. C) No. 73 (5 February 2001).
[51] IACtHR (Ser. C.) No. 221 (24 February 2011).

These two decisions allow us to focus more closely on the complex and overlapping interaction of different sites of constitutional authority, which complicates regional human rights courts' roles as democracy-builders. In particular, in a similar manner to the Brazilian State's arguments in *Gomes Lund*, we encounter arguments in both cases concerning the democratic credentials of the state and domestic decision-making processes, which attempt to 'immunise' the state from regional oversight by the Inter-American Court. Such arguments, evidently, do not appear in cases before domestic courts.

In the *Last Temptation of Jesus Christ*, the Chilean State, defending the censorship of a film through an administrative decision that had been upheld by the Supreme Court, relied on an audacious argument: responsibility for the violation could not be imputed to it on the basis that it had occurred as a result of a judicial decision with which it did not agree, but which the government was bound to respect due to a democratic concern for the separation of powers:

> In a pluralist society, such as that of Chile, the courts are independent and there are sectors of the magistrature whose concept of the legal system leads them to maintain that prohibitions may be ordered by invoking other constitutional guarantees, such as those in article 19(4) of the Constitution on honor and intimacy. The Chilean magistrature is extremely legalistic.
>
> [T]he fact that judges have delivered judgments contrary to those articles is not sufficient grounds for maintaining that the State violated the Convention ... [T]he context must be taken into consideration – which is that of a pluralist, democratic system with separation of powers – and the intention of the provision.
>
> ... In the instant case, Chile is not alleging its internal law in order to fail to perform the provisions of the American Convention. Formal legal texts include international norms, but, unfortunately, there are sectors of the profession and the magistrature in Chile that have not been receptive to this situation.

The State's solution – a constitutional amendment to replace the system of film censorship with a classification system – though recognised as important by the Court, did not prevent it from finding a violation given that the required change in the law had not been effected at the time of the judgment. The Court accordingly ordered the State to amend its domestic law 'within a reasonable period'.[52] The argument made here, as we have seen, led the Court to become increasingly concerned with the role of domestic courts as 'Inter-American' courts.

---

[52] *Olmedo-Bustos et al.* v. *Chile*, IACtHR (Ser. C) No. 73 (5 February 2001) para. 103.

In *Gelman* v. *Uruguay*, concerning the State's failure to investigate the disappearance of a heavily pregnant student during the authoritarian era, the Court was faced with an amnesty law (the Expiry Law[53]) that had not only been enacted by a democratic legislature one year after Uruguay's return to democratic rule in 1985, but also – due to repeated calls for its repeal and affirmation of its constitutionality by the Supreme Court in 1988 – had been upheld twice in referendums of 1989 and 2009. Each time it had been upheld by a relatively slim margin (fifty-seven per cent in the first and fifty-three per cent in the second); indicative, one scholar offers, 'of a widespread sentiment in Uruguay that the majority wants to move forward and focus on continuing to build a sustainable democracy.'[54] The second referendum, however, pitted 'the people' against the Supreme Court, which just days prior to the referendum had struck down the law as unconstitutional.[55]

The Inter-American Court expended little energy on the constitutional entanglement that had arisen in the state. Decided a number of months after its judgment in *Gomes Lund*, the judgment underscored once again the Court's refusal to bow to arguments stressing the democratic credentials of the challenged law; including those linked to popular sovereignty, as well as its insistence on a thick conception of 'true' democracy as based fundamentally on rights protection, reminiscent of Luigi Ferrajoli's conception discussed in Chapter 1, and the Brazilian Supreme Court's judgment in the *Electoral Thresholds Case*:

> 238. The fact that the Expiry Law of the State has been approved in a democratic regime and yet ratified or supported by the public, on two occasions, namely, through the exercise of direct democracy, does not automatically or by itself grant legitimacy under International Law. The participation of the public in relation with the law, using methods of direct exercise of democracy ... should be considered, as an act attributable to the State that give rise to its international responsibility.
>
> 239. The bare existence of a democratic regime does not guarantee, *per se*, the permanent respect of International Law, including International Law

---

[53] Law No. 15.848.

[54] D Soltman, 'Applauding Uruguay's Quest for Justice: Dictatorship, Amnesty, and Repeal of Uruguay Law No. 15.848' (2013) 12 *Washington University Global Studies Law Review* 829, 832.

[55] *Sabalsagaray Curutchet, Blanca Stela – Denuncia de Excepción de Inconstitucionalidad*, Judgment No. 365 (19 October 2009) 2325–79. The decision was subsequently reaffirmed in *Organización de los derechos humanos – Denuncia de Excepción de Inconstitucionalidad*, Judgment No. 1525 (29 October 2010) 5205–7.

of Human Rights ... The democratic legitimacy of specific facts in a society is limited by the norms of protection of human rights recognized in international treaties, such as the American Convention, in such a form that the existence of one true democratic regime is determined by both its formal and substantial characteristics, and therefore, particularly in cases of serious violations of nonrevocable norms of International Law, the protection of human rights constitutes a [sic] impassable limit to the rule of the majority, that is, to the forum of the 'possible to be decided' by the majorities in the democratic instance, those who should also prioritize 'control of conformity with the Convention' ... which is a function and task of any public authority and not only the Judicial Branch. In this sense, the Supreme Court of Justice has exercised an appropriate control of conformity with the Convention in respect to the Expiry law, by establishing, *inter alia*, that 'the limits of the sovereignty of the majority lies, essentially, in two aspects: the guardianship of the fundamental rights (first, amongst all, the right to life and personal liberty, and there is no will of the majority, nor the general interest, nor the common good wherein these can be sacrificed) and the subjection of the public authorities to the law.' Other domestic courts [the Constitutional Chamber of the Supreme Court of Costa Rica and the Constitutional Court of Colombia] have also referred to the limits of democracy in relation to the protection of fundamental rights.

In October 2011, five months after a parliamentary vote on a Bill to replace the Expiry Law resulted in a forty-nine to forty-nine deadlock, a law was enacted to repeal the Expiry Law,[56] lifting all bars on prosecutions, including application of the statute of limitations.[57]

4   Carving Out a Role for the Court: Four Observations

It should be evident from the brief discussion above that the Inter-American Court's capacity and means to support democratisation processes differ significantly from the capacity of a domestic court. Four observations might be made here.

First, it is important to appreciate that the Court's intervention in any one democratisation process tends to be infrequent. We can compare, for instance, the Colombian Constitutional Court's total of 9,442 judgments from 1992–2004 (an average of 840 decisions per year) with the three judgments by the Inter-American Court in cases against Colombia

---

[56] Law No. 18.831.   [57] Soltman, 'Uruguay's Quest for Justice' 836.

during the same period.[58] This means its greatest hope of an effective democratisation jurisprudence is for states to submit to all of its judgments, whether they are respondents or not before the Court.

Yet, second, while the Court has considerable success in achieving individual justice, as discussed in Chapter 3 it encounters significant difficulty in pursuing 'structural reform' to address systemic deficiencies in the new democracies that impede rights protection, the constraint of public power, and reckoning with the rights violations of the past. The analysis in this chapter provides a sense of the complex web of obstacles to the reception of such structural reform judgments at the domestic level, which encompasses not only outright political resistance to judgments, but also inconsistent reference to its case-law in domestic courts and an overall lack of co-ordination within the State to implement its decisions.

That said, even where aspects of implementation are lacking, as seen in Brazil's reaction to the *Gomes Lund* decision, the Court's decisions can have a notable impact, freeing up a form of 'bottleneck' in the domestic democratisation process by addressing matters that the political branches, judiciary, and civil society have been unable to address. In addition, the Court's externality to the constitutional order might be characterised as an asset at times. In the *Gelman* decision, for instance, the clash between the constituted power of the Supreme Court and the referendum as an expression of popular sovereignty was, once brought to the Court, transmuted from a constitutional clash to a simpler question of obeisance to international law. Yet, the ease with which the Court in each case dispenses with democratic concerns gives cause for significant pause. The idea that 'true' democracy simply depends on rights protection appears to be a simplification; an example of the tendency observed by Walker, discussed in Chapter 1, to 'define up' democracy rather than admitting the iterative relationship between democracy and constitutional law, and the tensions between them.

Third, the Court's externality to the democratisation process in any given state has a profound impact on its conception of its role, the justification for that role, and its limits. The Inter-American Court has had to push hard and shout loud to carve out any space for itself in domestic political orders and the regional space. Coupled with a docket full of severe and widespread rights violations, this has led to a generalised tendency toward assertiveness, which leaves little room

---

[58] Cepeda-Espinosa, 'Judicial Activism' 559.

for differential treatment for different states. From the *Gomes Lund*, *The Last Temptation*, and *Gelman* cases there is a clear sense of the Inter-American Court's unwillingness to investigate the democratic quality of the laws and acts that come before it for assessment, or to accord differential deference to states based on their democratic progress.

From its external perch, the only 'quality' issue is the compatibility of the domestic norm with the Convention; epitomised in its 'conventionality control' doctrine. This is ostensibly based on a principled adherence to international law as having overriding force, and on traditional understandings of responsibility under international law as based on the indivisibility of the state. However, it is perhaps also based on an understanding that to evince openness to such arguments would lead to every state in the region seeking special treatment due either to its democratic success, or, conversely, the difficulties of its democratisation process – which, we will see at the end of the chapter, is the reality in Europe.

Fourth, all courts as they carve out their role become, in a sense, hostage to an accretion of doctrinal development. This increasingly limits their freedom to manoeuvre, but they must retain some element of adjudicative flexibility in order to address different contexts. This is seen to starkest effect in the Court's judgment in *Almonacid*. The majority judgment affirming the Court's strong line on the incompatibility of amnesty laws with the Convention, penned by Justice Trindade, was, rather unusually, followed by a concurring opinion from the same judge, which appeared to suggest (albeit obliquely) that some amnesties might pass muster under the Convention. Eventually, in *Massacres of El Mozote v. El Salvador*[59] in 2012 the Court did make a distinction between the amnesty laws struck down in its early jurisprudence and amnesty laws aimed at ending armed conflict. This must all be considered in the context that Colombia had, for some time, been engaged in a peace process aimed at ending a half-century of violent conflict, which was expected to include some form of amnesty. Context, as ever, is fundamentally important.

5 Latin America in an Inter-Regional Context: Africa and Europe

This chapter thus far has provided a sense of how courts have operated and interacted, with one another and with other sites of constitutional

---

[59] IACtHR (Ser. C) No. 252 (25 October 2012).

authority, in Latin American democratisation processes since the 1980s. The very different settings, aims, and normative frameworks of domestic and regional courts, and how these impact their roles as democracy-builders, have been emphasised. It is clear that the validity of amnesty laws has been a particular preoccupation in the Inter-American context, bringing regional courts into conflict with governments and courts, domestic courts into conflict with 'the people', and bringing some domestic courts into conflict with the domestic constitution. In this section the aim is to show how similar patterns of interaction, and similar questions, can be seen in the elaboration of democratisation jurisprudence in Africa and Europe; although the former appears more similar to the Latin American experience than the latter.

In Africa the most striking case to date has concerned the disentrenchment of one-party rule and entrenchment of a multiparty system, in *Mtikila v. Tanzania*.[60] In Europe the main concern has been the struggle to achieve democratic rule in the aftermath of totalitarian Communist governance, which shines a light on the difficult balance that needs to be struck between entrenchment of the new democratic order and disentrenchment of the old order. The main decision examined here is *Ždanoka v. Latvia*.[61]

A   Africa: New Context, Familiar Patterns

As briefly discussed in Chapter 3, *Mtikila*, the first merits judgment of the African Court on Human and Peoples' Rights, issued in 2013, saw the Court adopt an assertiveness on a par with the Inter-American Court in *Velásquez-Rodriguez* a quarter-century previous, holding that Tanzania's constitutional ban on independent electoral candidacy constituted a violation of the African Charter on Human and Peoples' Rights. Even more strikingly, the case presents a mirror image of the three-dimensional interaction between judicial, political, and constituent power, discussed above.

The Domestic Decisions in *Mtikila*

The case, like *Gomes Lund*, had a long history before it reached the regional sphere, first arising in the context of Tanzania's transition to

---

[60] ACtHPR, App. 009/2011 and 011/2011 (14 June 2013). The Court's other judgments to date, briefly canvassed in Chapter 3, are not discussed here.

[61] (2007) 45 EHRR 17.

electoral democracy in 1995. Amendments in 1993 to the 1977 Constitution, paving the way from one-party to multi-party politics, had
required candidates in elections to hold membership of, and be spon-
sored by, a political party. On foot of a constitutional challenge, the High
Court in 1994, citing the Indian Supreme Court's 'basic structure' doctrine, found the amendments to be unconstitutional on the basis that
restricting candidacy to political party members held significant potential
for abuse and, in its view, would 'render illusory the emergence of a truly
democratic society.'[62]

However, a week before the High Court issued its judgment, the
government enacted a new bill to amend the Constitution,[63] which had
the effect of nullifying what was anticipated to be an adverse judgment.
In a further challenge brought by the same applicant the High Court in
2006 again struck down the amending act, on the basis that it infringed
electoral rights, was unnecessary and unreasonable and was therefore a
disproportionate measure.[64] It ordered the government to establish a
legislative framework to permit independent candidates to run in elections, setting the deadline as the date of the next general election in
October 2010.

This decision was subsequently overturned by the Court of Appeal
sitting *en banc* in a judgment of June 2010, on the basis that a court could
not declare a constitutional provision to be unconstitutional in a substantive sense; only where the procedure for constitutional amendment
has been violated.[65] The Court stressed that opening the electoral system
to independent candidates is a political question, to be addressed by
Parliament. However, as Makulilo notes, the Court took a shot across
the bows of the political branches:

> We give a word of advice to both the Attorney General and our Parlia-
> ment: The United Nations Human Rights Committee, in paragraph 21 of
> its General Comment No.25, of July 12, 1996, said as follows on Article 25
> of the International Covenant on Civil and Political Rights, very similarly
> worded as Art 23 of the American Convention and our Art 21 [of the
> African Charter]: The Right of persons to stand for election should not be
> limited unreasonably by requiring candidates to be members of parties
> or of specific parties. Tanzania is known for our good record on human

---

[62] *Mtikila* v. *The Attorney General*, Civil Case No. 5 of 1993 (24 October 1994); see 26.
[63] Eleventh Constitutional Amendment Act No. 34 of 1994.
[64] *Mtikila* v. *The Attorney General*, Miscellaneous Civil Cause No. 10 of 2005 (5 May 2006).
[65] *Attorney General* v. *Reverend Christopher Mtikila*, Civil Appeal No.45 of 2009 (17 June 2010).

rights and particularly our militancy for the right to self determination and hence our involvement in the liberation struggle. We should seriously ponder that comment from a Committee of the United Nations, that is, the whole world.[66]

The State, following the decision, made moves toward initiating a consultative process to seek the views of Tanzanian citizens concerning the possible amendment of the Constitution;[67] tabling a Constitutional Review Bill dated 2011 before Parliament in March 2011.[68]

The African Court's Decision

In June 2011 the same applicant (joined by two legal organisations) brought the matter to the African Court, claiming violation of the African Charter rights to freedom of association (Article 10), to participate in public and governmental affairs (Article 13) and the right against discrimination (Article 2), as well as a broader argument that the State had 'violated the rule of law by initiating a constitutional review process to settle an issue pending before the courts of Tanzania.'[69] Freedom of association, they argued, is 'a core democratic principle' designed to permit citizens to monitor the State, ensure proper discharge of its functions, and ensure that the government complies with legislation with the aim of achieving transparency and accountability.[70]

The State argued, *inter alia*, that the case should be deemed as inadmissible due to the failure to exhaust domestic remedies: the Court of Appeal judgment had left the matter to Parliament, which had yet to consider it, and the constitutional review process, the State contended, would not only permit the views of the applicant to be heard, but would occur within the operation of a Constituent Assembly, which would consider the provisions of a new constitution. The matter, the State stressed, had thus 'been left to the people of Tanzania.'[71]

Regarding the merits, the State argued – citing the Inter-American Court's judgment in *Castañeda Gutman v. Mexico*,[72] which had been relied on by the Court of Appeal – that the bar on independent candidates to stand in elections was based on 'the social needs of the country,

---

[66] A.B. Makulilo, 'Introductory Note to Tanganyika Law Society and the Legal and Human Rights Centre v. Tanzania and Rev. Christopher R. Mtikila v. Tanzania (Afr. Ct. H.R.)' (2013) 52(6) *International Legal Materials* 1327, 1328; 83.
[67] *Mtikila* (Court of Appeal) para. 74.   [68] Ibid. para. 80.1.
[69] ACtHPR, App. 009/2011 and 011/2011 (14 June 2013) para. 4.   [70] Ibid. para. 112.
[71] Ibid. para. 80.1.   [72] IACtHR (Ser.C) No. 184 (6 August 2008).

based on its historical reality',[73] and sought to achieve various aims, including the exigencies of national security, defence, public order, public peace, and morality, regional representation in a federal state, and avoidance of tribalism.[74] Of most relevance was the State's democratisation-based argument that at the time of the constitutional reform in 1992

> Tanzania was still in the throes of establishing a multiparty democracy. The country, at the time, was as yet to hold its very first general election under the multi-party system, and it was still at its infant stage of multi-party democracy, and there was not any compelling social need for independent candidature.[75]

In response to the applicants' rule of law argument, the State insisted that it respected the principle of the rule of law, the separation of powers, and independence of the judiciary as provided for by its Constitution, that the Constitution permitted amendment of its text, and that the 1994 amendment had followed the required constitutional procedure.[76] The Court, in its judgment of June 2013, unanimously found violations of freedom of association and the right to participate in public and governmental affairs, and by a majority of seven to two a violation of the non-discrimination provisions of the Charter. Addressing the admissibility argument concerning the failure to exhaust local remedies, the Court, citing a key decision of the African Commission on Human and Peoples' Rights and jurisprudence of the European and Inter-American human rights courts, emphasised that 'local remedies' referred primarily to *judicial* remedies, which must be 'available, effective and sufficient'; criteria it viewed the constitutional review process as incapable of fulfilling.[77] Having noted earlier in its judgment that the Constitution Review Bill of 2011 was still undergoing parliamentary scrutiny, the Court stated:

> The parliamentary process, which the Respondent states should also be exhausted is a political process and is not an available, effective and sufficient remedy because it is not freely accessible to each and every individual; it is discretionary and may be abandoned anytime; moreover, the outcome thereof depends on the will of the majority. No matter how democratic the parliamentary process will be, it cannot be equated to an independent judicial process for the vindication of the rights under the Charter.[78]

Arguments based on the social needs, historical reality, and federal structure of the State were given equally short shrift. Citing relevant

---

[73] ACtHPR, App. 009/2011 and 011/2011 (14 June 2013) para. 94.
[74] Ibid. para. 90.1, para. 102.   [75] Ibid. para. 105.   [76] Ibid. para. 120.
[77] Ibid. para. 82.   [78] Ibid. para. 82.

case-law of the European and Inter-American courts, the Court affirmed that limitations to the rights and freedoms in the African Charter are restricted to the parameters of Article 27(2) of the Charter,[79] can only be set out in the form of laws of 'general application', and must be proportionate to the legitimate aim pursued.[80]

Viewing the State as having failed to show the ban on independent candidates as falling within the scope of permissible restrictions in Article 27(2), the Court stressed that, in any case, it could not be deemed proportionate to the alleged aim of fostering national unity and solidarity, and, citing the same Human Rights Committee Resolution invoked by the Court of Appeal, that any limitations should be 'in consonance with international standards, to which the Respondent is expected to adhere.'[81] The Court further emphasised that the 'claw-back' clauses in the Charter, which textually provide a wide basis for rights restriction,[82] should not be interpreted against the Charter and that regulation of rights and freedoms 'may not be allowed to nullify the very rights and liberties they are to regulate'. Essentially, the Court asserted, there is a restriction on restrictions, echoing the German Constitutional Court's judgment in *Lüth* fifty-five years before.

In ascertaining a violation of the equality principle in the Charter, the Court again found no merit in the State's democratisation argument that the history, social reality, and federal structure of the State required 'a gradual construction of a pluralist democracy in unity'.[83] The Court declined to adjudicate on the 'rule of law' argument, on the basis that it was not connected to a specific right.[84] The Court therefore ordered the State to remedy the violations within a reasonable time through legislative, constitutional, and 'all other necessary measures', and to inform the Court of the measures adopted.[85] In effect, the State would have to amend the ban on independent candidates in the challenged electoral law and provisions of the Constitution to comply with the judgment.

Mtikila in Three Dimensions and Global Context

The African Court's judgment in *Mtikila* encapsulates the globalisation of the court-centric model of democratisation, and the complexity of elaborating democratisation jurisprudence in a three-dimensional space.

---

[79] 'The rights and freedoms of each individual shall be exercised with due regard to the rights of others, collective security, morality and common interest.'
[80] Ibid. para. 107.2.   [81] Ibid. para. 108.   [82] Discussed in Chapter 4.
[83] Ibid. para. 119, 51.   [84] Ibid. para. 121.   [85] Ibid. para. 126.

Here, we see contestation at the domestic level between different courts as to judging democratisation. We see the normative straitjacket on the domestic courts as constituted powers within the constitutional framework, compared to the freedom of externality enjoyed by the regional court, which has no qualms in assessing the validity of constitutional provisions or in 'short-circuiting' a nascent constitutional amendment process. We see state arguments invoking democratic processes and the particularities of the democratisation process itself as reasons for immunity from either any review by the regional court, or its finding of a rights violation. We see a complex interaction between the Court of Appeal, the government, and the African Court, where apparent judicial deference by the domestic court nevertheless puts the political branches on notice of international law violations, thus opening a space for assertive action by the African Court. We see the African Court's reference to its sister-courts in San José and Strasbourg, as well as the Human Rights Committee, in order to mitigate the deficiencies of the African Charter, while retaining the freedom to depart from external jurisprudence which does not serve its needs. Importantly, in this connection, like the Inter-American Court it has not adopted any margin of appreciation doctrine in the face of a hostile climate.

We can follow the thread all the way back to post-war Germany in the reliance on proportionality reasoning in both the domestic and regional courts, and in the African Court's assertion of the need for a 'restriction on restrictions'. Clearly, some sixty years after the Federal Constitutional Court's first judgment in 1951, its pioneering post-authoritarian jurisprudence continues to reverberate through the courts of the world.

Yet, interesting though this all is, as mentioned in Chapter 3 the decision appeared to achieve little on the ground. The State has vigorously resisted the judgment, and it remains to be seen whether it will effect any change in Tanzanian law given that enforcement mechanisms for the Court's judgments, and the political will to use them, remain weak.[86] The norm cascade is once again reduced to a trickle.

B   Europe as the Inter-Regional Outlier

Where does Europe fit in this global picture? At the end of his key work on the transitional jurisprudence of the European Court of Human Rights, James Sweeney suggests that his research 'provides a starting

[86] See Cole, 'The African Court'.

point to inquire into whether any of the lessons learned in Europe have relevance outside of it.'[87] The answer to this is, yes and no. The discussion in this chapter tends toward the conclusion that the European experience is of limited relevance to other regions. Set against the Inter-American and African experiences, it betrays three significant fundamental differences.

First, as discussed in Chapter 3, the European Court was well-established by the time it was required to elaborate a democratisation jurisprudence for the new democracies of post-Communist Europe. Submission to its jurisdiction was an accepted reality in Western Europe, and all aspirant members of the Council of Europe (and EU) were required to accept its jurisdiction. It therefore appears that it did not have to exert itself unduly to become a relevant actor in the domestic orders of the new democracies that submitted to its jurisdiction in the 1990s. Second, its case-law and doctrine had been slowly forged in a post-war Western Europe where democratisation proceeded apace with little call for its intervention until the 1970s, by which time it was engaging in fine-tuning domestic law to render it compatible with the European Convention. Its core doctrine, the margin of appreciation doctrine, was fundamentally a recognition, not just of cultural diversity across Western Europe, but of the democratic credentials of the states under its supervision. Third, the new democracies in Central and Eastern Europe have transitioned, not just from authoritarian rule, as seen in Latin America and Africa, but from totalitarian political systems that sought to occupy all available societal space, and which left an even stronger residue in the democratic era than military or strongman rule in other regions.

Even if we confine ourselves here solely to electoral matters, compared to the straightforward question before the African Court in *Mtikila* the European Court has faced a difficult mix of cases concerning: refusals to register new communist parties;[88] refusals to register other antidemocratic or merely minority organisations;[89] and prohibitions on the involvement of police officers in political activity;[90]

[87] Sweeney, *Post-Cold War Era* 253.
[88] *Partidul Comunistilor (Nepeceristi) and Ungureanu* v. *Romania* (2007) 44 EHRR 340; *Tsonev* v. *Bulgaria* (2008) 46 EHRR 8.
[89] *WP and others* v. *Poland*, ECtHR, App. No. 42264/98 (2 September 2004); *Gorzelik and Others* v. *Poland* (2005) 40 EHRR 4.
[90] *Rekvényi* v. *Hungary* (1997) 30 EHRR 519.

as well as lustration measures of differing severity.[91] This can involve somewhat different calculations as to the Court's role in disentrenching the old order and entrenching the new, especially when the two functions appear to clash. It has also seen the Court evince a limited willingness to accept arguments based on the exigencies and difficulties of the democratisation process, compared to the deaf ear turned to such arguments by the human rights courts in other regions.

A good example here is the European Court's Grand Chamber judgment in *Ždanoka* v. *Latvia*. In earlier decisions the Court had embraced the concept of 'self-defending democracy' or 'militant democracy', echoing the German Federal Constitutional Court's doctrine discussed in Chapter 2, under which certain restrictions to electoral rights in the European Convention could be permitted.[92] This led to different results depending on the context. The doctrine was invoked in *Refah Partisi (Welfare Party)* v. *Turkey*[93] in 2003 to uphold Turkey's outlawing of its biggest political party, on the basis that the party's aims were anti-democratic and its promotion of sharia law lay in fundamental conflict with the principle of secularism in the domestic constitution. However, in various post-Communist states the Court has adopted a 'tutelary' role in urging states to adopt an attitude of openness and tolerance of extreme political views,[94] where the danger posed by such views to the State is not 'imminent'[95] or there is no 'real threat' posed to the society or state.[96]

In *Ždanoka* the Grand Chamber of the Court swung back to a more hardline position, holding that a legal prohibition on candidates from standing for parliamentary elections who had participated in the Communist Party after 13 January 1991, when it had attempted a *coup d'état*, was not in violation of the Convention. The first judgment by the Chamber of the First Section had found the opposite, largely on the basis that the State had offered no evidence that the applicant had carried out any act capable of threatening the state, national security, or the domestic democratic order. That initial judgment had provoked, as Sweeney notes, significant dissent from Judge Bonello, arguing against blind promotion of human-rights ideals:

[91] See, in particular, chs. 7 and 8 in Sweeney, *Post-Cold War Era*.
[92] Article 3, Protocol 1.   [93] (2003) 37 EHRR 1.
[94] Sweeney, *Post-Cold War Era* 210–11.   [95] *Partidul Comunistilor* v. *Romania*.
[96] *Tsonev* v. *Bulgaria*.

> Even in defiance of historical realities, the weakness of emergent and fragile pluralisms and the contradictions faced by a democracy called to contain democratically those who consider democracy, at best, expendable and, at worst, wholly detrimental.[97]

We see here the significant challenges in facilitating the construction of a democratic public sphere while attempting to mediate the shift from the old order to the new order. In *Refah Partisi* the context concerned an entire party with millions of followers. In *Ždanoka*, by contrast, it is difficult to see how the voice of a single person – whose menace to Latvia's democratic system had not been proven by the State – could not be accommodated in the democratic order, even if it was linked to the past regime. It is hard to decide between the entrenchment value of allowing maximal respect to free speech, association, and the right to stand for election and participate in democratic deliberation, and the disentrenchment value of excluding anti-democratic voices from a democratic public sphere which is nascent and fragile, in a context where portions of the citizenry may view the new democratic order with distaste.

The lesson from Europe for the Inter-American and African regional human rights courts appears to be that greater sensitivity to democratisation processes, rather than a 'one-size-fits-all' approach, brings a new suite of difficulties and judgments into play. Uniformity, as best seen in the Inter-American jurisprudence, has the advantage of providing clear markers as to what is and is not acceptable, and signals greater respect for the universality of human rights, but lacks flexibility and can engender resistance as well as co-operation. Context-sensitivity and flexibility, on the other hand, can bring charges of inconsistency and unfairness, and opens a space for every state to plead for special treatment. In Europe, Sweeney observes, for instance, the Court's more understanding approach to Dutch lustration laws, as compared to Slovakian lustration laws.[98] There is different treatment in Europe, also, as between new democracies, with the Court's acceptance of electoral restrictions in the Latvian case of *Ždanoka* seemingly at odds with its finding of a violation in earlier Polish and Hungarian cases.[99]

The fundamental question underlying all these discussions is the capacity of a regional court to assess just what is possible in, and required

---

[97] See the First Section judgment, ECtHR, App. No. 58278/00 (17 June 2004) para. 2.2 of the dissent.

[98] See Sweeney, *Post-Cold War Era* 89.   [99] Ibid. ch. 8.

by, a new democracy to support the democratisation process – its ability to 'judge democratisation'. This point has been most vividly made as regards the Court's judgment in *Sejdić and Finci v. Bosnia and Herzegovina*.[100] In *Sejdić* the Court, placing significant emphasis on opinions of the Venice Commission, held that candidacy rules for the respondent State's tripartite presidency under consociational democratic arrangements, painstakingly established in the Dayton peace agreement to end the armed conflict which had ended over 100,000 lives in the mid-1990s, constituted discrimination contrary to the European Convention (Article 12 and Article 1 of Protocol No.12, in combination with Article 3 of Protocol No.1). McCrudden and O'Leary have taken the Court to task for a rash and poorly reasoned judgment; they argue that the decision not only threatened democratic governance (albeit intensely supervised by external actors) and the tense peace in Bosnia and Herzegovina, which had lasted just over a decade, thereby threatening the lives of those in the state, but that the Court's judgment also removed the decision on reform from those who should make it:

> [D]eciding when to make changes, who is to make them, and how they should be made should not be in the hands of a court.[101]

6 Conclusion: A Fundamental Question

The question above, of course, hovers over every controversial decision made by courts in any democratic order, but has a particular added bite when related to a young democracy and the role of any court in supporting democratisation.

Chapters 5 and 6 have sought to explore the nature of democratisation jurisprudence at both the domestic and regional levels to get a better sense of how the global model of court-centric democracy-building operates, through 'double review' across the two levels. Taking in the case-study as a whole, it is clear that significant limitations exist regarding the capacities of the courts at each level to 'build' democracy, but that nevertheless they are able to shape and support the democratisation process at critical points. This provides the basis for the exploration in the next chapter of the crucial question: what *should* courts do in new democracies?

---

[100] ECtHR, App. Nos. 27996/06 and 34836/06 (22 December 2009).
[101] McCrudden & O'Leary, *Courts & Consociations* 149.

7

What *Should* Courts Do in a Young Democracy? Rethinking Our Approach

> Lawfulness reveals all that is orderly and fitting, and often places fetters around the unjust. She makes the rough smooth, puts a stop to excess, dries up the blooming flowers of ruin, straightens out crooked judgments, tames deeds of pride, and puts an end to acts of sedition and to the anger of grievous strife. Under her all things among men are fitting and rational.
>
> Solon, Athenian law-giver and politician, 6th Century BC[1]

> Men will always prove bad unless, by necessity, they are compelled to be good.
>
> Niccolò Machiavelli, 1515[2]

> Judges may help us to become a truly democratic community without themselves becoming the unguarded guards of that community.
>
> Roberto Gargarella, 2004[3]

This book so far has been tethered to the existing reality of the world around us. We have been focused on how the global model of court-centric democratisation has developed from its primary roots in post-war Germany, to its migration across scores of new democracies in three world regions, and how it has retained a particular internal logic across time and space while mutating in reaction to each new context. It is important, however, not to remain too tethered to what we see around us. The aim of this chapter is to jump from the 'is' to the 'ought'; to examine how this global model might be made better, and why. In doing so, it canvasses existing normative

---

[1] Translation from Fragment 4 of Solon's poetry. See J.H. Blok & A.P.M.H. Lardinois (eds.), *Solon of Athens* (Brill, 2005) 458.
[2] *The Prince*: see H. Neville, *The Works of the Famous Nicolas Machiavel* (A. Churchill, 1720) 232.
[3] Gargarella, 'Democratic Justice' 184.

arguments for what courts should do as democracy-builders, and makes certain recommendations based on a clear-eyed view of the strengths and weaknesses of adjudication at each level. The final section of the chapter examines the existing model of court-centric democracy-building in its fundamentals, with a view to spurring exploration of how we can preserve what is best about the current model, while moving away from the current trend of excessive reliance on courts.

1 Aim of this Chapter: Framing the Problem

Although there has clearly been a normative thrust to the discussion in the book thus far, this chapter takes a much more expressly normative tack in addressing the question of what roles constitutional courts and regional human rights courts should play to support democratisation processes.

First, a quick recap of the discussion thus far. This book started out with three questions. First, how have domestic constitutional courts and regional human rights courts become such central actors in post-war democratisation processes? Second, what roles do these courts *actually* play in democratisation processes, and how does the democratisation context shape their roles? Third, what roles *should* courts play in a young democracy, as compared to a mature democracy? Chapters 1, 2, and 3 focused on the first question, while Chapters 2 to 6 together focused on the second question. This chapter focuses on the final question.

As Chapters 2 to 6 have shown, great expectations are placed on both constitutional courts and regional human rights courts to act as democracy-builders, but at each level they encounter significant institutional, political, and epistemic challenges in this task. More importantly, although commonly conceived of as a combined system, there are multiple asymmetries between their purposes, setting, embeddedness in the democratisation context, and capacity to impact on the domestic order. This leads, at times, to starkly divergent approaches to the same key democratisation issues and sub-optimal outcomes in the effort to constrain anti-democratic actors. We saw how adjudication at each level is fundamentally shaped by the context: for constitutional courts, their embeddedness in one state-bound constitutional order and democratisation process; for regional human rights courts, their externality to any one democratisation process and any domestic constitutional order.

We also got a sense of the complex normative landscape in which democratisation has taken place in the young democracies of the 1980s onward, involving multiple sites of constitutional authority across a three-dimensional political space.

Keeping in mind these key insights gained from the previous chapters, the problem addressed here is two-fold. First, certain prescriptions are offered concerning the roles courts at the domestic and regional levels should play within the existing framework, emphasising the strengths and weaknesses of adjudication at each level and the need for co-ordination between both levels. The second question, which evidently cannot be pursued at length in this work, is the deeper consideration of whether the global court-centric model of democratisation itself needs to be re-evaluated, and how we might go about redesigning courts in the future to act as more effective democracy-builders. The fundamental claim here is that we should embrace a position of 'dynamic conservatism' aimed at preserving the best of the judicialised post-war model for democratisation, while considering new possibilities for a broader-based system that pays more attention to interaction between the domestic and international levels, and which remains cognisant of the need to ensure that courts do not stifle the role of other actors in the democratisation process.

In approaching these questions, it is tempting to jump straight into the discussion of the various normative arguments made by scholars such as Kim Scheppele and Roberto Gargarella for the roles courts should play in a young democracy. However, to fully understand those arguments, it is important to first appreciate the essentials of the 'core' debate on the judicial role in a mature democracy. Although we will see that discussion of courts in young democracies is conducted in parallel to the core debate, and departs from it in vital respects, the core debate has shaped our frameworks for even approaching questions regarding the appropriate roles for courts in young democracies, and is linked in various ways to the parallel discussion.

The chapter therefore starts by briefly canvassing the core debate concerning the appropriate roles of courts in mature democracies, before contrasting it with the parallel discussion concerning the role of courts in young democracies. Two central claims are made regarding the parallel discussion. First, it fails to take sufficient account of relevant arguments by political constitutionalists in the core debate. Second, there is a fundamental failure, across this scholarship, to integrate regional human rights courts into the discussion.

2   The 'Core' Debate on the Role of the Courts in a Mature Democracy

The proper role of courts in a mature democracy has been at issue since the late nineteenth century, when the implications of the US Supreme Court's arrogation in *Marbury* v. *Madison* (1803) of the power of strong judicial review began to become manifest during the forty-year *Lochner* era, during which the Court consistently struck down legislation aimed at more expansive State intervention in economic activity on the basis that it violated economic liberty or private contract rights.[4] As briefly discussed in the Introduction to this book, the deviation of strong judicial review from the general principle of democratic governance – majoritarian decision-making – has since become a central obsession of constitutional scholars. That obsession has become increasingly intense and globalised in the post-war era, due to the exponential transfer of significant governance power from executives and legislatures to courts in recent decades, at both the domestic and regional levels, marking a move from the common pre-war role of policing basic legality to the contemporary reality where courts police law-making, policy-making, and even 'pure' politics.

A   *Legal Constitutionalism v. Political Constitutionalism*

As briefly discussed in the Introduction to the book, the core debate regarding strong judicial review is divided between 'political constitutionalists', such as Jeremy Waldron, Jeffrey Goldsworthy, and Mark Tushnet, and 'legal constitutionalists' such as Ronald Dworkin and John Hart Ely, who, while agreeing on the fundamental proposition that the powers of government should be subject to effective limits to protect the rights and liberties of the people, disagree on the institutional form such constraints should take.

Political constitutionalists, as briefly discussed in the Introduction, place their faith in the political process and the capacity of individuals in a political community for moral judgment, and thus perceive a fundamental conflict between democratic principles, such as the political equality of individuals in a political community, and the enjoyment of constitutional supremacy by unelected judges. Legal constitutionalists, for their part, argue that justiciable constitutional limits on governmental

---

[4] See Chapter 2.

power and action, embodied in the judicial power to invalidate unconstitutional laws, are necessary to counter dangerous majoritarian impulses and to provide sufficient protection for fundamental rights.

With respect to strong judicial review by regional human rights courts, political constitutionalists perceive heightened concerns regarding the legitimacy of such review, as against the domestic setting; while legal constitutionalists focus on questions of heterarchy and hierarchy as between domestic and international courts, and the challenge of managing co-existence and co-operation in a shared transnational judicial space. The aim here is not to re-tread this debate at length, but to capture its essentials.

B   Five Key Characteristics of the Debate

Five main points may help to orient the discussion in the following sections. First, due to intense engagement between both camps, each position has been constructed to a significant extent in an oppositional fashion; political constitutionalists construct a model of political constitutionalism as against the model of legal constitutionalism, and vice versa. As Graham Gee and Grégoire Webber have observed:

> it can sometimes seem as if, for many of its proponents, a political constitution is defined by the array of contrasts that can be drawn with a legal constitution, with much effort being made to rebut the challenges that appear to be posed to a political constitution by its legal counterpart. More emphasis tends to be placed on making sense of a political constitution obliquely, in terms of what it differs from, rather than in terms of its own possibilities.[5]

Second, to a significant extent, even today, the core debate remains a very American one, or at least a common law Anglosphere one, with the leading lights tending to be American scholars, or from other Anglosphere mature democracies but based in the United States (e.g. Waldron). This US-centred debate, though often couched in universal language, tends to speak in many ways to the very particular development of strong judicial review in the United States as a polity, and betrays acute concerns regarding the crucible of that power and its enduringly slim constitutional basis. The 'counter-majoritarian difficulty' of the US Supreme Court, as

---

[5] G. Gee & G.C.N. Webber, 'What is a Political Constitution?' (2010) 30 *Oxford Journal of Legal Studies* 273, 276.

Alexander Bickel put it, is heightened by the fact that it has no explicit textual basis in the US Constitution of 1789, unlike most constitutional courts in new democracies of the post-war era, which is our broad temporal and geographical focus here.[6] Most expressly, certain scholars such as Mark Tushnet and Larry Kramer 'thicken' their theoretical critiques with a particular focus on the empirical realities of the US context.[7]

By contrast, normative approaches to strong judicial review from scholars outside the Anglosphere, in states such as Germany and Italy, tend to have a different starting point given that the express grant of the strong judicial review powers to the courts lends it a less contested (though certainly not uncontested) legitimacy than the power as exercised by the US Supreme Court.[8]

Third, despite the emergence of various powerful international courts since the 1960s, this core debate has remained largely state-bound for decades, with constitutional courts, legislatures, and 'the people' – the source of democratic power – as the main protagonists.[9] In particular, the role of regional human rights courts tends to feature as a distant second to the primary focus on domestic constitutional courts. To a certain extent, this again reflects the fact that the United States remains the main intellectual and empirical centre of gravity of the legal v. political constitutionalism debate. The United States, after all, is not subject to the jurisdiction of any regional court with strong judicial review powers; in particular, it has never accepted the jurisdiction of the Inter-American Court of Human Rights.[10]

It should be relatively unsurprising then that the extension of the debate to regional human rights courts has been led by European scholars in mature democracies with a sceptical view of strong judicial review: Richard Bellamy hails from the United Kingdom, with its enduring tradition of parliamentary supremacy; while Andreas Føllesdal is from Norway, where a strong review system is coloured by much greater

---

[6] On Bickel and the counter-majoritarian difficulty see Delaney, 'Analyzing Avoidance'; and A. Bickel, *The Least Dangerous Branch: The Supreme Court at the Bar of Politics* (Bobbs-Merrill, 1962).

[7] See J. Waldron, 'The Core of the Case against Judicial Review' (2006) 115 *Yale Law Journal* 1346, 1351.

[8] See e.g. the discussion of Luigi Ferrajoli's work in Chapter 1.

[9] The vast scholarship on courts such as the European Court of Justice is considered a separate entity here from the 'core' debate on strong judicial review.

[10] The United States has signed the American Convention on Human Rights (ACHR), but has not ratified the Convention or recognised the Inter-American Court's jurisdiction.

deference to the legislature than the US system or 'mainstream' European systems such as the German or Spanish systems.[11]

To some extent the domestic debate maps on to strong judicial review as exercised by regional human rights courts, but the arguments are modified to take account of the different empirical context, with particular concerns focusing on the *problématique* of regional human rights courts as external to the democratic state system, less subject to the control of any electorate, freer to engage in dynamic treaty interpretation, subject to more diffuse professional norms, less familiar with the mores and particularities of domestic societies and legal systems, freer from even indirect forms of political accountability in the form of co-equal constitutional partners, and threatening the coherence of law by competing with domestic law.[12] Bellamy argues, for instance, that the very nature of regional human rights courts as outsiders raises the risk of the regional court misunderstanding the specificities of rights realisation at the domestic level. Worse, he argues that their externality means they lack the motivation to decide responsibly, given that they remain unaffected by the impact of their decisions.[13]

Importantly, outside the EU context, it is hard to find considered arguments supporting strong judicial review at the regional level, which squarely address the concerns of political constitutionalists. For instance, Føllesdal's defence of the review function of the European Court of Human Rights as 'central to the Rule of Law, and in turn as crucial to a domestic and international constitutionalism worth respecting', is rooted in his characterisation of that court's review function as 'weak' judicial review.[14] States, he observes, enjoy discretion as to how a decision finding a violation of the European Convention is to be implemented, and the Court's margin of appreciation doctrine is used to accommodate a diversity of opinion across Europe regarding rights issues.

Fourth, the debate is geared toward, and expressed in the language of, rights. It focuses on which form of constitutionalism is a more democratically legitimate means to ensure rights protection (a primary

---

[11] See R. Bellamy, 'Democratic Legitimacy'; and Føllesdal, 'Much Ado'. Both use the term 'international', but it appears that their arguments do not go beyond the particular case of strong judicial review at the regional level.

[12] See e.g. Føllesdal, 'Much Ado' 276–7; and chs. 25–8 in Huls, Adams & Bomhoff (eds.), *The Legitimacy of Highest Courts' Rulings*.

[13] Føllesdal, 'Much Ado' 248–61.   [14] Ibid. 293.

concern for political constitutionalists), and also which is the most *effective* for rights protection. Regarding democratic legitimacy, Jeremy Waldron famously characterises the ability of individuals in a political community to participate in ultimate decision-making on an equal basis as 'the right of rights', and insists that an objection to strong judicial review on the basis of democratic principles must be rights-based.[15] However, Jeffrey Goldsworthy argues that this can be somewhat reductive. For him, democracy is not only valued for its capacity to protect rights, but also on the basis that, by facilitating citizen participation in decision-making and debate, it aids in the development of central civic virtues, such as an appreciation of other points of view, and thereby promotes 'cooperation and compromise, a sense of responsibility to the community, and a more willing acceptance of group decisions.'[16]

Fifth, democracy here tends to mean *representative* democracy, with the particularities of electoral competition, rotations of power, and the deliberative, multi-actor and multi-stage nature of the legislative process as a decision-making procedure viewed as providing a better way of promoting the requisite civic virtues for a functioning democratic political community than alternatives such as direct democracy through referendums and plebiscites.[17]

As a result, the core debate tends to overlook significant complexities in the contexts in which many courts find themselves adjudicating. Key here, as discussed in Chapter 4, are the transfer of governance power from legislatures to executives in many democracies, the increasing use of direct democracy mechanisms such as referendums, and the flow of governance power outside the state.

C Arguing to a Stalemate

Although there is significant engagement by scholars in each camp with those from the other side, there is a certain sense that they argue one another to a stalemate. Waldron's concise conspectus of the core arguments for and against strong judicial review shows, for instance, that

[15] J. Waldron, 'A Right-Based Critique of Constitutional Rights' (1993) 13 *Oxford Journal of Legal Studies* 18 (1993); and J. Waldron, *Law and Disagreement* (Clarendon Press, 1999) 282. Cited in J. Goldsworthy, 'Judicial Review, Legislative Override, and Democracy' in T. Campbell, J. Goldsworthy & A. Stone (eds.), *Protecting Human Rights: Instruments and Institutions* (Oxford University Press, 2003) 265, 270.
[16] Goldsworthy, 'Judicial Review' 270.   [17] See e.g. ibid.

claims for courts as better moral reasoners can be countered with a claim for moral reasoning of at least equal, if not better, quality in parliaments.[18] Legal constitutionalists will assert the democratic credentials of strong judicial review, on the basis that courts are merely enforcers of a bill of rights adopted by the people, and that judicial decisions can be overturned by amending the bill of rights. The response is that bills of rights are merely focal points for disagreements concerning rights rather than settling them, and that amending a bill of rights tends to be a rather difficult process.[19]

Similarly, political constitutionalists such as Mark Tushnet argue that the very practice of strong judicial review can operate to reduce the sensitivity of both the people and their representatives to the importance of respecting rights, and their very capacity to engage in moral reasoning and deliberation concerning the meaning and scope of rights issues.[20] Legal constitutionalists assert the opposite. Irwin Stotzky, for example, opines that a constitutional court can help 'to create a moral consciousness in the citizenry through the process of rational discourse'.[21] Joseph Goldstein characterises judicial opinions as a means of maintaining an informed citizenry in accordance with the principle of popular sovereignty on which a (republican) democratic system rests.[22] However, none of these arguments, for or against strong review, is easy to verify, and would require extremely sophisticated sociological research to assess.

For Waldron, according the final say on constitutional matters to courts fundamentally violates the principle of political equality between citizens by disenfranchising current democratic majorities. Decision-making by legislatures, in his view, responds best to this challenge in that contemporary representative democracy realises, albeit imperfectly, the principle of political equality by means of elections, representation by elected persons, and the legislative process itself, with the result that the aggrieved citizen can be assured that she, and other aggrieved citizens, has been accorded the 'greatest say possible compatible with an equal say for each of the others.'[23] Yet scholars such as Richard Kay concede

---

[18] Waldron, 'Core of the Case' 1382ff.   [19] Ibid. 1386–91.

[20] See R.S. Kay, 'Rights, Rules and Democracy' in Campbell, Goldsworthy & Stone (eds.), *Protecting Human Rights* 122–3; and Goldsworthy, 'Judicial Review' 271.

[21] I. Stotzky, 'The Tradition' 349.

[22] J. Goldstein, 'The Opinion-Writing Function of the Judiciary of Latin American Governments in Transition to Democracy: *Martinez v. Provincia de Mendoza*' in Stotzky (ed.), *Transition to Democracy* 300ff.

[23] Waldron, 'Core of the Case' 1389.

that a particular democratic concern is raised where sitting democratic majorities are engaged in shaping legislation concerning the electoral system. Courts, in such cases, can pursue 'representation-reinforcing review' by placing constraints on attempts by elected actors to entrench themselves in power, by playing a vital role in reviewing legislation concerning the electoral process.[24] The latter point tends to show that opposition to strong judicial review can be, to a certain extent, context-specific.

D   Where Does the 'Core' Debate Apply?

The core debate is often expressly emphasised as relating to decision-making in well-functioning democratic systems, especially by political constitutionalists.

Waldron, for instance, emphasises that his argument against strong judicial review relates to a functioning democratic order, predicated on 'four quite demanding assumptions'.[25] These are: first and second, that representative institutions and unelected judicial institutions are in reasonably good working order; third, that most officials and members of society evince a commitment to the idea of individual and minority rights; and fourth, that there is 'persisting, substantial and good faith disagreement' concerning the implications of, and meaning of, the commitment to such rights. Where one or more of these preconditions is not met by a particular political community – what Waldron calls 'non-core cases' – his argument against strong judicial review does not apply. However, he stresses that this does not automatically mean that strong judicial review will be legitimate in such a community. For instance, it cannot be considered legitimate where judicial review will not address inadequacies in rights protection, or where corruption affects judicial organs to the same extent as legislative organs.[26]

While it is not easy to draw a bright line on the basis of Waldron's assumptions between what democracies would be included and excluded, they appear to exclude a significant number of young democracies of the post-1974 third wave of democratisation from the application of the core debate. How, then, do normative stances concerning the roles of courts in these young democracies differ from those in the core debate?

---

[24] Kay, 'Rights, Rules and Democracy' 122–3.   [25] Waldron, 'Core of the Case' 1402.
[26] Ibid.

3   A Parallel Discussion: The Role of Courts in a Young Democracy

A   *The Nature of this Parallel Discussion*

In a sense, the scholarship on the role of strong judicial review in young democracies occupies the space beyond the outer boundaries set by scholarship on the role of such review in mature democracies. However, this parallel discussion does not merely mirror the legal v. political constitutionalism debate canvassed above. A number of distinguishing features may be noted.

First, there is no neat debate, as found above, between so-called legal constitutionalists and political constitutionalists. Instead, we find a variety of normative arguments made by scholars in both law and political science, which take somewhat different approaches, although the majority of the arguments tend to support a role for strong judicial review in young democracies. There is less intense intersection between these arguments, with scholars tending to focus on their own proclivities rather than seeking to spark a specific discussion. There are thus no ideological camps marked out, or clear battle lines drawn, as one finds in the scholarship on mature democracies.

Second, unlike arguments for legal constitutionalism in mature democracies, these treatments often do not address at any length arguments against strong judicial review made by political constitutionalists regarding mature democracies; usually dispensing with such concerns in a rather cursory manner. Lach and Sadurski capture this well:

> In the initial period of the courts' functioning a convenient explanation of the legitimacy conundrum was the claim that there existed a transitional character to the legal and political environment in which the courts operated. As the argument went, in the period of dramatic transformation from an authoritarian to a democratic system, ordinary intuitions concerning the role of adjudication might need to be modified. This conviction ... certainly had some explanatory value as to the sudden rise and success of constitutional adjudication combined with a relative absence of critical reflection about [sic] legitimacy of this institutional system.[27]

Somewhat more stridently, Samuel Issacharoff asserts that constitutional courts in third wave democracies, granted an expressly central role and

---

[27] K. Lach and W. Sadurski, 'Constitutional Courts of Central and Eastern Europe: Between Adolescence and Maturity' in Harding & Leyland (eds.), *Constitutional Courts* 69; citing R Teitel, 'Transitional Jurisprudence'.

significant review powers by new democratic constitutions, are 'little detained by concerns over the authority for judicial review or over the countermajoritarian consequences of constitutional challenge.'[28] Even where scholars, such as Theunis Roux, argue that this is untrue, their claims are descriptive rather than normative:

> [T]hose concerns are real and pressing, and an appreciation for how post-1989 constitutional courts mediate them is crucial to a proper understanding of their capacity to act as a hedge against democratic authoritarianism.[29]

Third, although the majority of the key scholars in the area are American or based in the United States, such as Samuel Issacharoff, Kim Lane Scheppele, and Tom Ginsburg, there is a greater diversity of empirical referents in the form of young democracies worldwide, allowing a departure from the influence (whether direct or indirect) of the US experience. This parallel discussion also includes leading voices from Europe (e.g. Wojciech Sadurski), Latin America (e.g. Roberto Gargarella), and Africa (e.g. Theunis Roux).

Finally, the arguments concerning strong judicial review posited by such scholars are not expressed solely in the language of rights protection, but extend much more expressly to the structural elements of democratic governance, such as separation of powers, electoral rules, the power of constitutional amendment, and the overall capacity of majoritarian decision-making to overwhelm democratic rule itself in fragile new democracies.

B Constitutional Courts: Five Basic Approaches

When we canvass scholarship as a whole concerning the role of strong judicial review by constitutional courts, five basic positions can be identified.

First is an approach that simply expects constitutional courts in young democracies to operate in a similar manner to their counterparts in mature democracies, with limited tweaks. Second is the argument that innovations in strong review in states of the Global South should not be discounted as aberrant simply because they do not conform to Western norms. Third is a general argument from Kim Lane Scheppele that, where the elected organs are unable to fulfil their functions in the same manner as their counterparts in mature democracies, a constitutional

---

[28] Issacharoff, 'Democratic Hedging' 964.   [29] Roux, 'A Response' 12.

court can act as a substitute for deliberation and reflection of the popular will, with strong judicial review thus recast as a democratic process. Fourth is the argument for a more targeted role, from authors such as Samuel Issacharoff and Roberto Gargarella, aimed at shoring up the worst inadequacies of a new democratic political system and thus facilitating the persistence and development of democratic rule rather than its decay after the initial transition to electoral democracy. Fifth, and final, is an argument from Stephen Gardbaum that, rather than strong judicial review, weak review should be embraced as a means of establishing and maintaining the independence of the judiciary in a young democracy, by providing more '"dialogical" modes of judicial intervention'.[30]

For the purposes of clarity, and although there are certainly overlaps between them, these five approaches are called here the 'mirror', 'Global South', 'surrogate', 'scaffolding', and 'weak review' arguments.

'Mirror' Argument

The mirror argument generally argues for constitutional courts to approximate the role carried out by courts in mature democracies with systems of strong judicial review. That is, they are expected to play an active part in democratic governance, but to evince a clear respect for the constitutional role of the other actors in the system, and to avoid trenching upon their sphere of action. The difference, as compared to a mature democracy, is how the court can carve out such a role for itself in what can constitute a hostile institutional matrix, in a context where the court often has more extensive adjudication powers and a significantly thicker constitution to interpret than those of mature democracies. Due to the Hungarian experience, and that of serious missteps by courts in other states, such as Russia and Mongolia in the 1990s, Western authors tend to advise that caution and restraint are the route to effectiveness, allowing a constitutional court to engage in progressive institution-building.

In the European context, for example, Lach and Sadurski state: 'In the long run, doing less and in a more restrained manner might prove more effective than an excessive pro-activity'.[31] Sadurski opines elsewhere that rights protection constitutes 'the most important' aspect of constitutional adjudication, on the basis that constitutional rights are 'at the very centre of the self-definition of a polity, and of the construction of the status of

---

[30] Gardbaum, 'Strong Constitutional Courts' 311.
[31] Lach & Sadurski, 'Constitutional Courts' 79.

an individual vis-à-vis the state'.[32] This sentiment is echoed, to a significant extent, by Tom Ginsburg in his analysis of the East Asian experience, when he opines that caution is warranted 'on core issues of the political process for courts in new democracies', leaving 'attention to fundamental rights and constraint of state authority as the real roles the courts can play'.[33]

Under this view, courts need to engage in strategic behaviour to avoid addressing matters that will bring them into conflict with the other branches of government. This can be achieved by making use of Alexander Bickel's 'passive virtues' to simply duck the issue and leave it to the political branches. In supreme courts this can be achieved through the application of judicial tools such as a 'political question' doctrine. For Kelsenian constitutional courts it requires the application of other tools, such as strategic case management. A good example is the German Constitutional Court's stalling tactics approach to challenges to the EDC Treaty with France in the early 1950s, discussed in Chapter 2. As seen in Chapter 5, a court can also take a cautious approach to exercising express powers that raise the risk of clashes with the other branches; seen in the Brazilian Supreme Court's non-confrontational use of its power to address legislative omission in the 1990s.

'Global South' Argument

Scholars such as Sadurski and Ginsburg do acknowledge that courts in young democracies face some different challenges to their counterparts in mature democracies, but they do not appear to place any special weight on this fact. Other scholars place much greater weight on the different political and social context of young democracies.[34] Daniel Bonilla Maldonado, criticising in particular the 'closed and parochial nature of the US legal academy' (although this charge certainly cannot be levelled at many of the American scholars discussed here), has argued that the jurisprudence of the Indian, Colombian, and South African constitutional courts should be viewed as a 'constitutionalism of the

---

[32] Sadurski, *Rights Before Courts* xix.

[33] Ginsburg, 'Constitutional Courts in East Asia' 310.

[34] It may be noted here that India is (perhaps controversially) not considered a mature democracy under the framework set out in Chapter 1. South Africa is considered a young democracy. Colombia, although a 'thin' electoral democracy for decades before the 1991 Constitution, is considered a young democracy insofar as that constitution underpinned a new political settlement and a movement to a 'thick' constitutional democracy in the post-war mould.

Global South' that has sought to address political violence, high rates of poverty and inequality, cultural and religious diversity, and 'consolidation of the rule of law',[35] which, he contends, should not be discounted simply because it does not faithfully mirror the approaches in Western courts such as the US Supreme Court, the Federal Constitutional Court of Germany, and the European Court of Human Rights:

> The jurisprudence of [the Indian, Colombian, and South African courts] certainly moves within and is supported by modern constitutionalism's basic rules and principles. These Courts use and comply with modern constitutionalism's grammar. Consequently, as happens with all courts, many of the cases that they decide are doctrinally unimportant – they merely reiterate standard interpretations of rules and principles. . . . However, some of the interpretations offered by these Courts present modern constitutionalism's basic components in a new light, or at least rearrange them in novel ways [and] therefore, [have] something to contribute to the ongoing global conversation on constitutionalism. . . . Constitutional law scholars and other participants in this dialogue would discover, for example, interesting ways of interpreting the principle of separation of powers, appealing forms of interpreting the practical consequences of connecting social and economic rights with the principle of human dignity, and powerful strategies to allow poor individuals to access justice.[36]

It is true that the particular context of non-Western young democracies has often led to expansions in the exercise of judicial review and a willingness to exert greater control over political actors and governance questions. It is seen, for instance, in the Colombian Constitutional Court's assertive approach to social and economic rights since the 1990s and the Indian Supreme Court's basic structure doctrine of the 1970s, through which it asserted the power to review constitutional amendments. However, it clearly cuts both ways: the democratisation context has also, for instance, been provided as a reason for the South African Constitutional Court's refusal to issue structural injunctions to direct policy in the areas of health and housing policy, on the basis that the time is not yet ripe for such intervention. This approach has been strongly criticised by authors such as Upendra Baxi as a failure to realise the promise of a 'transformative constitutionalism' common to states such as Brazil, India, and South Africa.[37]

---

[35] D. Bonilla Maldonado, 'Introduction: Toward a Constitutionalism of the Global South' in Bonilla Maldonado (ed.), *Constitutionalism of the Global South* 11, 22.
[36] Ibid. 22–4.   [37] Baxi, 'Preliminary Notes' 46.

To complicate matters further, Latin American scholars tend to contest the value of caution and restraint, suggesting that strategic deferential behaviour in order to develop judicial power can be quite costly for courts, leading to perceptions that the court is partisan or reluctant to protect fundamental rights, and thereby hampering rather than furthering institution-building.[38] Conversely, incremental institution-building can be so successful as to lead to what some see as an *excessive* judicialisation of politics. For instance, as seen in Chapter 5, in recent years Brazilian scholars have begun warning of the perils of 'supremocracy', with the Supreme Court enjoying excessive power in the democratic order.[39] The Constitutional Chamber (*Sala Cuarta*) of the Costa Rican Supreme Court is similarly viewed as 'a victim of its own success'.[40] These arguments do not strike at the legitimacy of strong judicial review *per se*, but rather at the extent to which such review plays a part in governance. (They also suggest that, whatever approach a court takes, criticism is virtually inevitable).

'Surrogate' Argument

The surrogate argument is a radical theoretical position born of extreme circumstances. Writing in 2001 Kim Lane Scheppele, charting the remarkable development of the Hungarian Constitutional Court's dominant role in the governance of Hungary's young democracy from 1989 until the late 1990s, spoke of 'democracy by judiciary'.[41] As discussed in Chapter 2, the Court had struck down a third of all laws in its first six years, extended specific challenges against legislative provisions to a review of the entire law itself, and was empowered to weigh heavily in the legislative process by providing advisory opinions during deliberations and ordering the legislature to enact laws mandated by the Constitution.[42] As a new institution attempting to mark out a role for itself, the Court's approach tended to be unleavened by restraint, with an approach to the political branches characterised, in Scheppele's memorable term, as

---

[38] See e.g. J. Couso & L. Hilbink, 'From Quietism to Incipient Activism: The Institutional and Ideological Roots of Rights Adjudication in Chile' in Helmke & Ríos-Figueroa (eds.), *Courts in Latin America*.

[39] See Vilhena Vieira, 'Supremocracia'.

[40] R.A. Sanchez-Urribarri, 'Constitutional Courts in the Region: Between Power and Submissiveness' in R. Dixon & T. Ginsburg (eds.), *Comparative Constitutional Law in Latin America* (Edward Elgar Publishing, forthcoming, 2017).

[41] Scheppele, 'Democracy by Judiciary'.   [42] Ibid. 13–17.

'separation of powers as a contact sport'[43] – a more conflictual model of interaction than, for instance, Aharon Barak's view of constant tension between governmental branches as 'natural and desirable'.[44]

In Scheppele's view, the standard democratic critique of the vivid amplitude of the court's jurisprudence – that it constituted an undemocratic transfer of power to the judiciary – failed to account for two key particularities of a new democracy such as Hungary. First, political parties, as the main vehicles of representative democracy, were unable and unwilling to reflect the wishes of the electorate due to slim or non-existent electoral manifestos, and shifting alliances and formations. Second, a hard-pressed electorate, saddled with onerous workloads to stay financially afloat in a very difficult economic climate, had little time to build and take part in the vigorous civil society viewed as essential to a functioning democratic order in the Western mould.

She also argued that the standard critique – focusing on a procedural conception of democracy in which merely elections, the fundamental structures of democratic governance, and a small core of basic rights are guaranteed – failed to reflect the desire in new democracies for (and constitutional reflection of) a much thicker, substantive conception of democracy based on the recognition of a suite of rights 'to be treated decently and with respect', and detailed rules for the operation of democratic institutions.[45] An enduring focus on elections had to make way for a commitment to democratic values, motivated by a concern of 'back-sliding' to Communist-era modes of governance.[46]

Thus, for Scheppele, in the particular context of Hungary, citizens' ease of access to the Constitutional Court transformed it into an alternative forum for the mobilisation of the popular will. She notes for instance that, from a population of 10.5 million, some 1,500–2,500 petitions a year were brought to the Court, challenging virtually every major law enacted by parliament and seeking to hold the elected actors to 'a higher vision of politics'. In this altered reality, Scheppele is so bold as to say that 'the Court acted as a more popularly responsive, democratically thoughtful body than the Parliament', even to speak of the Court's 'democratic mandate'.[47]

As discussed in Chapter 2, in Hungary this did not prove to be a lasting governance arrangement, which suggests that the form of

---

[43] Scheppele, 'Guardians' 1760.
[44] A. Barak, *The Judge in a Democracy* (Princeton University Press, 2006) 216.
[45] Scheppele, 'Democracy by Judiciary' 32.   [46] Ibid. 8, 32.   [47] Ibid. 33–34.

'*über-Rechstaat*' model that Hungary embodied in the 1990s – which pushed the post-war West German *Rechtstaat* model to its extreme – is inherently unstable and unsustainable. However, this is evidently easy to see in hindsight. When Scheppele set out her defence of the model, there was much to applaud and the risks occasioned by excessively judicialised governance were not readily apparent.

'Scaffolding' Argument

Others argue for a more targeted role for constitutional courts, aimed not at substituting the court for the elected actors, mirroring adjudication in mature democracies, or a general expansion of the 'normal' Western boundaries of review to address particular societal problems, but at actively mitigating the *worst deficiencies* of new democracies. On this view, the constitutional court has a key role to play in preventing the elected organs from overwhelming the basic structure of democratic governance.

As briefly discussed in Chapter 4, Roberto Gargarella's concept of a 'democratic justice', hammered out on the empirical anvil of Argentina's problematic democratisation process from 1983 to 2002, suggests that in a young democracy a constitutional court should seek to counteract 'two particularly dangerous tendencies': first, the gradual establishment of restrictions on basic civil and political rights, such as the rights to freedom of expression and fair trial; and second, the executive's tendency to amplify its powers and distort or overcome democratic controls, such as the separation of powers, or even attempts to discontinue democratic rule.[48]

In a similar vein to Scheppele and Maldonado, Gargarella asserts that the mere fact that Anglo-American theories of democratic governance and the constitutional role of courts are attractive in the Anglo-American context does not necessarily render them attractive to Latin American contexts (and presumably other contexts), in which, for instance, the right to criticise government is always the first right to be curtailed by democratic regimes 'under stress'.[49] Thus, he argues, such moves should be subjected to the most intense scrutiny, requiring the courts to adopt an assertive posture and reduce the presumption of validity ordinarily associated with duly enacted laws.

---

[48] Gargarella, 'Democratic Justice' 182–3.   [49] Ibid.

The result should be, in his view, not an expansion of judicial power as compared to that seen in mature democracies, but a necessary *refinement* and redefinition of the role of constitutional adjudication in a different empirical context. It does not, he emphasises, necessitate the court to have the final say on all matters. It is also a role, he notes, that requires the mobilisation of civil society actors (e.g. social movements) to bring cases to the courts, echoing to some extent Scheppele's model, but falling far short of her justification of a constitutional court substituting for representative organs. As Gargarella expressly notes:

> [E]ven if we had democratically committed and well-prepared judges, they would not be able to transform our democracies into stronger ones by themselves.[50]

Samuel Issacharoff in his 'law of democracy' theory takes a somewhat similar approach to the second prong of Gargarella's 'democratic justice' by focusing on the role of constitutional courts in helping to mitigate specific structural deficiencies of the political system in a young democracy.[51] His approach is also strongly rooted in the empirical reality, being based on his observation that constitutional courts have appeared to take action to fill gaps in the structure of political governance in third wave democracies from South Africa to Romania to Colombia. Such courts have found themselves adjudicating on 'foundational' issues including impeachment, access to the electoral arena, the limits of governmental power, and minimum threshold requirements for parliamentary representation.[52]

For Issacharoff, the most crucial role courts can play, and one that should be 'unconstrained by a legitimacy concern over interceding in the political process', is protecting the 'vitality of democratic competition for electoral office and the ability of the political process to dislodge incumbents', to guard against the transition to electoral democracy merely providing a brief interregnum before the formation of a new autocracy, with the diminution of the opposition, partisan capture of all state power, and control of elections and the media:[53]

> The role of these constitutional courts is perhaps the most critical in the transition period [which would mean consolidation under the framework here] because of the immaturity and likely weakness of not only political

---

[50] Ibid. 184.   [51] See the works by Issacharoff at (n. 25) in the Introduction to the book.
[52] See Issacharoff, 'Democratic Hedging' 971–80.   [53] Ibid. 965, 992–3.

institutions, but the ancillary civil-society participants in democratic life – most notably, program-based political parties.[54]

Where Gargarella focuses on excessive concentration of power in the form of hyperpresidentialism, Issacharoff's particular focus is the ability of a court to limit distortion of democratic governance in a state, such as South Africa, where a single party dominates governance following the transition to democracy.

Noting courts' reticence to explicitly lay claim to this role, preferring to couch intervention in rights language, Issacharoff argues that the only means for a court to adequately constrain partisan capture of the democratic process in this way is the adoption of a version of the Indian 'basic structure' doctrine, in order to police the validity of constitutional amendments, and thereby to adequately address instances of Landau's 'abusive constitutionalism', discussed in Chapter 4. This, he contends, would empower courts to guard the fundamentals of democratic governance, such as plurality of representation, against majoritarian pressure – an approach he prefers to the enshrinement of 'eternity clauses' in the constitutional text on the basis that it affords the courts greater flexibility in their role.[55]

In elaborating this argument, Issacharoff places particular emphasis on the fact that constitutional courts in new democracies enjoy an express constitutional basis for exercising strong judicial review, and the argument that the establishment of such courts is itself integral to the constitutional pact facilitating the transition to electoral democracy, as briefly discussed in Chapter 1.[56] He is unconvinced by the arguments of other scholars, such as Sadurski, Scheppele, and Stone Sweet, for the democratic credentials of strong judicial review as, respectively, an alternative democratic expression of the majority will, an integral part of the legislative process, or as itself quasi-parliamentary, in the sense of the court's acting as a 'third chamber' reviewing draft legislation.[57]

'Weak Review' Argument

In contrast to the four previous approaches, which all envisage a role for the exercise of strong judicial review by a constitutional court in a young democracy, Stephen Gardbaum has recently argued that weak judicial review might be a better option for courts in some new democracies, allowing them to adjudicate in a bold and creative manner and maintain

---

[54] Ibid. 1003.   [55] Ibid. 1002–3.   [56] Ibid. 964, 980–92.   [57] Ibid. 1001.

the coherence of the constitution without the cost, seen in the strong judicial review systems of new democracies across the world, of antagonising the other State powers and undermining the principle of judicial independence. His argument, like the mirror argument, may be viewed as speaking to the third dimension of democratisation jurisprudence, set out in Chapter 4: the court's challenge in carving out a role for itself in the new democratic order.

For Gardbaum, the independence of the judiciary – both in terms of freedom from political interference and impartial performance of functions 'without political, partisan or personal bias' – is at greater risk in a strong review system, which accords a more central governance role to the court as a 'veto player', placing it in opposition to government and opening it to political attacks. It also, he asserts, heightens claims that the court should enjoy democratic legitimacy, which is met by politicising the judicial appointments process.[58]

Significantly, his argument does not rest on the normative basis, so familiar to Western discourse, that courts should not have the power of strong judicial review due to its democratic illegitimacy. Rather, his is a pragmatic argument that strong review can hamper rather than help the effectiveness of courts where they are unlikely to be able to withstand political attacks or unable or unwilling to exercise the self-restraint required in a febrile political atmosphere. Where Aharon Barak views inter-branch conflict as natural and desirable, and Kim Scheppele sees separation of powers as necessarily a 'contact sport' when the court is attempting to assert itself in the new order, Gardbaum sees unnecessary and damaging confrontation that is entirely avoidable. Departing from the mirror argument, he views as insufficient the attempt to temper or resolve such confrontation by employing caution and restraint, or techniques such as suspended declarations of invalidity regarding unconstitutional laws, which still leave courts with the final say on constitutional matters.

Nor, in his view, can the systemic conflict engendered by strong review be fully addressed by embedding the new democracy in a 'broader, supervisory international regime' to enhance compliance by the government with judicial decisions. Noting the 'general success' of accession to the Council of Europe and its human rights protection system (and the EU) in supporting democratisation processes in Central and Eastern

---

[58] Gardbaum, 'Strong Constitutional Courts' 303ff.

Europe, he nonetheless observes that this has not reined in authoritarian 'backsliding' in states such as Hungary and Romania, which have withstood pressure from these external sources.[59]

C Deficiencies in the Existing Discussion

A number of key criticisms may be made of existing scholarship on the role of strong judicial review in young democracies, as outlined above.

Taking Each Approach in Turn

First, pace Scheppele, in her defence of the 'surrogate' model as democratic, the post-war normative paradigm of 'constitutional democracy', in which constitutionalism 'defines up' democracy, is stretched past its breaking point. In Scheppele's account, the 'constitutional', instead of 'completing' democracy, tends to cannibalise its conceptual partner. Democracy in her account is reduced to, not a procedure in which aggregate political and moral preferences across the entire population can be fed into governance (particularly legislative and policy-making processes), but rather a procedure whereby the preferences and moral reasoning of shifting, atomised, and often unconnected sub-communities (or even single individuals) are fed into a judicial process. The latter system cannot be held to equate to the former, especially when viewed from the perspective of the core principle of democratic governance, that is, the equality of individuals within the political community.

Such a system may be argued to serve the interests of the rule of law and of constitutionalism – a veritable *Rechtstaat* – but it cannot be democratic. It is perhaps a sign of the symbolic power of democracy itself, as noted by Kay, that no author can bring themselves to make an argument for a governance system that is not characterised as democratic.[60] Indeed, the model can also be argued to offend against the core constitutional prohibition against excessive concentration of power in any one organ – here, a constitutional court. In many ways, it appears to bear unwholesome similarities to the model of hyperpresidentialism, which envisages a fundamentally dyadic system with a direct connection between 'the people' and a powerful president at the apex of the governance structure, unmediated by formal processes for representation, and sidelining other sites of governance power.[61] That said, it must be fully

---

[59] Ibid. 28–30.   [60] Kay, 'Rights, Rules and Democracy' 120.
[61] See Uprimny, 'Recent Transformation' 1606.

recognised that Scheppele's 'surrogate' model is not advanced as a general model, but as a defence of a governance model born of the very particular circumstances of post-1989 Hungary.

The mirror argument, in turn, appears to cleave strongly to understandings of judicial activism and judicial passivity in scholarship on mature democracies, which have been shown to have limited explanatory power in Chapter 5. The prescriptions of caution and restraint overlook the fact that such an approach is easier for some courts to practise than others. Courts endowed with the power of abstract review are more easily 'politicised', some courts have no control over their dockets, some courts are required to interpret particularly badly drafted constitutions, or constitutions which enjoy very weak legitimacy, some courts must grapple with constitutions that provide for an enormous raft of justiciable fundamental rights, especially social and economic rights, and so on.

In short, it is crucial to bear in mind that while some courts may actively seek to expand their jurisdiction and have the last say regarding the most contentious social, political, and moral questions of the day, others, by dint of constitutional design, have no real choice in being pulled endlessly into the political fray. Indeed, the literature is replete with examples illustrating the difficulties that certain constitutional design options raise for the courts in one way or another. We might note, by way of example, the undermining of the Slovakian Constitutional Court following its inescapable intervention in disputes between the executive powers in the new semi-presidential system under the 1992 Constitution.[62] In addition, as regards the practice of caution and restraint, as Latin American scholars have emphasised, standard models for analysing strategic decision-making in constitutional courts, based on research in mature democracies, 'wildly underpredict' the number of political attacks against the judiciary in that region, which have not curtailed courts in the way Western scholars may expect.[63]

Turning to the scaffolding argument, Issacharoff's main claim for the court as a 'stabilizer' of the 'basic structure' of democracy at one level has an intuitive appeal, when we appreciate its roots in the empirical contexts of India, Colombia, Belize, and other states where courts have been pushed into asserting the power to assess the validity of constitutional amendments in order to address different strains of 'abusive constitutionalism'. However, his argument has insufficiently defined boundaries.

---

[62] See e.g. Lach & Sadurski, 'Constitutional Courts' 71.
[63] Helmke & Staton, 'Judicial Politics of Latin America' 306.

Even if we accept that the courts should assume this role, it does not resolve the question of how far a constitutional court may go beyond the text of the constitution to fulfil this function. He also expends little energy on examining the extent to which this changes the court's role from a constituted entity tasked with acting as 'guardian of the constitution', to an entity *external* to the constitution tasked with acting as 'guardian of democracy'. One reading, based on the emphasis he places on constitutional courts as part of the political pact underpinning the democratic transition, is that he views such courts as meta-constitutional organs, but this is never expressly stated.[64]

Theunis Roux has also criticised Issacharoff for failing to fully appreciate how the democratisation context places the courts in a precarious position:

> [T]hey are assumed [by Issacharoff] to be in a position roughly equivalent to that of courts in mature democracies, with little threat to their independence and consequently free to focus their efforts on developing the required constitutional law doctrines. The problem with this assumption is that it ignores the fact that a constitutional court's capacity to act as a hedge against authoritarianism may be inhibited by the same political conditions that interventions of this sort are aimed at addressing. Not just that, but a court's intervention to protect the democratic system necessarily has an effect, either positive or negative, on its capacity to intervene in future cases.[65]

This lack of appreciation for the political context cannot be levelled at Gardbaum, for whom context is everything. However, his argument for weak review is, in many ways, more problematic than the mirror and scaffolding arguments. It is hard to see how political actors who refuse to submit to strong judicial review would submit to the softer touch of weak review. Surely, where courts and such actors have divergent views, the latter would easily discard any weak review constraints.

This is not mere conjecture. Although Gardbaum presents this weak review solution as a constitutional transplant from the mature democracy context (i.e. common law Westminster states including Canada and New Zealand),[66] it is important to recognise that regions such as Latin America are no strangers to weak review models. As Joel Colón-Ríos has observed, several nineteenth-century Latin American constitutions, such as the Colombian Constitution of 1858, featured a weak form of judicial

---

[64] See in particular Issacharoff, *Fragile Democracies*.   [65] Roux, 'A Response' 12.
[66] Gardbaum, 'Strong Constitutional Courts' 293.

review that explicitly institutionalised parliament as the ultimate arbiter of constitutional validity. As recently as 1945 the Ecuadorean Constitution installed a form of weak judicial review whereby a special court, where requested by a final appeals court, had the power to suspend a law or regulation temporarily, in order to permit Congress to decide on its validity.[67]

The historical breakdown of constitutionalism and democracy in virtually all of these states, and particularly the move to strong judicial review across Latin America in the post-war era, tends to suggest that wholesale adoption of weak review may not prove a good fit for any but the most mature democracies. Moreover, the Chilean experience, where the courts' traditional long-term strategy was to avoid politically controversial cases in order to preserve judicial independence, raises the question of what worth judicial independence has if a court cannot use it to engage in assertive adjudication when the occasion so requires.[68]

Four Common Deficiencies

Taken together, scholarship on constitutional courts in particular also suffers from four key common weaknesses.

First, there is little analysis of the temporal limits of the extraordinary context of democratisation; all scholars advocate a particular role for the courts based on the context of a new democracy, but do not address the end-point beyond which such a role may no longer be justifiable. This is particularly true of Scheppele's argument, which does not appear to recognise the inherent unsustainability of the 'surrogate' model even while acknowledging its end in reality.

Issacharoff and Gargarella's approaches appear to imply at the very least a subsisting 'scaffolding' role for the courts beyond the consolidation of democracy. It is particularly strongly implied by Issacharoff's enthusiasm for the basic structure doctrine in Indian jurisprudence, which is now over forty years old.[69] He does not address, for instance, whether fundamental structural developments (e.g. the fragmentation of a dominant party into two or more parties) would remove the case for such a role for the constitutional court. Similarly, Gardbaum's pragmatic approach leaves open the question as to whether weak review might cede to strong review at a point when attacks on the constitutional courts become less likely. At least in a functional sense, he appears to suggest so

---

[67] Colón-Ríos, 'A New Typology' 145–6.   [68] See Chavez, 'The Rule of Law' 71.
[69] The Indian Constitution itself is, of course, much older, dating from 1949.

when he states that the 'partial depoliticization' of a constitutional court, achieved by adopting a system of weak review,

> may even mean that the judicial review carries greater weight and author-
> ity among both legislatures and, more importantly, citizens so that the
> political costs of overriding it are further increased.[70]

Second, it may be said that all scholars, bar perhaps Gargarella, fail to engage particularly seriously with the arguments of political constitu-tionalists within the core debate. For instance, Scheppele's argument for 'democracy by judiciary' on the basis that elected actors are unable to carry out the same roles as their counterparts in mature democracies, does not engage with Waldron's position that the solution may be to address the deficiencies in these institutions, not to bypass them entirely.[71] However, Waldron himself notes the conundrum that some rights may be considered too important to leave to the hopeful emer-gence of a 'more responsible and representative legislature', which would necessitate a greater role for the courts. Yet, such a role for courts may itself hinder the development of the desired improvements in the legisla-ture.[72] This may be viewed as a democratisation variant of Tushnet's 'democratic debilitation' argument, with the emphasis more squarely on elected representatives than both parliaments and the people.

Scheppele's 'democracy by judiciary' also fails to answer Waldron's more general observation that people 'tend to look to judicial review when they want greater weight for their opinions than electoral politics would give them.'[73] To organise a governance system around litigation appears to offend the basic principle of equal respect and an equal voice for all individuals of a community.

Third is the weak explanatory power of the enduring strong review/ weak review distinction. The choice presented across the literature on young democracies discussed above tends to be an either/or dichotomy, failing to recognise that courts, including regional human rights courts, often have a mixture of weak review powers alongside the strong review power to strike down legislation (or, in the case of regional courts, to declare it invalid for incompatibility with the human rights con-vention).[74] Gardbaum's approach, advocating a wholesale adoption

---

[70] Gardbaum, 'Strong Constitutional Courts' 314.
[71] Waldron, 'Core of the Case' 1403ff.   [72] Ibid.   [73] Ibid. 1395.
[74] See e.g. Abebe & Fombad, 'Advisory Jurisdiction'.

of weak review, falls, as so much of the scholarship does, into this weak/strong binary conception.

Yet, as we have seen in Chapter 5 in particular, courts calibrate their use of the strong review power to invalidate legislation, using or declining to use it depending on the specific circumstances of the case before them. At times, when given the opportunity, a court will decline to invalidate a law, choosing instead to offer guidelines or suggestions to the political branches as to the law's problematic validity. In doing so, it transforms strong into weak review; and its capacity to have the final say on constitutional matters, into a more advisory role. That said, most courts, even those considered relatively quiescent, appear to be comfortable with striking down laws that are patently unconstitutional, and which offend against core democratic rights.

To a certain extent, the false binary focus on weak or strong review reflects the influence of the Anglosphere core debate, where strong and weak review are more sharply defined (as between the United States and United Kingdom, for example). It also underscores Bonilla Maldonado's observation that constitutional innovation in new democracies is not integrated into the debate, and the extent to which the debate remains, to some extent, tied to the forms and formulae of the core debate concerning courts in mature democracies.[75] Colón-Ríos, for instance, surveying the global picture of judicial review, argues that it is time to replace the weak/strong review typology with a more nuanced framework that includes two additional types of review as separate categories: 'strong basic structure review' such as that in India, where the constitutional court enjoys the power to make a final judgment on the validity of constitutional amendments, and 'weak basic structure review', present in certain Latin American countries, where the constitutional court is similarly empowered (or self-empowered) to strike down both ordinary and constitution-amending legislation, but accords the final say as to validity to the people, in the form of a constituent assembly.[76]

Fourth, all five approaches fail to fully account for the role of regional human rights courts. In Issacharoff's account, for instance, international law as a whole is peripheral, appearing fleetingly in passing mentions of references to treaty obligations in South African case-law, despite also focusing on the Colombian context where the Inter-American Court's jurisprudence has loomed large.[77] For those who advocate a generally

---

[75] Maldonado, 'Introduction' 11, 22.   [76] Colón-Ríos, 'A New Typology' 144, 158ff.
[77] See Issacharoff, 'Consolidated Power' 40.

muscular role for constitutional courts, such as Scheppele and Bonilla Maldonado, the question remains as to how such a system accommodates regional review. Would, for example, a court with overwhelming governance power under a 'surrogate' system, or expansive power under the Global South approach easily partner with, or submit to, the jurisprudence of a regional human rights court when the two conflict? Colombia suggests a positive answer, while Brazil suggests a negative answer. By contrast, how can the posture of caution and restraint advocated by Ginsburg and Sadurski operate in a region with a human rights court? It already appears problematic under the European system, where courts are expected to pay close attention to the European Convention on Human Rights, but appears most difficult to reconcile with the Inter-American doctrine of 'control of conventionality', which tends to push domestic courts toward more assertive decision-making. The limits of the cautious Chilean constitutional court's engagement in such conventionality control, for instance, was mentioned in Chapter 6.

On the other hand, Gardbaum's argument for weak judicial review at the domestic level is particularly vulnerable to the criticism that, in young democracies subject to strong judicial review by a regional human rights court, weak review at the domestic level would simply see adjudication power – and citizen demands for justice and good governance – flow from the domestic to the regional level. In a region such as Latin America, it would tend to place domestic constitutional courts in an even more invidious position than the mirror argument. Any such argument would have to integrate regional human rights courts, with the clearest way of resolving the domestic–regional adjudicative tension being to advocate weak review at *both* levels. However, to do so would simply replicate the difficulties with domestic weak review as discussed above.

D   Regional Human Rights Courts

As regards regional courts, there is little, if any, theoretical analysis of the democratic nature of review by regional human rights courts, especially in Latin America and Africa. Scholarship tends to be dominated by legal constitutionalist accounts which, to a significant extent, assume its legitimacy (democratic or otherwise) and focus on issues of effectiveness and the content of specific decisions.

Engagement with democratic legitimacy arguments tends to be rather cursory. For instance, Ezequiel Malarino's strident critique of review by the Inter-American Court of Human Rights, bemoaning its 'illiberal and antidemocratic tendencies', rests primarily on arguments as to the basic legality of the Court's case-law, concerning the Court's perceived illegitimate departure from the text of the American Convention on Human Rights and recognition of norms not expressly laid out therein, thus violating the sovereignty of states, which have not agreed to be bound by such norms.[78] He places limited and secondary emphasis on familiar democratic arguments against the Court's exercise of its review power, including the unelected status of judges, and the argument that its requirements for the creation of new criminal offences in domestic law violates the principle that any restrictions on individual liberties should be made by the organ most reflective of the popular will (i.e. the legislature).[79] While other authors, such as Huneeus, David Kosař, and Lucas Lixinski raise the legitimacy problems raised by the European and Inter-American courts' expansion into 'structural reform' adjudication in particular, they do not fully pursue this line of theoretical enquiry.[80]

The discussion in this chapter thus far underscores the highly problematic nature of the gulf between scholarship on domestic constitutional courts and regional human rights courts, emphasised in the Introduction to this book. Scholarship on regional courts tends to focus on the relationship between these courts and the state as a whole, rather than their relationship with domestic courts. Sweeney, for instance, makes no mention of domestic courts when he argues in the conclusion to his monograph that the European Court of Human Rights should

> engage far more robustly with the difficult question of when, and in what circumstances, national transitional policies that might secure peace or democratic consolidation are trumped by human rights concerns[81]

As discussed at the end of Chapter 6, this is also the central question at the heart of McCrudden and O'Leary's analysis of the European Court's judgment in *Sejdić and Finci*. These authors only pay passing attention to the fact that the European Court's judgment – finding the reservation of election to Bosnia and Herzegovina's tripartite presidency to the three

---

[78] E. Malarino, 'Judicial Activism, Punitivism and Supranationalisation: Illiberal and Anti-democratic Tendencies of the Inter-American Court of Human Rights' (2012) 12 *International Criminal Law Review* 665.

[79] Ibid. 686.

[80] See Huneeus, 'Reforming the State'; and D. Kosař & L. Lixinski, 'Domestic Judicial Design by International Human Rights Courts' (2015) 109 *The American Journal of International Law* 713.

[81] Sweeney, *Post-Cold War Era* 250.

'constituent peoples' a violation of the European Convention – also tended to bring into question the legitimacy of that State's constitutional court, which shares six of the nine court seats between the three constituent peoples (with three allocated to international judges).[82] There is no consideration of the additional possibility that the European Court's 'overruling' of the domestic court on a foundational constitutional question *in itself* tended to risk damaging the latter's institutional standing and development.

Others, such as Başak Çalı and Ximena Soley Echeverría, are more focused on the inter-court relationship between constitutional courts and regional courts. However, the dominant preoccupation is not about whether strong judicial review is justifiable *per se*, but rather about which level should have the ultimate say, the degree of deference that should be accorded by the court in each sphere (domestic or regional) to its putative partner, and the justifications regional courts provide for deferential and assertive stances.

As discussed in Chapter 4, these authors identify the democratic credentials of the state and the level of seriousness evinced by the domestic constitutional court regarding rights protection and the rule of law as criteria by which a deferential approach by the regional human rights court should be calibrated. The implication appears to be that a regional human rights court should play a more robust role concerning young democracies, whose courts may be unable to present sufficient credentials to claim greater subsidiarity (especially in the earlier years of the new democratic regime), or where the State itself cannot claim the required democratic pedigree. The regional court, in this way, can be viewed as playing a legitimate tutelary role in the new regime until democratic governance is sufficiently consolidated.

This, in turn, implies that a certain degree of democratic progress may justify a domestic court adopting a less deferential stance to the regional human rights court, shifting from a more hierarchical to a more heterarchical relationship as democratisation proceeds. However, we get no sense of how such a shift can be managed in practical terms. In the Inter-American context, Dulitzky has argued that the Inter-American Court's conventionality control doctrine, discussed in Chapter 3, leaves little space for meaningful dialogic interaction with the courts at the national level, and no room for domestic courts to follow alternative lines of

[82] McCrudden & O'Leary, *Courts & Consociations* 144–5.

reasoning regarding certain matters (e.g. recognising the validity of domestic amnesty laws).[83] In place of any notion of dialogue, the Court under this doctrine simply requires constitutional courts to act, not as gatekeepers of the domestic constitutional order, but foot soldiers of the regional human-rights order:

> My basic proposition is that the [Inter-American] Court must assume that Latin American judges are essential and central actors in this new framework. National judges are not merely robotic users of the Convention as interpreted by the Court.
>
> ...
>
> In order to succeed in the Convention's domestication process, the Court must recognize the important political role that judges play. As the judges are the ones deciding the content of constitutional and conventional rights, the prospect of success for the Court relies heavily on how those judicial authorities follow its determination. As such, the Court needs to become an ally of judicial authorities at the national level and also transform them into its own allies. The first step in this direction will be to take seriously what judges are saying and deciding in similar situations. It requires the Court to engage in a substantive bidirectional dialogue with national judges and to involve them as much as possible in the procedure of the tribunal.[84]

Huneeus has provided perhaps the most concrete prescriptions to support her normative argument for greater dialogue, arguing that the Inter-American Court needs to be more 'mindful' of domestic courts and 'less quick to impose its judgment' on the highest national courts, with the aim of fostering greater co-operation from these courts, while allowing for assertive decision-making where necessary. Key practical ways of doing so, she argues, is for the Inter-American Court to foster dialogue by generously and frequently citing domestic judgments that follow its rulings, and providing concrete examples in its judgments of how difficult issues have been addressed in other states.[85] Yet, it remains difficult to say precisely when the Court should accord deference to the domestic courts.

4   Points of Orientation for a Normative Stance

The range of positions above reveal the extent to which discussion of the roles of courts in young democracies diverges from the familiar debate on

---

[83] See Aguilar Cavallo, 'El Control de Convencionalidad'. For a trenchant critique of the doctrine, see Malarino, 'Judicial Activism'.

[84] Dulitzky, 'An Inter-American Constitutional Court?' 92.

[85] Huneeus, 'Courts Resisting Courts' 525–7.

this subject concerning courts in mature democracies, and provides a useful starting point for considering what role courts should play in supporting democratisation, which is the focus for the rest of the chapter. First, this section provides three points of orientation for setting out a normative stance, by indicating a preference for the scaffolding approach of Gargarella and Issacharoff, canvassing the key pathologies of new democracies, and revisiting the concepts of consolidation as our normative end-point and democratisation jurisprudence as our framework.

A Preference for the Scaffolding Argument

As a jumping-off point, Issacharoff's and Gargarella's conception of the court as scaffolding for the new democracy is arguably the most convincing. In essence, it justifies a particular role for strong judicial review in a young democracy, but does not place an unrealistic burden on the courts or discount any notion of meaningful limits to judicial power. Gargarella's approach in particular shows a sensitivity to the particular exigencies of a young democracy. While acknowledging that we must make certain adjustments to our adherence to standard theoretical accounts of the proper role of strong judicial review developed in the Western context, it also avoids using these contextual differences to abandon all concerns regarding not only the legitimacy of strong judicial review, but also the capacity of judges to carry out the task of democratic transformation on their own.

Gargarella's is, at heart, a negative account, seeking normative lessons from the perceived failures of the Argentine courts to protect rights and constrain the executive after the state transitioned to electoral democracy in 1983. Both Gargarella and Issacharoff's approaches dovetail with the more general observation of transitional justice theorists that constitutions in new democracies should act to disentrench the old constitutional order as well as entrenching the new. However, given the criticisms of Issacharoff's approach in particular, above, and the generally state-bound nature of the scaffolding argument, it is merely a starting point. This will be addressed in Sections 5 and 6 in this chapter.

B Key Pathologies of Young Democracies

If one of the central priorities of a court is disentrenchment and guarding against a return of authoritarianism, it is worthwhile recalling from Chapter 4 the key deficiencies that tend to afflict young democracies, and which sharply distinguish them from mature democracies.

First, at the constitutional level one finds, characteristically, a new or revised constitution that requires very significant interpretation, the legacy of an authoritarian constitution or prior façade constitution, a *residuum* of authoritarian-era laws of suspect constitutional validity, and often, as discussed in Chapter 4, certain countermajoritarian elements in the constitutional–legal order aimed at mediating the balance of power between the old and new regime (e.g. amnesty laws, or electoral posts for members of the previous regime).

Second, as compared to the empirical context to which much of the core debate refers (whether implicitly or explicitly), at the political level there is often no stable opposition of two political blocs with clearly defined agendas, which together represent the majority of the electorate, and which are able to reflect the popular will.[86] Rather, it is quite usual to have significant fragmentation of political parties with a lack of clarity concerning political platforms, oligarchical party politics where existing parties do not represent significant portions of the electorate, dominance of the electoral arena by one party, or diminution of the significance of party politics due to the existence of a directly elected president with broad governance powers, and whose role is supported by various parties with conflicting policies.

Third, at the societal level, commitment to rights and the rule of law tends to be underdeveloped, and civil society is usually weak owing to repression of non-state actors and popular movements under undemocratic rule. New democracies also often suffer from the impact of economic restructuring that often accompanies democratisation.

To say that these deficiencies commonly exist is not, of course, an automatic argument in favour of strong judicial review. It is simply to recognise their existence to enable a clear-eyed approach to the evils constitutionalism and the law may play a role in alleviating. It is also important to recall that these are not permanent nor static conditions; the hallmark of the democratisation context, as discussed in Chapters 1 and 4, is inordinate flux, compared to the relative stability of a mature democracy or authoritarian state. The key question, then, is how adjudication can operate so as to mitigate the pathologies of a new democracy

---

[86] The focus on representativeness here is to exclude states such as Colombia and Venezuela, where two opposing political blocs may exist, but in an electoral system that excludes other political groupings in a limited competitive 'partyarchy', as Landau calls it: D Landau, 'Constitution-Making Gone Wrong' (2012) 64 *Alabama Law Review* 923, 939.

without also actively undermining the democratisation process by preventing the very civic virtues, culture of constitutionalism, and respect for others' views and widespread commitment to rights that is required for a democratic system, as we understand it, to function. The experience of states such as Hungary has underlined that constitutionalism and legalism have very clear limits, but this has not led to any systematic consideration of what might work better, with the exception of Gardbaum's proposals, which suffer from multiple deficiencies, as discussed above.

C Our End-Point: Consolidated Democracy

We have a sense, then, of where our starting point lies. As discussed in Chapters 1 and 4, the question here is the role that courts can play, not in the aim to develop the political community into a democratic state comparable to the mature democracies of the Global North, but into a consolidated democracy where the essentials of democratic order are in place: a regime which

> allows for the free formulation of political preferences, through the use of basic freedoms or associations, information and communication, for the purpose of free competition between leaders to validate at regular intervals by non-violent means their claims to rule ... without excluding any effective political office from that competition or prohibiting members of the political community from expressing their preference.[87]

In Chapter 4, building on this notion of consolidation, the argument was made that the main roles constitutional courts could play in helping to achieve this level of democratic development involved eight core activities across three dimensions:

(i) Facilitating the creation of a democratic public sphere
1. Upholding core democratic rights
2. Shaping an inclusive electoral system
3. Curbing the re-emergence of authoritarianism
(ii) Mediating the shift from an undemocratic to democratic order
4. Articulating the relationship between the old and new constitutional order
5. Addressing/eliminating authoritarian legislation
6. Addressing key transitional justice questions

---

[87] Schneider, *Consolidation of Democracy* 10.

(iii) Carving out a role for the court in the new democratic order
    7. Delineating the Court's jurisdiction
    8. Addressing crises.

The core contribution of regional human rights courts was suggested as operating across the same three dimensions, but as tending to involve less frequent direct interventions and as approaching the democratisation process from the very different vantage point of an external entity in relation to the state-bound constitutional order.

D   Making Normative Arguments from Two Angles

With the above starting points in mind, the final two sections of this chapter consider the central question of what courts should do in a new democracy. Each section approaches this question from a different angle. Section 5, based on the existing reality of courts in new democracies, makes arguments for how constitutional courts and regional human rights courts might better approach the challenge of supporting democratisation, both separately and as a system. The final section goes beyond the existing reality to explore the question of how courts might be more fundamentally redesigned to act as more effective democracy-builders.

5   Three Lessons for Existing Courts: Targeting, Teamwork, and Temporality

If we had the ear of judges on existing domestic and regional courts faced with the challenge of supporting democratisation processes, what would we advise them to do? Three key lessons can be gleaned from the analysis in Chapters 2 to 6. The first is that, if we accept the framework laid out in Chapter 4, this provides some guidance to courts in young democracies as to when they should engage in assertive decision-making to support democratisation. The second is a need for greater sensitivity in courts at both levels to the context and nature of adjudication at the other level. Third is the need for sensitivity toward the temporal aspect of democratisation, which involves a complex dialectic between the courts at both levels, and an appreciation of the impact of their roles on other potential democracy-builders at the domestic level.

However, a very fundamental caveat is required here. To lay out detailed prescriptions for courts aimed at improving their effectiveness as democracy-builders, and their interaction in this task, may be helpful, but it risks overlooking the reality that courts at both the domestic and international levels are prisoners of legal culture, institutional culture, limited perspective, incomplete comparative knowledge, and simple knowledge of adjudication and the normative framework at the other level. As discussed later in this chapter, we cannot set the bar for judges at the highest level reached by the most prominent judges in the global pantheon. To do so is not just unreal but unfair. It is also crucially important to avoid the trap of duplicating the mode of thinking of which this book is a sustained critique; namely, the tendency to expect too much from courts. As the last portion of this book argues, we need to have a root-and-branch rethink of the court-centric model of democracy-building. With that fundamental caveat in mind, the following remarks can be taken as pointers for greater effectiveness.

A   Targeting: Criteria for Picking Battles

As discussed above, scholars tend to make rather general arguments concerning the roles courts can play in supporting democratisation. Sadurski suggests that rights protection is a primary function, but does not select any particular rights. Scholars such as Scheppele and Bonilla Maldonado, in advocating an expansive role for courts in a young democracy, make no selections as to what a court should accord priority in order to bolster the democratisation process. Issacharoff and Gargarella get closest, focusing in particular on core democratic rights, such as the rights of free speech, assembly, association, and fair trial, as well as the disentrenchment function of constraining the accretion of excessive power at any one site (whether by an executive or a dominant party).

The framework set out in Chapter 4, and its application to the Brazilian context in Chapter 5, emphasises that courts cannot do everything. The argument here is that courts should focus on the eight core activities set out in Section 4.C, and expend their institutional capital on adjudication that furthers these key objectives. This necessarily means that courts would have to strategically adopt deferential postures regarding other matters (e.g. economic governance, social and economic rights), in order to store their power for use when needed.

This approach can be differentiated from all five arguments discussed in Section 3. In addition, it is not an argument for courts to always stay within the 'tolerance level' of the political branches, as argued by

Epstein, Knight, and Shvetsova.[88] Nor does it equate to the idea of 'strategic deference' by constitutional courts, as discussed by Roux and Rodríguez-Raga in the South African and Colombian contexts, which refers to how courts adopt general assertiveness or deference based on the macropolitical context.[89] Rather, the argument here is for consistent robustness on the same core issues that strike to the core of the democratisation process. Such an approach would, in any state, still leave a court open to political censure, but it has to be accepted that there is no way of entirely immunising a court from such censure. At the level of the regional court, a consistent focus on these core issues could lead to greater resonance between the domestic and regional levels, and guard against overreaching on other matters with lower importance to democratic consolidation.

Overall, instead of expecting democratic progress to rely mainly on adjudication, this approach would allow courts to focus on progressively opening a societal space in which other actors, such as civil society organisations, the media, the political opposition, and individual citizens can also act as democracy-builders and pursue their conception of the good.

B   Teamwork: Negotiating Systemic Asymmetries

As discussed at the start of this chapter, there are various institutional and epistemic asymmetries between constitutional courts and regional courts, which cut across their capacity to work in tandem as democracy-builders. There is no easy answer to resolving these asymmetries, or achieving greater co-ordination, between domestic and regional courts in a way that is practically useful.

We can recall here the discussion in Chapter 4, concerning Krisch's presentation of the European regional legal order as a plural order characterised by heterarchy rather than hierarchical constitutional order, which manages to operate without excessive friction due to judicial strategy and mutual accommodation by all courts in the system.[90] However, his focus is on interaction between the European Court of Human Rights and courts in the mature democracies of Western Europe

---

[88] 'The Role of Constitutional Courts'.
[89] See Roux, 'A Response' 30; and Rodríguez-Raga, 'Strategic Deference' 95.
[90] Krisch, *Beyond Constitutionalism*.

(e.g. Germany, the United Kingdom). This provides a picture of domestic and regional courts as co-equal entities in the plural legal space, which does not appear to fully capture the reality of the relationship between regional human rights courts and constitutional courts outside Western Europe. As such, his analysis lacks a normative inflection capable of guiding us toward addressing the particular asymmetries between regional and domestic courts in the democratisation setting, where the relationship tends to take on a more hierarchical aspect.

For some, persistent and irresolvable tension between the two orders, international and domestic, is both positive and desirable. Alon Harel and Eyal Benvenisti, for instance, in a recent working paper make the argument for a 'discordant parity' between a 'robust constitutionalism', which claims superiority in the putative hierarchy between domestic and international law, and a 'robust internationalism', which would claim the converse.[91] 'Clarity', they say, 'is the enemy of discordant parity':

> The pursuit of 'hierarchy', 'harmony' and 'order' between the international and the constitutional is fundamentally at odds with the idea that individual freedom is founded on friction and discordance. ... The conflict between international and state norms need not be resolved; in fact it needs to be maintained and even intensified. This conflict is a permanent and desirable feature of the legal world.[92]

However, this approach appears of little assistance in the present context. Leaving aside its disregard for legal certainty as one of the core values of the rule of law, by refusing to make any value judgments as to the different ways in which domestic and international courts operate, it provides no orientation for any real position on the appropriateness of adjudication by the courts at each level on any given issue. Set against Krisch's description of co-equal courts in Western Europe, its prescription of a norm-tussle between domestic and international law is problematic when applied to Central and Eastern Europe, Latin America, and Africa. It would tend to leave a domestic court in a young democracy at a disadvantage as compared to a regional human rights court; frequently reduced to a passive recipient of norms rather than an active participant in norm-making. Where the regional court is a fledgling compared to the domestic courts, as is the case with the African Court of Human and

---

[91] E. Benvenisti & A. Harel, 'Embracing the Tension between National and International Human Rights Law: The Case for Parity', Global Trust Working Paper Series 04/2015.
[92] Ibid. 32.

Peoples' Rights, it would cut across the kind of co-operation needed to build effective regional jurisprudence.

Rather than the courts at each level seeking to maximise their power as against the other level, perhaps the only route to greater effectiveness as democracy-builders is for the courts at each level to develop a greater appreciation of the context of adjudication at the other level. This is especially important for regional human rights courts, which should be willing to recognise the limits of their epistemic and functional capacities, and which should be mindful of assuming a normative role that prevents domestic courts from developing their own jurisprudence, needlessly undermines domestic courts' authority, or precludes 'good faith' dis-agreement on rights matters that are not amenable to a single solution. In other words, this is yet another variant of the democratic debilitation argument. Regional courts faced with oversight of a significant number of new or young democracies should look, when adjudicating, beyond the immediate purpose of achieving individual justice, or even constitutional justice, to the impact of their adjudication on domestic courts themselves.

Domestic courts, in turn, should evince greater openness to some form of dialogue with the human rights court in their region. Although a much overused metaphor, dialogue captures the capacity of domestic courts to explain their positions to the regional court and to achieve accommoda-tions in regional adjudication.[93] A good example is the *Horncastle* deci-sion of the United Kingdom Supreme Court in 2009, where Lord Phillips took great pains to explain why the Court refused to follow a decision of the European Court, and the latter's subsequent modification of its position to accommodate the Supreme Court's decision.[94] As discussed in Chapter 4, existing literature suggests that such dialogue is rare between constitutional courts in young democracies and regional human rights courts, even in Europe.

It may be argued, for example, that, if the majority of the Brazilian Supreme Court in the *Amnesty Law Case* had provided a clear discussion of the relevant Inter-American jurisprudence on amnesty laws and offered arguments to distinguish the Brazilian scenario from that of previous amnesty law cases concerning Argentina, Peru, and Chile, it may have opened a dialogic space for the Inter-American Court to inject

---

[93] See D.S. Law & W.C. Chang, 'The Limits of Global Judicial Dialogue' (2011) 86 *Wash-ington Law Review* 523.

[94] See *R* v. *Horncastle* [2009] UKSC 14 (SC); and *Al-Khawaja and Tahery* v. *United Kingdom* (2012) 54 EHRR 23.

more nuance into its own position. As discussed in Chapter 6, Justice Trindade had already signposted a possible change of position in the *Almonacid* decision in 2006, some time before the *Amnesty Law Case* came before the Supreme Court, auguring the Court's shift of position in *El Mozote* in 2012.

There are, of course, limits regarding the extent to which a sensitivity within each court to the particular setting of the other level, and inter-court dialogue, can help to reconcile positions where possible and improve the overall functioning of the courts as a plural system. However, the prescriptions here are at least preferable to outright submission by domestic courts to the regional level, which may not understand the complexities of the domestic democratisation process, or a refusal by domestic courts to engage with regional jurisprudence, as seen in Brazil. The attempt to achieve greater understanding should also not be confined to the rather indirect method of dialogue through formal judgments, but should also encompass informal channels, such as judicial conferences, seminars, and organisations.[95]

Nor should the focus be exclusively on judges; also key are mechanisms to ensure adequate interaction and understanding between the staff of domestic and regional courts, which could be achieved through secondments, staff exchanges, meetings, conferences, and joint associations. Huneeus' insights regarding the central importance of the domestic legal profession in achieving openness to regional jurisprudence also suggests wider engagement is needed across legal communities as a whole if any regional court can make a meaningful contribution as a democracy-builder.[96] This, however, requires time and resources that many regional courts simply do not have, which means that they need to develop relationships with surrogate institutions at the domestic level, including not just courts, but also human rights commissions, NGOs, and government departments.

C   *Temporality: Toward Greater Democratisation Sensitivity*

The final core lesson from the previous chapters is the extent to which courts at both levels need to develop greater sensitivity to the temporal aspects of democratisation, and how the democratisation trajectory

---

[95] See further, Daly, 'Baby Steps'. See also Huneeus, 'Courts Resisting Courts' 529-30.
[96] Huneeus, 'Varied Authority'.

requires a continuous reassessment of the appropriateness of assertive and deferential decision-making at each level.

This is particularly important in negotiating the constitutional balance in young democracies between the old and new regimes. At the domestic level it places a heavy burden on the constitutional court to remain aware of the overall political context of the new democracy, and in assessing when addressing authoritarian-era laws and unravelling elements of the constitutional pact is timely and appropriate. At the regional level it requires the court to appreciate the overall nature of the constitutional settlement underpinning, and giving voice to, the democratic transition, and the need for the regional court to recognise the limits of its ability to judge when intervention is appropriate. Again, the context of each court is important, and regional human rights courts in particular should remain cognisant of their epistemic disadvantage when faced with such questions. Intervention may only be fully justifiable where the domestic court lacks the requisite independence to adjudicate freely on such questions.

The question remains, however, as to whether we can realistically expect courts to evince such sensitivity and perceptiveness. It must be borne in mind that judges are not, by and large, well trained for engaging in such strategic and broad cultural thinking. Although all courts show some ability to address highly important cases from a strategic perspective, courts with large dockets in particular are so busy simply dealing with the day-to-day business of keeping pace with their workload that to expect them to chart a fully fledged philosophical, cultural, transnational, and legal framework for their decision-making appears somewhat unrealistic. We end up again at risk of setting the bar too high for courts.

6   Thinking of the Future: Toward a Redesign of the Existing Model

The previous section laid out an argument for how courts should act as democracy-builders in existing young democracies. However, suppose we could start again. Knowing what we know from the discussion in this book so far, would we make any changes to the existing model? This section makes tentative initial steps toward consideration of constitutional frameworks for democracy-building in the future, with the emphasis on what might achieve a maximally effective role for courts as democracy-builders, while remaining cognisant of the fact that they cannot be the sole engines of democratisation. The aim is not to provide fully fledged solutions, but to point the way toward crucial fundamental questions in approaching this task. In considering this question it is first necessary to address trends in constitution-making in the post-war era, and their impact on the roles of courts.

A   Post-War Constitution-Making and the Utopian Burden

In Chapter 2 it was observed that a heavy democratisation burden has tended to be placed on courts in the post-war era, especially since the beginning of the third wave of democratisation. This is fundamentally rooted in the increasing post-war tendency toward thicker, longer, more ambitious, and more internationalised constitutions. We see ever more extensive bills of rights, including justiciable social and economic rights; enhanced review powers for constitutional courts; additional State organs such as ombudsmen; and direct democracy mechanisms such as referendums. There has been expansion across multiple dimensions. Constitutions are not only designed to provide a broader and more detailed blueprint for government, and to provide ever stronger checks on nakedly majoritarian decision-making; they are also designed to carry a greater symbolic weight as the legal expression of the new order, and to give a greater voice to current democratic majorities by moving beyond representative government alone.

We might call such texts 'utopian' constitutions, in the sense that they seek to provide the basis and blueprint for a fundamental transformation of society, the State, and political culture. The approach appears to place enormous faith in the capacity of law, and courts, to shape reality, echoing at some distance Solon's sixth-century elegy quoted at the start of the chapter, claiming that law 'makes the rough smooth, puts a stop to excess, dries up the blooming flowers of ruin, straightens out crooked judgments, tames deeds of pride', and all manner of other goods. This places courts in a 'Solonic trap', as the primary organ for ensuring the realisation and coherence of this new, dream-like, constitutional order.

Chapter 4 observed that, certainly, the constitutional text has path-dependent effects. Individual access, especially extremely open access (e.g. *actio popularis*), and powers of abstract review tend to lead to a central role for a court. Certain executive formats, such as the common third wave system of semi-presidentialism, can embroil a court in political power plays between the president and prime minister. A failure to settle 'first order' questions (such as executive format) heightens the risk of a court provoking a constitutional crisis. Excessive prolixity in the constitutional text can lead to a 'constitutionalisation' of what would best be left to the ordinary legislative and policy-making processes, overburdening the court with questions more suited to the political branches. In Chapter 6 we also saw (as in *Gelman* v. *Uruguay*) how the increased use of direct democracy mechanisms can cut across the court's role. This much is clear.

The following sections briefly consider five particular trends in postwar constitutions, and third wave constitution-making in particular, which place constitutional courts in a particularly invidious position: the recognition of social and economic rights; the extension of the Court's role beyond that of a 'negative legislator'; the notion of courts as public educators; the conception of such courts as programmable technology; and the idea that courts can not only facilitate democratic progress but also address democratic breakdown.

Courts as Purveyors of Social Justice

Arguments as to the transformational capacities of courts come together most clearly in arguments for and against the increasing tendency to enshrine justiciable social and economic rights in the new democratic constitution. As a voluminous literature now addresses, this accords a role to the courts regarding allocation of resources and policy choices that differs in many ways from those affecting the protection of civil and political rights (although, as recognised in Chapter 1, the difference should not be overstated). For some, the protection of such rights is perhaps the most important role a court can play in the context of a young democracy where existing levels of socio-economic development and income equality are low, or where economic restructuring alongside democratisation takes a significant toll on the economic well-being of individuals.

However, as briefly discussed in Chapter 2, the role has a significantly greater potential to bring a constitutional court into conflict with the political branches than adjudication on civil and political rights, and to undermine popular support for the court. As discussed in Chapter 2, Ferraz' argument that requiring courts to adjudicate on such rights places them in an unenviable position, requiring them to choose between 'usurpation' and 'abdication', gains added traction in the democratisation context, where the very existence of such rights in the constitution raises the stakes for a court's performance in the new democratic dispensation, complicating its task in carving out a role for itself in the new order.[97]

---

[97] See the discussion in Chapter 2, Section 3.B.

Perhaps more importantly, the added pressure such rights place on a constitutional court does not seem to be worth the results they produce. Not only does robust social rights jurisprudence appear to provoke increased political attacks on courts; but it also, focused as it is on individual cases, can do more harm than good, by leading to irrational resource allocation, creating distortions in slim state budgets, and adversely affecting public spending in areas which are not litigated; thereby threatening to undermine the democratic project of the constitution as a whole. Time and again, courts have been shown to have limited capacity to protect vulnerable sectors of the population; for instance, the Romanian Constitutional Court's invalidation of laws aimed at cutting pensions in 2010 simply led to the alternative of a general value added tax increase for the entire population.[98] Such rights are also prone to 'capture' and can easily come to offend the basic principle of political equality. Indeed, as Ferraz has observed, health litigation in Brazil has become a middle-class phenomenon, facilitated by greater access to justice in the more prosperous areas of the country, thus exacerbating rather than alleviating severe social inequalities.[99]

This is not to deny arguments by scholars such as Jeff King that courts are capable of providing a useful means of advancing social justice, under certain conditions.[100] However, his particular prescriptions appear most relevant to adjudication in mature democracies, as part of the overall constitutional fine-tuning role that constitutional courts play in such polities, in a context where they enjoy considerable institutional security (although he does suggest that South Africa might come within his framework). As King himself emphasises from the outset: 'any theory of judging ... must fit with the institutional and political constraints under which [courts] operate'.[101] Indeed, it appears that what he deems good arguments against fully justiciable social and economic rights – concerns regarding democratic legitimacy, the need for a polycentric approach that avoids according decisions to a single institution, questions of judicial expertise, the need for flexibility, and doubts as to why we should look to courts first – all take on a particular added edge in the democratisation context.[102]

---

[98] Gardbaum, 'Strong Constitutional Courts' 298.

[99] See Ferraz, 'Between Usurpation and Abdication?' 396; and O. Ferraz, 'Harming the Poor Through Social Rights Litigation: Lessons from Brazil' (2011) 89(7) *Texas Law Review* 1643.

[100] J. King, *Judging Social Rights* (Cambridge University Press, 2012).   [101] Ibid. 1.

[102] Ibid. 5–6.

It is also fully acknowledged here that it is natural that individuals facing low levels of social and economic development in young democracies will seek to pursue their claims for better treatment when an avenue is provided; especially in contexts where the political process is unable or unwilling to hear their demands. However, considering the significant downsides and uncertainties concerning the social value of such adjudication, and set against the already daunting task and limited institutional capital of a court in a fledgling democracy, this choice between usurpation and abdication, as discussed in Chapter 2, appears a high price to pay.

Courts as Positive Legislators

The trend toward conferring a role for courts as positive legislators, beyond the negative legislative role of addressing the constitutionality of enacted laws, also appears to leave courts in a difficult position. Beyond abstract review of legislation, which turns the court into a form of third chamber of parliament, there is the power to address legislative omission, under which the court can order the state to enact legislation. Refusal to use such powers leads to criticism, while using such powers appears to place the court in competition with the legislature. As Julian Zaiden Benvindo has noted in the Brazilian context, Justice Gilmar Mendes asserted in a 2008 decision seeking the Supreme Court to make legislative recommendations to Congress under its 'legislative omission' power, that this tended to transform it into a quasi-legislature:

> in cases like that one, the [Supreme Court] turns into a 'house of commons, as the parliament,' where the 'multiple social claims and the political, ethical and religious pluralism find refuge in the debates procedurally and argumentatively organized through previously established norms,' such as the public hearings, the amicus curiae intervention, and the participation of society through different civil organizations during the procedure.[103]

The similarities to Scheppele's surrogate argument are striking, in the sense of public democratic deliberation shifting from the parliamentary to the judicial sphere. However, Justice Mendes is clearly not suggesting in this quotation, as Scheppele does, that the Court can be an *overall* substitute for the legislature.

---

[103] Zaiden Benvindo, *On the Limits* 128.

The trend is also seen in the movement toward holding public hearings as part of constitutional court proceedings. A recent phenomenon seen in Brazil, Argentina, Colombia, and Mexico, it is a remarkable move that increasingly blurs the functional division of duties as between the judiciary and the legislature. Gargarella has characterised it as a further 'dialogic' constitutional mechanism, to add to existing mechanisms such as weak judicial review, with a particular focus on linking disadvantaged groups with decision-making processes. However, he notes that its use in states such as Argentina has been hampered by the centralisation of power and a 'top-down' approach to addressing communities' demands.[104] The use of public hearings by the Supreme Court of Brazil has also been criticised as doing little to enhance the democratic legitimacy or openness of its adjudication.[105] Echoing the criticism of Scheppele's surrogate argument above, it might be offered that, rather than transforming courts into quasi-parliaments, it may be better to focus on ameliorating the deficiencies of parliaments themselves.

Courts as Public Educators

A further example of the inflated perceptions of constitutional courts is found in the arguments by scholars such as Stotzky and Goldstein that a court can educate the citizenry on the ideals of democratic governance. As well as being difficult to verify, such claims appear to make a serious error of overlooking reality. They appear to assume, surely incorrectly, that individuals in a political community pay particular attention not just to the outcome, but also to the *content*, of judicial decisions; as though key judicial decisions are to be found on every kitchen table in a young democracy. Beyond practical realities, such as the often extremely poor analysis of judgments in the media, such arguments also place the court in a rather tutelary role, with the individual citizen reduced to a passive recipient of its teachings. This overlooks the basic fact that democratic governance, like dance, can only be learnt through active practice. Even if citizens were to pay close attention to court judgments, this is no substitute for their participation in democratic order through civil society

---

[104] See R. Gargarella, "We the People" Outside of the Constitution: The Dialogic Model of Constitutionalism and the System of Checks and Balances' (2014) *Current Legal Problems* 1.

[105] See T.L. Sombra, 'Why Should Public Hearings in the Brazilian Supreme Court Be Understood as an Innovative Democratic Tool in Constitutional Adjudication?' (2016) 17(4) *German Law Journal* 657.

organisations, social movements, protest, elections, and, perhaps (to a limited extent), mechanisms of direct democracy or deliberative democracy (discussed further below).

Courts as Programmable Technology

At the root of the tendency to overburden constitutional courts in the post-war era is the fundamental misconception of courts as 'devices' or 'mechanisms'. In Chapter 2, for instance, the metaphor of democratisation technology was used to refer to the perception of constitutional courts as key means to support and shape democratisation processes in a positive way. The metaphor speaks to a certain mode of thinking, common among practitioners as well as scholars, which conceives of courts as monolithic entities that can be 'programmed' to pursue particular ends, through the design of their 'operating system' (the constitution or international convention) and procedures for ensuring the appointment of high-quality members to the court.

Yet, while it is possible to seek as far as possible to avoid inordinate design deficiencies in the constitutional text, and the institutional set-up of the court itself, it is important to recognise that design has significant limits. As emphasised in Chapters 4 to 6, it is impossible to predict how a court, once established, will use its powers. We may, as Conrado Hübner Mendes and others have sought, set down principles for courts in carrying out their role – such as toeing the line between 'prudence' and 'courage'.[106] However, as Miguel Schor offers: '[C]ourts are not automatons whose job can be engineered *ex ante* by constitution makers.'[107] The messy reality is that courts are human institutions, where principles of legality, professionalism, and collegiality can be interpreted in various ways depending on the particular perspective of the individuals appointed. We cannot fully plan for judges to have the perceptive delicacy, adjudicative dexterity, political nous, and flair for strategic thinking required to pull off effective jurisprudence of the highest quality. Nor can we design judges to adhere to any one conception of the judicial role. The likes of England's Lord Coke, the US Justice Brandeis, Ireland's Judge Walsh, Brazil's Justice Pertence, and India's Raj Khanna cannot simply be created. Dworkin's Judge Hercules – who can always find the 'right' answer – does not exist.[108]

---

[106] Hübner Mendes, *Constitutional Courts* 15.
[107] Schor, 'Emergence of Constitutional Courts' 193.
[108] R. Dworkin, *Law's Empire* (Harvard University Press, 1986).

In addition, courts cannot meet an ever increasing raft of adjudicative burdens without a noticeable slide in the quality and consistency of their case-law – as seen to greatest effect in the European Court of Human Rights.[109]

Courts as the Last Line of Democratic Defence

Finally, it is important to recognise that law and courts can often do little if democratic breakdown is inevitable. It is true that in recent decades, in many states, courts worldwide have appeared as the sole domestic institutions capable of challenging an excessive concentration of political power that threatens to subvert democratic rule.[110] However, the capacity of strong judicial review, rights guarantees, eternity clauses, judicial doctrines, and international oversight has clear limits. In the 1980s the South African scholar A.R. Blackshield, for instance, noted:

> The South African history is not a failure of the courts; rather it demonstrates that if a real breakdown in human rights emerges, Bills of Rights and courts are ineffective.[111]

In today's world, examples of possible democratic breakdown, or at least decay, abound – in Hungary, Kenya, and, again, South Africa – all of which have been endowed with systems of strong review. In some states the constitutional court's achievement of overweening power is a sign of rot at the heart of the democratic order; as seen in Brazil, where a stalled and asymmetric democratisation process[112] has now degenerated into an alarming democratic crisis.[113] It is true that in many states constitutional courts have appeared to provide some bulwark against democratic decay and breakdown, as discussed in Chapter 2. However, it appears naïve, foolhardy, or even pernicious not only to place the lion's share of our faith in constitutional courts, but also to expend our time focusing on constitutional courts to the exclusion of all else. If broad design choices are 'at the heart of the constitutionalist's pharmacopeia', as Andrew Reynolds puts it, strong judicial review alone is clearly no panacea.[114]

---

[109] See Chapter 3. [110] Issacharoff, *Fragile Democracies* 272.
[111] Sturgess & Chubb, *Judging the World* 120.
[112] See P. Kingstone, *Democratic Brazil Revisited* (University of Pittsburgh Press, 2008).
[113] See e.g. P. McInerny, 'What's behind Brazil's Economic and Political Crises?' *UCLA Newsroom* 16 May 2016 http://newsroom.ucla.edu/stories/what-s-behind-brazil-s-economic-and-political-crises.
[114] A. Reynolds, 'Constitutional Medicine', in Diamond & Plattner (eds.), *Democracy* 50.

Notwithstanding the five key criticisms above, to say that courts cannot achieve everything does not mean that they can achieve nothing. It has been recognised throughout this study that there are core roles courts can play. However, to make the most of their advantages it is not enough to prescribe guidelines for adjudication. It is necessary to revisit the dominant modes of constitutional design to address structural deficiencies.

B   Avoiding the Solonic Trap: Design Principles for a Post-Authoritarian Constitution

The lesson from the above is that there are clear limits to what any one institution can achieve, and the relentless urge in the post-war era to stuff constitutions with promises and rights lays an impossible expectation on the courts to deliver; setting them up to disappoint, if not fail outright. A growing chorus of voices has begun to question the modes and motives of constitution-making in the contemporary world. As far back as 1993, Cass Sunstein had argued that in any state 'a constitution should be "negative" in the sense that it should be directed against the deepest risks in the relevant nation's political culture'.[115] More recently, in 2013, David Landau has argued for a tamping down of transformational promises and the move toward a more pragmatic approach to constitutional design for post-authoritarian societies:

> Constitution-making moments should not be idealized; they are often traumatic events. In these situations, the central challenge of constitution-making is not to achieve a higher form of lawmaking but rather to constrain unilateral exercises of power.[116]

Instead of attempting to achieve perfection, Landau offers that it is 'probably more fruitful to focus on avoiding a worst-case outcome.'[117] The move might be characterised as a shift from 'utopian' or 'transformational' constitution-making to a more 'Machiavellian' approach, in the sense that the focus turns to expediency in terms of what successful democratisation requires, rather than a bloated statement of values that achieves few concrete results. It appears to suggest that we should adopt a position of 'conservative dynamism', seeking to retain what works and discard what is unhelpful.

---

[115] See Sunstein, 'The Negative Constitution' 367–8.
[116] D. Landau, 'Constitution-Making' 923.   [117] Ibid. 926.

The central features of such an approach, in light of the discussion thus far, would be to: avoid excessive prolixity in the constitutional text; avoid the enshrinement of justiciable social and economic rights; avoid transforming the court into a 'positive legislator' in designing its formal powers; and to focus on aberrations in the specific political order of the new democracy, rather than seeking perfection. It might be considered that the court's purview over matters outside the core democracy-building functions discussed under the concept of democratisation juris-prudence might be reduced simply to a weak review advisory function. However, for the reasons discussed in connection with Gardbaum's argument, and the tendency of such an approach still to overburden the court, does not appear to be a viable option.

This all, of course, flies in the face of many nostrums of contemporary constitution-making, and may be a hard sell in constitutional negoti-ations that seek an expansive constitutional settlement that chimes with what has become democratic 'normality' in third wave states. It would also be hard to reconcile with the global trend toward ever greater public participation in constitution-drafting, which has been an increasingly central factor in the enactment of utopian, expansive texts.[118] These matters cannot be addressed here. Instead, the focus is on two central matters: first, the possibility of achieving greater balance, coherence, and transparency in constitutional texts, so as to optimise their capacity to underpin democracy-building (and the constitutional court's role in particular); and second, the possibility of seeking greater formal co-ordination between the domestic and regional spheres (and courts in particular).

Balance, Coherence, and Transparency

Gardbaum is correct when he states:

> Especially within a thin and fragile democratic culture, it is important to 'spread' constitutional sensibilities and the practice of principled political deliberation more broadly than in the single institution of the consti-tutional court.[119]

---

[118] See e.g. J. Gluck & M. Brandt, *Participatory and Inclusive Constitution Making: Giving Voice to the Demands of Citizens in the Wake of the Arab Spring* (United States Institute of Peace, 2015) www.usip.org/publications/participatory-and-inclusive-constitution-making.

[119] Gardbaum, 'Strong Constitutional Courts' 314.

Post-war constitutionalism has tended to set up the constitutional court as the sole guardian of the constitution, leading other actors in the political order to eschew any role in this regard. A post-authoritarian constitution should attempt to spread this role. This is not an argument for more state organs; some innovations, such as ombudsmen, have had little success in various third wave states in acting as additional constraints on the state.[120] Rather, the emphasis should be on reconfiguring the constitutional balance and coherence between existing powers.

In terms of greater coherence in the constitutional text, more attention needs to be given to complementarity between judicial action, legislative oversight, and mechanisms of direct democracy, with particular attention paid to the role of 'the people' as democracy-builders.[121] Some aspects are procedural, for instance, learning from the Uruguayan experience, it should not be constitutionally permissible to hold a referendum concerning a law where a challenge to its validity is *sub judice*. More thought needs to be given to which actors can petition the court; individual petitions (and *actio popularis* in particular) can lead to enormous backlogs, but closing off any individual access can limit the court's ability to address rights issues in particular.[122] Perhaps 'third way' options, such as 'class action' constitutional challenges against legislation or state action could be considered. The numerical threshold for such action would, of course, need to be carefully designed. Carefully calibrated mechanisms for civil society actors and citizen groupings to table debates in parliament, or to seek repeal of certain legislation, might also be considered.[123]

In a more experimental vein, we also need to consider whether 'constitutional juries' and 'citizens' assemblies', which provide a new avenue for giving voice and agency to 'the people' as a constitutional actor by providing an additional forum for structured democratic deliberation, could be an option for new and young democracies, as a way of cutting across an approach to democracy-building as an elite project, and fostering a less top-down form of constitutionalism.[124]

---

[120] See e.g. F. Uggla, 'The Ombudsman in Latin America' (2004) 36 *Journal of Latin American Studies* 423.

[121] Denis Galligan has begun this conversation in a more general way in 'The Sovereignty Deficit of Modern Constitutions' (2013) 33 *Oxford Journal of Legal Studies* 703.

[122] T. Ginsburg, 'Introduction' in Ginsburg (ed.), *Constitutional Design* 9.

[123] Such constitutional mechanisms already exist in a minority of democratic states: see Galligan, 'Sovereignty Deficit' 723ff.

[124] See e.g. E. Ghosh, 'Judicial Reference to Community Values – A Pointer Towards Constitutional Juries?' in T. Bustamante & B. Gonçalves Fernandes (eds.), *Democratizing*

More transparency may also be required in post-authoritarian constitutions. In the Chilean context, for instance, the open inclusion of 'authoritarian enclaves' in the text (such as reserved legislative seats for members of the old regime) allowed for a progressive removal of these provisions as democratisation progressed.[125] By contrast, the Brazilian Constitution's failure to make any mention of the Amnesty Law of 1979 left it with a special status outside the formal bounds of the constitutional structure, rendering review and reform more difficult. It also left a contradictory normative framework that shielded the old order from prosecution for the crimes of torture and murder, yet simultaneously voiced a strident approach to such crimes, including them among 'non-bailable' offences in Article 5.XLIII. In addition, countermajoritarian measures designed to shield the old order from the new in the transition to democratic governance could be time limited, at a sufficient distance (e.g. fifteen years) to provide an adequate incentive for their relinquishment of power, while also avoiding their acting as an ongoing constitutional irritant in the early years of the democratisation process.

Similarly, rather than leaving the courts to decide whether they should adopt some form of basic structure doctrine to address abusive constitutionalism, we should consider whether such a power should be expressly accorded to the court in the constitutional text. While this would evidently be at odds with the theoretical limits of the court as a 'constituted' entity under the constitution, given that courts are pushed into arrogating the power to themselves, it is perhaps the lesser of two evils to provide the power expressly in order to remove the impression of judicial sleight of hand.

The overall aim, then, in designing a post-authoritarian constitution, should be to seek a 'joined up' settlement, in which different elements work together, rather than a wilderness of single institutions, whose values and operation are considered in isolation from one another, and which reflects the particular aberrations of the new democracy.

Toward a More Co-ordinated Pluralism?

Where do regional human rights courts, and international law more generally, fit into this scheme? Is it possible, given the above discussion,

---

Constitutional Law: Perspectives on Legal Theory and the Legitimacy of Constitutionalism (Springer, 2016). See information on Ireland's Citizens' Assembly at www.citizens assembly.ie/en/.

[125] Alberts, Warshaw & Weingast, 'Democratization and Countermajoritarian Institutions'.

to achieve more formal co-ordination between the domestic and regional courts? At present, the courts at each level operate on two parallel tracks, with regional human rights courts generally used for addressing contentious cases, making little use of advisory powers, and generally suffering a significant 'time lag' in elaborating democratisation jurisprudence due to the requirement to exhaust domestic remedies. The state, in this respect, is reduced to an oubliette from which individuals must escape in order to seek justice.

Building on some recent innovations might be useful. For instance, Protocol 16 to the ECHR (which has yet to enter into force) has introduced a variant of the EU preliminary reference procedure, by allowing domestic courts to send questions concerning the interpretation of Convention law to the European Court of Human Rights in Strasbourg. This could enable domestic courts to seek interpretations of the regional human rights court's case-law, with the refinement that, when drafting court rules for its operation, they should be given the opportunity to offer their own interpretation when making the referral.

Indeed, in her discussion of the Korean Constitutional Court's push for the establishment of an Asian Court of Human Rights, Maartje de Visser pays particular attention to design options that would ensure structured interaction and a 'dialogic judicial culture' between such a court and existing domestic courts, including a Protocol 16-style procedure, a discursive style for the Asian Court's judgments as an effective tool of 'soft' conflict management, citation of national judgments (a point also made by Huneeus), and a carefully calibrated deference doctrine.[126] Like Huneeus, she also emphasises the importance of face-to-face meetings to humanise the relationship between the regional court and domestic courts.

We might also consider two further options. First, given that regional human rights court judgments seeking action by multiple state organs have the lowest compliance rates, we might consider a specific state agency, with sufficient clout, for assisting the executive and legislature to co-ordinate state action. Second, to relieve some of the burden from constitutional courts, a procedure for challenging the validity of constitutional amendments before a regional human rights court would make sense, by allowing us to escape the domestic difficulty of a constituted entity arrogating this power to itself. This possibility appears, in part, to underlie the (now defunct) proposal for an International Constitutional

---

[126] de Visser, 'Cultivating Judicial Conversations'.

Court, as mentioned in the Introduction. However, it is important to recognise that such prescriptions may prove politically difficult to achieve, and may make more sense in the Inter-American and African contexts, where the regional courts do not have unduly busy dockets. For the European Court of Human Rights, it would not seem possible to add competences without some accompanying reform reducing its jurisdiction concerning individual applications. The tension between individual and constitutional justice would need to be carefully managed.

Once again, it is important to remain aware of the capacity of nonjudicial organs to act as democracy-builders and democracy-defenders. At the regional level, significant frameworks for both democracy promotion and democratic protection have been elaborated by organisations including the AU, OAS, Council of Europe, and EU,[127] as well as transregional frameworks by organisations such as the Commonwealth and La Francophonie.[128] We have seen, for instance, the growing role of the Council of Europe's official think tank, the Venice Commission, in reviewing the validity of constitutional amendments under a concept of 'constitutional justice', which appears specifically designed to address the phenomenon of abusive constitutionalism. Incorporating the action of governance bodies within each organisation (secretary generals, executive councils, parliamentary assemblies), human rights commissions, human rights commissioners, special thematic rapporteurs, and advisory bodies such as the Venice Commission and the AU's Panel of the Wise, scholarship and policy is still grappling with how these systems operate – and perhaps more crucially, how they can be made more effective.[129]

Courts remain only one element in such systems, albeit a core element, and we need to consider how they might be better integrated into such systems – could we conceive of domestic constitutional courts being empowered to trigger the EU's 'pre-Article 7' rule of law monitoring process,[130] for instance, or to bring matters before the Commonwealth

---

[127] See e.g. E.R. McMahon & S.H. Baker, *Piecing a Democratic Quilt?*: Regional Organizations and Universal Norms (Kumarian Press, 2006).

[128] See e.g. A. Banerji, 'The Commonwealth of Nations: A Force for Democracy in the 21st Century?' (2008) 97 *The Round Table* 813.

[129] See in particular an International IDEA report by Micha Wiebusch: *The Role of Regional Organizations in the Protection of Constitutionalism* (July 2016) www.idea .int/sites/default/files/publications/the-role-of-regional-organizations-in-the-protection-of-constitutionalism.pdf.

[130] See e.g. D. Kochenov & L. Pech, 'Upholding the Rule of Law in the EU: On the Commission's "Pre-Article 7 Procedure" as a Timid Step in the Right Direction'. EUI working papers, RDCAS 2015/24.

Ministerial Action Group (CMAG)?[131] To date, little attention has been paid to such possibilities.

7   Conclusion: Law, Democracy-Building, and the Limits of Our Imaginations

This book, ultimately, boils down to what we expect the law, and courts, to do in the effort to achieve meaningful democratic governance from the ashes of authoritarianism. It is not a question we can answer in the abstract. Indeed, a rather minor point made by Nijman and Nollkaemper concerning monism and dualism gains added importance in the democratisation context. The scholarly turn toward monism by thinkers such as Hans Kelsen and Georges Scelle in the early twentieth century had, at least partly, its roots in a more general attempt to shore up shaky European democracies by enhancing the power of international law to achieve the ends of constitutionalism – chiefly, the constraint of political power at the domestic level.[132] Nijman and Nollkaemper observe, for instance, that Scelle's argument for the hierarchical superiority of international law was part of an attempt to address the political and democratic crisis in the French Third Republic arising from parliamentary absolutism:

> Monism came to be understood as a relative denial of a fundamental divide between international and domestic law, connected with universal, cosmopolitan, or even utopian connotations. Dualism tends to be understood as an articulation and appreciation of a solid divide between international and domestic law, connected with a conceptual (apologetic) affirmation of state sovereignty and international law as inter-State law.
>
> However, as the terms are used today, the models are disconnected from their contextual origins and the urgent problem of endangered European democracy with which they actually dealt. What was in origin an intensely political and moral debate became an issue approached rather pragmatically. From being a debate loaded with political and moral elements it became a more 'normal' doctrinal topic although marked, consciously or subconsciously, by a conviction of either the moral supremacy of international law or the supremacy of the State will.[133]

When we recall the case-studies in Chapters 5 and 6 it might be said that this intellectual heritage from a century ago – characterising

---

[131] See Banerji, 'Commonwealth'.
[132] 'Introduction' in Nijman & Nollkaemper (eds.), *New Perspectives* 9.   [133] Ibid. 10.

international law as serving domestic constitutional purposes to buttress democratic governance – has found a second life in the democratisation jurisprudence of the past three decades. It is also found, more widely, in the myriad ways international law and organisations seek to shore up the deficiencies of domestic law in young democracies. The 'urgent problem' of endangered Western European democracy in the post-World War I era has, in a way, been replaced by the urgent project in post-1945 young democracies, in all world regions, to consolidate and entrench democratic rule on a par with democratic systems of the Global North.

Rather than endlessly rehearsing theoretical debates that denigrate post-national constitutionalism as a postmodern mash-up with no meaningful boundaries, or which applaud it as a brave new world of plural law, the immediate challenge is to marshal our efforts at designing new ways of combining domestic and international law, in practical ways, which can provide support to societies that seek to leave authoritarian rule behind, while still ascribing meaningful independent value to the fundamental meaning of democracy as self-government by the people. In this task, as in previous eras, we are only held back by the limits of our constitutional imaginations.

~

Concluding Thoughts: Moving Beyond Our Court Obsession

I suppose it is tempting, if the only tool you have is a hammer, to treat everything as if it were a nail.

Abraham H. Maslow, 1966[1]

I get nervous when I see people viewing judges as heroes. Hercules is not the right image.

Justice Susanne Baer, Federal Constitutional
Court of Germany, 2016[2]

This book, having begun with a tale from the past, ends with a tale from the future.

* * *

In January 2037, after years of escalating internecine power struggles in the Politburo Standing Committee and the wider Communist Party, growing Uighur and Tibetan unrest, two decades of sputtering economic growth, a severe four-year clampdown on citizens' liberties, and, finally, a mass state-wide pro-democracy movement sparked by Hong Kong's Statue Square protests of 2029, the People's Republic of China held the first full, free, and fair elections in its history.

At that point in time, twenty years from today, will the current court-centric paradigm still be our model for supporting this nascent democratisation process? Will we be advocating a thick constitution that seeks to constitute the new democracy with all the trappings of the rule of law, an extensive bill of rights including rafts of justiciable social and economic rights, and comprehensive provisions concerning how the new democratic order should function? Will we be proposing that a new

---

[1] A.H. Maslow, *The Psychology of Science: A Reconnaissance* (Harper, 1966) 15.
[2] Speech at I-CON International Society of Public Law Conference, Plenary Session II: 'Inequalities', 18 June 2016.

constitutional court (or a repurposed Supreme People's Court) will act as the centrepiece of this new democratic order, capable of guarding its coherence and delivering on its promises? If an Asian Court of Human Rights has been established, as various scholars desire, will we be promoting it to the new democracy as a back-up system? Will we continue to claim that, together, these courts will bind the authoritarian Gulliver with ropes, and lead the Chinese state to a brighter democratic future?

* * *

We cannot know the answers to these questions. However, all signs indicate that the ground is already shifting beneath our feet. If the hallmark of governance in the late modern period was the wresting of power from monarchs by (increasingly) representative parliaments, and the twentieth century was marked by the transfer of significant governance power from parliaments to courts, the twenty-first century may yet see the pendulum swing back to a less central role for courts, as their limits as democracy-builders become more widely acknowledged.

Various signs point to the need for a new model for democracy-building: the backlash against the court-centric model in states worldwide; worrying levels of democratic decay in highly judicialised democracy-building projects (e.g. in Hungary, Brazil, South Africa); enduring resistance to robust adjudication in Africa and Asia; the uncertainties of the newer democratic projects in Tunisia and Sri Lanka, and the way they are challenging our 'democratisation toolkit'; and the emergence of new non-judicial democratisation technologies, including international democratic charters and a form of 'constitutional review' by intergovernmental think tanks, such as the Venice Commission.

As urged in the final chapter of this book, we must begin to seriously consider the enduring viability of our current thinking on courts as central institutions for democracy-building, and how we can move to a model, or perhaps multiple models, for sharing the democracy-building burden more evenly. Courts will remain key institutions in any attempt to build democracy on the ashes of an authoritarian regime, but we need to move beyond a model in which courts and judicial review are touted as the first solution to any challenge encountered or expected in this endeavour. That fuller discussion is, however, for another time and place.

BIBLIOGRAPHY

Monographs

Acemoğlu, D. & Robinson, J.A., *Why Nations Fail* (Crown Business, 2012).

Aiyede, R. & Isumonah, V., *Towards Democratic Consolidation in Nigeria: Executive-Legislative Relations and the Budgetary Process* (Development Policy Centre, 2002).

Alexander, G., *The Sources of Democratic Consolidation* (Cornell University Press, 2002).

Amr, M.S.M., *The Role of the International Court of Justice as the Principal Judicial Organ of the United Nations* (Martinus Nijhoff, 2003).

Barak, A., *The Judge in a Democracy* (Princeton University Press, 2006).

Barros, R., *Constitutionalism and Dictatorship: Pinochet, the Junta, and the 1980 Constitution* (Cambridge University Press, 2002).

Bates, E., *The Evolution of the European Convention on Human Rights. From its Inception to the Creation of a Permanent Court of Human Rights* (Oxford University Press, 2010).

Bell, C., *On the Law of Peace: Peace Agreements and the Lex Pacificatoria* (Oxford University Press, 2008).

Bickel, A., *The Least Dangerous Branch: The Supreme Court at the Bar of Politics* (Bobbs-Merrill, 1962).

Blokker, P., *New Democracies in Crisis? A Comparative Constitutional Study of the Czech Republic, Hungary, Poland, Romania and Slovakia* (Routledge 2013).

Bobek, M., *Comparative Reasoning in European Supreme Courts* (Oxford University Press, 2013).

Borges, N., *Damião Ximenes: Primeira Condenação do Brasil na Corte Interamericana de Direitos Humanos* (Editora Revan, 2009). [Trans. Damião Ximenes: The First Condemnation of Brazil in the Inter-American Court of Human Rights].

Bradford Burns, E., *A History of Brazil* (3rd edn, Columbia University Press, 1993).

Brewer-Carías, A.R., *Dismantling Democracy in Venezuela: The Chávez Authoritarian Experiment* (Cambridge University Press, 2010).

Brown, G.W. & Held, D., *The Cosmopolitanism Reader* (Polity, 2010).

Brown, K.B. & Snyder, D.V., *General Reports of the XVIIIth Congress of the International Academy of Comparative Law* (Springer, 2011).

Bugorgue-Larsen, L. & Úbeda de Torres, A., *The Inter-American Court of Human Rights: Case Law and Commentary* (Oxford University Press, 2011).

Butt, S., *The Constitutional Court and Democracy in Indonesia* (Brill, 2015).

Calleros, J.C., *The Unfinished Transition to Democracy in Latin America* (Routledge, 2009).

Cappelletti, M., *Judicial Review in the Contemporary World* (Bobbs-Merrill, 1971).

Chavez, R.B., *The Rule of Law in Nascent Democracies: Judicial Politics in Argentina* (Stanford University Press, 2004).

Coelho, R.M.G, *Proteção Internacional dos Direitos Humanos: A Corte Interamericana e a Implementação de Suas Sentenças no Brasil* (Juruá Editora, 2007). [Trans. International Protection of Human Rights: The Inter-American Court and the Implementation of its Judgments in Brazil].

Collings, J., *Democracy's Guardians: A History of the German Federal Constitutional Court, 1951–2001* (Oxford University Press, 2015).

Dahl, R.A., *On Democracy* (Yale University Press, 2000).

Da Silva, V.A., *The Constitution of Brazil: A Contextual Analysis* (Hart Publishing, forthcoming).

De Magalhães, J.C., *O Supremo Tribunal Federal e o Direito Internacional: Uma Análise Crítica* (Livreria do Advogado, 2002). [Trans. The Supreme Federal Court and International Law: A Critical Analysis].

De Oliveira, F.L., *Supremo Tribunal Federal: Do Autoritarismo à Democracia* (Elsevier, 2012). [Trans. Supreme Federal Court: From Authoritarianism to Democracy].

De Visser, M., *Constitutional Review in Europe: A Comparative Analysis* (Hart, 2014).

Diamond, L., *Developing Democracy: Toward Consolidation* (John Hopkins University Press, 1999).

Do Amaral Júnior, A. & Jubilut, L.L., *STF e o Direito Internacional dos Direitos Humanos* (Quartier Latin, 2009). [Trans. The Supreme Court and International Human Rights Law].

Dolenec, D., *Democratic Institutions and Authoritarian Rule in Southeast Europe* (ECPR Press, 2013).

Dorman, S.R., *Democracy in Comparative Perspective* (Cengage Learning, 2012).

Dworkin, R., *Law's Empire* (Harvard University Press, 1986).

Elster, J., Offe, C. & Preuss, U.K., *Institutional Design in Post-Communist Societies: Rebuilding the Ship at Sea* (Cambridge University Press, 1998).

Ferreres Comella, V., *Constitutional Courts and Democratic Values: A European Perspective* (Yale University Press, 2009).

Fitch, J.S. & Fontana, A., *Military Policy and Democratic Consolidation in Latin America* (Centro de Estudos y Sociedad, 1990).

Fowkes, J., *Building the Constitution: The Practice of Constitutional Interpretation in Post-Apartheid South Africa* (Cambridge University Press, 2016).

Gargarella, R., *Latin American Constitutionalism, 1810–2010: The Engine Room of the Constitution* (Oxford University Press, 2013).

Gerards, J.H. & Fleuren, J., *Implementation of the European Convention on Human Rights and of the Judgments of the ECtHR in National Case Law* (Intersentia, 2014).

Ginsberg, R.H., *Demystifying the European Union: The Enduring Logic of Regional Integration* (Rowman & Littlefield Publishers, 2010).

Ginsburg, T., *Judicial Review in New Democracies: Constitutional Courts in Asian Cases* (Cambridge University Press, 2003).

Gomes, L.F. & Piovesan, F., *O Sistema Interamericano de Proteção dos Direitos Humanos e o Direito Brasileiro* (Editora Revista dos Tribunais, 2000). [Trans. The Inter-American System of Human Rights Protection and Brazilian Law].

Gomes, L.F. & de Oliveira Mazzuoli, V., *Comentários à Convenção Americana sobre Direitos Humanos (Pacto de San Jose de Costa Rica)* (2nd edn, Editora Revista dos Tribunais, 2009). [Trans. Commentaries on the American Convention on Human Rights (Pact of San José, Costa Rica)].

Góngora Mera, M.E., *Inter-American Judicial Constitutionalism: On the Constitutional Rank of Human Rights Treaties in Latin America Through National and Inter-American Adjudication* (Inter-American Institute of Human Rights, 2011).

Grabowski, A. & Kieltyka, M., *Juristic Concept of the Validity of Statutory Law: A Critique of Contemporary Legal Nonpositivism* (Springer, 2013).

Hailbronner, M., *Traditions and Transformations: The Rise of German Constitutionalism* (Oxford University Press, 2015).

Hart Ely, J., *Democracy and Distrust. A Theory of Judicial Review* (Harvard University Press, 1981).

Helmke, G., *Courts Under Constraints: Judges, Generals, and Presidents in Argentina* (Cambridge University Press, 2012).

Hilbink, L., *Judges Beyond Politics in Democracy and Dictatorship: Lessons from Chile* (New York: Cambridge University Press, 2007).

Hirschl, R., *Towards Juristocracy: The Origins and Consequences of the New Constitutionalism* (Harvard University Press, 2004).

Hohmann, J., *The Right to Housing: Law, Concepts, Possibilities* (Bloomsbury Publishing, 2013).

Hübner Mendes, C., *Constitutional Courts and Deliberative Democracy* (Oxford University Press, 2013).

Controle de Constitucionalidade e Democracia (Campus Elsevier, 2007).

Huntington, S., *The Third Wave: Democratization in the Late Twentieth Century* (Oxford University Press, 1991).

Issacharoff, S., *Fragile Democracies: Contested Power in the Era of Constitutional Courts* (Cambridge University Press, 2015).

Jacob, H., Blankenberg, E., Kritzer, H.M., Provine, D.M. & Sanders, J., *Courts, Law and Politics in Comparative Perspective* (Yale University Press, 1996).

Jackson, V.C., *Constitutional Engagement in a Transnational Era* (Oxford University Press, 2010).

King, J., *Judging Social Rights* (Cambridge University Press, 2012).

Kingstone, P., *Democratic Brazil Revisited* (University of Pittsburgh Press, 2008).

Kiwinda Mbondenyi, M., *International Human Rights and their Enforcement in Africa* (LawAfrica, 2011).

Klabbers, J., Peters, A. & Ulfstein, G., *The Constitutionalization of International Law* (Oxford University Press, 2009).

Klug, H., *Constituting Democracy: Law, Globalisation and South Africa's Political Reconstruction* (Cambridge University Press, 2000).

Kommers, D., *Judicial Politics in Western Germany: A Study of the Federal Constitutional Court* (Sage Publications, 1976).

Kommers, D.P., Finn, J.E. & Jacobsohn, G.J., *American Constitutional Law: Essays, Cases, and Comparative Notes* (Rowman & Littlefield, 2009).

Kommers, D.P., *The Constitutional Jurisprudence of the Federal Republic of Germany* (2nd edn, Duke University Press, 1997).

The Constitutional Jurisprudence of the Federal Republic of Germany (1st edn, Duke University Press, 1989).

Kommers, D.P. & Miller, R.A., *The Constitutional Jurisprudence of the Federal Republic of Germany* (3rd edn, Duke University Press, 2012).

Koskenniemi, M., *From Apology to Utopia: The Structure of Legal Argument* (Cambridge University Press, 1989).

Krisch, N., *Beyond Constitutionalism: The Pluralist Structure of Postnational Law* (Oxford University Press, 2010).

Loughlin, M., *The Idea of Public Law* (Oxford University Press, 2003).

Lowe, K., *Savage Continent: Europe in the Aftermath of World War II* (Viking, 2012).

Markesinis, B. & Fedtke, J., *Judicial Recourse to Foreign Law: A New Source of Inspiration?* (Routledge, 2012).

Maslow, A.H., *The Psychology of Science: A Reconnaissance* (Harper, 1966).

Mavčič, A. *The Constitutional Review* (2nd edn, Vandeplas Publishing, 2013).

Slovenian Constitutional Review: Its Position in the World and its Role in the Transition to a New Democratic System (Nova revija, 1995).

McCrudden, C. & O'Leary, B., *Courts and Consociations: Human Rights versus Power-Sharing* (Oxford University Press, 2013).

McMahon, E.R. & Baker, S.H., *Piecing a Democratic Quilt?: Regional Organizations and Universal Norms* (Kumarian Press, 2006).

Møller, J. & Skaaning, S.-E., *Democracy and Democratization in Comparative Perspective: Conceptions, Conjunctures, Causes and Consequences* (Routledge 2012).

Mondaini, M., *Direitos Humanos no Brasil Contemporâneo* (Editora Universitária UFPE, 2008). [Trans. Human Rights in Contemporary Brazil].

Neville, H., *The Works of the Famous Nicolas Machiavel* (A. Churchill, 1720).

Pasqualucci, J., *Practice and Procedure of the Inter-American Court of Human Rights* (Cambridge University Press, 2012).

Pereira, A., *Political (In)Justice: Authoritarianism and the Rule of Law in Brazil, Chile, and Argentina* (University of Pittsburgh Press, 2005).

Pildes, R., *The Law of Democracy: Legal Structure of the Political Process* (Foundation Press, 1998).

Przeworski, A., *Sustainable Democracy* (Cambridge University Press, 1995).

Pridham, G., *The Dynamics of Democratization* (Continuum, 2000).

Prillaman, W.C., *The Judiciary and Democratic Decay in Latin America: Declining Confidence in the Rule of Law* (Greenwood Publishing Group, 2000).

Rapport, M., *1848: Year of Revolution* (Hachette, 2010).

Ríos-Figueroa, J., *Constitutional Courts as Mediators: Armed Conflict, Civil-Military Relations, and the Rule of Law in Latin America* (Cambridge University Press, 2016).

Roux, T., *The Politics of Principle: The First South African Constitutional Court, 1995–2005* (Cambridge University Press, 2013).

Sadurski, W., *Constitutionalism and the Enlargement of Europe* (Oxford University Press, 2012).

  Rights Before Courts: A Study of Constitutional Courts in Postcommunist States of Central and Eastern Europe (Springer, 2008).

Schneider, C., *The Consolidation of Democracy: Comparing Europe and Latin America* (Routledge, 2008).

Schumpeter, J., *Capitalism, Socialism, and Democracy* (Harper & Row, 1942).

Shapiro, M. & Stone Sweet, A., *On Law, Politics and Judicialization* (Oxford University Press, 2002).

Shelton, D., *The Regional Protection of Human Rights* (Oxford University Press, 2013).

Skidmore, T.E., *The Politics of Military Rule in Brazil, 1964–85* (Ebsco Publishing, 1988).

Stelzer, M., *The Constitution of the Republic of Austria* (Hart, 2011).

Stone Sweet, A. *Governing with Judges: Constitutional Politics in Europe* (Oxford University Press, 2000).

  The Birth of Judicial Politics in France (Oxford University Press, 1994).

Sturgess, G. & Chubb, P., *Judging the World: Law and Politics in the World's Leading Courts* (Butterworth, 1988).

Sun, H.T., *The Political Economy of Democratic Consolidation: Dynamic Labour Politics in South Korea* (Chonnam National University Press, 2002).

Sundaram, A., *Bad News: Last Journalists in a Dictatorship* (Bloomsbury Publishing, 2016).

Sweeney, J.A., *The European Court of Human Rights in the Post-Cold War Era: Universality in Transition* (Routledge, 2013).

Tate, N.C. & Vallinder, T., *The Global Expansion of Judicial Power* (New York University Press, 1995).

Tatham, A.F., *Central European Constitutional Courts in the Face of EU Membership: The Influence of the German Model in Hungary and Poland* (Martinus Nijhoff, 2013).

Taylor, M., *Judging Policy: Courts and Policy Reform in Democratic Brazil* (Stanford University Press, 2008).

Teitel, R. *Humanity's Law* (Oxford University Press, 2011).
  Transitional Justice (Oxford University Press, 2000).

Thorson, C.L, *Politics, Judicial Review, and the Russian Constitutional Court* (Palgrave MacMillan, 2012).

Tierney, S., *Constitutional Referendums. The Theory and Practice of Republican Deliberation* (Oxford University Press, 2012).

Todorakov, V., *The Bulgarian Constitutional Court: In the Context of Democratic Consolidation During Transition (1991–2005)* (Lambert Academic Publishing, 2010).

Tomkins, A., *Our Republican Constitution* (Oxford University Press, 2005).

Tsagourias, N., *Transnational Constitutionalism: International and European Perspectives* (Cambridge University Press, 2007).

Tully, J., *Strange Multiplicity: Constitutionalism in the Age of Diversity* (Cambridge University Press, 1995).

Vanberg, G., *The Politics of Constitutional Review in Germany* (Cambridge University Press, 2004).

Vergniaud, P.V., *Oeuvres de Vergniaud* (A Vermorel edn, A. Faure, 1867).

Vilhena Vilheira, O., *Supremo Tribunal. Jurisprudência Política* (2nd edn, Malheiros, 1994). [Trans. The Supreme Court. Political Jurisprudence].

Viola, S.E.A., *Direitos Humanos e Democracia no Brasil* (Editora UNISINOS, 2008). [Trans. Human Rights and Democracy in Brazil].

Waldron, J., *Law and Disagreement* (Clarendon Press, 1999).

Walker, N., *Intimations of Global Law* (Cambridge University Press, 2014).

Wiebelhaus-Brahm, E., *Truth Commissions and Transitional Societies: The Impact on Human Rights and Democracy* (Routledge Security and Governance Series, 2010).

Winter, S., *Transitional Justice in Established Democracies* (Palgrave 2014).

Wolfe, C., *The Rise of Modern Judicial Review: From Constitutional Interpretation to Judge-made Law* (Rowman & Littlefield, 1994).

Yap, P.J., *Judicial Review of Elections in Asia* (Routledge, 2016).

Zaiden Benvindo, J., *On the Limits of Constitutional Adjudication: Deconstructing Balancing and Judicial Activism* (Springer, 2010).

Edited Collections

Andenas, M. & Fairgrieve, D. (eds.) *Tom Bingham and the Transformation of the Law: A Liber Amicorum* (Oxford University Press, 2009).

Judicial Review in International Perspective Vol. 2 (Kluwer Law International, 2000).

Angell, A., Schjolden, L. & Sieder, R. (eds.), *The Judicialization of Politics in Latin America* (Palgrave MacMillan, 2009).

Badinter, R. & Breyer, S. (eds.), *Judges in Contemporary Democracy: An International Conversation* (New York University Press, 2004).

Barahona de Brito, A., González Enríquez, C. & Aguilar, P. (eds.), *The Politics of Memory: Transitional Justice in Democratizing Societies* (Oxford University Press, 2001).

Beneyto, J.M. & Kennedy, D. (eds.), *New Approaches to International Law: The European and the American Experiences* (Springer, 2012).

Blok, J.H. & Lardinois, A.P.M.H. (eds.), *Solon of Athens* (Brill, 2005).

Bonilla Maldonado, D. (ed.), *Constitutionalism of the Global South: The Activist Tribunals of India, South Africa, and Colombia* (Cambridge University Press, 2013).

Brewer, S. (ed.), *Evolution and Revolution in Theories of Legal Reasoning: Nineteenth Century Through the Present* Vol. 4 (Taylor & Francis, 1998).

Brewer-Carías, A.R. (ed.), *Constitutional Courts as Positive Legislators: A Comparative Law Study* (Cambridge University Press, 2013).

Bustamante, T. & Gonçalves Fernandes, B. (eds.), *Democratizing Constitutional Law: Perspectives on Legal Theory and the Legitimacy of Constitutionalism* (Springer, 2016).

Buyse, A. & Hamilton, M. (eds.), *Transitional Jurisprudence and the ECHR: Justice, Politics and Rights* (Cambridge University Press, 2011).

Caldeira, A., Kelemen, R.D. & Whittington, K.E. (eds.), *The Oxford Handbook of Law and Politics* (Oxford University Press, 2008).

Campbell, T., Goldsworthy, J. & Stone, A. (eds.), *Protecting Human Rights: Instruments and Institutions* (Oxford University Press, 2003).

Christoffersen, J. & Rask Madsen, M. (eds.), *The European Court of Human Rights: Between Law and Politics* (Oxford University Press, 2011).

Claes, M., de Visser, M., Popelier, P. & Van de Heyning, C. (eds.), *Constitutional Conversations in Europe: Actors, Topics and Procedures* (Intersentia 2012).

Couso, J., Huneeus, A. and Sieder, R. (eds.), *Cultures of Legality: Judicialization and Political Activism in Latin America* (Cambridge University Press, 2010).

Crawford, G. & Lynch, G. (eds.), *Democratization in Africa: Challenges and Prospects* (Routledge, 2013).

Croissant, A. & Bünte, M. (eds.), *The Crisis of Democratic Governance in Southeast Asia* (Palgrave Macmillan, 2011).

Cuadras-Morató, X. (ed.), *Catalonia: A New Independent State in Europe?* (Routledge, 2016).

Diamond, L. & Morlino, L. (eds.), *Assessing the Quality of Democracy* (Johns Hopkins University Press, 2005).

Diamond, L. & Plattner, M. (eds.), *Democracy: A Reader* (Johns Hopkins University Press, 2009).

Dixon, R. & Ginsburg, T. (eds.), *Comparative Constitutional Law in Latin America* (Edward Elgar Publishing, forthcoming, 2017).

Dolinger, J. & Rosenn, K. (eds.), *A Panorama of Brazilian Law* (Lynne Rienner, 1992).

Dorsen, N. & Gifford, P. (eds.), *Democracy & The Rule of Law* (CQ Press, 2001).

Dunoff, J.L. & Trachtman, J.P. (eds.), *Ruling the World? Constitutionalism, International Law and Global Governance* (Cambridge University Press, 2009).

Eberhard, H., Lachmayer, K. & Thallinger, G. (eds.), *Transitional Constitutionalism: Proceedings of the 2nd Vienna Workshop on International Constitutional Law* (Nomos, 2007).

Elster, J. & Slagstad, R. (eds.), *Constitutionalism and Democracy* (Cambridge University Press, 1993).

Federico, V. & Fusaro, C. (eds.), *Constitutionalism and Democratic Transitions: Lessons from South Africa* (Firenze University Press, 2006).

Flogaitis, S.I., Zwart, T. & Fraser, J. (eds.), *The European Court of Human Rights and its Discontents: Turning Criticism into Strength* (Edward Elgar Publishing, 2013).

Føllesdal, A., Peters, B., Karlsson Schaffer, J. & Ulfstein, G. (eds.), *The Legitimacy of International Human Rights Regimes: Legal, Political and Philosophical Perspectives* (Cambridge University Press, 2013).

Føllesdal, A., Peters, B. & Ulfstein, G. (eds.), *Constituting Europe: The European Court of Human Rights in a National, European and Global Context* (Cambridge University Press, 2013).

Fortes, P., Boratti, L., Palacios Lleras, A. & Daly, T.G. (eds.), *Law and Policy in Latin America: Transforming Courts, Institutions, and Rights* (Palgrave MacMillan, 2017).

Friedman, L.M. & Pérez-Perdomo, R. (eds.), *Legal Culture in the Age of Globalization. Latin America and Latin Europe* (Stanford University Press, 2003).

Fung, E.S.K. & Drakeley, S. (eds.), *Democracy in Eastern Asia: Issues, Problems and Challenges in a Region of Diversity* (Routledge, 2013).

Galligan, D. & Versteeg, M. (eds.), *Social and Political Foundations of Constitutions* (Cambridge University Press, 2013).

Gargarella, R., Domingo, P. & Roux, T. (eds.), *Courts and Social Transformation in New Democracies: An Institutional Voice for the Poor?* (Ashgate, 2006).

Ginsburg, T. (ed.), *Comparative Constitutional Design* (Cambridge University Press, 2012).

Ginsburg, T. & Dixon, R. (eds.), *Comparative Constitutional Law* (Edward Elgar, 2011).

Ginsburg, T. & Huq, A. (eds.), *Assessing Constitutional Performance* (Cambridge University Press, 2016).

Ginsburg, T. & Simpser, A. (eds.), *Constitutions in Authoritarian Regimes* (Cambridge University Press, 2013).

Gloppen, S., Gargarella, R. & Skaar, E. (eds.), *Democratization and the Judiciary: The Accountability Function of Courts in New Democracies* (Routledge, 2004).

Gloppen, S., Wilson, B.M., Gargarella, R., Skaar, E. & Kinander, M. (eds.), *Courts and Power in Latin America and Africa* (Palgrave MacMillan, 2010).

Groppi, T. & Ponthereau, M.C. (eds.), *The Use of Foreign Precedents by Constitutional Judges* (Hart Publishing, 2013).

Hamad, M. & Al-Anani, K. (eds.), *Elections and Democratization in the Middle East: The Tenacious Search for Freedom, Justice, and Dignity* (Palgrave MacMillan, 2014).

Hanke, L., *Bartolomé de las Casas: An Interpretation of his Life and Writings* (1951, H Hanke edn, Springer, 2013).

Harding, A. & Leyland, P. (eds.), *Constitutional Courts: A Comparative Study* (Wildy, Simmonds & Hill Publishing, 2009).

Harding, A. & Nicholson, P. (eds.), *New Courts in Asia* (Routledge, 2010).

Hasan, Z., Sridharan, E. & Sudarshan, R. (eds.), *India's Living Constitution: Ideas, Practices, Controversies* (Anthem Press, 2005).

Haynes, J. (ed.), *Routledge Handbook of Democratization* (Routledge, 2012).

Heckman, J.J., Nelson, R.L. & Cabatingan, L. (eds.), *Global Perspectives on the Rule of Law* (Routledge, 2010).

Helmke, G. & Ríos-Figueroa, J. (eds.), *Courts in Latin America* (Cambridge University Press, 2011).

Higley, J. & Gunther, R. (eds.), *Elites and Democratic Consolidation in Latin America and Southern Europe* (Cambridge University Press, 1991).

Holló, A. & Erdei, Á. (eds.), *Selected Decisions of the Constitutional Court of Hungary (1998–2001)* (Akadémiai Kiadó, 2005).

Hucko, E.M. (ed.), *The Democratic Tradition. Four German Constitutions* (Berg Publishers Limited, 1987).

Huls, N., Adams, M. & Bomhoff, J. (eds.), *The Legitimacy of Highest Courts' Rulings: Judicial Deliberations and Beyond* (TMC Asser Press, 2009).

Jovanović, M.A., Pavićević, Đ. & Đorđević, B. (eds.), *Crisis and Quality of Democracy in Eastern Europe* (Eleven International Publishing, 2012).

Kapiszewski, D., Silverstein, G. & Kagan, R.A. (eds.), *Consequential Courts: Judicial Roles in Global Perspective* (Cambridge University Press, 2013).

Killander, M. (ed.), *International Law and Domestic Human Rights Litigation in Africa* (Pretoria University Law Press, 2010).

Kingstone, P. & Power, T. (eds.), *Democratic Brazil: Actors, Institutions, and Processes* (University of Pittsburgh Press, 2000).

Lamont, C.K., van der Harst, J. & Gaenssmantel, F. (eds.), *Non-Western Encounters with Democratization: Imagining Democracy after the Arab Spring* (Ashgate, 2015).

Lettinga, D. & van Troost, L. (eds.), *Can Human Rights Bring Social Justice? Twelve Essays* (Amnesty International, 2015).

Levine, D.H. & Molina, J.E. (eds.), *The Quality of Democracy in Latin America* (Lynne Rienner Publishers, 2011).

Linnan, D.K. (ed.), *Legitimacy, Legal Development and Change: Law and Modernization Reconsidered* (Routledge, 2016).

Linz, J. & Stepan, A. (eds.), *Problems of Democratic Transition and Consolidation. Southern Europe, South America, and Post-Communist Europe* (Johns Hopkins University Press, 1996).

The Breakdown of Democratic Regimes (Johns Hopkins University Press, 1978).

Mainwaring, S. & Soberg Shugart, M. (eds.), *Presidentialism and Democracy in Latin America* (Cambridge University Press, 1997).

Mainwaring, S., O'Donnell, G. & Valenzuela, J. (eds.), *Issues in Democratic Consolidation: The New South American Democracies in Comparative Perspective* (University of Notre Dame Press, 1992).

Morison, J., MacEvoy, K. & Anthony, G. (eds.), *Judges, Transition, and Human Rights* (Oxford University Press, 2007).

Nervo Codato, A. (ed.), *Political Transition and Democratic Consolidation: Studies on Contemporary Brazil* (Nova Science, 2006).

Nijman, J. & Nollkaemper, A. (eds.), *New Perspectives on the Divide between National and International Law* (Oxford University Press, 2007).

O'Donnell, G., Schmitter, P. & Whitehead, L. (eds.), *Transitions from Authoritarian Rule* (re-issue, Johns Hopkins University Press, 2013).

Transitions from Authoritarian Rule (Johns Hopkins University Press, 1986).

O'Donnell, G., Vargas Cullell, J. & Iazzetta, O.M. (eds.), *The Quality of Democracy: Theory and Applications* (University of Notre Dame Press, 2004).

Popelier, P., Mazmanyan, A. & Vandenbruwaene, W. (eds.), *The Role of Constitutional Courts in Multilevel Governance* (Intersentia, 2013).

Pridham, G. (ed.), *Transitions to Democracy: Comparative Perspectives from Southern Europe, Latin America and Eastern Europe* (Dartmouth, 1995).

Securing Democracy: Political Parties and Democratic Consolidation in Southern Europe (Routledge, 1990).

Qvortrup, M. (ed.), *The British Constitution: Continuity and Change. A Festschrift for Vernon Bogdanor* (Hart, 2013).

Rodriguez Garavito, C. (ed.), *Law and Society in Latin America: A New Map* (Routledge, 2014).

Romano, C., Alter, K. & Shany, Y. (eds.), *The Oxford University Press Handbook of International Adjudication* (Oxford University Press, 2014).

Rosas, A., Levits, E. & Bot, Y. (eds.), *The Court of Justice and the Construction of Europe: Analyses and Perspectives on Sixty Years of Case-law* (Springer, 2012).

Rosenfeld, M. & Sajó, A. (eds.), *The Oxford Handbook of Comparative Constitutional Law* (Oxford University Press, 2012).

Russell, P. & O'Brien, D.M. (eds.), *Judicial Independence in the Age of Democracy. Critical Perspectives from Around the World* (University of Virginia Press, 2001).

Sadurski, W. (ed.), *Constitutional Justice, East and West: Democratic Legitimacy and Constitutional Courts in Post-Communist Europe in a Comparative Perspective* (Springer, 2002).

Sadurski, W. & Febbrajo, A. (eds.), *Central and Eastern Europe After Transition: Towards a New Socio-legal Semantics* (Ashgate Publishing, 2013).

Sadurski, W., Czarnota, A. & Krygier, M. (eds.), *Spreading Democracy and the Rule of Law?: The Impact of EU Enlargement for the Rule of Law, Democracy and Constitutionalism in Post-Communist Legal Orders* (Springer, 2006).

Sadurski, W., Krygier, M. & Czarnota, A. (eds.), *Rethinking the Rule of Law in Post-Communist Europe: Past Legacies, Institutional Innovations, and Constitutional Discourses* (Central European University Press, 2005).

Scheinin, M. & Aksenova, M. (eds.), *Judges as Guardians of Constitutionalism and Human Rights* (Edward Elgar Publishing, 2016).

Schilling-Vacaflor, A. & Nolte, D. (eds.), *New Constitutionalism in Latin America: Promises and Practices* (Ashgate, 2012).

Seibert-Fohr, A. (ed.), *Judicial Independence in Transition* (Springer, 2012).

Sellers, M. & Tomaszewski, T. (eds.), *The Rule of Law in Comparative Perspective* (Springer, 2010).

Serrano, M. & Popovski, V. (eds.), *Human Rights Regimes in the Americas* (United Nations University Press, 2010).

Shelton, D. (ed.), *The Oxford Handbook of International Human Rights Law* (Oxford University Press, 2013).

Sólyom, L. & Brunner, G. (eds.), *Constitutional Judiciary in a New Democracy: The Hungarian Constitutional Court* (University of Michigan Press, 2000).

St John McDonald, R. & Johnston, D.M. (eds.), *Towards World Constitutionalism* (Martinus Nijhoff, 2005).

Stoner, K. & McFaul, M. (eds.), *Transitions to Democracy: A Comparative Perspective* (Johns Hopkins University Press, 2013).

Stotzky, I. (ed.), *Transition to Democracy in Latin America: The Role of the Judiciary* (Westview Press, 1993).

Suumann, G. (ed.), *15 Years of Constitutional Review in the Supreme Court of Estonia. Systematized Extracts of Constitutional Review Judgments and*

Rulings of the Supreme Court En Banc and the Constitutional Review Chamber in 1993–2008 (Supreme Court of Estonia, 2009).

Terris, D., Romano, C.P.R. & Swigart, L. (eds.), *The International Judge: An Introduction to the Men and Women Who Decide the World's Cases* (Brandeis University Press, 2007).

Vilhena Vilheira, O., Viljoen, F. & Baxi, U. (eds.), *Transformative Constitutionalism: Comparing the Apex Courts of Brazil, India and South Africa* (Pretoria University Law Press, 2013).

Volcansek, M.L. (ed.), *Judicial Politics and Policy-Making in Western Europe* (Cass, 1992).

Von Bogdandy, A., Ferrer, E., Morales, M. & Piovesan, P. (eds.), *Transformative Constitutionalism in Latin America: A New Latin American Ius Commune* (Oxford University Press, forthcoming, 2017).

Von Bogdandy, A. & Sonnevend, P. (eds.), *Constitutional Crisis in the European Constitutional Area: Theory, Law and Politics in Hungary and Romania* (Bloomsbury Publishing, 2015).

Von Bogdandy, A. & Venzke, I. (eds.), *International Judicial Lawmaking: On Public Authority and Democratic Legitimation in Global Governance* (Springer, 2012).

Walker, N. & Loughlin, M. (eds.), *The Paradox of Constitutionalism: Constituent Power and Constitutional Form* (Oxford University Press, 2007).

Williams, M. & Nagy, J.E. (eds.), *Transitional Justice* (New York University Press, 2012).

Woolman, S. & Bishop, M. (eds.), *Constitutional Conversations* (Pretoria University Law Press, 2008).

Zielonka, J. (ed.), *Democratic Consolidation in Eastern Europe, Vol. 1: Institutional Engineering* (Oxford University Press, 2001).

Book Chapters

Alberts, S., Warshaw, C. & Weingast, B.R., 'Democratization and Countermajoritarian Institutions' in T. Ginsburg (ed.), *Comparative Constitutional Design* (Cambridge University Press, 2012).

Alston, L.J., Melo, M.A., Mueller, B. & Pereira, C., 'On the Road to Good Governance: Recovering from Economic and Political Shocks in Brazil' in E. Stein, M. Tommasi, C.G. Scartascini & P.T. Spiller (eds.), *Policymaking in Latin America: How Politics Shapes Policies* (Inter-American Development Bank, 2008).

Ayala, C., 'The Judicial Dialogue between International and National Courts in the Inter-American Human Rights System' in M. Scheinin & M. Aksenova (eds.), *Judges as Guardians of Constitutionalism and Human Rights* (Edward Elgar Publishing, 2016).

Baker, A., 'GIs in West Germany' in T. Adam (ed.), *Germany and the Americas: O-Z* (ABC-CLIO, 2005).

Baxi, U., 'Preliminary Notes on Transformative Constitutionalism' in O. Vilhena Vilheira, F. Viljoen & U. Baxi (eds.), *Transformative Constitutionalism: Comparing the Apex Courts of Brazil, India and South Africa* (Pretoria University Law Press, 2013).

Bellamy, R., 'The Democratic Legitimacy of Regional Human Rights Conventions: Political Constitutionalism and the *Hirst* case' in A. Føllesdal, B. Peters, J. Karlsson Schaffer & G. Ulfstein (eds.), *The Legitimacy of International Human Rights Regimes: Legal, Political and Philosophical Perspectives* (Cambridge University Press, 2013).

Binder, C., 'The Prohibition of Amnesties by the Inter-American Court of Human Rights' in A. von Bogdandy & I. Venzke (eds.), *International Judicial Lawmaking: On Public Authority and Democratic Legitimation in Global Governance* (Springer, 2012).

Björgvinsson, D.T., 'The Role of Judges of the European Court of Human Rights as Guardians of Fundamental Rights of the Individual' in M. Scheinin & M. Aksenova (eds.), *Judges as Guardians of Constitutionalism and Human Rights* (Edward Elgar Publishing, 2016).

Blankenburg, E., 'Changes in Political Regimes and Continuity of the Law in Germany' in H. Jacob, E. Blankenberg, H.M. Kritzer, D.M. Provine. & J. Sanders, *Courts, Law and Politics in Comparative Perspective* (Yale University Press, 1996).

Bonilla Maldonado, D., 'Introduction: Toward a Constitutionalism of the Global South' in D. Bonilla Maldonado (ed.), *Constitutionalism of the Global South: The Activist Tribunals of India, South Africa, and Colombia* (Cambridge University Press, 2013).

Bossacoma i Busquets, P., 'The Secession of Catalonia: Legal Strategies and Barriers' in X. Cuadras-Morató (ed.), *Catalonia: A New Independent State in Europe?* (Routledge, 2016).

Botelho Junqueira, E., 'Brazil: The Road of Conflict Bound for Total Justice' in L.M. Friedman & R. Pérez-Perdomo (eds.), *Legal Culture in the Age of Globalization. Latin America and Latin Europe* (Stanford University Press, 2003).

Breuer, A., 'South America' in J. Haynes (ed.), *Routledge Handbook of Democratization* (Routledge, 2012).

Brown, W., 'Seeking Socioeconomic Justice' in D. Lettinga & L. van Troost (eds.), *Can Human Rights Bring Social Justice? Twelve Essays* (Amnesty International, 2015).

Chavez, R.B., 'The Rule of Law and Courts in Democratizing Regimes' in A. Caldeira, R.D. Kelemen & K.E. Whittington (eds.), *The Oxford Handbook of Law and Politics* (Oxford University Press, 2008).

Chong, D., 'How Human Rights Can Address Socioeconomic Inequality' in D. Lettinga & L. van Troost (eds.), *Can Human Rights Bring Social Justice? Twelve Essays* (Amnesty International, 2015).

Daly, T.G., 'Brazilian Supremocracy and the Inter-American Court of Human Rights: Unpicking an Unclear Relationship' in P. Fortes, L. Boratti, A. Palacios Lleras & T.G. Daly (eds.), *Law and Policy in Latin America: Transforming Courts, Institutions, and Rights* (Palgrave Macmillan, 2017).

De Franciscis, M.E. & Zannini, R., 'Judicial Policy-Making in Italy: The Constitutional Court' in M.L. Volcansek (ed.), *Judicial Politics and Policy-Making in Western Europe* (Cass, 1992).

De Lange, R., 'Judicial Deliberations, Legitimacy and Human Rights Adjudication' in N. Huls, M. Adams & J. Bomhoff (eds.), *The Legitimacy of Highest Courts' Rulings: Judicial Deliberations and Beyond* (TMC Asser Press, 2009).

Ferraz, O.L.M., 'Between Usurpation and Abdication? The Right to Health in the Courts of Brazil and South Africa' in O. Vilhena Vilheira, F. Viljoen & U. Baxi (eds.), *Transformative Constitutionalism: Comparing the Apex Courts of Brazil, India and South Africa* (Pretoria University Law Press, 2013).

Ferreres Comella, V., 'The Rise of Specialized Constitutional Courts' in T. Ginsburg & R. Dixon (eds.), *Comparative Constitutional Law* (Edward Elgar Publishing, 2011).

Føllesdal, A., 'Much Ado about Nothing? International Judicial Review of Human Rights in Well-Functioning Democracies' in A. Føllesdal, B. Peters, J. Karlsson Schaffer & G. Ulfstein (eds.), *The Legitimacy of International Human Rights Regimes: Legal, Political and Philosophical Perspectives* (Cambridge University Press, 2013).

Frosini, J. & Pegoraro, L, 'Constitutional Courts in Latin America: A Testing Ground for New Parameters of Classification?' in A. Harding & P. Leyland (eds.), *Constitutional Courts: A Comparative Study* (Wildy, Simmonds & Hill Publishing, 2009).

Galligan, D.J. & Versteeg, M., 'Theoretical Perspectives on the Social and Political Foundations of Constitutions' in D.J. Galligan & M. Versteeg (eds.), *Social and Political Foundations of Constitutions* (Cambridge University Press, 2013).

García-Sayan, D., 'Una Viva Interacción: Corte Interamericana y Tribunales Internos' in *La Corte Interamericana de Derechos Humanos: Un Cuarto de Siglo: 1979–2004* (Inter-American Court of Human Rights, 2005). www.corteidh .or.cr/docs/libros/cuarto%20de%20siglo.pdf.

Gargarella, R., 'In Search of a Democratic Justice – What Courts Should Not Do: Argentina, 1983–2002' in S. Gloppen, R. Gargarella & E. Skaar (eds.), *Democratization and the Judiciary: The Accountability Function of Courts in New Democracies* (Routledge, 2004).

Ghosh, E., 'Judicial Reference to Community Values – A Pointer Towards Constitutional Juries?' in T. Bustamante & B. Gonçalves Fernandes (eds.), *Democratizing Constitutional Law: Perspectives on Legal Theory and the Legitimacy of Constitutionalism* (Springer, 2016).

Ginsburg, T., 'The Politics of Courts in Democratization: Four Junctures in Asia' in D. Kapiszewski, G. Silverstein & R.A. Kagan, (eds.), *Consequential Courts: Judicial Roles in Global Perspective* (Cambridge University Press, 2013).

'The Politics of Courts in Democratisation', in J.J. Heckman, R.L. Nelson & L. Cabatingan (eds.), *Global Perspectives on the Rule of Law* (Routledge, 2010).

'The Global Spread of Constitutional Review' in A. Caldeira, R.D. Kelemen & K.E. Whittington (eds.), *The Oxford Handbook of Law and Politics* (Oxford University Press, 2008).

Goldstein, J., 'The Opinion-Writing Function of the Judiciary of Latin American Governments in Transition to Democracy: *Martinez* v. *Provincia de Mendoza*' in I. Stotzky (ed.), *Transition to Democracy in Latin America: The Role of the Judiciary* (Westview Press, 1993).

Goldsworthy, J., 'Judicial Review, Legislative Override, and Democracy' in T. Campbell, J. Goldsworthy & A. Stone (eds.), *Protecting Human Rights: Instruments and Institutions* (Oxford University Press, 2003).

González-Salzberg, D.A., 'Complying (Partially) with the Compulsory Judgments of the Inter-American Court of Human Rights' in P. Fortes, L. Boratti, A. Palacios Lleras & T.G. Daly (eds.), *Law and Policy in Latin America: Transforming Courts, Institutions, and Rights* (Palgrave Macmillan, 2017).

Grimm, D., 'Address' in N. Dorsen & P. Gifford (eds.), *Democracy & The Rule of Law* (CQ Press, 2001).

'Constitutional Adjudication and Democracy' in M. Andenas & D. Fairgrieve (eds.), *Judicial Review in International Perspective*, Vol. 2 (Kluwer Law International, 2000).

Groppi, T., 'The Italian Constitutional Court: Towards a 'Multilevel System' of Constitutional Review?' in A. Harding & P. Leyland (eds.), *Constitutional Courts: A Comparative Study* (Wildy, Simmonds & Hill Publishing, 2009).

Halmai, G. & Scheppele, K., 'Living Well is the Best Revenge: The Hungarian Approach to Judging the Past' in A.J. McAdams (ed.), *Transitional Justice and the Rule of Law in New Democracies* (University of Notre Dame Press, 1997).

Harding, A., Leyland, P. & Groppi, T., 'Constitutional Courts: Forms, Functions and Practice in Comparative Perspective' in A. Harding & P. Leyland (eds.), *Constitutional Courts: A Comparative Study* (Wildy, Simmonds & Hill Publishing, 2009).

Helmke, G. & Staton, J.K., 'The Puzzling Judicial Politics of Latin America: A Theory of Litigation, Judicial Decisions, and Interbranch Conflict' in G. Helmke & J. Ríos-Figueroa, *Courts in Latin America* (Cambridge University Press, 2011).

Herz, M., 'The Organization of American States and Democratization' in J. Haynes (ed.), *Routledge Handbook of Democratization* (Routledge, 2012).

Horowitz, D., 'Constitutional Courts: A Primer for Decision Makers' in L. Diamond & M. Plattner (eds.), *Democracy: A Reader* (Johns Hopkins University Press, 2009).

Huneeus, A., 'Rejecting the Inter-American Court: Judicialization, National Courts, and Regional Human Rights' in J. Couso, A. Huneeus & R. Sieder (eds.), *Cultures of Legality: Judicialization and Political Activism in Latin America* (Cambridge University Press, 2010).

Kapiszewski, D., 'How Courts Work: Institutions, Culture and the Brazilian *Supremo Tribunal Federal*' in J. Couso, A. Huneeus & R. Sieder (eds.), *Cultures of Legality: Judicialization and Political Activism in Latin America* (Cambridge Studies in Law and Society, 2010).

'Power Broker, Policy Maker, or Rights Protector: the Brazilian *Supremo Tribunal Federal* in Transition' in G. Helmke & J. Ríos-Figueroa, *Courts in Latin America* (Cambridge University Press, 2011).

Kay, R.S., 'Rights, Rules and Democracy' in T. Campbell, J. Goldsworthy & A. Stone (eds.), *Protecting Human Rights: Instruments and Institutions* (Oxford University Press, 2003).

Killander, M. & Adjolohoun, H., 'International Law and Domestic Human Rights' in M. Killander (ed.), *International Law and Domestic Human Rights Litigation in Africa* (Pretoria University Law Press, 2010).

Kommers, D.P. & Miller, R.A., '*Das Bundesverfassungsgericht*: Procedure, Practice and Policy of the German Federal Constitutional Court' in A. Harding & P. Leyland (eds.), *Constitutional Courts: A Comparative Study* (Wildy, Simmonds & Hill Publishing, 2009).

Kuhm, M., 'The Best of Times and the Worst of Times: Between Constitutional Triumphalism and Nostalgia' in P. Dobner & M. Loughlin (eds.), *The Twilight of Constitutionalism?* (Oxford University Press, 2010).

Lach, K. & Sadurski, W., 'Constitutional Courts of Central and Eastern Europe: Between Adolescence and Maturity' in Harding & P. Leyland (eds.), *Constitutional Courts: A Comparative Study* (Wildy, Simmonds & Hill Publishing, 2009).

Lettinga, D. & van Troost, L., 'Introduction' in D. Lettinga & L. van Troost (eds.), *Can Human Rights Bring Social Justice? Twelve Essays* (Amnesty International, 2015).

Maruste, R., 'The Outset of Constitutional Judicial Review' in G. Suumann (ed.), *15 Years of Constitutional Review in the Supreme Court of Estonia. Systematized Extracts of Constitutional Review Judgments and Rulings of the Supreme Court En Banc and the Constitutional Review Chamber in 1993–2008* (Supreme Court of Estonia, 2009).

Monclaire, S., 'Democracy, Transition and Consolidation' in A. Nervo Codato (ed.), *Political Transition and Democratic Consolidation: Studies on Contemporary Brazil* (Nova Science, 2006).

O'Donnell, G., 'Transitions, Continuities, and Paradoxes' in S. Mainwaring, G. O'Donnell & J. Valenzuela (eds.), *Issues in Democratic Consolidation: The New South American Democracies in Comparative Perspective* (University of Notre Dame Press, 1992).

Oliver, D., 'The United Kingdom Constitution in Transition: From Where to Where?' in M. Andenas & D. Fairgrieve (eds.), *Tom Bingham and the Transformation of the Law: A Liber Amicorum* (Oxford University Press, 2009).

Overy, R., 'Interwar, War, Postwar: Was there a Zero Hour in 1945?' in D. Stone (ed.), *The Oxford Handbook of Postwar European History* (Oxford University Press, 2012).

Reynolds, A., 'Constitutional Medicine' in L. Diamond & M. Plattner (eds.), *Democracy: A Reader* (Johns Hopkins University Press, 2009).

Riddell, P., 'The Constitution and the Public – How Voters Forgot the Constitution' in M. Qvortrup (ed.), *The British Constitution: Continuity and Change. A Festschrift for Vernon Bogdanor* (Hart Publishing, 2013).

Robinson, W.I., 'Global Capitalism and the Oromo Liberation Struggle: Theoretical Notes on US Policy Towards the Ethiopian Empire' in A. Jalata (ed.), *State Crises, Globalisation and National Movements in North-East Africa: The Horn's Dilemma* (Routledge, 2004).

Rodríguez-Pinzón, D., 'The Inter-American Human Rights System and Transitional Processes' in A. Buyse & M. Hamilton (eds.), *Transitional Jurisprudence and the ECHR: Justice, Politics and Rights* (Cambridge University Press, 2011).

Rodríguez-Raga, R., 'Strategic Deference in the Colombian Constitutional Court, 1992–2006' in G. Helmke & J. Ríos-Figueroa, *Courts in Latin America* (Cambridge University Press, 2011).

Rosenn, K., 'Conflict Resolution and Constitutionalism: The Making of the Brazilian Constitution of 1988', in L.E. Miller & L. Aucoin (eds.) *Framing the State in Times of Transition: Case Studies in Constitution Making* (US Institute of Peace Press, 2010).

Roux, T., 'The Principle of Democracy in South African Constitutional Law' in S. Woolman. & M. Bishop (eds.), *Constitutional Conversations* (Pretoria University Law Press, 2008).

Sanchez-Urribarri, R.A., 'Constitutional Courts in the Region: Between Power and Submissiveness' in R. Dixon & T. Ginsburg (eds.), *Comparative Constitutional Law in Latin America* (Edward Elgar Publishing, forthcoming, 2017).

Santiso, C., 'Economic Reform and Judicial Governance in Brazil: Balancing Independence and Accountability' in S. Gloppen, R. Gargarella & E. Skaar (eds.),

Democratization and the Judiciary: The Accountability Function of Courts in New Democracies (Routledge, 2004).

Scheppele, K.L., 'Democracy by Judiciary (Or Why Courts Can Sometimes Be More Democratic than Parliaments)' in W. Sadurski, M. Krygier & A. Czarnota (eds.), *Rethinking the Rule of Law in Post-Communist Europe: Past Legacies, Institutional Innovations, and Constitutional Discourses* (Central European University Press, 2005).

Schmitter, P., 'The Consolidation of Political Democracies: Processes, Rhythms, Sequences and Types' in G. Pridham (ed.), *Transitions to Democracy: Comparative Perspectives from Southern Europe, Latin America and Eastern Europe* (Dartmouth, 1995).

Stack, J.F., 'Judicial Policy-Making and the Evolving Protection of Human Rights: The European Court of Human Rights in Comparative Perspective' in M.L. Volcansek (ed.), *Judicial Politics and Policy-Making in Western Europe* (Cass, 1992).

Stone Sweet, A. 'Constitutions and Judicial Power' in D. Caramani (ed.), *Comparative Politics* (3rd edn, Oxford University Press, 2014).

'Constitutional Courts' in M. Rosenfeld & A. Sajó (eds.), *The Oxford Handbook of Comparative Constitutional Law* (Oxford University Press, 2012).

Stotzky, I.P., 'Lessons Learned and the Way Forward' in S. Gloppen, R. Gargarella & E. Skaar (eds.), *Democratization and the Judiciary: The Accountability Function of Courts in New Democracies* (Routledge, 2004).

'The Tradition of Constitutional Adjudication' in I. Stotzky (ed.), *Transition to Democracy in Latin America: The Role of the Judiciary* (Westview Press, 1993).

Sunstein, C., 'The Negative Constitution: Transition in Latin America' in I. Stotzky (ed.), *Transition to Democracy in Latin America: The Role of the Judiciary* (Westview Press, 1993).

Thio, L.-A., 'Constitutionalism in Illiberal Polities' in M. Rosenfeld & A. Sajó (eds.), *The Oxford Handbook of Comparative Constitutional Law* (Oxford University Press, 2012).

Tierney, S., "The Three Hundred and Seven Year Itch': Scotland and the 2014 Independence Referendum' in M. Qvortrup (ed.), *The British Constitution: Continuity and Change. A Festschrift for Vernon Bogdanor* (Hart, 2013).

Torelly, M., 'Gomes Lund vs. Brasil Cinco anos Depois: Histórico, impacto, evolução jurisprudencial e críticas' in F. Piovesan & I.V. Prado Soares, *Impacto das Decisões da Corte Interamericana de Direitos Humanos na Jurisprudência do STF* (Editora Juspodium, 2016). [Trans. Impact of Decisions of the Inter-American Court of Human Rights on the Jurisprudence of the STF].

Tushnet, M., 'Authoritarian Constitutionalism: Some Conceptual Issues' in T. Ginsburg & A. Simpser (eds.), *Constitutions in Authoritarian Regimes* (Cambridge University Press, 2014).

Uprimny, R., 'The Constitutional Court and Control of Presidential Extraordinary Powers in Colombia' in S. Gloppen, R. Gargarella & E. Skaar (eds.),

Democratization and the Judiciary: The Accountability Function of Courts in New Democracies (Routledge, 2004).

Vilhena Vieira, O., 'Descriptive Overview of the Brazilian Constitution and Supreme Court' in O. Vilhena Vilheira, F. Viljoen & U. Baxi (eds.), *Transformative Constitutionalism: Comparing the Apex Courts of Brazil, India and South Africa* (Pretoria University Law Press, 2013).

Zimmermann, A., 'Constitutions without Constitutionalism: The Failure of Constitutionalism in Brazil' in M. Sellers & T. Tomaszewski (eds.), *The Rule of Law in Comparative Perspective* (Springer, 2010).

Journal Articles

Abebe, A.K. & Fombad, C.M., 'The Advisory Jurisdiction of Constitutional Courts in Sub-Sahara Africa' (2013) 46 *George Washington International Law Review* 55.

Abramovich, V., 'From Massive Violations to Structural Patterns: New Approaches and Classic Tensions in the Inter-American Human Rights System' (2009) 11 *SUR – International Journal on Human Rights* 7.

Ackerman, B., 'The New Separation of Powers' (2000) 113 *Harvard Law Review* 633.

Aguilar Cavallo, G, 'El Control de Convencionalidad: Análisis en Derecho Comparado' (2013) 9 *Revista Direito GV* 721.

Allain, J., 'Laurence Burgorgue-Larsen & Amaya Úbeda de Torres, The Inter-American Court of Human Rights: Case-Law and Commentary' (2013) 17 *Edinburgh Law Review* 115.

Alshehri, S., 'An Arab Court of Human Rights: The Dream Desired' (2016) 30 *Arab Law Quarterly* 34.

Alter, K.J., Gathli, J.T. & Helfer, L., 'Backlash against International Courts in West, East and Southern Africa: Causes and Consequences' (2016) 27(2) *European Journal of International Law* 293.

Alvira, G., 'Toward a New Amnesty: The Colombian Peace Process and the Inter-American Court of Human Rights' (2013) 22 *Tulane Journal of International & Comparative Law* 119.

An-Na'im, A.A., 'Human Rights in the Arab World: A Regional Perspective' (2001) 23 *Human Rights Quarterly* 701.

Anderson, J., 'Catholicism and Democratic Consolidation in Spain and Poland' (2003) 26(1) *West European Politics* 137.

Arden, Rt. Hon. Lady Justice, 'Peaceful or Problematic? The Relationship between National Supreme Courts and Supranational Courts in Europe' (2010) 29 *Yearbook of European Law* 3.

Baek, B.-S., 'Mere Ritual or Gradual Change: Why Has Asia Failed to Establish Regional Human Rights Institutions Thus Far?' (2012) 5 *Northwestern Interdisciplinary Law Review* 145.

Banerji, A., 'The Commonwealth of Nations: A Force for Democracy in the 21st Century?' (2008) 97 *The Round Table* 813.

Barbosa, J., 'Reflections on Brazilian Constitutionalism' (2007) 12 *UCLA Journal of International Law and Foreign Affairs* 181.

Barker, R.S., 'Judicial Review in Costa Rica: Evolution and Recent Developments' (2000) 7 *Southwestern Journal of Law and Trade in the Americas* 267.

Baudenbacher, C., 'Judicial Globalization: New Development or Old Wine in New Bottles?' (2003) 39 *Texas International Law Journal* 505.

Bekker, G., 'The African Commission on Human and Peoples' Rights and Remedies for Human Rights Violations' (2013) 13 *Human Rights Law Review* 499.

Bell, C., Campbell, C. & Ní Aoláin, F., 'Transitional Justice: (Re)Conceptualising the Field' (2007) 3(2) *International Journal of Law in Context* 81.

Benda, E., 'Constitutional Jurisdiction in Western Germany' (1981) 19 *Columbia Journal of Transnational Law* 1.

Benvenisti, E. & Downs, G.W., 'National Courts, Domestic Democracy, and the Evolution of International Law' (2009) 20 *European Journal of International Law* 59.

Bernardes, M.N., 'Inter-American Human Rights System as a Transnational Public Sphere: Legal and Political Aspects of the Implementation of International Decisions' (2011) 15 *SUR – International Journal on Human Rights* 131.

Burke, T.P., 'The Origins of Social Justice: Taparelli d'Azeglio' (2010) 52(2) *Modern Age* 97.

Bustamante, T. & de Godoi Bustamante, E., 'Constitutional Courts as "Positive/Negative Legislators": The Brazilian Case' (2011) 3 *Revista Forumul Judecatorilor* 89.

Cançado Trindade, A.A., 'The Developing Case Law of the Inter-American Court of Human Rights' (2003) 3 *Human Rights Law Review* 1.

Carothers, T., 'The End of the Transition Paradigm' (2002) 13 *Journal of Democracy* 5.

Carter, E., 'Actual Malice in the Inter-American Court of Human Rights' (2013) 18 *Communication Law and Policy* 395.

Cavallaro, J.L., 'Toward Fair Play: A Decade of Transformation and Resistance in International Human Rights Advocacy in Brazil' (2002) 3 *Chicago Journal of International Law* 481.

Cavallaro, J. & Brewer, S.E., 'Reevaluating Regional Human Rights Litigation in the Twenty-First Century: The Case of the Inter-American Court' (2008) 102 *American Journal of International Law* 768.

Cepeda-Espinosa, M.J., 'Judicial Activism in a Violent Context: The Origin, Role, and Impact of the Colombian Constitutional Court' (2004) 3 *Washington University Global Studies Law Review* 529.

Cerna, C.M., 'The Inter-American System for the Protection of Human Rights' (2004) 16 *Florida Journal of International Law* 195.

Chiam, S., 'Asia's Experience in the Quest for a Regional Human Rights Mechanism' (2009) 49 *Victoria University Wellington Law Review* 127.

Coelho Filho, P., 'The Truth Commission in Brazil. Individualizing Amnesty, Revealing the Truth' (2012) 2 *Yale Review of International Studies* 47.

Coimbra, E.M., 'Inter-American System of Human Rights: Challenges to Compliance with the Court's Decisions in Brazil' (2013) 19 *SUR – International Journal on Human Rights* 57.

Cole, R.G.V., 'The African Court on Human and Peoples' Rights: Will Political Stereotypes Form an Obstacle to the Enforcement of its Decisions?' (2010) 43 *The Comparative and International Law Journal of Southern Africa* 23.

Colomer, J.M., 'Disequilibrium Institutions and Pluralist Democracy' (2001) 13 *Journal of Theoretical Politics* 235.

Colón-Ríos, J.I., 'A New Typology of Judicial Review of Legislation' (2014) 3 *Global Constitutionalism* 143.

Couso, J., 'Models of Democracy and Models of Constitutionalism: The Case of Chile's Constitutional Court, 1970–2010' (2011) 89 *Texas Law Review* 1517.

da Silva, V.A., 'Deciding without Deliberating' (2013) 11 *International Journal of Constitutional Law* 557.

'Discovering the Court: Or How Rights Awareness Puts the Brazilian Supreme Court in the Spotlight' (2012) 1 *This Century's Review* 16.

Daly, T.G., 'Baby Steps Away from the State: Regional Judicial Interaction as a Gauge of Postnational Order in South America and Europe' (2014) (3)4 *Cambridge Journal of International and Comparative Law* 1011.

Dawson, E.C., 'Adjusting the Presumption of Constitutionality Based on Margin of Statutory Passage' (2013) 16 *University of Pennsylvania Journal of Constitutional Law* 97.

de Oliveira Mazzuoli, V., 'The Inter-American Human Rights Protection System: Structure, Functioning and Effectiveness in Brazilian Law' (2011) 11 *African Human Rights Law Journal* 194.

de Visser, M., 'Cultivating Judicial Conversations on Human Rights Protection under the Auspices of a Regional Rights Regime' *The Asian Yearbook of Human Rights and Humanitarian Law* (forthcoming, 2017).

de Zela Martínez, H., 'The Organization of American States and its Quest for Democracy in the Americas' (2013) 8 *Yale Journal of International Affairs* 23.

Delaney, E.F., 'Analyzing Avoidance: Judicial Strategy in Comparative Perspective' (2016) 66(1) *Duke Law Journal* 1.

Delgado, J.L., 'The Inter-American Court of Human Rights' (1999) 5 *ILSA Journal of International & Comparative Law* 541.

Deodhar, N.S., 'First Contentious Cases before the International American Court of Human Rights' (1998) 3 *American University Journal of International Law and Policy* 283.

Diamond, L., 'Facing Up to the Democratic Recession' (2015) 26(1) *Journal of Democracy* 141.

Dick Howard, A.E., 'Constitution-Making in Central and Eastern Europe' (1994) 28 *Suffolk University Law Review* 5.

Dolinger, J., 'Brazilian Supreme Court Solutions for Conflicts between Domestic and International Law: An Exercise in Eclecticism' (1993) 22 *Capital University Law Review* 1041.

Domingo, P., 'Judicialization of Politics, or Politicization of the Judiciary? Recent Trends in Latin America' (2004) 11 *Democratization* 104.

Dulitzky, A., 'An Inter-American Constitutional Court? The Invention of the Conventionality Control by the Inter-American Court of Human Rights' (2015) 50(1) *Texas International Law Journal* 45.

Dunshee de Abranches, C., 'The Inter-American Court of Human Rights' (1980) 30 *American University Law Review* 79.

Dürr, S.R., 'Comparative Overview of European Systems of Constitutional Justice' (2011) 5 *Vienna Journal on International Constitutional Law* 159.

Dwyer, A.S., 'The Inter-American Court of Human Rights: Towards Establishing an Effective Regional Contentious Jurisdiction' (1990) 13 *Boston College International and Comparative Law Review* 127.

Elias, J.S., 'Constitutional Changes, Transitional Justice, and Legitimacy: The Life and Death of Argentina's "Amnesty" Laws' (2008) 31 *Hastings International and Comparative Law Review* 587.

Epstein, L., Knight, J. & Shvetsova, O., 'The Role of Constitutional Courts in the Establishment and Maintenance of Democratic Systems of Government' (2001) 35 *Law & Society Review* 117.

Farer, T., 'The Rise of the Inter-American Human Rights Regime: No Longer a Unicorn, Not Yet an Ox' (1997) 19 *Human Rights Quarterly* 510.

Faro de Castro, M., 'The Courts, Law, and Democracy in Brazil' (1997) 49 *International Social Science Journal* 241.

Feinrider, M., 'Judicial Review and the Protection of Human Rights Under Military Governments in Brazil and Argentina' (1981) 5 *Suffolk Transnational Law Quarterly* 187.

Faundez, J., 'Book Review: Roberto Gargarella, Pilar Domingo and Theunis Roux (eds.), Courts and Social Transformation in New Democracies: An Institutional Voice for the Poor? (Aldershot: Ashgate, 2006)' (2007) 39 *Journal of Latin American Studies* 419.

Ferrajoli, L., 'The Normative Paradigm of Constitutional Democracy' (2011) 17 *Res Publica* 355.

Ferraz, O., 'Harming the Poor through Social Rights Litigation: Lessons from Brazil' (2011) 89(7) *Texas Law Review* 1643.

Ferreira Santos, G., 'Treaties X Human Rights Treaties. A Critical Analysis of the Dual Stance on Treaties in the Brazilian Legal System' (2013) 15 *European Journal of Law Reform* 20.

Fombad, C.M., 'Internationalization of Constitutional Law and Constitutionalism in Africa' (2012) 60 *American Journal of Comparative Law* 439.

Franck, T., 'The Emerging Right to Democratic Governance' (1992) 86(1) *Journal of International Law* 46.

Frost, L.E., 'The Evolution of the Inter-American Court of Human Rights: Reflections of Present and Former Judges' (1992) 14 *Human Rights Quarterly* 171.

Galligan, D., 'The Sovereignty Deficit of Modern Constitutions' (2013) 33 *Oxford Journal of Legal Studies* 703.

'Authoritarianism in Government and Administration: The Promise of Administrative Justice' (2001) 54(1) *Current Legal Problems* 79.

García-Sayan, D., 'The Role of the Inter-American Court of Human Rights in the Americas' (2012) 19 *UC Davis Journal of International Law & Policy* 103.

'The Inter-American Court and Constitutionalism in Latin America' (2011) 89 *Texas Law Review* 1835.

Gardbaum, S., 'Are Strong Constitutional Courts Always a Good Thing for New Democracies?' (2015) 53 *Columbia Journal of Transnational Law* 285.

Gargarella, R., "We the People" Outside of the Constitution: The Dialogic Model of Constitutionalism and the System of Checks and Balances' (2014) 67(1) *Current Legal Problems* 1.

Gee, G. & Webber, G.C.N., 'What is a Political Constitution?' (2010) 30 *Oxford Journal of Legal Studies* 273.

Gelinsky, K., 'Interview with Professor Dr. Christoph Mollers, Humboldt University, Berlin, Faculty of Law: On the Occasion of the 60th Anniversary of the German Federal Constitutional Court (Bundesverfassungsgericht)' (2012) 13 *German Law Journal* 165.

Ginsburg, T., 'Locking in Democracy: Constitutions, Commitment, and International Law' (2006) 38 *New York University Journal of International Law and Politics* 707.

Ginsburg, T. & Ganzorig, G., 'When Courts and Politics Collide: Mongolia's Constitutional Crisis' (2001) 14 *Columbia Journal of Asian Law* 309.

Ginsburg, T. & Versteeg, M., 'Why Do Countries Adopt Constitutional Review?' (2014) 30(3) *The Journal of Law, Economics and Organization* 587.

Goldman, R.K., 'History and Action: The Inter-American Human Rights System and the Role of the Inter-American Commission on Human Rights' (2009) 31 *Human Rights Quarterly* 856.

González-Salzberg, D.A., 'The Implementation of Decisions from the Inter-American Court of Human Rights in Argentina: An Analysis of the Jurisprudential Swings of the Supreme Court' (2011) 15 *SUR – International Journal of Human Rights* 113.

Greer, S. & Wildhaber, L., 'Revisiting the Debate about 'Constitutionalising' the European Court of Human Rights' (2012) 12 *Human Rights Law Review* 655.

Grossman, C., 'Challenges to Freedom of Expression within the Inter-American System: A Jurisprudential Analysis' (2012) 34 *Human Rights Quarterly* 361.

'The Inter-American System and Its Evolution' (2009) 2 *Inter-American and European Human Rights Journal* 49.

'Freedom of Expression in the Inter-American System for the Protection of Human Rights' (2001) 25 *Nova Law Review* 411.

Habermas, J., 'Constitutional Democracy: A Paradoxical Union of Contradictory Principles?' (2001) 29 *Political Theory* 766.

Harvey, P., 'Militant Democracy and the European Court of Human Rights' (2004) 29 *European Law Review* 407.

Helfer, L.R. & Slaughter, A-M, 'Toward a Theory of Effective Supranational Adjudication' (1997) 107 *Yale Law Journal* 273.

Helmke, G., 'Public Support and Judicial Crises in Latin America' (2010) 13 *University of Pennsylvania Journal of Constitutional Law* 397.

Hillebrecht, C., 'The Domestic Mechanisms of Compliance with International Human Rights Law: Case Studies from the Inter-American Human Rights System' (2012) 34(4) *Human Rights Quarterly* 959.

Hirschl, R., 'The New Constitutionalism and the Judicialization of Pure Politics Worldwide' (2006) 75 *Fordham Law Review* 721.

Hübner Mendes, C., 'Judicial Review of Constitutional Amendments in the Brazilian Supreme Court' (2005) 17 *Florida Journal of International Law* 449.

Huneeus, A. 'Constitutional Lawyers and the Inter-American Court's Varied Authority' (2016) 79 *Law and Contemporary Problems* 179.

'Reforming the State from Afar: Structural Reform Litigation at the Human Rights Courts' (2015) 40(1) *Yale Journal of International Law* 1.

'Courts Resisting Courts: Lessons from the Inter-American Court's Struggle to Enforce Human Rights' (2011) 44 *Cornell International Law Journal* 493.

Hydén, G., 'Top-Down Democratization in Tanzania' (1999) 10(4) *Journal of Democracy* 142.

Isiksel, T., 'Between Text and Context: Turkey's Tradition of Authoritarian Constitutionalism' (2013) 11(3) *International Journal of Constitutional Law* 702.

Issacharoff, S., 'Constitutional Courts and Democratic Hedging' (2011) 99 *Georgetown Law Journal* 961.

'Constitutionalizing Democracy in Fractured Societies' (2004) 82 *Texas Law Review* 1861, abridged in (2004) 58 *Journal of International Affairs* 73.

Jackson, V.C., 'What's in a Name? Reflections on Timing, Naming, and Constitution-Making' (2008) 49 *William & Mary Law Review* 1249.

Jakab, A. & Sonnevend, P., 'Continuity with Deficiencies: The New Basic Law of Hungary' (2013) 1 *European Constitutional Law Review* 102.

Kalb, J., 'The Judicial Role in New Democracies: A Strategic Account of Comparative Citation' (2013) 38 *Yale Journal of International Law* 423.

Keane, R., 'Judges as Lawmakers: The Irish Experience' (2004) 2 *Judicial Studies Institute Journal* 1.

Klug, H., 'Finding the Constitutional Court's Place in South Africa's Democracy:
    The Interaction of Principle and Institutional Pragmatism in the Court's
    Decision Making' (2010) 3 *Constitutional Court Review* 1.
Kommers, D.P., 'The Federal Constitutional Court: Guardian of German Demo-
    cracy' (2006) 603 *Annals of the American Academy of Political & Social
    Science* 111.
Kosař, D. & Lixinski, L., 'Domestic Judicial Design by International Human Rights
    Courts' (2015) 109 *The American Journal of International Law* 713.
Krsticevic, V., 'How Inter-American Human Rights Litigation Brings Free
    Speech to the Americas' (1997) 4 *Southwest Journal of Law & Trade in
    the Americas* 209.
Landau, D., 'Abusive Constitutionalism' (2013) 47 *UC Davis Law Review* 189.
    'Constitution-Making Gone Wrong' (2012) 64 *Alabama Law Review* 923.
Larkins, C., 'The Judiciary and Delegative Democracy in Argentina' (1998) 31
    Comparative Politics 423.
    'Judicial Independence and Democratization: A Theoretical and Conceptual
    Analysis' (1996) 44 *American Journal of Comparative Law* 605.
Law, D.S. & Chang, W.-C., 'The Limits of Global Judicial Dialogue' (2011) 86
    Washington Law Review 523.
Law, D.S. & Versteeg, M., 'The Declining Influence of the US Constitution' (2012)
    87 *New York University Law Review* 762.
Lessa, F., Olsen, T.D., Payne, L.A & Pereira, G., 'Persistent or Eroding Impunity;
    The Divergent Effects of Legal Challenges to Amnesty Laws for Past Human
    Rights Violations' (2014) 47 *Israel Law Review* 105.
Leuprecht, P., 'Innovations in the European System of Human Rights Protection:
    Is Enlargement Compatible with Reinforcement?' (1998) 8 *Transnational
    Law and Contemporary Problems* 313.
Levitsky, S., 'Argentina: From Kirchner to Kirchner' (2008) 19 *Journal of
    Democracy* 16.
Levitt, B.S., 'A Desultory Defense of Democracy: OAS Resolution 1080 and the
    Inter-American Democratic Charter' (2006) 48(3) *Latin American Politics &
    Society* 93.
Linz, J., 'Democracy Today: An Agenda for Students of Democracy' (1997) 20(2)
    Scandinavian Political Studies 115.
    'Transitions to Democracy' (1990) 13 *The Washington Quarterly* 143.
López Guerra, L., 'The Application of the Spanish Model in the Constitutional
    Transitions in Central and Eastern Europe' (1998) 19 *Cardozo Law Review*
    1937.
Luci Oliveira, F., 'Justice, Professionalism, and Politics in the Exercise of Judicial
    Review by Brazil's Supreme Court' (2008) 2(2) *Brazilian Political Science
    Review* 93.

MacDowell Santos, C., 'Transnational Legal Activism and the State: Reflections on Cases against Brazil in the Inter-American Commission on Human Rights' (2007) 7 *SUR - International Journal on Human Rights* 29.

Mace, G., 'Sixty Years of Protecting Human Rights in the Americas' (2011) *Quebec Journal of International Law* 1.

Makulilo, A.B., 'Introductory Note to Tanganyika Law Society and the Legal and Human Rights Centre v. Tanzania and Rev. Christopher R. Mtikila v. Tanzania (Af. Ct. H.R.)' (2013) 52(6) *International Legal Materials* 1327.

Malarino, E., 'Judicial Activism, Punitivism and Supranationalisation: Illiberal and Antidemocratic Tendencies of the Inter-American Court of Human Rights' (2012) 12 *International Criminal Law Review* 665.

Massadas, J., 'Between Legal Authority and Epistemic Competence: A Case Study of the Brazilian Supreme Court' (2015) 9(6) *International Journal of Social, Behavioural, Educational, Economic, Business and Industrial Engineering* 2197.

Maveety, N. & Grosskopf, A., '"Constrained" Constitutional Courts as Conduits for Democratic Consolidation' (2004) 38 *Law and Society Review* 463.

McFaul, M., 'The Fourth Wave of Democracy and Dictatorship: Noncooperative Transition in the Postcommunist World' (2002) 54 *World Politics* 212.

McWhinney, E., 'Judicial Restraint and the West German Constitutional Court' (1961) 75 *Harvard Law Review* 5.

Melish, T.J., 'Rethinking the "Less as More" Thesis: Supranational Litigation of Economic, Social, and Cultural Rights in the Americas' (2006) 39 *New York University Journal of International Law and Politics* 171.

Mezarobba, G., 'Between Reparations, Half Truths and Impunity: The Difficult Break with the Legacy of the Dictatorship in Brazil' (2010) 13 *SUR - International Journal on Human Rights* 7.

Mietzner, M., 'Political Conflict Resolution and Democratic Consolidation in Indonesia: The Role of the Constitutional Court' (2010) 10 *Journal of East Asian Studies* 397.

Mohallem, M.F., 'Immutable Clauses and Judicial Review in India, Brazil and South Africa: Expanding Constitutional Courts' Authority' (2011) 15(5) *The International Journal of Human Rights* 765.

Monteiro de Matos, S., 'Anístia Democrática? Sobre a (I)legitimade da Lei da Anistia Brasileira' (2012) 7 *Revista Anistia Política e Justiça de Transição* 136.

Moreira Maués, A., 'Supra-legality of International Human Rights and Constitutional Interpretation' (2013) 18 *SUR - International Journal of Human Rights* 205.

Munck, R., 'Introduction: A Thin Democracy' (1997) 24(6) *Latin American Perspectives* 5.

Murray, J.L., 'The Influence of the European Convention on Fundamental Rights on Community Law' (2011) 33 *Fordham International Law Journal* 1388.

Neuman, G.L., 'Human Rights and Constitutional Rights: Harmony and Dissonance' (2003) 55 *Stanford Law Review* 1863.

Nmehielle, V.O., 'Saddling the New African Regional Human Rights Court with International Criminal Jurisdiction: Innovative, Obstructive, Expedient' (2014) 7 *African Journal of Legal Studies* 7.

Nowak, M., 'On the Creation of a World Court of Human Rights' (2012) 7 *National Taiwan University Law Review* 257.

O'Donnell, G., 'The Perpetual Crises of Democracy' (2007) 18 *Journal of Democracy* 5.

'Illusions About Consolidation' (1996) 7(2) *Journal of Democracy* 34.

Ogowewo, T.I., 'Why the Judicial Annulment of the Constitution of 1999 is Imperative for the Survival of Nigeria's Democracy' (2000) 44(2) *Journal of African Law* 135.

Olsen, T.A., Payne, L.A., Reiter, A.G. & Weibelhaus-Brahm, E., 'When Truth Commissions Improve Human Rights' (2010) 4(3) *International Journal of Transitional Justice* 457.

Osiel, M.J., 'Dialogue with Dictators: Judicial Resistance in Argentina and Brazil' (1995) 20 *Law and Social Inquiry* 481.

Pauw, E.J. & Shapiro, A.C., 'Defamation, the Free Press, and Latin America: A Roadmap for the Inter-American Court of Human Rights and Emerging Democracies' (1998) 30 *University of Miami Inter-American Law Review* 203.

Peters, A., 'Supremacy Lost: International Law Meets Domestic Constitutional Law' (2009) 3 *Vienna Journal on International Constitutional Law* 170.

Peters, B., 'Germany's Dialogue with Strasbourg: Extrapolating the Bundesverfassungsgericht's Relationship with the European Court of Human Rights in the Preventive Detention Decision' (2012) 13 *German Law Journal* 757.

Pettit, P., 'Democracy, National and International' (2006) 89 *The Monist* 301.

Phan, H.D., 'A Blueprint for a Southeast Asian Court of Human Rights' (2009) 10 *Asian-Pacific Law & Policy Journal* 384.

Phillips Mandaville, A. & Mandaville, P.P., 'Introduction: Rethinking Democratization and Democracy Assistance' (2007) 50 *Development* 5.

Pollicino, O., 'The New Relationship between National and the European Courts after the Enlargement of Europe: Towards a Unitary Theory of Jurisprudential Supranational Law?' (2010) 29(1) *Yearbook of European Law* 65.

Prado Verbicaro, L., 'Um Estudo Sobre as Condições Facilitadoras da Judicialização da Política no Brasil' (2008) 4 *Revista Direito GV* 389–90. [Trans. A Study Concerning the Conditions Facilitating the Judicialisation of Politics in Brazil].

Rask Madsen, M., 'The Challenging Authority of the European Court of Human Rights: From Cold War Legal Diplomacy to the Brighton Declaration and Backlash' (2016) 79(1) *Law and Contemporary Problems* 141.

Rishmawi, M., 'The Arab Charter on Human Rights and the League of Arab States: An Update' (2010) 10 *Human Rights Law Review* 169.

Robertson, A.H., 'The European Court of Human Rights' (1960) 9 *American Journal of Comparative Law* 1.

Rodríguez-Rescia, V.M., 'Reparations in the Inter-American System for the Protection of Human Rights' (1999) 5 *ILSA Journal of International & Comparative Law* 583.

Rodriguez Rescia, V. & Seitles, M.D., 'The Development of the Inter-American Human Rights System: A Historical Perspective and a Modern-Day Critique' (2000) 16 *New York Law School Journal of Human Rights* 593.

Rosato, C.M. & Cerqueira Correia, L., 'The Damião Ximenes Lopes Case: Changes and Challenges following the First Ruling against Brazil in the Inter-American Court of Human Rights' (2011) 15 *SUR – International Journal on Human Rights* 91.

Rosenn, K., 'Recent Important Decisions by the Brazilian Supreme Court' (2014) 45 *Inter-American Law Review* 297.

'Separation of Powers in Brazil' (2009) 47 *Duquesne Law Review* 839.

'Judicial Review in Brazil: Developments under the 1988 Constitution' (2000) 7 *Southwestern Journal of Law and Trade in the Americas* 291.

'Brazil's New Constitution: An Exercise in Transient Constitutionalism for a Transitional Society' (1990) 38 *American Journal of Comparative Law* 773.

Roux, T., 'Constitutional Courts as Democratic Consolidators: Insights from South Africa Twenty Years On' (2016) 42(1) *Journal of Southern African Studies* 5.

'The South African Constitutional Court's Democratic Rights Jurisprudence: A Response to Samuel Issacharoff' (2014) 5 *Constitutional Court Review* 33.

'Principle and Pragmatism on the Constitutional Court of South Africa' (2009) 7 *International Journal of Constitutional Law* 106.

Ruiz-Chiriboga, O., 'The Conventionality Control: Examples of (Un)Successful Experiences in Latin America' (2010) 3 *Inter-American and European Human Rights Journal* 200.

Safjan, M., 'Politics and Constitutional Courts (Judge's Personal Perspective)' (2009) 165 *Polish Sociological Review* 3.

Sagües, N.P., 'Obligaciones Internacionales y Control de Convencionalidad' (2010) 8 *Estudios Constitucionales* 117. [Trans. International Obligations and Control of Conventionality].

Sato, M., 'Judicial Review in Brazil. Nominal and Real' (2003) 3(1) *Global Jurist Advances* 1535–1661.

Schedler, A., 'What Is Democratic Consolidation?' (1998) 9(2) *Journal of Democracy* 91.

Scheppele, K.L., 'The Constitutional Role of Transnational Courts: Principled Legal ideas in Three-Dimensional Political Space' (2010) 28 *Penn State International Law Review* 451.

'Guardians of the Constitution: Constitutional Court Presidents and the Struggle for the Rule of Law in Post-Soviet Europe' (2006) 154 *University of Pennsylvania Law Review* 1757.

'The New Hungarian Constitutional Court' (1999) 8 *Eastern European Constitutional Review* 81.

Schmitter, P. & Santiso, J., 'Three Temporal Dimensions to the Consolidation of Democracy' (1998) 19(1) *International Political Science Review* 69.

Schneider, B., 'Democratic Consolidations: Some Broad Comparisons and Sweeping Arguments' (1995) 30 *Latin American Research Review* 215.

Schneider, N., 'Impunity in Post-authoritarian Brazil: The Supreme Court's Recent Verdict on the Amnesty Law' (2011) 90 *European Review of Latin American and Caribbean Studies* 39.

Schönsteiner, J., Alma y Puga, A. & Lovera, D.A., 'Reflections on the Human Rights Challenges of Consolidating Democracies: Recent Developments in the Inter-American System of Human Rights' (2011) 11 *Human Rights Law Review* 362.

Schor, M., 'An Essay on the Emergence of Constitutional Courts: The Cases of Mexico and Columbia' (2009) 16 *Indiana Journal of Global Legal Studies* 173.

'Mapping Comparative Judicial Review' (2008) 7 *Washington University Global Studies Law Review* 257.

'Constitutionalism Through the Looking Glass of Latin America' (2006) 41 *Texas International Law Journal* 1.

Shapiro, M. & Stone, A., 'The New Constitutional Politics of Europe' (1994) 26 *Comparative Political Studies* 397.

Shaver, L., 'The Inter-American Human Rights System: An Effective Institution for Regional Rights Protection' (2010) 9 *Washington University Global Studies Law Review* 639.

Shelton, D., 'Jurisprudence of the Inter-American Court of Human Rights' (1994) 10 *American University Journal of International Law & Policy* 333.

Slaughter, A.-M., 'A Global Community of Courts' (2003) 44 *Harvard International Law Journal* 191.

Soltman, D., 'Applauding Uruguay's Quest for Justice: Dictatorship, Amnesty, and Repeal of Uruguay Law No. 15.848' (2013) 12 *Washington University Global Studies Law Review* 829.

Sólyom, L., 'The Role of Constitutional Courts in the Transition to Democracy: With Special Reference to Hungary' (2003) 18 *International Sociology* 133.

Sombra, T.L., 'Why Should Public Hearings in the Brazilian Supreme Court Be Understood as an Innovative Democratic Tool in Constitutional Adjudication?' (2016) 17(4) *German Law Journal* 657.

Ssenyonjo, M., 'Direct Access to the African Court on Human and Peoples' Rights by Individuals and Non Governmental Organisations: An Overview of the Emerging Jurisprudence of the African Court 2008–2012' (2013) 2(1) *International Human Rights Law Review* 17.

Staton, J.K. & Moore, W.H., 'Judicial Power in Domestic and International Politics' (2011) 65 *International Organization* 553.

Stone Sweet, A., 'A Cosmopolitan Legal Order: Constitutional Pluralism and Rights Adjudication in Europe' (2012) 1 *Global Constitutionalism* 53.

Tan, M., 'Member State Compliance with Judgments of the Inter-American Court of Human Rights' (2005) 33 *International Journal of Legal Information* 319.

'Upholding Human Rights in the Hemisphere: Casting Down Impunity through the Inter-American Court of Human Rights' (2008) 43 *Texas International Law Journal* 243.

Teitel, R., 'Transitional Justice in a New Era' (2003) 26(4) *Fordham International Law Journal* 893.

'Transitional Jurisprudence: The Role of Law in Political Transformation' (1997) 106 *Yale Law Journal* 2035.

Tittemore, B.D., 'Ending Impunity in the Americas: The Role of the Inter-American Human Rights System in Advancing Accountability for Serious Crimes Under International Law' (2006) 12 *South Western Journal of Law and Trade in the Americas* 429.

Toth, G.A., 'Historicism or Art Nouveau in Constitutional Interpretation; A Comment on Zoltan Szente's *The Interpretive Practice of the Hungarian Constitutional Court – A Critical View*' (2013) 14 *German Law Journal* 1615.

Trombetas, T., 'The United States Supreme Court and the Federal Constitutional Court of Germany' (1964) 17 *Revue Hellenique de Droit International* 281.

Úbeda de Torres, A., 'Freedom of Expression under the European Convention on Human Rights: A Comparison with the Inter-American System of Protection of Human Rights' (2003) 10 *Human Rights Brief* 6.

Uggla, F., 'The Ombudsman in Latin America' (2004) 36 *Journal of Latin American Studies* 423.

Uprimny, R., 'The Recent Transformation of Constitutional Law in Latin America: Trends and Challenges' (2011) 89 *Texas Law Review* 1587.

Vanberg, G., 'Constitutional Courts in Comparative Perspective: A Theoretical Assessment' (2015) 18 *Annual Review of Political Science* 167.

Vidmar, J., 'Judicial Interpretations of Democracy in Human Rights Treaties' (2014) 3 *Cambridge Journal of International and Comparative Law* 532.

Vilhena Vieira, O., 'Supremocracia' (2009) 8 *Revista Direito GV* 441. [Trans. Supremocracy].

Vincze, A., 'Wrestling with Constitutionalism: The Supermajority and the Hungarian Constitutional Court' (2014) 8 *Vienna Journal on International Constitutional Law* 86.

Wa Mutua, M., 'The African Human Rights System in a Comparative Perspective' (1993) 3 *Review of the African Commission on Human and Peoples' Rights* 5.

Waldron, J., 'Can there be a Democratic Jurisprudence?' (2009) 58 *Emory Law Journal* 675.

'The Core of the Case against Judicial Review' (2006) 115 *Yale Law Journal* 1346.

'Foreign Law and the Modern *Ius Gentium*' (2005) 119 *Harvard Law Review* 129.

'A Right-Based Critique of Constitutional Rights' (1993) 13 *Oxford Journal of Legal Studies* 18.

Walker, C.J., 'Toward Democratic Consolidation – The Argentine Supreme Court, Judicial Independence, and the Rule of Law' (2008) 4 *High Court Quarterly Review* 54.

Walker, N., 'Constitutionalism and the Incompleteness of Democracy: An Iterative Relationship' (2010) 39 *Rechtsfilosofie & Rechtstheorie* 206.

Waters, M.A., 'Creeping Monism: The Judicial Trend Toward Interpretive Incorporation of Human Rights Treaties' (2007) 107 *Columbia Law Review* 628.

Windridge, O., 'A Watershed Moment for African Human Rights: Mtikila & Others v Tanzania at the African Court on Human and Peoples' Rights' (2015) 15(2) *African Human Rights Law Journal* 299.

Witteman, C., 'West German Television Law: An Argument for Media as Instrument of Self-Government' (1983) 7 *Hastings International and Comparative Law Review* 145.

Zakaria, F., 'The Rise of Illiberal Democracy' (1997) *Foreign Affairs* 22.

Conference Papers, Presentations & Working Papers

Baer, S., Speech at I-CON International Society of Public Law Conference, Plenary Session II: 'Inequalities', 18 June 2016.

Benvenisti, E., 'The Margin of Appreciation and the Facilitation of Democratic Deliberation', 'Margin of Appreciation and Democracy: Conference on Human Rights and Deference to Political Bodies', iCourts, University of Copenhagen, 13 April 2016.

Benvenisti, E. & Harel, A., 'Embracing the Tension between National and International Human Rights Law: The Case for Parity'. Global Trust Working Paper Series 04/2015.

Bossacoma i Busquets, P., 'Constitutional Roads to Independence: The Problematic Catalan Case in the Light of the Scottish Experience', Constitutional Law Discussion Group, Edinburgh Law School, 14 November 2014.

Daly, T.G., 'The Differential Openness of Brazil's Supreme Federal Court to External Jurisprudence'. International Association of Constitutional Law (IACL) World Congress 2014, Oslo, Norway, 16–20 June 2014 www.jus.uio .no/english/research/news-and-events/events/conferences/2014/wccl-cmdc/ wccl/papers/ws5/w5-daly.pdf.

Engstrom, P., 'Brazilian Post-Transitional Justice and the Inter-American Human Rights System'. Remarks for a conference on Post-Transitional Justice in Brazil, Brazil Institute, King's College, University of London 4 March 2013 www.academia.edu/2907644/Brazilian_Post-Transitional_Justice_and_the_ Inter-American_Human_Rights_System.

Ghai, Y., 'Human Rights and Social Development: Toward Democratization and Social Justice', Democracy, Governance and Human Rights Programme Paper Number 5 (October 2001), United Nations Research Institute for Social Development.

Ginsburg, T., 'Courts and New Democracies: Recent Works'. Public Law and Legal Theory Working Papers, University of Chicago, June 2012 http://chicago unbound.uchicago.edu/cgi/viewcontent.cgi?article=1078&context=public_ law_and_legal_theory.

Hentrei, S., 'The Conventionality Control of the Inter-American Court of Human Rights as a Manifestation of Complementarity', 'Latin American Constitutionalism: Between Law and Politics', University of Glasgow, 2 July 2014.

Issacharoff, S., 'Constitutional Courts and Consolidated Power', NYU Public Law and Legal Theory Working Papers, Paper 459 (2014).

'The Democratic Risk to Democratic Transitions', NYU Public Law and Legal Theory Working Papers, Paper 418 (2013).

Jayawickrama, N., 'Establishing a Constitutional Court: The Impediments Ahead', CPA Working Papers on Constitutional Reform No. 13, January 2017 www.constitutionalreforms.org/wp-content/uploads/2016/06/Working-Paper-13-1.pdf.

Kochenov, D. & Pech, L., 'Upholding the Rule of Law in the EU: On the Commission's "Pre-Article 7 Procedure" as a Timid Step in the Right Direction'. EUI working papers, RDCAS 2015/24.

Konder Comparato, B. & Sarti, C., 'Amnesty, Memory, and Reconciliation in Brazil: Dilemmas of an Unfinished Political Transition'. International Studies Association (ISA) Annual Convention, San Diego, 1–4 April 2012. http:// files.isanet.org/ConferenceArchive/f2ecc7f25f6147f9ac79067fb7142135.pdf.

O'Meara, N., 'Reforming the ECtHR: The Impacts of Protocols 15 and 16 to the ECHR', iCourts Working Paper Series, No. 31, 2015.

Pettai, V., 'Estonia's Constitutional Review Mechanisms: A Guarantor of Democratic Consolidation?'. European University Institute (EUI), Robert Schuman Centre for Advanced Studies, Working Paper No.2000/59 (2000).

Reis Freire, A., 'Evolution of Constitutional Interpretation in Brazil and the Employment of a Balancing "Method" by Brazilian Supreme Court in Judicial Review', VIIth International Association of Constitutional Law (IACL) World Congress, Athens, Greece, 2007 www.academia.edu/8306512/ Evolution_of_Constitutional_Interpretation_in_Brazil_and_the_Employment_ of_Balancing_Method_by_Brazilian_Supreme_Court_in_Judicial_Review.

Romano, C.P., 'International Judicialization in the Arab World: An Initial Assessment', iCourts Working Paper Series, No. 49, 2016.

Rua Wall, I., 'Constituent Power and the Question of Andean Constitutionalism' www.academia.edu/5472698/Constituent_Power_and_the_Question_ of_Andean_Constitutionalism.

Soley Echeverría, X., 'The Legitimatory Discourse of Inter-American Constitutional Adjudication'. 'Latin American Constitutionalism: Between Law and Politics', University of Glasgow, 2 July 2014.

Stone Sweet, A., 'On the Constitutionalisation of the Convention: The European Court of Human Rights as a Constitutional Court'. Yale Law School Faculty Scholarship Series. Paper 71, 2009.

Torelly, M., 'Transnational Legal Process and Constitutional Engagement in Latin America: How do Domestic Constitutional Regimes deal with International Human Rights Law?'. Society of Legal Scholars (SLS) Second Graduate Conference on Latin American Law and Policy, St Antony's College, Oxford, 7 March 2014.

Wa Mutua, M. 'The African Human Rights System: A Critical Evaluation'. United Nations Development Programme Occasional Paper Series (2000).

Ph.D Theses & Academic Dissertations

Cha, D., 'The Role of the Korean Constitutional Court in the Democratization of South Korea'. Ph.D thesis, University of Southern California, 2005.

Couso, J., 'The Politics of Judicial Review in Latin America: Chile in Comparative Perspective'. Ph.D thesis, University of California, Berkeley, 2002.

Toda Castán, D., 'The Transformation of the Inter-American System for the Protection of Human Rights: The Structural Impact of the Inter-American Court's Case Law on Amnesties'. E.MA thesis, European Inter-University Centre for Human Rights and Democratisation (EUIC), 2010/2011.

Reports

Boutros-Ghali, B., *An Agenda for Democratization* (United Nations, 1996).

Democratic Governance and Rights Unit, *Has the South African Constitutional Court Over-reached? A Study of the Court's Application of the Separation of Powers Doctrine between 2009 and 2013* (28 August 2014) www.dgru.uct .ac.za/sites/default/files/image_tool/images/103/Separation%20of%20Powers %20Draft%20August%202014.pdf.

European Court of Human Rights, *References to the Inter-American Court of Human Rights in the Case-Law of the European Court of Human Rights* (Council of Europe, 2012).

Freedom House, *Discarding Democracy: Return to the Iron Fist. Freedom in the World 2015* https://freedomhouse.org/sites/default/files/01152015_FIW_ 2015_final.pdf.

Gluck, J. & Brandt, M., *Participatory and Inclusive Constitution Making: Giving Voice to the Demands of Citizens in the Wake of the Arab Spring* (United States Institute of Peace, 2015) www.usip.org/publications/participatory-and-inclusive-constitution-making.

International Commission of Jurists. *The Draft Libyan Constitution: Procedural Deficiencies, Substantive Flaws* (December 2015) http://icj.wpengine.net dna-cdn.com/wp-content/uploads/2015/12/Lybia-Draft-Constitution-Flaws-Deficiencies-Publications-Reports-2015-ENG.pdf.

The Arab Court of Human Rights: A Flawed Statute for an Ineffective Court (8 April 2015) http://icj.wpengine.netdna-cdn.com/wp-content/uploads/ 2015/04/MENA-Arab-Court-of-Human-Rights-Publications-Report-2015-ENG.pdf.

International Forum for Social Development, *Social Justice in an Open World: The Role of the United Nations* (United Nations, 2006) www.un.org/esa/socdev/ documents/ifsd/SocialJustice.pdf.

International Institute for Democracy and Electoral Assistance (IDEA) *The Judiciary and Constitutional Transitions* (2016, author: T.G. Daly) www.idea.int/sites/default/files/publications/the-judiciary-and-constitutional-transitions.pdf.

The Role of Regional Organizations in the Protection of Constitutionalism (2016, author: M. Wiebusch) www.idea.int/sites/default/files/publications/the-role-of-regional-organizations-in-the-protection-of-constitutionalism.pdf.

Constitutional Courts After the Arab Spring (Center for Constitutional Transitions at NYU Law, (2014, author: S. Choudhry) www.idea.int/sites/default/ files/publications/constitutional-courts-after-the-arab-spring.pdf.

Legal and Human Rights Centre (LHRC) & Tanzania Civil Society Consortium for Election Observation (TACCEO), *Report on the United Republic of Tanzania General Elections of 2015* (March 2016) www.humanrights.or.tz/user

files/file/Report%20on%20the%20Observation%20of%20the%202015%20
General%20Elections%20in%20Tanzania.pdf.

Lock, T. & Daly, T.G., *Brexit and the British Bill of Rights* (Edinburgh Law School and Bingham Centre for the Rule of Law, February 2017).

National Truth Commission (Brazil), *Relatório da Comissão Nacional da Verdade*, 10 December 2014 www.cnv.gov.br.

Organization of American States, *Tenth Anniversary of the Inter-American Democratic Charter* (OAS, 2011).

Think-Tank Task Force, *Smart Power – Ways of Enhancing the Council of Europe's Impact* (Advisory report, Council of Europe, 2014).

Third Congress of the World Conference on Constitutional Justice, 'Seoul Communiqué' (30 September 2014) www.venice.coe.int/wccj/seoul/WCCJ_Seoul_Communique-E.pdf.

Venice Commission, 'The Role of the Constitutional Court in the Consolidation of the Rule of Law', Bucharest, 8–10 June 1994. CDL-STD(1994)010.

Blog Posts

Barbosa C.M., 'The Brazilian Supreme Court: Between Activism and Judicial Responsibility' *International Journal of Constitutional Law Blog* 25 December 2012 www.iconnectblog.com/2012/12/the-brazilian-supreme-court-between-activism-and-judicial-responsibility.

Barroso, L.R., 'The Roles of Supreme Courts and Constitutional Courts in Contemporary Democracies' *International Journal of Constitutional Law Blog* 21 October 2016 www.iconnectblog.com/2016/10/the-roles-of-supreme-courts-and-constitutional-courts-in-contemporary-democracies.

Çalı, B., 'Domestic Courts and the European Court of Human Rights: Towards Developing Standards of Weak International Judicial Review?' *Opinio Juris* 11 January 2013 www.opiniojuris.org/2013/01/11/domestic-courts-and-the-european-court-of-human-rights-towards-developing-standards-of-weak-international-judicial-review.

Daly, T.G., 'The Democratic Recession and the "New" Public Law: Toward Systematic Analysis' *International Journal of Constitutional Law Blog* 22 April 2016 www.iconnectblog.com/2016/04/the-democratic-recession-and-the-new-public-law-toward-systematic-analysis.

'Repression in Bahrain: The End of Any Hope for an Effective Arab Court of Human Rights?' *International Journal of Constitutional Law Blog*, 22 July 2016 www.iconnectblog.com/2016/07/repression-in-bahrain-the-end-of-any-hope-for-an-effective-arab-court-of-human-rights/.

Demirtaş, S., 'New Turkish constitution to redefine powers of constitutional court and judiciary' *ConstitutionNet* 29 March 2016 www.constitutionnet.org/news/new-turkish-constitution-redefine-powers-constitutional-court-andjudiciary.

Denniston, L., 'Opinion Analysis: Leaving a Constitutional Ideal Still Undefined' *SCOTUS blog* 4 April 2016 www.scotusblog.com/2016/04/opinion-analysis-leaving-a-constitutional-ideal-still-undefined.

Douglas-Scott, S., 'Opinion 2/13 on EU Accession to the ECHR: A Christmas Bombshell from the European Court of Justice' *UK Constitutional Law Blog* 24 December 2014 www.ukconstitutionallaw.org.

Ferreres Comella, V., 'The Spanish Constitutional Court Faces Direct Democracy' *International Journal of Constitutional Law Blog* 23 September 2009 www.iconnectblog.com/2009/09/the-spanish-constitutional-court-faces-direct-democracy.

'The Secessionist Challenge in Spain: An Independent Catalonia?', *International Journal of Constitutional Law Blog* 22 November 2012 www.iconnectblog.com/2012/11/the-secessionist-challenge-in-spain-an-independent-catalonia.

Koncewicz, T.T., 'Living under the Unconstitutional Capture and Hoping for the Constitutional Recapture' *Verfassungsblog* 3 January 2017 www.verfassungs blog.de/living-under-the-the-unconstitutional-capture-and-hoping-for-the-constitutional-recapture.

Mekki, N., 'The Tunisian Constitutional Court at the Center of the Political System – and Whirlwind' *ConstitutionNet* 9 February 2016 www.constitutionnet.org/news/tunisian-constitutional-court-center-political-system-and-whirlwind?utm_source=newsletter&utm_medium=email.

O'Donnell, K., 'Thoughts on a New Ireland: Oral History and the Magdalene Laundries' *Human Rights in Ireland* 22 August 2011 www.humanrights.ie/law-culture-and-religion/thoughts-on-a-new-ireland-oral-history-and-the-magdalene-laundries.

Riquelme Cortado, R., 'Central American Court of Justice (1907–18)', *Oxford Public International Law* http://opil.ouplaw.com/view/10.1093/law:epil/9780199231690/law-9780199231690-e15.

Windridge, O., 'Protecting the Safety of Journalists: the Role of the African Court' *ACtHPR Monitor* 20 September 2016 www.acthprmonitor.org/protecting-the-safety-of-journalists-the-role-of-the-african-court.

'2015 at the African Court on Human and Peoples' Rights–A Year in Review' *The ACtHPR Monitor* 25 January 2016 www.acthprmonitor.org/2015-at-the-african-court-on-human-and-peoples-rights-a-year-in-review.

'Guest Post: 2014 at The African Court on Human and Peoples Rights–a Year in Review' *Opinio Juris* 10 January 2015 www.opiniojuris.org/2015/01/10/guest-post-2014-african-court-human-peoples-rights-year-review.

Zaiden Benvindo, J., 'Abusive Judicial Activism and Judicial Independence in Brazil' *International Journal of Constitutional Law Blog* 22 December 2016 www.iconnectblog.com/2016/12/abusive-judicial-activism-and-judicial-independence-in-brazil.

'Abusive Impeachment? Brazilian Political Turmoil and the Judicialization of Mega-Politics' *International Journal of Constitutional Law Blog* 23 April 2016 www.iconnectblog.com/2016/04/abusive-impeachment-brazilian-polit ical-turmoil-and-the-judicialization-of-mega-politics.

Media Reports & Speeches

Akyol, M., 'The Rage against the Constitutional Court' *Hürriyet Daily News* 12 March 2016 www.hurriyetdailynews.com/the-rage-against-the-constitu tional-court.aspx?pageID=238&nid=96345.

Amnesty International, 'Brazil: Historic Efforts by Federal Prosecutors to Challenge Decades of Impunity for Military Regime' *Amnesty International* 25 April 2012 www.amnesty.org/en/latest/news/2012/04/brazil-historic-efforts-federal-prosecutors-challenge-decades-impunity-military-regime.

Arab News (unattributed), 'Plan to Establish Arab Court of Human Rights in Final Stage' 23 February 2016 www.arabnews.com/saudi-arabia/news/ 884921.

Arslan, Z., 'Constitutional Complaint in Turkey: A Cursory Analysis of Essential Decisions', Conference on 'Best Individual Complaint Practices to the Constitutional Courts in Europe', Strasbourg 7 July 2014 www.coe.int/t/dgi/hr-natimplement/Source/echr/Conference_07072014_Speech_Arslan.pdf.

Ben Hamadi, M., 'Tunisie: Les "gardiens de la Constitution" essuient un flot de critiques' *HuffPost Maghreb* 27 May 2014 www.huffpostmaghreb.com/2014/ 05/27/tunisie-instance-controle-constitutionnalite_n_5395843.html.

Bertoni, E., 'Setbacks and Tension in the Inter-American Court of Human Rights' *Media Legal Defence Initiative* 17 December 2013 www.mediadefence.org/ blog/setbacks-and-tension-inter-american-court-human-rights#.VUvAQ_ lVjDV.

Centre for Human Rights University of Pretoria, 'Report: Rwanda's Withdrawal of its Acceptance of Direct Individual Access to the African Human Rights Court' 22 March 2016 www.chr.up.ac.za/index.php/centre-news-a-events-2016/1604-report-rwandas-withdrawal-of-its-acceptance-of-direct-individ ual-access-to-the-african-human-rights-court.html.

Duffy, G., 'Brazil Truth Commission Arouses Military Opposition' *BBC News* 11 January 2010 http://news.bbc.co.uk/2/hi/8451109.stm.

Duke Law News, 'Helfer Project Examines the Evolution of International Human Rights Courts in Africa' *Duke Law News* 11 September 2013 www.law.duke .edu/news/helfer-project-examines-evolution-international-human-rights-courts-africa.

European Court of Human Rights, press release, 'President Raimondi Presents the Court's Results for 2016', ECHR 037 (2017) 26 January 2017.

Friedman, U., 'The Slow Implosion of Brazilian Politics' *The Atlantic* 19 April 2016 www.theatlantic.com/international/archive/2016/04/brazil-impeachment-dilma-rousseff/478677/.

Hürriyet Daily News (unattributed), 'Top Court Refuses Appeal by Families of Uludere Victims' 26 February 2016 www.hurriyetdailynews.com/top-court-refuses-appeal-by-families-of-uludere-victims-.aspx?pageID=238&nID=95773&NewsCatID=509.

International Federation of Journalists, 'IFJ and FAJ Welcomes African Court's Landmark Decision in Favour of Freedom of Expression' *International Federation of Journalists* 10 December 2014 www.ifj.org/nc/news-single-view/backpid/1/article/ifj-lauds-african-courts-landmark-decision-in-favor-of-freedom-of-expression-in-africa/.

International Justice Resource Center, 'OAS Concludes Formal Inter-American Human Rights 'Strengthening' Process, but Dialogue Continues on Contentious Reforms', 24 March 2013 www.ijrcenter.org/2013/03/24/oas-concludes-formal-inter-american-human-rights-strengthening-process-but-dialogue-continues-on-contentious-reforms.

Louw, R., 'Meddling with Constitutional Court Powers a Threat to All', Rhodes University graduation, South Africa, 22 April 2012 www.ru.ac.za/media/rhodesuniversity/content/communications/documents/Raymond_Louw%20Grad%20Address.pdf.

Lowe, R., 'Bassiouni: New Arab Court for Human Rights Is Fake "Potemkin Tribunal"' *International Bar Association* 1 October 2014 www.ibanet.org/Article/Detail.aspx?ArticleUid=c64f 9646-15a5-4624–8c07-bae9d9ac42df.

Lutyens, S. & Tlili, H., 'Torture and Police Abuse Still a Reality, Five Years after Tunisia's Revolution' *France 24* 14 January 2016 www.france24.com/en/20160114-focus-tunisia-police-abuse-torture-violence-security-forces-revolution-ben-ali.

McInerny, P., 'What's behind Brazil's Economic and Political Crises?' *UCLA Newsroom* 16 May 2016 http://newsroom.ucla.edu/stories/what-s-behind-brazil-s-economic-and-political-crises.

Murungi, M., 'Report from Kenya: Constitutional Court Considers the Legitimacy of the Trial of Jesus' *The Court* 28 September 2007 www.thecourt.ca/report-from-kenya-constitutional-court-considers-the-legitimacy-of-the-trial-of-jesus.

Ndlovu, R., 'Sadc Tribunal Back with Mandate Reduced to Interstate Cases' *BDLive* 20 August 2014 www.bdlive.co.za/africa/africannews/2014/08/20/sadc-tribunal-back-with-mandate-reduced-to-interstate-cases.

Pio, C., 'The Impeachment Vote in Brazil Is Definitely Not a Coup' *New York Times* 19 April 2016 www.nytimes.com/roomfordebate/2016/04/18/in-brazil-a-house-cleaning-or-a-coup/the-impeachment-vote-in-brazil-is-definitely-not-a-coup.

Politi, D., 'Uncomfortable Truths' *New York Times* 28 September 2012 http://
latitude.blogs.nytimes.com/2012/09/28/brazils-truth-commission-gets-to-
work/?_r=0.

Ryklief, S., 'South Africa's 2016 Municipal Elections – Why the Excitement?'
GroundUp 23 August 2016 www.groundup.org.za/article/south-africas-2016-
municipal-elections-why-excitement.

Saad Filho, A., 'The Mass Protests in Brazil in June–July 2013' *Global Research
Project* 15 July 2013 www.globalresearch.ca/the-mass-protests-in-brazil-in-
june-july-2013/5342736.

Stone, H., 'Brazil Prosecutes Retired Colonel Over Disappearances in Challenge to
Amnesty Law' *The Pan-American Post* 14 March 2012 www.panamerican
post.blogspot.com/2012/03/brazil-prosecutes-retired-colonel-over.html.

Stork, J., 'New Arab Human Rights Court is Doomed from the Start' *International
Business Times* 26 November 2014 www.ibtimes.co.uk/new-arab-human-
rights-court-protects-rulers-doomed-fail-1476728.

Watts, J. & Bowater, D., 'Brazil's Dilma Rousseff Impeached by Senate in Crushing
Defeat' *The Guardian* 1 September 2016 www.theguardian.com/world/2016/
aug/31/dilma-rousseff-impeached-president-brazilian-senate-michel-temer.

Worley, W., 'Theresa May "Will Campaign to Leave the European Convention on Human Rights in 2020 Election"' *The Independent* 30 December
2016 www.independent.co.uk/news/uk/politics/theresa-may-campaign-leave-
european-convention-on-human-rights-2020-general-election-brexit-a74999
51.html.

Webpages

East African Community, 'Political Federation. What is Political Federation?'
www.eac.int/integration-pillars/political-federation.

European Court of Human Rights Press Country Profile: Turkey www.echr.coe
.int/Documents/CP_Turkey_ENG.pdf.

International Commission of Jurists, 'The Tunis Declaration on the Arab Court
of Human Rights' http://icj.wpengine.netdna-cdn.com/wp-content/uploads/
2015/05/MENA-Arab-Court-Tunis-Declaration-Advocacy-2015-ENG.pdf.

Koh, T.B., 'A Constitution for the Oceans', 6 December 2012 www.un.org/depts/
los/convention_agreements/texts/koh_english.pdf.

United Nations, 'Growth in United Nations Membership, 1945–Present'
www.un.org/en/members/growth.shtml#1980.

INDEX

343